Hiking Mount Rainier National Park

Second Edition

Heidi Schneider and Mary Skjelset

FALCONGUIDE®

GUILFORD, CONNECTICUT
HELENA, MONTANA
AN IMPRINT OF THE GLOBE PEQUOT PRESS

/IFALCONGUIDE®

Spine Photo: ©2004 Michael DeYoung
All interior photos are by the authors unless otherwise
noted.

Maps by XNR Productions, Inc. © Morris Book Publishing,
LLC.

Library of Congress Cataloging-in-Publication Data
is available.
ISBN 0-7627-3626-7

Manufactured in the United States of America
Second Edition/First Printing

The authors and The Globe Pequot Press assume no liability for accidents happening to,
or injuries sustained by, readers who engage in the activities described in this book.

Contents

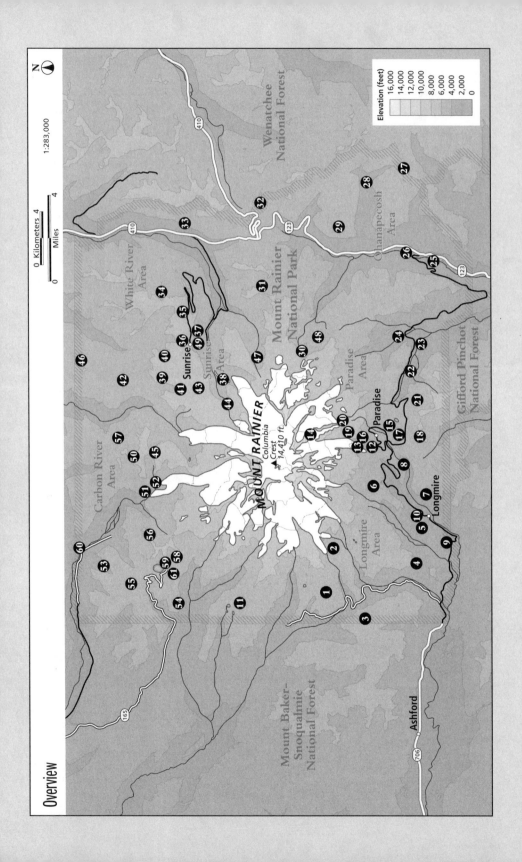

Overview

1:283,000

Dedicated to our parents.

Acknowledgments (revised edition)

Again, we would like to thank all the rangers and staff from Mount Rainier National Park for assisting us in the revision process. In particular, we would like to acknowledge the individual contributions of two park employees: Angela Johnson for meticulously editing and revising the mileages in our revised edition and Elizabeth Demsetz for answering our numerous questions. Thanks to Russell Flint and Chad Harkcom for their generosity and to our family and friends for their support and feedback.

Acknowledgments (original edition)

First and foremost, we want to thank the rangers and staff of Mount Rainier National Park. National Park Service employees spent many hours poring over this manuscript to ensure its accuracy. Special thanks to John Wilcox for coordinating the editorial efforts and to his co-workers, Debbie Brenchley and Rick Kirschner. Their expertise was invaluable to the formation of a quality hiking guide to Mount Rainier National Park.

We would also like to thank those people who offered their time, energy, companionship, and sometimes vehicles to help us hike the more than 260 miles of maintained trails in Mount Rainier National Park: Denise Peterson, Bill and Margaret Schneider, Marika Engelhardt, Stefan Durham, and Adela Soliz. Special thanks to John Caldwell and Bill Schneider for contributing photography.

On the home front, we would like to thank many people for their love and support. Thanks to Nikki Wallin, Alexandra Folias, Miles Norton, Miriam Aronoff, Alison Madsen, and our housemates, Esther Harlow and Daphne Stanford. We love you and appreciate you all.

Introduction

The Mountain

Mount Rainier is, above all else, eclectic. Rising from the Cascade foothills, the mountain's broad shoulders carry steep-sloped forests, meadowed parks, U-shaped river valleys, jagged ridges, and a deceptively smooth-looking cap of ice and snow. This varied terrain harbors an array of habitats, from extensive montane and subalpine forests to bands of tundra and swatches of temperate rain forest. At higher elevations, glaciers and permanent snowfields exist in an Arctic environment just 40 miles from the mild, humid shores of Puget Sound.

Although its stature and majesty seem exceptional, Mount Rainier is only one of more than 400 volcanoes that constitute the "Ring of Fire" around the Pacific Ocean. The collision of oceanic and continental plates created this string of volcanoes. Almost a million years ago, Mount Rainier rose from a weak spot between the Juan de Fuca plate and the North America continental plate. By then the rugged Cascades, including the Tatoosh Range, had already been created by carving rivers.

The Pleistocene epoch, the ice age that began three million years ago and continued until 10,000 years ago, bore Mount Rainier. The first eruption sent massive amounts of lava cascading over a 15-mile radius around the small cone. Lava filled the ancient streambeds and canyons, only to be carved again by new streams into the jutting ridges surrounding Mount Rainier. Ensuing smaller eruptions slowly built the cone to heights far above present calculations. Considerable erosion from glaciation, explosion, collapse, and the creation of riverbeds reduced Mount Rainier to its present zenith, 14,411 feet above sea level.

Mount Rainier was not undergoing these drastic changes alone. Mount St. Helens, Mount Adams, and Mount Baker were also forming. In fact, much of the pumice and ash found on Mount Rainier did not originate from its own volcanic eruptions, but from those of neighboring mountains, including Mount Mazama (home now to Crater Lake) and Mount St. Helens. These materials, although deadly and scorching to contemporary wildlife, create a fecund landscape for successive organisms. Below timberline, in areas temperate enough for plant growth, vegetation prospered. As a result of dramatic elevation and climatic disparities on Mount Rainier, an incredible variety of species developed in four distinct ecological zones: temperate rain forest, silver fir forest, subalpine forest, and the alpine zone.

As you hike the trails that traverse such a diverse land, keep in mind the dynamics of the past. The National Park Service has preserved this culmination of millions of years of evolution for the public to enjoy. Please, obey park regulations while you delight in this marvel of nature.

The Human Presence on Mount Rainier

While becoming familiar with the geography of Mount Rainier National Park, you may notice the distinctive blend of cultural influences on place names. The human history of Mount Rainier divides into two discrete periods: pre– and post–Manifest Destiny. Before the arrival of Europeans, the ten surrounding Native American tribes revered the mountain, using its abundant resources only as a means of sustenance. Subsequent English and American explorers found Mount Rainier a challenge. Hence, those features with English titles were named for prominent summit-climbers, while Native American names bear witness to the spiritual veneration held for Rainier by local peoples.

Most of the tribes near Mount Rainier knew it as *Tahoma,* or a similar derivation. This word has been translated variously as "the Great Snow" or "the Great Snowy Peak," but these dry translations do not portray the reverence with which the word was spoken. The original name for the south flank of Mount Rainier, *Saghalie Illahe,* or "Land of Peace," designated a place of armistice. Today we call this area Paradise. All tribal wars or skirmishes ended when Paradise was entered.

Carbon dating indicates Native American presence on the mountain for 6,000 years. Never were these settlements permanent, nor was the use damaging. With the summer melt-off, coastal and plains tribes alike set out for the high mountain meadows in pursuit of berries and game. The mountain provided an abundance of resources, which the plains tribes east of Mount Rainier depended upon for survival.

After the discovery of Mount Rainier by Captain George Vancouver, sustainable use gave way to commercialization, and concerns about survival arose only on the ascent to the summit. With the exception of Rear Admiral Peter Rainier, a little-known English naval officer who fought against the United States in the American Revolution, the names of features are those of summit-climbers. James Longmire, a prominent local who advocated the use of Mount Rainier's hot springs as a panacea, led the first two climbers to scale the mountain to what is now called Sluiskin Falls. From this point on August 17, 1870, General Hazard Stevens and Philemon Van Trump completed the first ascent to the summit of Mount Rainier.

With the publicity of later summit attempts and the building of Longmire-Paradise and Paradise Valley Roads, the popularity of Mount Rainier grew. The need for the preservation of Mount Rainier and its surrounding area became evident, advocated by conservationists such as John Muir. With wide popular support, President McKinley signed into law the act declaring Mount Rainier the fifth national park on March 2, 1899.

Attempting to keep up with the mountain's increasing inundation of visitors, the management of Mount Rainier is in a constant state of flux. Lenient regulations of the past led to activities as damaging, dangerous, and frivolous as a ski-race from Camp Muir to Paradise Valley. The ski lift is now gone, as are the motorcycle track and the boat rentals, yet their legacies remain. Some of the earth was nearly irreparably scarred.

Mount Rainier from atop Tolmie Peak.

An attempt to convert all the mileage signs to kilometers many years ago has resulted in some discrepancies in what the signs read, as well as mislabeled, unlabeled, or incorrect mileages. The National Park Service has nearly completed the process of returning all the distance readings to miles. The mileages that we have compiled came directly from the National Park Service's database and should reflect the most accurate numbers.

The National Park Service has also experimented with various reservation systems. Fees, permits, and regulations are apt to change, so call ahead for the most recent information on these systems. Appreciate the conservation attempts of the National Park Service, and preserve Mount Rainier National Park accordingly.

Seasons and Weather

The most severe weather on Mount Rainier occurs in the winter months. An immense elevated mass, Mount Rainier stands in the midst of a temperate lowland forest. The surrounding area receives massive amounts of rain in winter, while the nature of the mountain's situation leads to incredible amounts of snow. Moisture-laden air from the Pacific Ocean bombards Mount Rainier. As the air is pushed above the mountain, it cools, and the moisture falls as snow. The western flank of the mountain, Paradise in particular, receives record-level snowfalls yearly. In winter 1971–1972 Paradise saw the most snowfall ever recorded: 1,122 inches.

This book is targeted at those who visit Mount Rainier National Park in the summer months. Compared with winter, the weather in summer is relatively mild. The heavier rainfall in early summer abates by mid-July. In July and August Mount Rainier sees many nice, clear days. That is not to say that you will not encounter fog. Many visitors to Mount Rainier never actually see the mountain. If lenticular clouds, those that form a saucerlike disc on the summit, do not obscure the peak, thick blankets of fog that rise from the humid lower levels may. You still can experience the beauty of Mount Rainier National Park on such days: crashing waterfalls, subalpine fields of flowers, wildlife, and mountain lakes. If you seek views of the mountains or the surrounding forests, however, hope for a clear day

Season List

May:

9 Twin Firs Loop
10 Trail of the Shadows
23 Stevens Creek
24 Box Canyon
25 Silver Falls
26 Grove of the Patriarchs
53 Green Lake and Ranger Falls
54 Paul Peak Trail
60 Chenuis Falls

June:

5 Rampart Ridge
22 Stevens Canyon

Early July:

8 Narada Falls
12 Nisqually Vista
13 Alta Vista Summit
16 Dead Horse Creek
29 Shriner Peak
38 Emmons Moraine
44 Glacier Basin
59 Spray Falls

Mid-July:

1 Klapatche Park
2 Emerald Ridge
3 Gobbler's Knob
4 Indian Henry's Hunting Ground
6 Comet Falls and Van Trump Park
7 Eagle Peak
15 Lakes Trail
17 High Lakes Trail
19 Skyline Trail
20 Paradise Glacier

21 Snow Lake
27 Three Lakes
31 Owyhigh Lakes
33 Crystal Lakes
34 Palisades Lakes
35 Dege Peak
36 Sourdough Ridge Nature Trail
37 Silver Forest
41 Berkeley Park
42 Grand Park
45 Northern Loop
46 Lake Eleanor
47 Summerland
50 Yellowstone Cliffs and Windy Gap
51 Carbon Glacier and Moraine
52 Mystic Lake
55 Tolmie Peak
57 Lake James

Late July:

11 West Wonderland
14 Camp Muir
18 Pinnacle Peak Saddle
28 Pacific Crest Trail
30 Ohanapecosh Park
32 Naches Peak
39 Mount Fremont Lookout
40 Forest Lake
48 Indian Bar
49 Sunrise Rim
56 Mother Mountain
58 Spray Park
61 Wonderland Trail

August:

43 Burroughs Mountain

Getting There

Mount Rainier is located in central-western Washington and has four entrance stations—one at each corner of the park. The southwest entrance, Nisqually Entrance Station, is open year-round. The other three—Carbon River Entrance Station (northwest), Stevens Canyon Entrance Station (southeast), and White River Entrance Station (northeast)—are generally open mid- to late June or early July. It is an easy drive from Seattle, Tacoma, or Portland to any of the four entrance stations. It is also possible to fly into either Portland or the Seattle/Tacoma airport, where you can rent a car, take a shuttle, or ride a bus into the park. Although paved and well maintained, the park roads are winding two-lanes and often crowded with traffic, including slow-moving vehicles. During the daytime, expect a leisurely drive through the park.

Following is a detailed description of how to reach each entrance station.

Stevens Canyon Entrance Station: From the north (Seattle or Tacoma), go south on Interstate 5 until you reach Highway 512, which originates in Tacoma. Go east on Highway 512 to Highway 410. The park entrance is 33.0 miles from Enumclaw. Go east on Highway 410, which starts going east and then bends south as it nears the park. After entering the park, continue on Highway 410 east for 9.0 miles until the Highway 123 junction. Turn right (south) onto Highway 123 and travel for 11.2 miles to Stevens Canyon Road. Turn right (west) onto Stevens Canyon Road; the Stevens Canyon Entrance Station is directly in front of you. *DeLorme: Washington Atlas and Gazetteer:* Page 48 C4.

From the south (Portland), go about 80 miles north on I–5 to U.S. Highway 12. Go east on US 12 through Packwood (the last town—and gas, camping supplies, etc.—before entering the park), and continue 7.0 miles to Highway 123. Go left (north) on Highway 123 and in 3.0 miles enter Mount Rainier National Park. In another mile go left (west) onto Stevens Canyon Road; the entrance station is directly in front of you. *DeLorme: Washington Atlas and Gazetteer:* Page 48 C4.

From the east (Yakima), drive west on Highway 410. The park boundary is 13.0 miles past the hamlet of American River. From the park boundary continue 3.6 miles west on Highway 410 and turn left (south) onto Highway 123. Drive 11.2 miles, and turn right (west) onto Stevens Canyon Road; the entrance station is directly in front of you. *DeLorme: Washington Atlas and Gazetteer:* Page 48 C4.

Nisqually Entrance Station: From the north (Seattle or Tacoma), go south on I–5 to Highway 512, just south of Tacoma. Drive 2.0 miles east on Highway 512 and turn south onto Highway 7. Drive 31.0 miles south to Elbe and go east on Highway 706. Continue 13.0 miles to the park boundary. The last town before entering the park is Ashford, so be sure to stock up on supplies. The Nisqually Entrance Station is 5.0 miles east of Ashford. Once inside the Mount Rainier National Park, Highway 706 becomes the Longmire-Paradise Road. *DeLorme: Washington Atlas and Gazetteer:* Page 48 C1.

Aurora Lake. BILL SCHNEIDER

From the south (Portland), drive about 80 miles north on I–5 to US 12. Go 30.0 miles east on US 12, then turn north onto Highway 7. Drive 17.0 miles north to Elbe and turn east onto Highway 706. Drive 13.0 miles to the park boundary. The last town before entering the park is Ashford, so be sure to stock up on supplies. The Nisqually Entrance Station is 5.0 miles east of Ashford. *DeLorme: Washington Atlas and Gazetteer:* Page 48 C1.

From the East (Yakima), drive west on US 12 to Highway 123. Turn right (north) onto Highway 123 and drive 3.0 miles to the park entrance. Turn left (west) onto Stevens Canyon Road. Pay the entrance fee at the Stevens Canyon Entrance Station and continue west on Stevens Canyon Road, which eventually becomes Longmire-Paradise Road. The Nisqually Entrance Station is 6.7 miles west of the Longmire Historic District. *DeLorme: Washington Atlas and Gazetteer:* Page 48 C1.

Carbon River Entrance Station: Whether you are coming from the north or south, the best route starts from Tacoma. From Tacoma go east on Highway 512 to Highway 410. Go about 16 miles east on Highway 410 to Highway 165 in the town of Buckley. Go right (south) on Highway 165 until you reach Wilkeson. Continue from Wilkeson for 9.0 miles to where the road forks. Go to the left (east) onto Carbon River Road. Continue 8.0 miles to the Carbon River Entrance Station. *DeLorme: Washington Atlas and Gazetteer:* Page 48 A1.

From the east (Yakima), drive west on Highway 410 to Buckley. The junction with Highway 165 is in the middle of Buckley. Turn left and drive south on Highway 165 until you reach Wilkeson. Continue 9.0 miles to where the road forks. Go to the left (east) onto Carbon River Road. Continue 8.0 miles to the Carbon River Entrance Station. *DeLorme: Washington Atlas and Gazetteer:* Page 48 A1.

White River Entrance Station: From the north (Seattle or Tacoma), go south on I–5 to Highway 512, which originates in Tacoma. Drive east on Highway 512 until you reach Highway 410. Go east on Highway 410, which starts going east and then bends south as it nears the park. The road enters Mount Rainier National Park and continues 4.5 miles to White River Road. Turn right (west) and go 1.5 miles to the White River Entrance Station. *DeLorme: Washington Atlas and Gazetteer:* Page 48 A4.

From the south (Portland), drive about 80 miles north on I–5 to US 12. Go 72.0 miles east on US 12 and turn left (north) onto Highway 123, 7.0 miles east of Packwood. Continue 14.2 miles north on Highway 123 and stay left (west) on Highway 410. Drive 1.9 miles and turn left (west) onto White River Road. Continue 1.5 miles to the White River Entrance Station. *DeLorme: Washington Atlas and Gazetteer:* Page 48 A4.

From the east (Yakima), drive west on Highway 410. The park boundary is 13.0 miles past the hamlet of American River. From the park boundary continue west on Highway 410 3.6 miles to the junction with Highway 123. Stay on Highway 410 to the right and drive 1.9 miles to White River Road. Turn left (west) onto White River Road and drive 1.5 miles to the White River Entrance Station. *DeLorme: Washington Atlas and Gazetteer:* Page 48 A4.

Here are a few services that provide transportation to and from Mount Rainier:

- **Grayline Bus Services:** Bus service from downtown Seattle. Call for rates and reservations: (800) 231–2222; (206) 628–5526.
- **Rainier Overland:** Operates shuttles by reservation between Sea-Tac Airport and Ashford, as well as points within Mount Rainier National Park. Call for rates and reservations: (360) 569–0851.
- **Rainier Shuttle:** Operates shuttles by reservation between Sea-Tac Airport and Ashford, as well as points within Mount Rainier National Park. Call for rates and reservations: (360) 569–2331.

Visitor Facilities

Ranger Stations

Paradise Climbing Ranger Station: (360) 569–2211, ext. 2314

The Paradise Climbing Ranger Station mainly issues climbing permits for routes starting from Paradise, but you can obtain Wilderness Camping Permits and information here as well. This ranger station is open mid-May to late September. From the Nisqually Entrance Station (see Getting There), drive 15.9 miles east on Longmire-Paradise Road to the intersection with Stevens Canyon Road. Stay to the left and head 2.2 miles up to the Paradise complex. From the Stevens Canyon Entrance Station (see Getting There), drive nearly 19 miles west on the Stevens Canyon Road to the intersection with the Longmire-Paradise Road. Turn right (north) and follow the signs to Paradise.

Mowich Ranger Station

The Mowich Ranger Station, located on the west side of Mowich Lake, does not issue permits or provide wilderness information. It does, however, serve as a location to pick up food caches along the Wonderland Trail. From Wilkeson drive 9.0 miles south on Highway 165 to where the road forks. Stay to the right (south) at this fork, the way to Mowich Lake. After 3.2 miles the road becomes a well-maintained dirt road, although it can be slippery when muddy. Follow this road for another 8.8 miles to the Paul Peak trailhead on the right (south) side of the road. Pause at the fee station here and pay the park entrance fee, then continue southeast 5.3 miles to Mowich Lake, a total of 26.3 miles from Wilkeson.

Sunrise Ranger Station: (360) 663–2425

The Sunrise Ranger Station is located in the Sunrise Complex and shares a phone number with the Sunrise Visitor Center. This facility does occasionally issue permits if someone is available, but your best bet is to stop at the White River Wilderness Information Center in order to obtain Wilderness Camping Permits. The Sunrise Ranger Station opens in early July, about the time the White River Road opens, and stays open throughout the summer. From the White River Entrance Station (see Getting There), drive 13.8 miles west on White River Road to the Sunrise complex.

Wilderness Information Centers

Longmire Wilderness Information Center: (360) 569–HIKE (4453)

Open late May to October, the Longmire Wilderness Information Center issues Wilderness Camping Permits primarily for backpacking. The center has rangers equipped to help with any questions you might have, as well as a large relief map of the park. The Longmire Wilderness Information Center is located in the Longmire Historic District, along Longmire-Paradise Road. From the Nisqually Entrance Station (see Getting There), drive 6.7 miles east to the Longmire Historic District.

White River Wilderness Information Center: (360) 569–6030
This center issues permits primarily for backpacking and north-side climbing routes. Open late May through summer, the White River Wilderness Information Center is located next to the White River Entrance Station (see Getting There).

Wilkeson Wilderness Information Center: (360) 829–5127
Staff issues permits primarily for backpacking and north-side climbing routes. This center opens mid-May and stays open until the end of September. Drive to Wilkeson on Highway 165. The Wilkeson Wilderness Information Center is located in the center of Wilkeson's quaint downtown strip at 569 Church Street.

Visitor Centers and Museums
Sunrise Visitor Center: (360) 663–2425
The Sunrise Visitor Center provides a wealth of historical and geological information about Mount Rainier National Park. It opens in early July, about the time the White River Road opens, and stays open throughout the summer. From the White River Entrance Station, drive 13.8 miles west on White River Road to the Sunrise Complex.

Ohanapecosh Visitor Center: (360) 569–6046
The Ohanapecosh Visitor Center provides a variety of exhibits and information about Mount Rainier National Park. In some cases you can also get permits at the Ohanapecosh Visitor Center, but plan on getting your permit from one of the main locations listed above. The visitor center usually opens after Memorial Day and stays open until Labor Day. From the Stevens Canyon Entrance Station (see Getting There), drive 1.8 miles south on Highway 123 to the turnoff for Ohanapecosh Campground. The road forks just after you turn in; go right (north) and drive until the Ohanapecosh Visitor Center appears directly in front of you.

Jackson Visitor Center: (360) 569–6036
The Jackson Visitor Center is located in the Paradise Complex and offers a variety of natural and cultural information through exhibits, guided walks, and nature talks. The visitor center is open year-round on weekends, but usually opens daily after Memorial Day weekend until Labor Day weekend. From the Nisqually Entrance Station (see Getting There), drive 15.9 miles east on Longmire-Paradise Road to the intersection with Stevens Canyon Road. Stay to the left and head 2.2 miles up to the Paradise Complex. From the Stevens Canyon Entrance Station (see Getting There), drive nearly 19 miles west on the Stevens Canyon Road to the intersection with the Longmire-Paradise Road. Turn right (north) and follow the signs to Paradise.

◀ *Ranger Falls.*

Longmire Museum: (360) 569–2211, ext. 3314.

The Longmire Museum offers a range of information, such as natural history, cultural history, backpacking, hiking, and trail conditions. It issues permits only when the Longmire Wilderness Information Center is closed. The Longmire Museum is located in the Longmire Historic District, along Longmire-Paradise Road. From the Nisqually Entrance Station (see Getting There), drive 6.7 miles east to the Longmire Historic District.

Fees and Permits

Entry Fees

You must pay an entry fee to enter Mount Rainier National Park. The fees fund services and projects that directly benefit both the visiting public and park resources. The fee depends basically on how long you want to stay and how you are arriving. All persons traveling in single, privately owned automobiles pay $10.00 for a seven-day pass. Individual persons traveling on foot, bicycle, or motorcycle or in a vehicle owned by a nonprofit organization pay only $5.00 for the same seven-day pass. For avid Mount Rainier lovers, the park sells a $30 annual pass. Mount Rainier National Park honors and sells the National Parks Pass, Golden Eagle sticker, Golden Age Passport, and Golden Access Passport.

Wilderness Camping Permits

In Mount Rainier National Park, you must have a permit for any overnight stay in the backcountry. You can either make a reservation or obtain a permit twenty-four hours before starting your hike. Although the permits are free, the park charges a $20 fee for reservations.

Wilderness Camping Permit Reservations

Most people find making reservations well worth the extra charge because many campsites fill up by the end of April, especially camps along the Wonderland Trail. The park accepts reservation requests for any time from May 1 to September 1 beginning on April 1. Approximately 60 percent of all wilderness campsites and zones are reservable, but the permits for the remaining portion are issued on a first-come, first-served basis. You can download the reservation form at www.nps .gov/mora/recreation/rsvpform.htm. The park accepts reservation forms in person at the Longmire Wilderness Information Center beginning Memorial Day weekend. For your convenience, completed forms can be faxed to (360) 569–3131 or sent to the following address:

Longmire Wilderness Information Center
Mount Rainier National Park Tahoma
Woods, Star Route
Ashford, WA 98304–9751

Within one week of submitting your form, you will receive either a confirmation or a rejection letter. Keep in mind that reservations cannot be confirmed until payment has been received.

Wilderness Camping Permit Guidelines

- There is no charge for Wilderness Camping Permits. Permits may be obtained within twenty-four hours of your hike at either a ranger station or a wilderness information center. They are issued on a first-come, first-served basis unless previously reserved.

- Reservations cost $20 per party, which covers up to twelve persons in a single group for up to fourteen consecutive nights. This fee is nonrefundable. The park allows one change to a reservation for no additional fee, but subsequent changes require an additional $20 fee. Reservations that are not picked up by 10:00 A.M. on the first day of the trip will be canceled, unless you request a late pickup. Late pickups can be arranged by calling any park station or wilderness information center.

- Permits are issued for specific locations and nights. During summer, the number of permits is limited due to high demand.

- No more than five persons are allowed to stay at an individual site. If you have more than five persons, you will have to obtain a group permit. A group permit is subject to the same wilderness guidelines as individual sites but allows six to twelve persons. Mount Rainier currently has more than twenty-five backcountry group sites.

Cross-country Camping Permits

For campers especially well versed in zero-impact camping practices who want a more genuine wilderness experience, the park offers Cross-country Camping Permits. These permits allow you to pitch your tent and make your campsite outside the established wilderness camping areas. Due to overuse of delicate subalpine meadows and destructive camping practices, cross-country camping is not an option if you plan to hike one-third or more of the Wonderland Trail. These permits, like Wilderness Camping Permits, are free and can be obtained at the nearest ranger station or wilderness information center. You must first watch a nine-minute video refresher on zero-impact camping before you can receive a Cross-country Camping Permit.

Closest Wilderness Information Center or Ranger Station

The following list will help you obtain your permit in the fastest, easiest way possible by directing you to the wilderness information center or ranger station closest to the hike you plan to take.

Wilderness Use Regulations

Wilderness use regulations are not intended to complicate your life. They help preserve the natural landscape and protect park visitors. The following is a list of Mount Rainier National Park's wilderness use regulations.

- Have a permit for all overnight use of the backcountry.

- Camp in designated campsites.

- Hang your food at night on the established food-storage poles.

- Carry out all trash. If you can pack it in, you can pack it out.

- Fish by hook and line only. This is permitted without a license, but some waters are closed. Check with a ranger to be certain.

- Do not take pets into the backcountry. Leashed pets are allowed on the Pacific Crest Trail and a portion of Naches Peak loop trail that travels out of the park.

- Do not possess or operate a motorized vehicle, bicycle, wheeled vehicle, skateboard, roller skates, or cart in any undeveloped area or on any backcountry trail.

Mount Rainier from a meadow near Mystic Lake.

- Do not drive off any park road.
- Do not pick wildflowers.
- Do not destroy, injure, deface, remove, dig, or disturb from its natural state any plant, rock, animal, mineral, cultural, or archaeological resource.
- Do not violate a closure, designation, use, or activity restriction or condition, schedule of visiting hours, or public use limit.
- Do not use or possess weapons.
- Do not pollute or contaminate any water source (with soap, waste, etc.).
- Never shortcut on any trail.
- Do not dispose of waste within 100 feet of water or within sight of a trail.

Trail Finder

Mountain Lakes
Easy
17 High Lakes Trail
21 Snow Lake
32 Naches Peak
53 Green Lake and Ranger Falls

Moderate
 3 Gobbler's Knob
46 Lake Eleanor
27 Three Lakes
28 Pacific Crest Trail
31 Owyhigh Lakes
33 Crystal Lakes
34 Palisades Lake
40 Forest Lake
55 Tolmie Peak

Strenuous
 1 Klapatche Park
11 West Wonderland
50 Yellowstone Cliffs and Windy Gap
52 Mystic Lake
57 Lake James
61 Wonderland Trail

Waterfalls
Easy
 8 Narada Falls
23 Stevens Creek
25 Silver Falls
53 Green Lake and Ranger Falls
59 Spray Falls
60 Chenuis Falls

Moderate
 6 Comet Falls and Van Trump Park
19 Skyline Trail
22 Stevens Canyon

Strenuous
30 Ohanapecosh Park
48 Indian Bar
61 Wonderland Trail

Alpine Country
Easy
39 Mount Fremont Lookout

Moderate
19 Skyline Trail
20 Paradise Glacier
43 Burroughs Mountain
47 Summerland
48 Indian Bar

Strenuous
14 Camp Muir
30 Ohanapecosh Park
11 West Wonderland
45 Northern Loop
61 Wonderland Trail

Peaks
Easy
18 Pinnacle Peak Saddle
35 Dege Peak
39 Mount Fremont Lookout

Moderate
 3 Gobbler's Knob
55 Tolmie Peak

Strenuous
 7 Eagle Peak
29 Shriner Peak

Overnight Backpacking Trips
Easy
21 Snow Lake
40 Forest Lake

Mount Rainier from Silver Forest Trail.

Moderate
58 Spray Park

Glaciers
Easy
12 Nisqually Vista

Moderate
19 Skyline Trail
51 Carbon Glacier and Moraine
20 Paradise Glacier

Strenuous
 2 Emerald Ridge
11 West Wonderland
14 Camp Muir
30 Ohanapecosh Park
45 Northern Loop
52 Mystic Lake
48 Indian Bar
61 Wonderland Trail

Trails That Allow Pets
Easy
32 Naches Peak
     Pets are allowed on the portion of the Naches Peak loop that leaves the park.

Moderate
28 Pacific Crest Trail

Wildflowers (in season)
Easy
21 Snow Lake
37 Silver Forest
40 Forest Lake

Moderate
 3 Gobbler's Knob
31 Owyhigh Lakes
33 Crystal Lakes
41 Berkeley Park

42 Grand Park
46 Lake Eleanor
55 Tolmie Peak
58 Spray Park

Strenuous
 1 Klapatche Park
 2 Emerald Ridge
 4 Indian Henry's Hunting Ground
11 West Wonderland
29 Shriner Peak
30 Ohanapecosh Park
45 Northern Loop
48 Indian Bar
56 Mother Mountain
61 Wonderland Trail

Great Views of Mount Rainier
Easy
18 Pinnacle Peak Saddle
32 Naches Peak

Moderate
19 Skyline Trail
42 Grand Park
55 Tolmie Peak
58 Spray Park

Strenuous
 1 Klapatche Park
 2 Emerald Ridge
 4 Indian Henry's Hunting Ground
11 West Wonderland
14 Camp Muir
29 Shriner Peak
30 Ohanapecosh Park
48 Indian Bar
56 Mother Mountain
61 Wonderland Trail

For a Good Chance of Seeing a Bear
Moderate
 2 Emerald Ridge
42 Grand Park

How to Use This Guide

To use this book effectively, please note the following categorical descriptions.

Types of Hikes

Suggested hikes have been split into the following categories:

Loop—Starts and finishes at the same trailhead, with no (or very little) retracing of your steps. Sometimes the definition of loop is stretched to include "lollipops" and trips that involve a short walk on a road at the end of the hike to get back to your vehicle.

Shuttle—A point-to-point trip that requires two vehicles (one left at the other end of the trail) or a prearranged pickup at a designated time and place. One good way to manage the logistical problems of shuttles is to arrange for another party to start at the other end of the trail. The two parties meet at a predetermined point and then trade keys. When finished, they drive each other's vehicles home.

Out-and-back—Traveling to a specific destination, then retracing your steps back to the trailhead.

Ratings

To help you plan your trip, trails are rated according to difficulty; however, the ratings serve as a general guide only, not the final word. What is difficult to one hiker may be easy to the next. In this guidebook, difficulty ratings consider both how long and how strenuous the route is. Here are general definitions of the ratings.

Easy—Suitable for any hiker, including children or elderly persons, without serious elevation gain, hazardous sections, or places where the trail is faint.

Moderate—Suitable for hikers who have some experience and at least an average fitness level. Probably not suitable for children or the elderly unless they have an above-average level of fitness. The hike may have some short sections where the trail is difficult to follow and often includes some hills.

Strenuous—Suitable for experienced hikers with an above-average fitness level, often with sections of trail that are difficult to follow or even some off-trail sections that could require knowledge of route-finding with topographic map and compass. The hike may have serious elevation gain and possibly some hazardous conditions.

Distances

The distances displayed in this book are derived from the National Park Service's database. Currently the National Park Service is correcting the mileage on all signs in the park to correspond to distances listed in the database. Keep this in mind when trail signs do not correlate with the numbers listed in this guide. Our distances are current and accurate, although they are rounded to the nearest 0.1 mile.

How to Use the Maps

The maps in this book use elevation tints, called hypsometry, to portray relief. Each gray tone represents a range of equal elevation, as shown in the scale key with the map. These maps will give you a good idea of elevation gain and loss. The darker tones are lower elevations and the lighter greys are higher elevation. The lighter the tone, the higher the elevation. Narrow bands of different gray tones spaced closely together indicate steep terrain, whereas wider bands indicate areas of more gradual slope.

Where to Get Maps

Most maps of Mount Rainier are available at park visitor centers, sporting goods stores around the park, or online. You can usually special-order any USGS quad from your local sporting goods store or directly from the USGS at the following address:

Map Distribution
U.S. Geological Survey
Box 25286, Federal Center
Denver, CO 80225
http://store.usgs.gov/

Elevation Charts

Most—but not all—hike descriptions include elevation charts. These charts do not give a detailed picture of elevation gain and loss on a hike, but they do provide a general idea of how much climbing or descending you face on a trail. Out-and-back hike profiles only show the way out/up until the turnaround point.

Map Legend

Boundaries

///////////. National/Wilderness Boundary

Transportation

—(410)— State Highway

——— Primary Roads

——— Other Roads

===== Unpaved Road

= = = = = Unimproved Road

━━━━━ Featured Unpaved Road

▬ ▬ ▬ ▬ Featured Trail

- - - - - - - Other Trail

• • • • • • • Nature Trail

············ Off-trail Hike

—+——+— Tunnel

Hydrology

〜〜 River/Creek

＼ 〜 ＼ Intermittent Stream

ℓ Spring

∥ Falls

⬭ Lake

🗺 Glacier

⁂⁂ Marsh/Swamp

Physiography

∧ Cavern/Natural Bridge

⌒⌒⌒ Cliff

)(Pass

▲ Peak

Symbols

🚶 Trailhead

❷ 58 Trail Locator

↻ Trail Turnaround

🅿 Parking

📷 Ranger Station

❓ Visitor Center

▲ Back Country Campground

△ Campground

⬧ Cabin/Lodge

🎪 Picnic Area

○ Town

👁 Viewpoint

■ Point of Interest

🏛 Museum

•—• Gate

⋈ Bridge

Longmire

Originally the home of a hot springs resort founded by James Longmire, the Longmire Historic District now houses the Longmire Museum, the Longmire Wilderness Information Center, and the National Park Inn. The Longmire family built the Longmire Springs Hotel in 1888, only to watch it go up in flames and consequently be condemned in 1920. James Longmire built a rough wagon track from Ashford to the hot springs, a significant improvement over packhorses for resortgoers. This road was improved in 1906, allowing a comfortable passage to the Longmire Springs Hotel. Although James Longmire's panacea of mineral waters is no longer available, the Longmire Historic District offers visitors a variety of services and attractions. This area continues to be a popular place for people to visit, whether they plan to day hike or begin the celebrated Wonderland Trail.

The unique backcountry in the Longmire area contains a plethora of gorgeous flower-filled meadows—Sunset Peak, Indian Henry's Hunting Ground, St. Andrews Park, Emerald Ridge, and Klapatche Park. This corner of the park offers spectacular views of the southwestern glaciers, including the massive Tahoma Glacier, as well as the pebbly creeks originating from these glaciers, all of which provide a breathtaking contrast to the subalpine meadows.

Mud slides, a common occurrence in Mount Rainier National Park, occur less than every one hundred years in the Longmire area. These slides originating from volcanoes are often referred to by the Indonesian word for lava, *lahar*, although they are not usually associated with eruptions in Mount Rainier National Park. These mud slides, glacial outburst floods that gather rock and debris, result from either especially high autumn rainfall or especially warm summer weather.

The glacial creeks of Longmire, such as Kautz and Tahoma Creeks, constantly reroute themselves due to glacial outburst floods caused by geological activity. Longmire has experienced more washouts of this kind than any other area of the park, but fortunately the National Park Service responds quickly to restore bridges and footlogs.

1 Klapatche Park

This hike to Klapatche Park is all uphill and a strenuous but worthwhile climb. The tranquil waters of Aurora Lake and the beautiful subalpine meadows of Klapatche Park are popular destinations for park visitors. The trail takes you up the Westside Road and through old-growth forest with fascinating rock formations, colonade, formed from cooled lava of past eruptions. You'll also feast on the majestic deep-blue waters of St. Andrews Lake and the scenic meadows of St. Andrews Park.

Start: Westside Road closure.
Distance: 19.6-mile out-and-back.
Approximate hiking time: 2- to 4-day back-pack.
Difficulty: Strenuous.
Seasons: Mid-July through September.
Nearest town: Ashford.
Fees and permits: $10.00 vehicle or $5.00 individual entry fee (seven days); $30.00 annual entry fee, Wilderness Camping Permits free—reservations recommended ($20.00 fee).

Maps: USGS: Mount Wow, WA; Trails Illustrated Mount Rainier National Park; Astronaut's Vista: Mount Rainier National Park, Washington; Earthwalk Press Hiking Map & Guide.
Trail contacts: Longmire Wilderness Information Center, (360) 569-HIKE (4453).
Trail conditions: www.nps.gov/mora/trail/tr _cnd.htm; weather, www.nps.gov/mora/ current/weather.htm.

Finding the trailhead: From the Nisqually Entrance Station (see Getting There), drive east on Longmire-Paradise Road 1.0 mile to the Westside Road. Turn left (north) onto Westside Road and drive 3.3 miles to the road closure. Directly before the Westside Road closure is a gravel parking lot that often fills up in summer. *DeLorme: Washington Atlas and Gazetteer:* Page 48 B1.

The National Park Service originally closed the road in 1967 because of a glacial outburst flood that washed out pieces of the road. The road reopened but was closed again due to a washout in 1987. Every three years a geologist evaluates the road to determine if it is safe to reopen. The road has remained closed since the 1987 washout, but you might want to call ahead or visit the Mount Rainier Web site to check the status of the Westside Road. If the road has reopened, you can continue up the road for 7.8 miles (a little over 11 miles from the Longmire-Paradise Road) and start your hike at the St. Andrews trailhead.

Although bikes are not allowed on the park's backcountry trails, the closed portion of the Westside Road has become a popular route to bike. You may opt to bicycle to either the Round Pass or St. Andrews trailhead. The park has installed bike racks at the Lake George trailhead, located just before the Round Pass trailhead, for your convenience.

Special considerations: Historically, the western part of the park experiences numerous washouts due to glacial outburst floods, and footlogs across rivers or streams originating from glaciers frequently wash out. The National Park Service does not advise fording glacial rivers due to the high concentration of debris and risk of large glacial boulders in the water. If you must cross, the Park Service recommends crossing early in the day and using any fallen logs to assist you. Also, always wear boots to protect yourself from any debris suspended in the river.

Aurora Lake. Bill Schneider

Be aware that cougars are often seen along Westside Road. (Refer to Appendix B: Being Prepared for cougar safety information.)

The Hike

Depending on how many miles you want to travel per day and your skill level, this hike can be either a one-night or a three-night backpack. If you go for only one night, you will stay at Klapatche Park and hike 10 miles per day. If you spread your hike out over three nights, you can stay at South Puyallup Camp the first and third nights, averaging about 5 miles per day.

From the Westside Road closure, you will hike uphill on the now-closed road until you reach the Round Pass trailhead. The road, although all uphill, slopes at a nice grade and is easy to follow. The road parallels Tahoma Creek at the beginning, but then diverges from the creek into the forest up to Round Pass. About halfway up the road, you will encounter the abandoned Tahoma Creek Picnic Area.

The Round Pass trailhead is located between the Lake George trailhead and the Marine Memorial. This memorial, dedicated to the thirty-two U.S. Marines killed

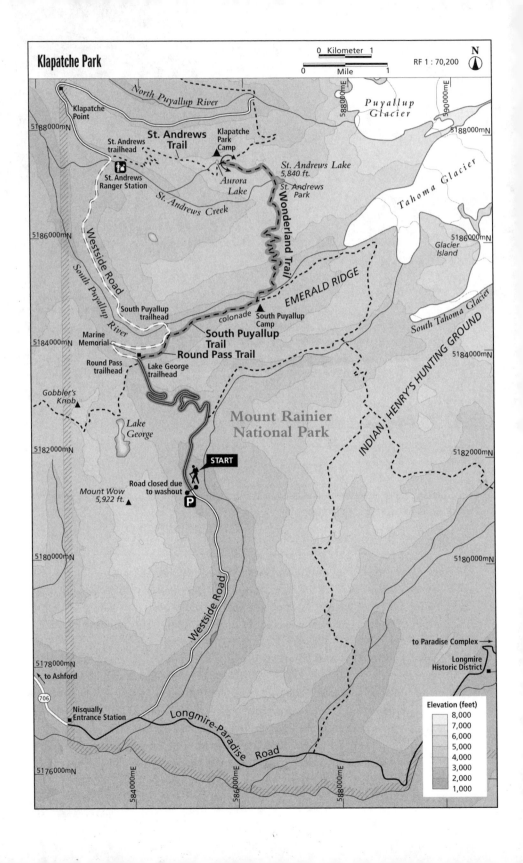

Klapatche Park

0 Kilometer 1

0 Mile 1

RF 1 : 70,200

N

North Puyallup River

Puyallup Glacier

Klapatche Point

5188000mN

St. Andrews trailhead

Klapatche Park Camp

St. Andrews Trail

St. Andrews Lake 5,840 ft.

Tahoma Glacier

St. Andrews Ranger Station

Aurora Lake

St. Andrews Park

St. Andrews Creek

Wonderland Trail

5186000mN

Glacier Island

5186000mN

South Puyallup River

Westside Road

EMERALD RIDGE

South Puyallup trailhead

colonade

South Puyallup Camp

South Tahoma Glacier

5184000mN

Marine Memorial

South Puyallup Trail

Round Pass Trail

5184000mN

Round Pass trailhead

Lake George trailhead

INDIAN HENRY'S HUNTING GROUND

Gobbler's Knob

Mount Rainier National Park

Lake George

5182000mN

5182000mN

START

Road closed due to washout

Mount Wow 5,922 ft.

P

5180000mN

5180000mN

to Paradise Complex →

Longmire Historic District

5178000mN

← to Ashford

Westside Road

706

Nisqually Entrance Station

Longmire-Paradise Road

Elevation (feet)

8,000
7,000
6,000
5,000
4,000
3,000
2,000
1,000

5176000mN

in a plane crash on the South Tahoma Glacier in 1946, offers a spectacular view of the very glacier these unfortunate Marines encountered.

Hike 0.6 mile northeast on the Round Pass Trail to the junction with the South Puyallup Trail. The Round Pass Trail continues left, heading west. Go to the right and take the South Puyallup Trail, which continues northeast. This rocky trail climbs through beautiful old-growth forest for 1.6 miles to South Puyallup Camp.

About 0.3 mile shy of the camp, watch for slanted angular rock formations on the right that assemble in fascinating geometric configurations. The formations, called colonade, are columnar pieces of andesite rock that were formed thousands of years ago when hot lava flowing through the area cooled. As lava flows, it pours into the valley, shrinks slightly, and then breaks into long columns. The columnar andesite makes up Mount Rainier's cone.

▶ Glacial outburst floods, sometimes referred to by the Icelandic term *jokulhlaups,* occur when water pours into the ice cavities of a glacier or between the glacier and bedrock during either heavy autumn rains or summer heat. This results in a churning, concretelike mix of mud, rocks, and uprooted trees. Anytime you are near a river and notice a rapid rise in water level or hear a roaring sound coming from upvalley—often described as sounding similar to a fast-moving train—move quickly to higher ground.

After you pass South Puyallup Camp, you will come to the Wonderland Trail. Go left (north) onto the Wonderland Trail and cross the South Puyallup River. The next 2.0 miles of trail, consisting entirely of steep switchbacks and bordered by brush, take you up to St. Andrews Park. Once atop the ridge, the trail levels out and the breathtaking scenery fills your senses completely. In July avalanche lilies fill the meadows of St. Andrews Park, while Mount Rainier towers majestically above all these natural wonders.

You reach the deep-blue waters of St. Andrews Lake 3.2 miles from the junction with the Wonderland Trail and 9.0 miles into your hike. Previous hikers have greatly impacted this subalpine lake by creating numerous social trails along its fragile banks. Minimize your impact by admiring the lake from the designated trail. West-side climbing routes weave up the side of the mountain above the heavenly lake.

Your destination, Klapatche Park Camp, is 0.8 mile from St. Andrews Lake, and the trail slopes downhill the rest of the way. Colorful subalpine wildflowers fill the meadows of Klapatche Park and surround Aurora Lake in mid-July. This lake, really only a shallow pool of snowmelt, could not be more astonishing, partnered with Mount Rainier above it and the serene meadows of Klapatche Park around it. Mountain goats occasionally graze in the meadows visible from Klapatche Park. The backcountry campsites are located at the west end of the lake.

On the return trip you can either head back the way you came or take the St. Andrews Trail to the Westside Road and hike the remainder of your trip on a gravel road. The second half of this hike is almost entirely downhill, thus either option may be hard on your knees. Although the Westside Road option offers a change of scenery and will likely take less time, it also features an 800-foot elevation gain up to Round Pass and offers less of a wilderness experience.

Miles and Directions

0.0 Start at the Westside Road closure. Continue hiking uphill for 3.6 miles to the top of Round Pass.

3.6 At the Round Pass trailhead, hike 0.6 mile northeast on the Round Pass Trail to the junction with the South Puyallup Trail.

4.2 When the Round Pass Trail meets the South Puyallup Trail, go to the right and take the South Puyallup Trail, which continues northeast.

5.8 Go left (north) onto the Wonderland Trail and cross the South Puyallup River when the South Puyallup Trail dead-ends into the Wonderland Trail. (See Option for a possible side trip to Emerald Ridge.)

9.0 Reach the deep-blue waters of St. Andrews Lake 3.2 miles from the junction with the Wonderland Trail. You will pass St. Andrews Trail to your left (west) just as you reach the west end of Aurora Lake. Continue hiking north on the Wonderland Trail.

9.8 Arrive at Klapatche Park Camp, your turnaround point.

19.6 Arrive back at the road closure.

Option: Take a side trip to Emerald Ridge by turning right (east) at the junction with the Wonderland Trail. Although it lengthens your trip, the emerald-green meadow, with a close-up view of the South Tahoma Glacier, will enchant you. See Hike 2: Emerald Ridge.

Wilderness camping: Fires are prohibited in backcountry camps, and Klapatche Park is no exception. Bring a stove for cooking. The Klapatche Park Camp is amazing, by far our favorite campground in the park. If you can, stay in Site 1. Mount Rainier is most clearly visible from this campsite, which overlooks the lake, but all the sites offer enjoyable views. Sites 3 and 4 have a nice view of the north side of Klapatche Ridge. All the sites are relatively close together, and Klapatche Park Camp

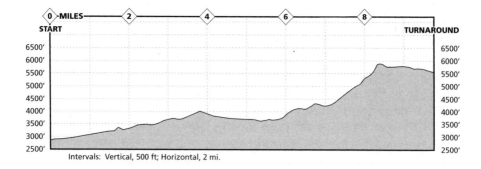

Intervals: Vertical, 500 ft; Horizontal, 2 mi.

has both an outhouse and a food storage pole. Aurora Lake is the water source, but keep in mind that it usually dries up by mid- to late September.

South Puyallup Camp has four individual sites and one group site. Site 1 is probably the best due to its private location and close water source. Be forewarned that the toilet is a 0.1-mile hike from all the campsites. Site 2 also has its own water source and good tent sites. Sites 3 and 4 have just been improved, and if seclusion is your primary concern, Site 4 is your best bet.

Hike Information

Local Information

Mount Rainier National Park Web site, www.nps.gov/mora; twenty-four-hour visitor information, (360) 569-2211.

Gifford Pinchot National Forest, www.fs.fed.us/gpnf.

Longmire Museum, (360) 569-2211, ext. 3314.

Lodging

National Park Inn, (360) 569-2275; Paradise Inn, (360) 569-2275. For a list of accommodations outside the park, visit www.nps.gov/mora/general/accom.htm.

Campgrounds

You can stay at a campground inside the park if you wish to day hike and car camp. Sunshine Point Campground is located in the southwest corner of the park, 0.25 mile inside the Nisqually Entrance. Register at the campground. Cougar Rock Campground is located in the southwest corner of the park, 2.3 miles north of the Longmire Historic District. Reserve a site at Cougar Rock Campground online at http://reservations.nps.gov, or call (800) 365-CAMP (2267) 7:00 A.M. to 7:00 P.M. PST.

2 Emerald Ridge

Befittingly, Emerald Ridge boasts deep-green meadows, yet this precious gem also houses subalpine wildflowers and hoary marmots. The ridge offers spectacular views of Tahoma Glacier, South Tahoma Glacier, and Glacier Island. Additionally, the hike to Emerald Ridge takes you up the Westside Road and through old-growth forest with fascinating rock formations, colonade, formed from cooled lava from past eruptions. Although the hike to Emerald Ridge is all uphill and relatively strenuous, the rewards are well worth the effort.

Start: Westside Road closure.
Distance: 15.0-mile out-and-back.
Approximate hiking time: 2-day backpack.
Difficulty: Strenuous.
Seasons: Mid-July through September.
Nearest town: Ashford.
Fees and permits: $10.00 vehicle or $5.00 individual entry fee (seven days); $30.00 annual entry fee. Wilderness Camping Permits free—reservations recommended ($20 fee).

Maps: USGS: Mount Rainier West; Trails Illustrated Mount Rainier National Park; Astronaut's Vista: Mount Rainier National Park, Washington; Earthwalk Press Hiking Map & Guide.
Trail contacts: Longmire Wilderness Information Center, (360) 569-HIKE (4453).
Trail conditions:
ww.nps.gov/mora/trail/tr_cnd.htm; weather, www.nps.gov/mora/current/weather.htm.

Finding the trailhead: From the Nisqually Entrance Station (see Getting There), drive east on Longmire-Paradise Road 1.0 mile to the Westside Road. Turn left (north) onto Westside Road and drive 3.3 miles to the road closure. Directly before the Westside Road closure is a gravel parking lot that often fills up in summer. *DeLorme: Washington Atlas and Gazetteer:* Page 48 B1.

The National Park Service originally closed the road in 1967 because of a glacial outburst flood that washed out pieces of the road. The road reopened, but was closed again due to a washout in 1987. Every three years a geologist evaluates the road to determine if it is safe to reopen. The road has remained closed since the 1987 washout, but you might want to call ahead or visit the Mount Rainier Web site to check the status of the Westside Road. If the road has reopened, you can continue up the road for 3.6 miles to the parking lot to the left of the Lake George trailhead and start your hike at the Round Pass trailhead.

Although bikes are not allowed on the park's backcountry trails, the closed portion of the Westside Road has become a popular route to bike. You may opt to bicycle from the road closure to the Round Pass trailhead. The park has installed bike racks at the Lake George trailhead, located just before the Round Pass trailhead on the left (west) side of the road, for your convenience.

Special considerations: Historically, the western part of the park experiences numerous washouts due to glacial outburst floods, and footlogs across rivers or streams originating from glaciers frequently wash out. The National Park Service does not advise fording glacial rivers due to the high concentration of debris and risk of large glacial boulders in the water. If you must cross, the Park Service recommends crossing early in the day and using any fallen logs to assist you. Also, always wear boots to protect yourself from any debris suspended in the river.

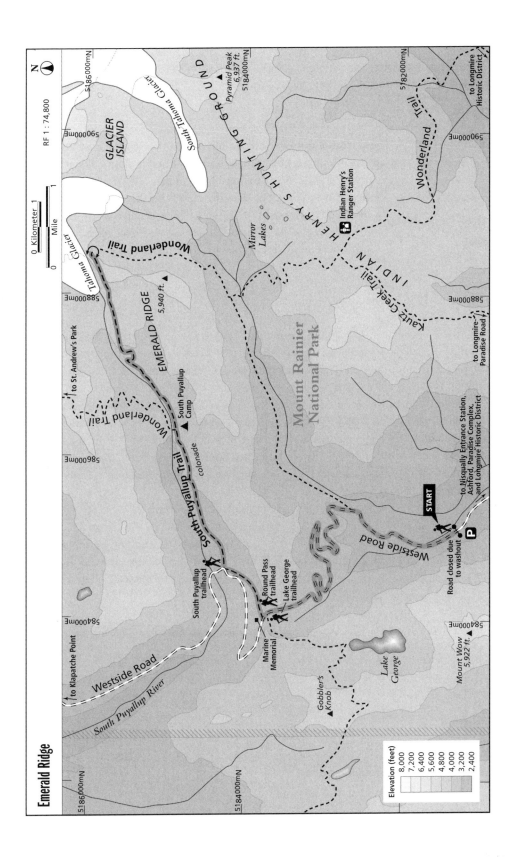

Emerald Ridge

RF 1 : 74,800

0 Kilometer 1
0 Mile 1

GLACIER ISLAND

South Tahoma Glacier

Pyramid Peak
6,937 ft.

HENRY'S HUNTING GROUND

Indian Henry's Ranger Station

Mirror Lakes

Wonderland Trail

to Longmire Historic District

Tahoma Glacier

Wonderland Trail

EMERALD RIDGE

5,940 ft.

South Puyallup Camp

South Puyallup Trail

colonade

INDIAN

Kautz Creek Trail

to Longmire, Paradise Road

Mount Rainier National Park

to St. Andrew's Park

Wonderland Trail

South Puyallup trailhead

Round Pass trailhead

Lake George trailhead

Marine Memorial

START

to Nisqually Entrance Station, Ashford, Paradise Complex, and Longmire Historic District

Westside Road

Road closed due to washout

P

to Klapatche Point

Westside Road

South Puyallup River

Gobbler's Knob

Lake George

Mount Wow
5,922 ft.

Elevation (feet)
8,000
7,200
6,400
5,600
4,800
4,000
3,200
2,400

Be aware that cougars are often seen along Westside Road. (Refer to Appendix B: Being Prepared for cougar safety information.)

The Hike

From the Westside Road closure, you will hike uphill on the now-closed road until you reach the Round Pass trailhead. The road, although all uphill, slopes at a nice grade and is easy to follow. The road parallels Tahoma Creek at the beginning, but then diverges from the creek into the forest up to Round Pass. About halfway up the road, you will encounter the abandoned Tahoma Creek Picnic Area.

▶ **Andesite is an igneous rock named for the Andes Mountains.**

The Round Pass trailhead is located between the Lake George trailhead and the Marine Memorial. This memorial, dedicated to thirty-two U.S. Marines killed in a plane crash on the South Tahoma Glacier in 1946, offers a spectacular view of the very glacier these unfortunate Marines encountered.

Hike 0.6 mile northeast on the Round Pass Trail to the junction with the South Puyallup Trail. The Round Pass Trail continues left, heading west. Go to the right and take the South Puyallup Trail, which continues northeast. This rocky trail climbs through beautiful old-growth forest for 1.6 miles to South Puyallup Camp.

About 0.3 mile shy of the camp, watch for slanted angular rock formations on the right that assemble in fascinating geometric configurations. The formations, called colonade, are columnar pieces of andesite rock that were formed thousands of years ago when hot lava flowing through the area cooled. As lava flows, it pours into the valley, shrinks slightly, and then breaks into long columns. Columnar andesite makes up the Mount Rainier's cone.

After you pass the South Puyallup Camp, you will come to the Wonderland Trail. Go right (east) toward Emerald Ridge. From here hike 1.7 miles to the top of Emerald Ridge, 7.5 miles into your hike. The Tahoma Glacier and its moraine are to your left (north). Tahoma Glacier resides in a land scar carved out by a previous mud slide. The trail borders the moraine and traverses the north side of Emerald Ridge. This

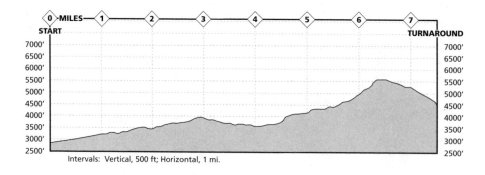

Intervals: Vertical, 500 ft; Horizontal, 1 mi.

part of the trail has washed out many times and has a steep, unstable ledge. Take the new trail that traverses diagonally across the ridge.

The emerald-green meadows speckled with wildflowers, especially subalpine lupine in mid-July, house tons of human-friendly hoary marmots. Please do not feed these wild animals; they need to be self-sufficient to survive in their natural habitat.

Looking up, behold the magnificent view of Tahoma Glacier above you and South Tahoma Glacier to the right. To date, twenty-three glacial outburst floods have exploded from South Tahoma Glacier. Couched between the two glaciers rests a small oasis of green pasture in a sea of ice. Mountain goats often graze in this green haven, and if you look closely you can see fields of lupine giving it a purple hue.

Miles and Directions

0.0 Start at the Westside Road closure. Continue hiking uphill for 3.6 miles to the top of Round Pass.

3.6 At the Round Pass trailhead, hike 0.6 mile northeast on the Round Pass Trail to the junction with the South Puyallup Trail.

4.2 When the Round Pass Trail meets the South Puyallup Trail, go to the right and take the South Puyallup Trail, which continues northeast.

5.8 Go right (east) onto the Wonderland Trail when the South Puyallup Trail dead-ends into the Wonderland Trail. From here hike 1.7 miles to the top of Emerald Ridge. (See the Option below for a possible side trip to Klapatche Park.)

7.5 Arrive at Emerald Ridge, your turnaround point.

15.0 Arrive back at the road closure.

Option: If you decide to stay at South Puyallup Camp, you might want to take an additional day hike. Klapatche Park is amazing. You pass through St. Andrews Park and by St. Andrews Lake, two natural wonders guaranteed to astound you. Klapatche Park is 4.0 miles from the South Puyallup Camp, making it an 8.0-mile round-trip day hike. You might consider making this trip a two- or three-night backpack trip in order to stay at Klapatche Park. See Hike 1: Klapatche Park.

Wilderness camping: Fires are prohibited in the backcountry, and the South Puyallup Camp is no exception. Bring a stove for cooking. There are four individual sites at South Puyallup Camp and one group site. Site 1 is probably the best campsite. It is private, with a close water source. Be forewarned that the toilet is more than 0.1 mile from all the campsites. Site 2 also has its own water source and good tent sites. Sites 3 and 4 have just been improved, and if seclusion is your primary concern, Site 4 is your best bet.

Hike Information

Local Information

Mount Rainier National Park Web site, www.nps.gov/mora; twenty-four-hour visitor information, (360) 569-2211.
Gifford Pinchot National Forest, www.fs.fed.us/gpnf.
Longmire Museum, (360) 569-2211, ext. 3314.

Lodging

National Park Inn, (360) 569-2275; Paradise Inn, (360) 569-2275. For a list of accommodations outside the park, visit www.nps.gov/mora/general/accom.htm.

Campgrounds

You can stay at a campground inside the park if you wish to day hike and car camp. Sunshine Point Campground is located in the southwest corner of the park, 0.25 mile inside the Nisqually Entrance. Register at the campground. Cougar Rock Campground is located in the southwest corner of the park, 2.3 miles north of the Longmire Historic District. Reserve a site at Cougar Rock Campground online at http://reservations.nps.gov, or call (800) 365-CAMP (2267) 7:00 A.M. to 7:00 P.M. PST.

3 Gobbler's Knob

The hike to Gobbler's Knob passes the clear waters of Lake George and ascends to a peak with panoramic views of Mount St. Helens, the Goat Rocks, the North Cascades, the Olympics, Mount Hood, and Mount Rainier. Lake George, a beautiful mountain lake, is one of the few places to fish in Mount Rainier National Park.

Start: Westside Road closure.
Distance: 12.0-mile out-and-back.
Approximate hiking time: 5 to 8 hours.
Difficulty: Moderate.
Seasons: Mid-July through September.
Nearest town: Ashford.
Fees and Permits: $10.00 vehicle or $5.00 individual entry fee (seven days); $30.00 annual entry fee. Wilderness Camping Permits free—reservations recommended ($20 fee).

Maps: USGS: Mount Wow; Trails Illustrated Mount Rainier National Park; Astronaut's Vista: Mount Rainier National Park, Washington; Earthwalk Press Hiking Map & Guide.
Trail contacts: Longmire Wilderness Information Center, (360) 569-HIKE (4453).
Trail conditions: www.nps.gov/mora/trail/tr_cnd.htm; weather, www.nps.gov/mora/current/weather.htm.

Finding the trailhead: From the Nisqually Entrance Station (see Getting There), drive east on Longmire-Paradise Road 1.0 mile to the Westside Road. Turn left (north) onto Westside Road and drive 3.3 miles to the road closure. Directly before the Westside Road closure is a gravel parking lot that often fills up in summer. *DeLorme: Washington Atlas and Gazetteer:* Page 48 B1.

Mount Rainier from Gobbler's Knob. ▶

ainier National Park

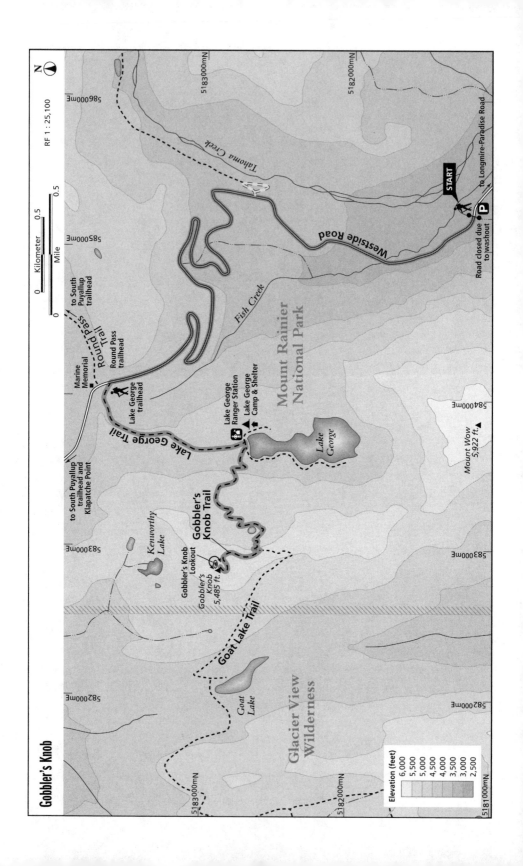

Gobbler's Knob

RF 1 : 25,100

N

Kilometer 0   0.5   0.5
Mile   0   0.5

to South Puyallup trailhead

Round Pass Trail

Marine Memorial

Round Pass trailhead

Lake George trailhead

to South Puyallup trailhead and Klapatche Point

Lake George Trail

Kenworthy Lake

Gobbler's Knob Lookout

Gobbler's Knob 5,485 ft.

Gobbler's Knob Trail

Lake George Ranger Station

Lake George Camp & Shelter

Lake George

Mount Rainier National Park

Fish Creek

Tahoma Creek

Westside Road

START

Road closed due to washout

to Longmire-Paradise Road

P

Mount Wow 5,922 ft.

Goat Lake Trail

Goat Lake

Glacier View Wilderness

Elevation (feet)
6,000
5,500
5,000
5,000
4,500
4,000
3,500
3,000
2,500

5186000mE
5185000mE
5184000mE
5183000mE
5182000mE

583000mE
584000mE
585000mE
586000mE

5183000mN
5182000mN
5181000mN

The National Park Service originally closed the road in 1967 because of a glacial outburst flood that washed out pieces of the road. The road reopened but was closed again due to a washout in 1987. Every three years a geologist evaluates the road to determine if it is safe to reopen. The road has remained closed since the 1987 washout, but you might want to call ahead or visit the Mount Rainier Web site to check the status of the Westside Road. If the road has reopened, you can continue up the road for 3.6 miles to the parking lot to the left of the Lake George trailhead and start your hike at the Round Pass trailhead.

Although bikes are not allowed on the park's backcountry trails, the closed portion of the Westside Road has become a popular route to bike. You may opt to bicycle from the road closure to the Round Pass trailhead. The park has installed bike racks at the Lake George Trailhead, located just before the Round Pass trailhead on the left (west) side of the road, for your convenience.

Special considerations: Historically, the western part of the park experiences numerous washouts due to glacial outburst floods. Footlogs across rivers or streams originating from glaciers frequently wash out. The National Park Service does not advise fording glacial rivers due to the high concentration of debris in them due to the risk of large glacial boulders in the water. If you must cross, the National Park Service recommends crossing early in the day and using any fallen logs. Also, always wear your boots to protect yourself from any debris suspended in the river.

Be aware that cougars are often seen along Westside Road. (Refer to Appendix B: Being Prepared for cougar safety information.)

The Hike

From the Westside Road closure, you will hike uphill on the now-closed road until you reach the Lake George trailhead. The road, although all uphill, slopes at a nice grade and is easy to follow. The road parallels Tahoma Creek at the beginning, but then diverges from the creek into the forest up to Round Pass. About halfway up the road, you will encounter the abandoned Tahoma Creek Picnic Area.

▶ In 1986 a 12-foot boulder landed at Tahoma Creek Picnic Area during a glacial outburst flood.

The first section of the trail to Lake George is less than 0.9 mile and ascends at a nice grade. You can steal a couple glimpses of Mount Rainier along the way. Take a break at Lake George, especially if you like to fish. The fish were rising like crazy the last time we were here, and you do not need a permit to fish in Mount Rainier National Park.

For the next 1.5 miles to Gobbler's Knob, the trail ascends a steep hill. After hiking for 1.1 miles up the hill, you encounter the Goat Lake Trail (Forest Service Trail 249). Go right (north) and stay on the Lake George Trail. The Goat Lake Trail leaves the park and continues on to Goat Lake.

After the junction, you travel through several meadows filled with beautiful wildflowers. In July lupine, magenta paintbrush, and an occasional Columbia lily color these meadows. From the last meadow, you clearly see the huge rock that makes up Gobbler's Knob, your destination.

From the lookout tower atop the knob, a variety of landmarks ring the horizon. Refer to your map to identify them. If it is a clear day, you can see Mount St. Helens to the southwest, the Goat Rocks to the southeast, the Cascades to the north, and magnificent Mount Rainier to the northeast. There is also a fabulous view of Lake George and Mount Wow, sloping steeply over Lake George. When you have had your fill of natural wonders, head back the way you came. If you have the time and energy, take the option to Goat Lake.

▶ **The *wow* of Mount Wow is a Native American term for goat.**

Miles and Directions

0.0 Start at the Westside Road closure. Continue hiking uphill for 3.6 miles to the top of Round Pass.

3.6 At the top of Round Pass, you will encounter the Lake George trailhead to your left (west). Follow the Lake George Trail for the next 0.9 mile to Lake George.

4.5 Reach Lake George. The next 1.5 miles of trail to Gobbler's Knob ascends a steep hill.

5.6 Before you reach the top of Gobbler's Knob, the Goat Lake Trail forks off to the left (west). Stay right heading north. (See Option for a possible side trip to Goat Lake.)

6.0 Reach Gobbler's Knob lookout tower. Enjoy the view before retracing your steps.

12.0 Arrive back at the road enclosure.

Option: Experience a taste of the Glacier View Wilderness, just west of the park, by taking a side trip to Goat Lake, adding only 3.8 miles to your hike. From the junction with the Goat Lake Trail, head west on the Goat Lake Trail. Travel uphill for just a couple of steps, and then go downhill all the way to Goat Lake. The descent is relatively steep, with only a few switchbacks. Be aware that the ledge of the trail drops off rather abruptly in places. At Goat Lake you can enjoy the tranquility of the lake or take your chances fishing from the banks.

It is also possible to access Goat Lake and Gobbler's Knob from Forest Road 59, which is about 2.0 miles east of Ashford and before you reach the Nisqually Entrance Station. After more than 8 miles, this forest road takes you to Forest Service Trail 248. This trail dead-ends into Forest Service Trail 249. Go left (north) on Forest Service Trail 249, the trail to Goat Lake.

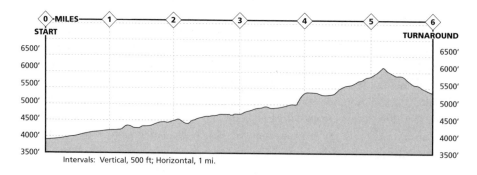

Intervals: Vertical, 500 ft; Horizontal, 1 mi.

Wilderness camping: Lake George has five individual campsites and one group site. Campsite 5 is closest to the lake but has semislanted tent sites. The rest of the campsites are along the ridge and require a short hike to water and the toilet. If possible, avoid Site 4, which lacks a good tent site. Campsite 3 is as flat as a board and has a view of Mount Rainier. The group site is to the east of the individual sites on its own hill and has at least one good tent site, possibly two.

Hike Information

Local Information

Mount Rainier National Park Web site,
www.nps.gov/mora; twenty-four-hour visitor information, (360) 569–2211.
Gifford Pinchot National Forest,
www.fs.fed.us/gpnf.
Longmire Museum, (360) 569–2211, ext. 3314.

Lodging

National Park Inn, (360) 569–2275; Paradise Inn, (360) 569–2275. For a list of accommodations outside the park, visit www.nps.gov/mora/general/accom.htm.

Campgrounds

You can stay at a campground inside the park if you wish to day hike and car camp. Sunshine Point Campground is located in the southwest corner of the park, 0.25 mile inside the Nisqually Entrance. Register at the campground. Cougar Rock Campground is located in the southwest corner of the park, 2.3 miles north of the Longmire Historic District. Reserve a site at Cougar Rock Campground online at http://reservations.nps.gov, or call (800) 365–CAMP (2267) 7:00 A.M. to 7:00 P.M. PST.

4 Indian Henry's Hunting Ground

Start: Kautz Creek trailhead.
Distance: 11.4-mile out-and-back.
Approximate hiking time: 5 to 8 hours.
Difficulty: Strenuous.
Seasons: Mid-July through September.
Nearest town: Ashford.
Fees and permits: $10.00 vehicle or $5.00 individual entry fee (seven days); $30.00 annual entry fee. Wilderness Camping Permits free—reservations recommended ($20 fee).

Maps: USGS: Mount Wow; Trails Illustrated Mount Rainier National Park; Astronaut's Vista: Mount Rainier National Park, Washington; Earthwalk Press Hiking Map & Guide.
Trail contacts: Longmire Wilderness Information Center, (360) 569–HIKE (4453).
Trail conditions: www.nps.gov/mora/trail/tr_cnd.htm; weather, www.nps.gov/mora/current/weather.htm.

Finding the trailhead: From the Nisqually Entrance Station (see Getting There), drive east on Longmire-Paradise Road 3.5 miles to the paved parking lot for Kautz Creek Picnic Area and Exhibit, which, unfortunately, often fills up on sunny summer weekends. Park and walk across the road to the trailhead. *DeLorme: Washington Atlas and Gazetteer: Page 48 C2.*

Kautz Creek.

The Hike

For avid hill climbers, this hike gives you a large dosage of uphill medicine. The trail takes you to the picturesque meadows of Indian Henry's Hunting Ground. Mount Rainier's Sunset Amphitheater is visible from the meadows on a clear day, as are Copper and Iron Mountains. This area was named for Indian Henry (Sutelik), the Native American who taught James Longmire about the trails in Mount Rainier.

The trailhead is across the road from the Kautz Creek Picnic Area. Cross Longmire-Paradise Road to the wooden boardwalk. Follow the wooden walkway for 100 feet; the trail will be on the right side. The boardwalk to your left was constructed by volunteers in 1994 and leads to a viewpoint of the Kautz Creek Mudflow. Unless you want to check out the viewpoint first, take the Kautz Creek Trail heading north.

The first mile of the trail takes you through the remnants of the Kautz Creek Mudflow. In October 1947 a glacial outburst flood wiped out the forest all around Kautz Creek. Glacial ice from the center of Kautz Creek crashed down the river, cutting a deep channel into the earth while picking up dirt, rocks, foliage, and other debris. The sheer power of this twenty-hour-long flood knocked down trees and

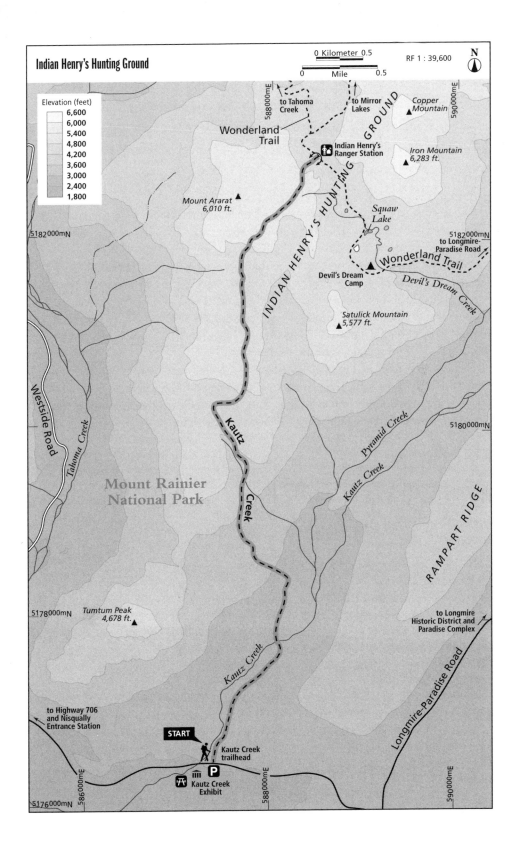

Indian Henry's Hunting Ground

0 Kilometer 0.5

0 Mile 0.5

RF 1 : 39,600

N

Elevation (feet)
- 6,600
- 6,000
- 5,400
- 4,800
- 4,200
- 3,600
- 3,000
- 2,400
- 1,800

to Tahoma Creek

to Mirror Lakes

Copper Mountain

Wonderland Trail

588000mE

590000mE

Indian Henry's Ranger Station

INDIAN HENRY'S HUNTING GROUND

Iron Mountain 6,283 ft.

Mount Ararat 6,010 ft.

Squaw Lake

5182000mN

5182000mN

to Longmire-Paradise Road

Wonderland Trail

Devil's Dream Camp

Devil's Dream Creek

Satulick Mountain 5,577 ft.

Westside Road

Tahoma Creek

Kautz Creek

Pyramid Creek

Kautz Creek

5180000mN

Mount Rainier National Park

RAMPART RIDGE

5178000mN

Tumtum Peak 4,678 ft.

Kautz Creek

to Longmire Historic District and Paradise Complex

to Highway 706 and Nisqually Entrance Station

START

Kautz Creek trailhead

Longmire-Paradise Road

586000mE

Kautz Creek Exhibit

588000mE

590000mE

5176000mN

▶ In 1857 Lt. August Valentine Kautz attempted to summit Mount Rainier and reached within 400 feet of the Columbia Crest. The Kautz Creek and Glacier commemorates his valiant attempt. Just east of the Kautz Glacier, the Wapowety Cleaver bears the name of the Nisqually Indian who guided the Kautz party up the mountain. Unlike other known Native American guides, Wapowety showed little fear of climbing Mount Rainier. Wapowety nearly died from the attempt despite his decision to exit early due to snowblindness.

deposited a blanket of debris around them. These piles of silt and rock around the roots eventually killed the trees, but you will notice that a new forest is emerging from the aftermath of the mudflow.

After you cross Kautz Creek, 1.0 mile into your hike, the trail turns into steep switchbacks that last for almost 4 miles. For the first part of your ascent, the trail takes you through a mature forest unaffected by the Kautz Creek Mudflow. As the forest disappears to reveal beautiful meadows with colorful wildflowers, you have reached Indian Henry's Hunting Ground. Mount Ararat rising from the northwest side of the trail and Satulick Mountain from the southeast side.

The last 0.7 mile of the hike is a slightly downhill relief. After enjoying the impressive scenery and the meadow's showcase of flowers, you might want to hike north up the Wonderland Trail to Mount Rainier's oldest patrol cabin, which is still in use. Another option includes a short hike to Mirror Lakes.

Miles and Directions

0.0 Start at the Kautz Creek Picnic Area and Exhibit. The trailhead is across the road from the picnic area. Cross Longmire-Paradise Road to the wooden boardwalk. Follow the wooden walkway for 100 feet; the trail will be on the left side.

1.0 You will cross Kautz Creek 1.0 mile into your hike. From this point on, the trail ascends steeply.

5.0 As the trees disappear and the scenery unfolds, you are stepping into Indian Henry's Hunting Ground.

5.7 At the junction with Wonderland Trail, you have a variety of options. You may choose to simply admire the view and then head back. Other options include visiting an old rustic patrol cabin located north on the Wonderland Trail, heading south to Devil's Dream, or taking a short side trip to Mirror Lakes.

11.4 Arrive back at the picnic area.

Option: You can take a side trip to Mirror Lakes, adding 1.8 miles to your hike. These small pools are surrounded by beautiful flower-filled meadows. Go left (north) at the junction with the Wonderland Trail and go 0.2 mile to the Mirror Lakes Trail. Go right (northeast) 0.6 mile to the lakes. Follow the Mirror Lakes Trail to its end, where there is a great view of Pyramid Peak and Mount Rainier.

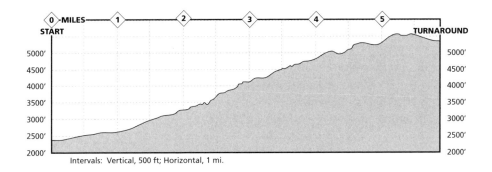

Intervals: Vertical, 500 ft; Horizontal, 1 mi.

Wilderness camping: The nearest camp is Devil's Dream Camp, a little over a mile southeast from the end of the Kautz Creek Trail. All seven individual campsites at Devil's Dream Camp, as well as the group site, are very pleasant and flat. Sites 5 and 6 offer the most privacy. There are two pit toilets, and the camp is often filled with Wonderland Trail hikers. Be careful when you use the toilet near Site 4—it is likely that the residents there can see you! All the other sites are next to the trail, spacious, and flat. Usually the water source for Devil's Dream Camp is near Site 1, but it often dries up in late summer. If this is the case, you will have to hike about 0.25 mile to Squaw Lake or to the creek directly after Squaw Lake, depending on where you prefer to obtain your water.

Hike Information

Local Information

Mount Rainier National Park Web site, www.nps.gov/mora; twenty-four-hour visitor information, (360) 569-2211.

Gifford Pinchot National Forest, www.fs.fed.us/gpnf.

Longmire Museum, (360) 569-2211, ext. 3314.

Lodging

National Park Inn, (360) 569-2275; Paradise Inn, (360) 569-2275. For a list of accommodations outside the park, visit www.nps.gov/mora/general/accom.htm.

Campgrounds

You can stay at a campground inside the park if you wish to day hike and car camp. Sunshine Point Campground is located in the southwest corner of the park, 0.25 mile inside the Nisqually Entrance. Register at the campground. Cougar Rock Campground is located in the southwest corner of the park, 2.3 miles north of the Longmire Historic District. Reserve a site at Cougar Rock Campground online at http://reservations.nps.gov, or call (800) 365-CAMP (2267) 7:00 A.M. to 7:00 P.M. PST.

5 Rampart Ridge

One of the few hikes that are snow free in June, this short but steep hike up to Rampart Ridge affords you splendid views of Eagle Peak, Mount Rainier, and the Nisqually River Valley. The trail takes you through a quiet, dense forest to two viewpoints offering the possibility of viewing a variety of flora and fauna.

Start: Longmire Historic District.
Distance: 4.8-mile loop.
Approximate hiking time: 2 to 3 hours.
Difficulty: Moderate.
Seasons: June through September.
Nearest town: Ashford.
Fees and permits: $10.00 vehicle or $5.00 individual entry fee (seven days); $30.00 annual entry fee.

Maps: USGS: Mount Rainier West; Trails Illustrated Mount Rainier National Park; Astronaut's Vista: Mount Rainier National Park, Washington; Earthwalk Press Hiking Map & Guide.
Trail contacts: Longmire Wilderness Information Center, (360) 569–HIKE (4453).
Trail conditions: www.nps.gov/mora/trail/tr_cnd.htm; weather, www.nps.gov/mora/current/weather.htm.

Finding the trailhead: From Nisqually River Entrance Station (see Getting There), drive 6.7 miles east on the Longmire-Paradise Road to the Longmire Historic District. Turn right (southeast) into the parking lot around the Longmire Historic District, which includes Longmire Wilderness Information Center, the Longmire Museum, and the National Park Inn. Walk on one of the two crosswalks across the Longmire-Paradise Road to the Rampart Ridge trailhead, located across the street from the inn. Finding a parking space at the Longmire Historic District is a potential problem on sunny summer weekends. *DeLorme: Washington Atlas and Gazetteer:* Page 48 C2.

Special considerations: There are no water sources along this trail.

The Hike

This hike is great for people who like to climb hills, enjoy great scenery, and need a hike that is snow-free in June. In less than 2 miles the trail takes you up 1,200 feet and allows you to peer into the valley you just ventured from, as well as the valley on the other side of Rampart Ridge. The ridge itself, also known as the "Ramparts," is a remnant of ancient lava flow from Mount Rainier. The switchbacks are steep, but definitely bearable. Remember to bring plenty of water, because this hike has no water sources.

Stay to your left (west) after crossing the street. A small section of the first part of the Rampart Ridge Trail is also part of the Trail of the Shadows, but the Rampart Ridge Trail veers off to the left after only 0.1 mile. The Trail of the Shadows (see Hike 10: Trail of the Shadows) is a self-guided hike that takes you around a field of mineral springs.

Rampart Ridge Viewpoint.

At the junction with the Rampart Ridge Trail, go right (north). For more than 1.5 miles there are relatively steep switchbacks, although they level out at the end just before the viewpoints. This part of the trail is mainly in the trees, but at one point you may catch a glimpse of Tumtum Peak to the west. After hiking 1.8 miles you reach a spur trail that goes to a viewpoint. Take a break and enjoy the scenery from the viewpoint. On a clear day you can see Eagle Peak, the Nisqually River, the Longmire Historic District, and Mount Rainier.

The next 1.2 miles along the ridge are flat and very pleasant. You can see down into the valley on the other side of Rampart Ridge along this section. A glimpse of Kautz Creek can be had 0.2 mile after the viewpoint. You arrive at the Wonderland Trail junction after traveling a little over a mile from the viewpoint. Go right (south) at this junction. This turn takes you off the Rampart Ridge Trail and onto the Wonderland Trail. From this point on, the trail loses elevation all the way back to the Longmire Historic District. About 0.2 mile after joining the Wonderland Trail, a trail leading to Van Trump Park splits off to the left (northeast). Stay to the right (south) here, and continue down the Wonderland Trail. At 4.6 miles cross Longmire-

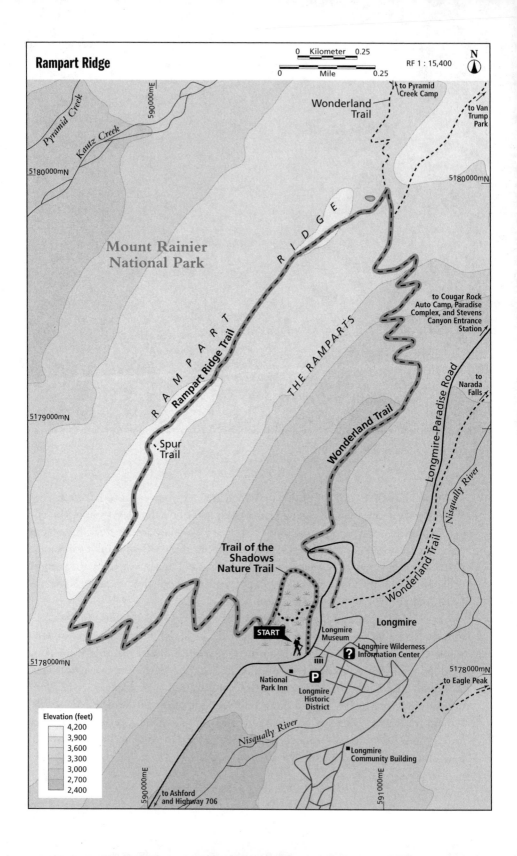

Rampart Ridge

RF 1 : 15,400

N

Kilometer 0.25

Mile 0.25

Pyramid Creek

Kautz Creek

590000mE

to Pyramid Creek Camp

Wonderland Trail

to Van Trump Park

5180000mN

5180000mN

Mount Rainier National Park

R I D G E

R A M P A R T

Rampart Ridge Trail

T H E   R A M P A R T S

to Cougar Rock Auto Camp, Paradise Complex, and Stevens Canyon Entrance Station

5179000mN

Spur Trail

Wonderland Trail

Longmire-Paradise Road

Nisqually River

to Narada Falls

Trail of the Shadows Nature Trail

START

Longmire Museum

Longmire Wilderness Information Center

Wonderland Trail

Longmire

?

National Park Inn

P

Longmire Historic District

5178000mN

5178000mN

to Eagle Peak

591000mE

Nisqually River

Longmire Community Building

590000mE

to Ashford and Highway 706

Elevation (feet)
4,200
3,900
3,600
3,300
3,000
2,700
2,400

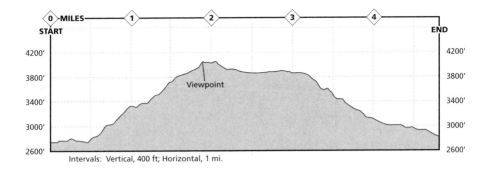

Intervals: Vertical, 400 ft; Horizontal, 1 mi.

Paradise Road and continue hiking on the Wonderland Trail back to the Longmire Historic District. There are many signs to point the way on this last stretch.

Miles and Directions

0.0 Start at the Longmire Historic District. Hike across the Longmire-Paradise Road; stay to the left, heading west on the Trail of the Shadows until you reach the Rampart Ridge Trail.

0.1 At the junction with the Rampart Ridge Trail, go right (north).

1.8 A spur trail to the right goes to a viewpoint. Continue on the Rampart Ridge Trail, hiking northeast.

3.0 Arrive at the Wonderland Trail junction after traveling a little over a mile from the viewpoint. Go right (south) at this junction. (See Options for a possible side trip to Indian Henry's Hunting Ground.)

3.2 A trail that leads to Van Trump Park heads off to the left (northeast). Stay to the right, heading south. (See Options for a possible side trip to Van Trump Park.)

4.6 Cross the Longmire-Paradise Road and continue hiking on the Wonderland Trail. There are many signs to point the way on this last stretch.

4.8 Arrive back at the Longmire Historic District.

Options: Take the trail to Van Trump Park, 3.2 miles into your hike. This hike takes you to beautiful flower-filled meadows with great views of the Tatoosh Range, Mount Adams, Mount St. Helens, and Mount Rainier. (See Hike 6: Comet Falls and Van Trump Park.) This side trip is 3.2 miles one-way, adding 6.4 miles to your hike.

You can also walk up to Indian Henry's Hunting Ground from the Wonderland Trail junction. This scenic area is about 5 miles from the junction, making it an almost 10-mile side trip. From Indian Henry's Hunting Ground there are fabulous views of Mount Rainier, beautiful meadows filled with lupine, and views of Copper and Iron Mountains. (See Hike 4: Indian Henry's Hunting Ground.) If you choose to take this option, turn left (north) at the Wonderland Trail junction (Milepoint 3.0).

Hike Information

Local Information

Mount Rainier National Park Web site, www.nps.gov/mora; twenty-four-hour visitor information, (360) 569–2211.

Gifford Pinchot National Forest, www.fs.fed.us/gpnf.

Longmire Museum, (360) 569–2211, ext. 3314.

Lodging

National Park Inn, (360) 569–2275; Paradise Inn, (360) 569–2275. For a list of accommodations outside the park, visit www.nps.gov/mora/general/accom.htm.

Campgrounds

You can stay at a campground inside the park if you wish to day hike and car camp. Sunshine Point Campground is located in the southwest corner of the park, 0.25 mile inside the Nisqually Entrance. Register at the campground. Cougar Rock Campground is located in the southwest corner of the park, 2.3 miles north of the Longmire Historic District. Reserve a site at Cougar Rock Campground online at http://reservations.nps.gov, or call (800) 365-CAMP (2267) 7:00 A.M. to 7:00 P.M. PST.

6 Comet Falls and Van Trump Park

This hike takes you by Comet Falls and up to Van Trump Park, a series of beautiful flower-filled meadows with great views of the Tatoosh Range, Mount Adams, Mount St. Helens, and Mount Rainier. Van Trump Park also offers you ample viewing of Kautz and Van Trump Glaciers.

Start: Van Trump Park trailhead (otherwise known as Comet Falls trailhead).

Distance: 5.8-mile out-and-back.

Approximate hiking time: 2.5 to 4 hours.

Difficulty: Moderate.

Seasons: Mid-July through September.

Nearest town: Ashford.

Fees and permits: $10.00 vehicle or $5.00 individual entry fee (seven days); $30.00 annual entry fee.

Maps: USGS: Mount Rainier West; Trails Illustrated Mount Rainier National Park; Astronaut's Vista: Mount Rainier National Park, Washington; Earthwalk Press Hiking Map & Guide.

Trail contacts: Longmire Wilderness Information Center, (360) 569–HIKE (4453).

Trail conditions: www.nps.gov/mora/trail/tr_cnd.htm; weather, www.nps.gov/mora/current/weather.htm.

Finding the trailhead: From the Nisqually Entrance Station, (see Getting There) drive 10.7 miles east on Longmire-Paradise Road. The parking lot is on your left, but it is often overcrowded on sunny weekends. If you cannot find a space in the parking lot or in the few spaces across the road, you might have to select an alternate hike. *DeLorme: Washington Atlas and Gazetteer:* Page 48 B2.

Special considerations: The footlog over a small tributary of Van Trump Creek above Comet Falls has been known to wash out, making the side trip to Mildred Point unavailable.

Comet Falls.

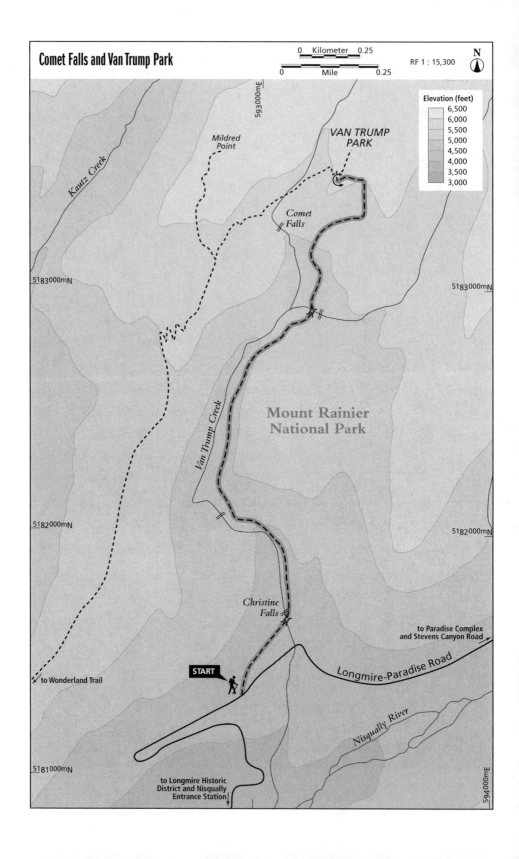

Comet Falls and Van Trump Park

0   Kilometer   0.25

0   Mile   0.25

RF 1 : 15,300

N

Elevation (feet)
6,500
6,000
5,500
5,000
4,500
4,000
3,500
3,000

593000mE

Kautz Creek

Mildred Point

VAN TRUMP PARK

Comet Falls

5183000mN

5183000mN

Van Trump Creek

Mount Rainier National Park

5182000mN

5182000mN

Christine Falls

to Paradise Complex and Stevens Canyon Road

Longmire-Paradise Road

START

to Wonderland Trail

Nisqually River

5181000mN

to Longmire Historic District and Nisqually Entrance Station

594000mE

The Hike

The trail takes you through beautiful forest to several waterfalls, including Comet Falls, one of the tallest falls in the park. From the flower-filled meadows of Van Trump Park, you can view both the Tatoosh Range and Mount Rainier on a clear day.

From the Van Trump Park parking lot, travel north up the Van Trump Park Trail. In less than 0.3 mile you come to a bridge over the top of Christine Falls. The trail stays mainly in the forest all the way, but it opens up just before you view Comet Falls. At that point you can relish Van Trump Creek on your left and the bushes of salmonberries to your right.

You come to a bridge before you reach Comet Falls. The trail seems to fork before the bridge, but stay to the left (north). The trail to the right (east) is a small spur trail that wraps around the bend to the foot of an unnamed falls. You have a nice view of the falls from the bridge.

When you reach your first view of Comet Falls, 1.7 miles from the beginning of your hike, several viewing areas await. The white waters of Comet Falls resemble the tail of a comet, the inspiration for its name. The spectacular falls are visible from the bottom of the switchbacks, but you have to travel 0.2 mile up the steep switchbacks adjacent to the falls to receive a close-up—and likely wet—view.

The switchbacks continue to ascend steeply, and the grade stays that way for the remainder of the trip to Van Trump Park. The trail affords a clear view of the Tatoosh Range to the southeast, and this part of the trail is often lined with wildflowers in mid- to late summer. Travel up the switchbacks for the next 0.7 mile, 2.6 miles total into your hike, until the Van Trump Trail splits off to the right. At the junction go right (north) up to Van Trump Park. If you are taking the spectacular option to Mildred Point, stay to the left. (See Option.)

From Van Trump Park you may see Mount St. Helens, Mount Adams, and the Tatoosh to the south. The park also offers you ample viewing of Kautz and Van Trump Glaciers. The maintained spur trail continues for only 0.3 mile. After this point, the trail is unmaintained and you travel at your own risk. Practice zero-impact principles in order to cause minimal impact. The unmaintained trail leads to a ridge with an excellent view of Mount Rainier.

Miles and Directions

0.0 Start at the Van Trump Park trailhead (sometimes referred to as Comet Falls trailhead). Travel north up the Van Trump Park Trail.

1.9 Reach Comet Falls. (There are numerous viewing opportunities before you actually reach the falls.)

2.6 To the right, the Van Trump Trail splits off, taking you north up through Van Trump Park.

2.9 The end of the Van Trump Park is also the end of the Van Trump Trail. From here head back the way you came, or take the option to Mildred Point.

5.8 Arrive back at the trailhead.

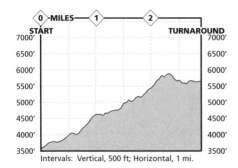

Intervals: Vertical, 500 ft; Horizontal, 1 mi.

Option: The side trip to Mildred Point is a must-do. The trail is extremely steep and not very well maintained, but the view is spectacular. Deer are commonly seen grazing in the grassy meadows along the trail. The knoll up to Mildred Point is filled with an array of wildflowers, from lupine to Columbia lilies. The top of Mildred Point provides a great view of the Kautz Glacier and Mount Rainier.

Hike Information

Local Information

Mount Rainier National Park Web site, www.nps.gov/mora; twenty-four-hour visitor information, (360) 569-2211.

Gifford Pinchot National Forest, www.fs.fed.us/gpnf.

Longmire Museum, (360) 569-2211, ext. 3314.

Lodging

National Park Inn, (360) 569-2275; Paradise Inn, (360) 569-2275. For a list of accommodations outside the park, visit www.nps.gov/mora/general/accom.htm.

Campgrounds

You can stay at a campground inside the park if you wish to day hike and car camp. Sunshine Point Campground is located in the southwest corner of the park, 0.25 mile inside the Nisqually Entrance. Register at the campground. Cougar Rock Campground is located in the southwest corner of the park, 2.3 miles north of the Longmire Historic District. Reserve a site at Cougar Rock Campground online at http://reservations.nps.gov, or call (800) 365-CAMP (2267) 7:00 A.M. to 7:00 P.M. PST.

7 Eagle Peak

This hike is a constant and strenuous ascent through varied terrain, ending with a spectacular view in the saddle between two peaks.

Start: Eagle Peak trailhead.
Distance: 7.2-mile out-and-back.
Approximate hiking time: 3 to 5 hours.
Difficulty: Strenuous.
Seasons: Mid-July through September.
Nearest town: Ashford.
Fees and permits: $10.00 vehicle or $5.00 individual entry fee (seven days); $30.00 annual entry fee.

Maps: USGS: Mount Rainier West; Trails Illustrated Mount Rainier National Park; Astronaut's Vista: Mount Rainier National Park, Washington; Earthwalk Press Hiking Map & Guide.
Trail contacts: Longmire Wilderness Information Center, (360) 569–HIKE (4453).
Trail conditions: www.nps.gov/mora/trail/tr_cnd.htm; weather, www.nps.gov/mora/current/weather.htm.

Finding the trailhead: From the Nisqually Entrance Station (see Getting There), drive 6.7 miles east along Longmire-Paradise Road to the Longmire Historic District on the right. Turn right (east) into the Longmire Historic District. Park in any of the number of parking spots around the Longmire Historic District. Walk on the road that takes you by the Longmire Wilderness Information Center, and continue beyond the parking lots and employee housing. The road narrows and curves right (south). Cross the bridge over the Nisqually River, and in less than 0.1 mile look for the trailhead on the left (east). *DeLorme: Washington Atlas and Gazetteer:* Page 48 C2.

The Hike

The now-anglicized Eagle Peak was once referred to by the Native Americans term *sim-layshe,* which literally means eagle. George Longmire changed *sim-layshe* to Eagle Peak. One of the most interesting attributes of this hike is the variety in the surroundings. You begin in dense virgin forest and end in subalpine rocky terrain. The trail itself, however, changes little, holding to a steady climb.

For the first 2.0 miles the trail makes a moderate to steep ascent by means of long switchbacks. On the north end of most of the switchbacks, you can catch an obscured glimpse of an unnamed tributary of the Nisqually River. A full view of this tributary will come 2.1 miles into the hike as you cross the wooden bridge just past the halfway point.

▶ The Tatoosh Range is composed of Tatoosh pluton, a coarse-grained igneous rock formed from granitelike magma that mixed with older volcanic rocks. Because of its geological composition, geologists think that the Tatoosh Range may represent a magma reservoir of previous volcanoes possibly fourteen million to twenty-five million years old.

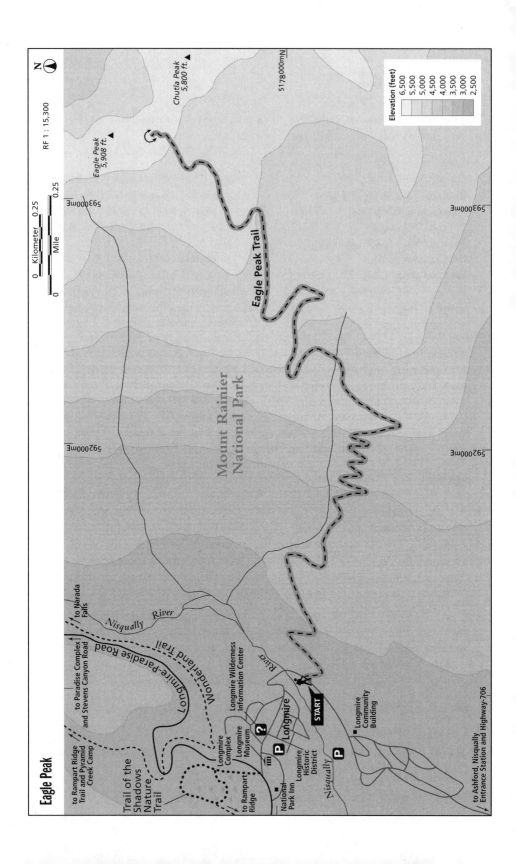

Eagle Peak

RF 1 : 15,300

Elevation (feet)
6,500
5,500
5,000
4,500
4,000
3,500
3,000
2,500

Chutla Peak
5,800 ft.

Eagle Peak
5,908 ft.

Eagle Peak Trail

Mount Rainier
National Park

to Narada
Falls

to Paradise Complex
and Stevens Canyon Road

to Rampart Ridge
Trail and Pyramid
Creek Camp

Nisqually River

Wonderland Trail

Longmire-Paradise Road

Trail of the Shadows
Nature Trail

to Rampart Ridge

Longmire
Complex

Longmire
Museum

Longmire Wilderness
Information Center

Longmire

Longmire Historic
District

National Park Inn

Nisqually River

START

Longmire Community
Building

to Ashford, Nisqually
Entrance Station and Highway-706

5178000mN

593000mE

592000mE

593000mE

592000mE

N

0   Kilometer   0.25

0   Mile   0.25

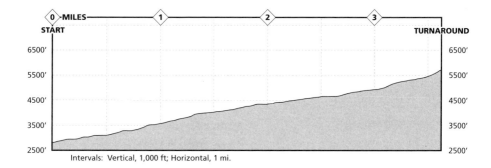

Intervals: Vertical, 1,000 ft; Horizontal, 1 mi.

Another mile of hiking in forest suddenly ends as the trees are exchanged for a mountain meadow and subalpine fields of wildflowers. After 0.5 mile of very steep hiking along a rocky face, you reach the saddle of Eagle Peak.

For the sake of aesthetics, hope for a clear day. The Eagle Peak saddle provides a fantastic view of the Nisqually Valley, the Nisqually Glacier, the Tatoosh Range, Mount St. Helens, and Mount Rainier.

Miles and Directions

0.0 Start at Eagle Peak trailhead. Follow the Eagle Peak Trail.

3.0 At this point the forest opens up and you enter a mountain meadow.

3.6 Reach the Eagle Peak saddle. (FYI: There is no maintained trail to the summit; the steep climb requires climbing experience. See Option.)

7.2 Arrive back at the trailhead.

Option: If you feel the need to conquer the peak, the climb to the summit is a scramble up a rocky face. You should have some climbing experience before attempting the summit. This option adds about 0.5 mile to your hike, raising the total round-trip hike to nearly 8 miles.

Hike Information

Local Information

Mount Rainier National Park Web site, www.nps.gov/mora; twenty-four-hour visitor information, (360) 569-2211.

Gifford Pinchot National Forest, www.fs.fed.us/gpnf.

Longmire Museum, (360) 569-2211, ext. 3314.

Lodging

National Park Inn, (360) 569-2275; Paradise Inn, (360) 569-2275. For a list of accommodations outside the park, visit www.nps.gov/mora/general/accom.htm.

Campgrounds

You can stay at a campground inside the park if you wish to day hike and car camp. Sunshine Point Campground is located in the southwest corner of the park, 0.25 mile inside the Nisqually Entrance. Register at the campground. Cougar Rock Campground is located in the southwest corner of the park, 2.3 miles north of the Longmire Historic District. Reserve a site at Cougar Rock Campground online at http://reservations.nps.gov, or call (800) 365-CAMP (2267) 7:00 A.M. to 7:00 P.M. PST.

8 Narada Falls

This completely downhill hike (with a vehicle shuttle) passes three waterfalls and runs through the scenic Paradise and Nisqually River Valleys.

Start: Narada Falls trailhead.
Distance: 4.5-mile shuttle.
Approximate hiking time: 2 to 3 hours.
Difficulty: Easy.
Seasons: Early July through September.
Nearest town: Ashford.
Fees and permits: $10.00 vehicle or $5.00 individual entry fee (seven days); $30.00 annual entry fee. Wilderness Camping Permits free—reservations recommended ($20 fee).

Maps: USGS: Mount Rainier West and Mount Rainier East; Trails Illustrated Mount Rainier National Park; Astronaut's Vista: Mount Rainier National Park, Washington; Earthwalk Press Hiking Map & Guide.
Trail contacts: Longmire Wilderness Information Center: (360) 569-HIKE (4453).
Trail conditions: www.nps.gov/mora/trail/ tr_cnd.htm; weather, www.nps.gov/mora/ current/weather.htm.

Finding the trailhead: Hiking this trail one-way requires a short two-car shuttle. From the Nisqually Entrance Station (see Getting There), drive 6.7 miles east on Longmire-Paradise Road to the Longmire Historic District on the right (south). Park one car here. *DeLorme: Washington Atlas and Gazetteer:* Page 48 C2.

In the second vehicle continue roughly 8 miles east on Longmire-Paradise Road and turn right (east) into the parking lot signed for Narada Falls. The Narada Falls Trail is on the far east side of the parking lot before the restrooms. Park and walk over the bridge until you see the trailhead on the right (south). *DeLorme: Washington Atlas and Gazetteer:* Page 48 B2.

The Hike

This hike passes three waterfalls and travels all downhill. You begin at the astonishing Narada Falls and then hike by two other waterfalls, Madcap and Carter Falls. The only disadvantage of this hike is that it requires two vehicles. If you do not have access to two cars, consider starting at the Longmire Historic District and doing an out-and-back hike. Other options include arranging a shuttle pickup or leaving a bike at the end of the hike and having one person ride back to pick up the car.

From the Narada Falls parking lot, go down the stone steps of the Narada Falls Trail that run along the falls. Narada Falls is wondrous, and on a hot day the cool spray of the falls is very refreshing. Do be careful on the slippery rocks. The first 0.2 mile on the Narada Falls Trail is usually extremely crowded, considering how close the magnificent falls are to the road.

▶ **The Native American term *narada* translates as "uncontaminated."**

Fortunately the traffic nearly disappears when you join the Wonderland Trail. Go right and head west on the Wonderland Trail. You can hear the Paradise River flowing directly to your right, which you cross about 1.0 mile into your hike (about 0.1 mile past Paradise River Camp on the left).

Bridge over the Nisqually River.

Three bridges take you over the relatively calm forks of the Paradise River. About 0.5 mile from here you encounter Madcap Falls, where the Tatoosh Creek flows into the Paradise River. Instead of dropping straight down, Madcap Falls slope at a diagonal. The water gushes over the rocks to create a white wonder.

Soon after Madcap Falls you come to Carter Falls. A sign reaffirms that the gorgeous waters you see dropping straight down are in fact Carter Falls. You might come upon a number of people here, considering the proximity to Cougar Rock Campground.

The next 1.1 miles are a pleasant walk along the Paradise River, despite some metal drain pipes and power lines along the trail. When you are 2.8 miles into your hike, you come to another set of bridges that take you across the Nisqually River. The waters of the Nisqually are thick with "glacial flour," fine sediments deposited by active glaciers at the river's source. The wide Nisqually River Valley is scattered with debris and downed trees from previous floods.

After you cross the bridges, climb up to Longmire-Paradise Road. The Wonderland Trail continues left (west). There is a sign to help you continue on the Wonderland Trail to Longmire. In less than 0.25 mile, you come to another junction. The

Narada Falls

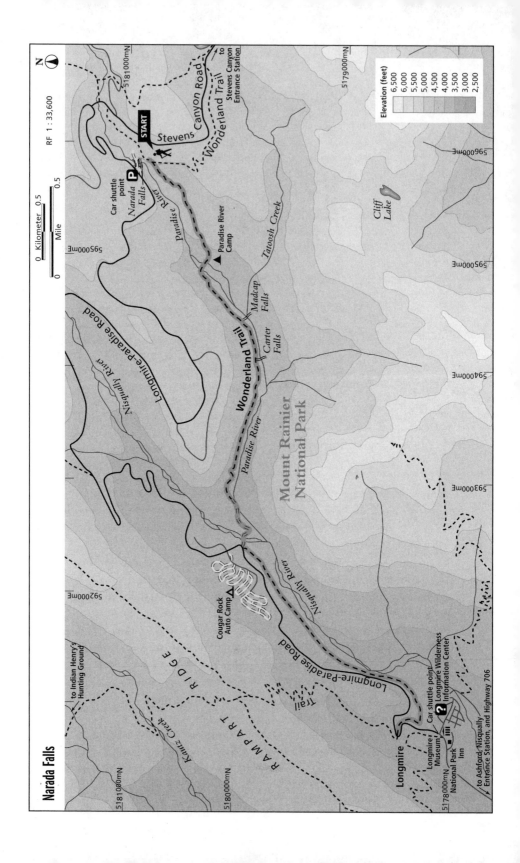

RF 1 : 33,600

N

Car shuttle point
Narada Falls

START

Stevens

Stevens Canyon Road

to Stevens Canyon Entrance Station

Wonderland Trail

P

Paradise River

Paradise River Camp

Tatoosh Creek

Madcap Falls

Carter Falls

Wonderland Trail

Paradise River

Mount Rainier National Park

Cliff Lake

Longmire-Paradise Road

Nisqually River

Cougar Rock Auto Camp

Nisqually River

RAMPART RIDGE

Kautz Creek

to Indian Henry's Hunting Ground

Trail

Longmire-Paradise Road

Car shuttle point

Longmire

Longmire Museum

Longmire Wilderness Information Center

?

National Park Inn

to Ashford, Nisqually Entrance Station, and Highway 706

0 Kilometer 0.5

0 Mile 0.5

5181000mN

5180000mN

595000mE

592000mE

5181000mN

5180000mN

5178000mN

Elevation (feet)
6,500
6,000
5,500
5,000
4,500
4,000
3,500
3,000
2,500

5179000mN

596000mE

595000mE

594000mE

593000mE

trail to your right (north) goes to Cougar Rock Campground; the trail left (south) goes to an old horse ford across the Nisqually River. Continue heading southwest on the Wonderland Trail through beautiful forest all the way to the Longmire Historic District.

Miles and Directions

0.0 Start at the Narada Falls trailhead. Hike down the trail past Narada Falls. (See Option for an alternative starting location.)

0.2 The Narada Falls Trail meets the Wonderland Trail. Turn right onto the Wonderland Trail, heading west.

0.9 A trail to Paradise River Camp heads to the left (south). Stay on the Wonderland Trail, traveling west.

1.5 Encounter Madcap Falls.

1.7 Arrive at Carter Falls.

2.8 A trail to Longmire-Paradise Road. Stay to the left, hiking west on the Wonderland Trail.

4.5 Arrive at Longmire Historic District.

Option: Start at the Paradise Complex instead of Narada Falls, making your trip 1.2 miles longer. This allows you to travel all the way from the Paradise Complex to the Longmire Historic District. Park one car at the Longmire Historic District, and park the other car at the Paradise Complex. To get to the Paradise Complex from the Longmire Historic District, drive 11.4 miles east on Longmire-Paradise Road. Park in the parking lot in front of the Paradise Ranger Station and the Paradise Inn. Walk to the Lakes trailhead, located in the southeast corner of the parking lot. Stay on the Lakes Trail for less than 0.6 mile until you intersect the Narada Falls Trail. Go west on the Narada Falls Trail for a little over 0.1 mile, until you reach the Longmire-Paradise Road. After you cross the road, travel along the Narada Falls Trail for another 0.5 mile until you reach Narada Falls. At this point, refer to the above hike description.

Wilderness camping: If you choose to stay overnight, you can stay at Paradise River Camp. Fires are not permitted, as in all the wilderness camps in Mount Rainier National Park. Paradise River Camp has three individual sites and one group

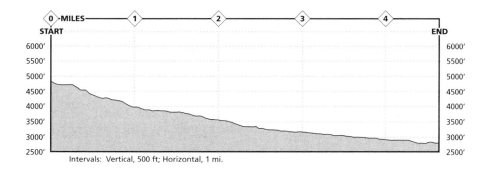

Intervals: Vertical, 500 ft; Horizontal, 1 mi.

site. All the sites are small and flat. Site 2 is the most secluded, but it overlooks Site 1. Site 3 is nearest to the restrooms and directly off the spur trail. The Paradise River is the water source for this wilderness camp. The Park Service closes the Paradise River Camp periodically to protect a pair of spotted owls seen nesting there.

Hike Information

Local Information

Mount Rainier National Park Web site, www.nps.gov/mora; twenty-four-hour visitor information, (360) 569-2211.

Gifford Pinchot National Forest, www.fs.fed.us/gpnf.

Longmire Museum, (360) 569-2211, ext. 3314.

Lodging

National Park Inn, (360) 569-2275; Paradise Inn, (360) 569-2275. For a list of accommodations outside the park, visit www.nps.gov/mora/general/accom.htm.

Campgrounds

You can stay at a campground inside the park if you wish to day hike and car camp. Sunshine Point Campground is located in the southwest corner of the park, 0.25 mile inside the Nisqually Entrance. Register at the campground. Cougar Rock Campground is located in the southwest corner of the park, 2.3 miles north of the Longmire Historic District. Reserve a site at Cougar Rock Campground online at http://reservations.nps.gov, or call (800) 365-CAMP (2267) 7:00 A.M. to 7:00 P.M. PST.

9 Twin Firs Loop

This short loop takes you through an old-growth, low-elevation forest. Along the trail you will see a variety of flora such as vine maple, skunk cabbage, giant ferns, mossy logs, Douglas fir, western hemlock, and western red cedar, as well as numerous squirrels darting across the trail.

Start: Twin Firs Loop trailhead.
Distance: 0.4-mile loop.
Approximate hiking time: 20 minutes.
Difficulty: Easy.
Seasons: May through October.
Nearest town: Ashford.
Fees and permits: $10.00 vehicle or $5.00 individual entry fee (seven days); $30.00 annual entry fee.

Maps: USGS: Mount Wow; Trails Illustrated Mount Rainier National Park; Astronaut's Vista: Mount Rainier National Park, Washington; Earthwalk Press Hiking Map & Guide.
Trail contacts: Longmire Wilderness Information Center, (360) 569-HIKE (4453).
Trail conditions: www.nps.gov/mora/trail/tr_cnd.htm; weather, www.nps.gov/mora/current/weather.htm.

Finding the trailhead: From the Nisqually Entrance Station (see Getting There), drive east for 4.5 miles on the Longmire-Paradise Road. You will see a turnout on the left of the road. If you

Twin Firs Loop.

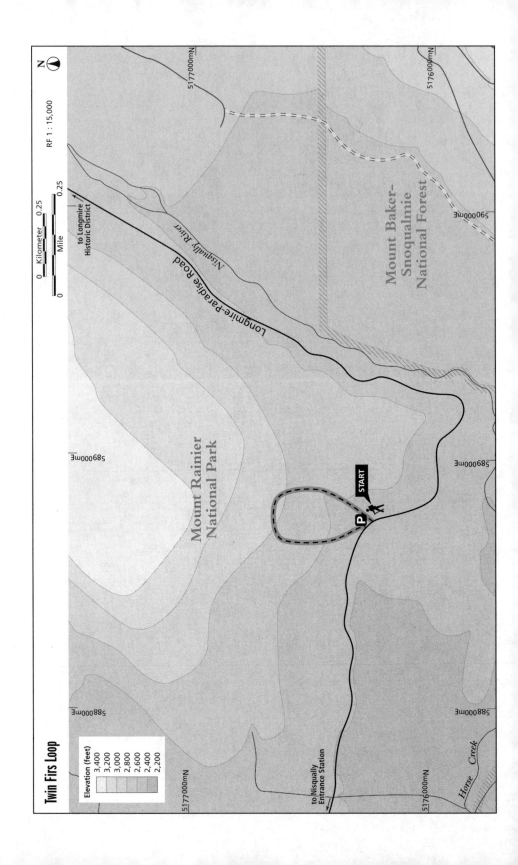

reach the Longmire Historic District, you have gone too far. *DeLorme: Washington Atlas and Gazetteer:* Page 48 C2.

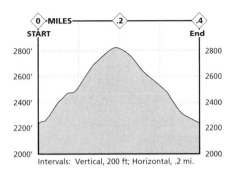

Intervals: Vertical, 200 ft; Horizontal, .2 mi.

The Hike

At the trailhead, take the time to read a wonderful exhibit describing the flora of low-elevation forests. Through pictures and written description, the exhibit recommends ways to differentiate between the Douglas fir, western hemlock, and western red cedar.

The trail weaves around majestic trees, some fallen and some standing tall. You will see mossy logs and big ferns lining both sides of the trail. Less than halfway into your hike, a log takes you across a small creek to where the trail becomes steeper. You will cross this gurgling creek again just before you return to the Longmire-Paradise road, directly west of where you begin your hike.

Miles and Directions

0.0 Start at the Twin Firs Loop trailhead.

0.4 Return to the Longmire Paradise Road.

Hike Information

Local Information

Mount Rainier National Park Web site, www.nps.gov/mora; twenty-four-hour visitor information, (360) 569-2211.

Gifford Pinchot National Forest, www.fs.fed.us/gpnf.

Longmire Museum, (360) 569-2211, ext. 3314.

Lodging

National Park Inn, (360) 569-2275; Paradise Inn, (360) 569-2275. For a list of accommodations outside the park, visit www.nps.gov/mora/general/accom.htm.

Campgrounds

You can stay at a campground inside the park if you wish to day hike and car camp. Sunshine Point Campground is located in the southwest corner of the park, 0.25 mile inside the Nisqually Entrance. Register at the campground. Cougar Rock Campground is located in the southwest corner of the park, 2.3 miles north of the Longmire Historic District. Reserve a site at Cougar Rock Campground online at http://reservations.nps.gov, or call (800) 365-CAMP (2267) 7:00 A.M. to 7:00 P.M. PST.

10 Trail of the Shadows

A thirty-minute stroll around the Longmire Meadow, with attractions that inform you about the Longmire family and its stake in the park.

Start: Longmire Historic District.
Distance: 0.7-mile loop.
Approximate hiking time: 30 minutes.
Difficulty: Easy.
Seasons: May through October.
Nearest town: Ashford.
Fees and permits: $10.00 vehicle or $5.00 individual entry fee (seven days); $30.00 annual entry fee.

Maps: USGS: Mount Rainier West; Trails Illustrated Mount Rainier National Park; Astronaut's Vista: Mount Rainier National Park, Washington; Earthwalk Press Hiking Map & Guide.
Trail contacts: Longmire Wilderness Information Center, (360) 569-HIKE (4453).
Trail conditions: www.nps.gov/mora/trail/tr_cnd.htm; weather, www.nps.gov/mora/current/weather.htm.

Finding the trailhead: From the Nisqually Entrance Station (see Getting There), drive 6.7 miles east on Longmire-Paradise Road. Look for the Longmire Historic District on the right (east). Park in one of the many spaces around the Longmire Wilderness Information Center, the Longmire Museum, and the National Park Inn, then cross the road along one of the two crosswalks to find the trailhead. *DeLorme: Washington Atlas and Gazetteer:* Page 48 C2.

The Hike

If you are a history buff who likes casual strolls, you will enjoy this hike. The trail winds around an enchanting meadow, while taking you to many informative stations. The theme of the stations is James Longmire, his crusade for a natural health spa, and his love of the mountain.

Starting to the right (north), the first stop is a work of stone masonry with bubbling water, said in the nineteenth century to cure any illness. But as the sign ironically reads, DO NOT DRINK THIS WATER; IT CAN MAKE YOU VERY ILL.

The next stop, 0.2 mile into the hike, is the cabin that Longmire built. It still has the original furniture, also constructed by Longmire. Next door is Iron Mike, a spring that is tinted orange by iron minerals.

A very small side trip at 0.5 mile from the trailhead leads to the Travertine Mound, another orange mass bursting with mineral water. A bench here provides a nice place to sit and view the meadow.

The home stretch of the loop includes a variety of interesting wild vegetation. After completing the loop, cross the Longmire-Paradise Road again to get back to

View of Rampart Ridge from the Trail of the Shadows. ▶

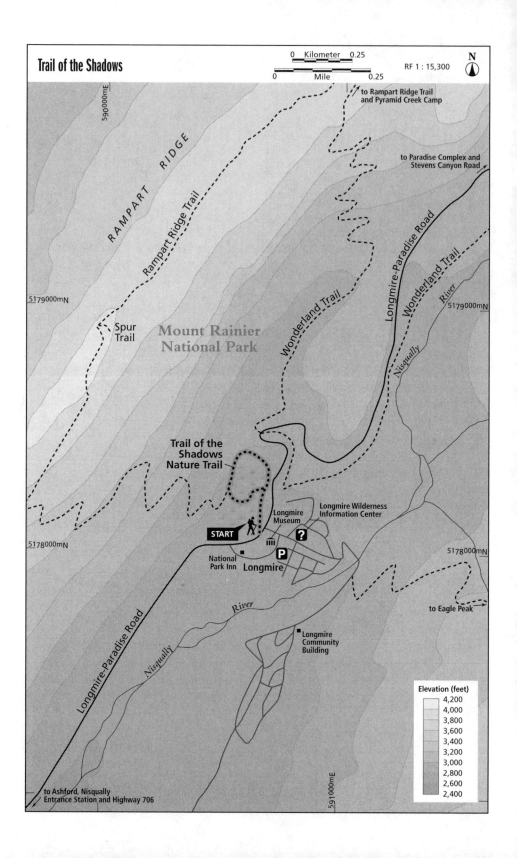

Trail of the Shadows

0   Kilometer   0.25

0   Mile   0.25

RF 1 : 15,300

N

590000mE

to Rampart Ridge Trail
and Pyramid Creek Camp

to Paradise Complex and
Stevens Canyon Road

R A M P A R T   R I D G E

Rampart Ridge Trail

Longmire-Paradise Road

Wonderland Trail

5179000mN

Spur
Trail

Mount Rainier
National Park

Wonderland Trail

Nisqually

River

5179000mN

Trail of the
Shadows
Nature Trail

Longmire Wilderness
Information Center

Longmire
Museum

START

?

5178000mN

National
Park Inn

P

Longmire

5178000mN

River

to Eagle Peak

Nisqually

Longmire
Community
Building

Elevation (feet)

4,200
4,000
3,800
3,600
3,400
3,200
3,000
2,800
2,600
2,400

591000mE

to Ashford, Nisqually
Entrance Station and Highway 706

your car and the large present-day Longmire Historic District. Notice the great disparity between the present-day edifices and the shadows of the past.

Intervals: Vertical, 25 ft; Horizontal, .25 mi.

Miles and Directions

0.0 Start at the Longmire Historic District. Cross the road on one of the two crosswalks to find the trailhead.

0.1 At this point, you're standing before the masonry spring.

0.2 Pass Longmire's cabin.

0.2 Reach Iron Mike.

0.5 A small spur trail takes you to the Travertine Mound.

0.7 Return to the trailhead. Head back across the road to the Longmire Historic District.

11 West Wonderland

This outstanding backpack trip covers the entire west side of the Wonderland Trail, which has been coined the "piecrust" by previous hikers. This hike, starting at Mount Rainier's largest mountain lake, Mowich Lake, travels through a multitude of natural wonders. Such attractions include pebbly river valleys, subalpine meadows, and close-up views of Mount Rainier's western glaciers.

Start: Mowich Lake.
Distance: 34.1-mile one-way, with lengthy vehicle shuttle.
Approximate hiking time: 4 to 6 days.
Difficulty: Strenuous.
Seasons: Late July through September.
Nearest town: Wilkeson at the start; Ashford at the end.
Fees and permits: $10.00 vehicle or $5.00 individual entry fee (seven days); $30.00 annual entry fee. Wilderness Camping Permits free—reservations recommended ($20 fee).

Maps: USGS: Mount Wow and Golden Lakes; Trails Illustrated Mount Rainier National Park; Astronaut's Vista: Mount Rainier National Park, Washington; Earthwalk Press Hiking Map & Guide.
Trail contacts: Longmire Wilderness Information Center, (360) 569–HIKE (4453). Wilkeson Wilderness Information Center, (360) 569-6020.
Trail conditions: www.nps.gov/mora/trail/tr_cnd.htm; weather, www.nps.gov/mora/current/weather.htm.

Finding the trailhead: This hike requires a two-car shuttle between the start and finish. First leave a car at the end of your hike, the Longmire Historic District. From the Nisqually Entrance Station (see Getting There), drive 6.7 miles east on Longmire-Paradise Road to the Longmire Historic District; park one car here. *DeLorme: Washington Atlas and Gazetteer:* Page 48 C2.

From here the drive to the hike's start in the northwestern section of the park can take more than two hours—make sure you account for this time when planning your trip. Drive back to the Nisqually Entrance Station and continue 13 miles west on Highway 706. In the town of Elbe stay to the right when the road forks and drive north, now on Highway 7. Continue about 10 miles north on Highway 7, and take the exit for Eatonville and Highway 161. Drive north on Highway 161 and take the exit for Kapowsin on your right. Continue north through Electron to the town of Orting and Highway 162. Turn right and drive about 10 miles east on Highway 162 to the junction with Highway 165. Go right (south) on Highway 165, through Wilkeson. From Wilkeson drive 9 miles south on Highway 165 until the road forks. Stay to the right (south) at this fork, the way to Mowich Lake. After 3.2 miles the road becomes a well-maintained dirt road, although it can be very slippery when muddy. Follow this road for another 8.8 miles to the Paul Peak trailhead on the right (south) side of the road. Pause here to pay the entrance fee at the fee station. Then continue 5.3 miles south and east to Mowich Lake, a total of 26.3 miles from Wilkeson. Although there is a big parking lot, you might have to park along the road on a sunny weekend. *DeLorme: Washington Atlas and Gazetteer:* Page A1.

Special considerations: Historically, the western part of the park experiences numerous washouts due to glacial outburst floods, and footlogs across rivers or streams originating from glaciers frequently wash out. The National Park Service does not advise fording glacial rivers due to the high concentration of debris and risk of large glacial boulders in the water. If you must cross, the Park Service recommends crossing early in the day and using any fallen logs to assist you. Also, always wear boots to protect yourself from any debris suspended in the river.

Do not filter water from creeks or rivers cloudy with glacial silt, referred to as glacial flour, suspended in them; it will ruin your filter. Bring iodine tablets and an extra filter along in the unfortunate event that your filter fails.

The Hike

This is a fantastic hike if you want to experience the Wonderland Trail but do not have the time or facilities to hike the entire trail, described in Hike 61: Wonderland Trail. This 34.1-mile hike takes you along the entire west side of the Wonderland Trail, commonly called the "piecrust" due to its severe elevation changes. The trail gives you spectacular views of Mount Rainier, Klapatche Park, St. Andrews Park, and other astonishing backcountry in Mount Rainier National Park.

Most hikers need anywhere from three to five nights to complete this trip. If you choose to go for three nights, you must average more than 10 miles per day. We recommend staying at Golden Lakes, Klapatche Park, and Devil's Dream Camps. If you choose to take five nights, you will hike 4 to 7 miles per day and stay at South Mowich River, Golden Lakes, Klapatche Park, South Puyallup, and Devil's Dream Camps. Of course, you might have to adjust according to what camps are available.

Head to the south end of Mowich Lake Campground and find the Wonderland Trail. At the junction, follow the Wonderland Trail. You will soon meet the Spray

North Puyallup River. BILL SCHNEIDER

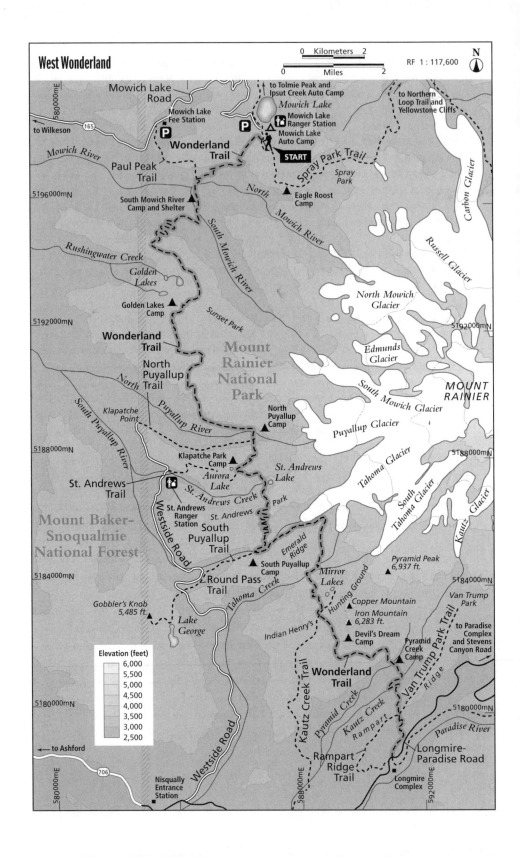

West Wonderland

Kilometers 2
Miles 2
RF 1 : 117,600
N

Mowich Lake Road

to Tolmie Peak and
Ipsut Creek Auto Camp

to Northern
Loop Trail and
Yellowstone Cliffs

Mowich Lake

Mowich Lake
Fee Station

Mowich Lake
Ranger Station

Carbon Glacier

to Wilkeson
165

**Wonderland
Trail**

Mowich Lake
Auto Camp

START

Spray Park Trail

Spray
Park

Russell Glacier

Mowich River

Paul Peak
Trail

North Mowich River

Eagle Roost
Camp

5196000mN

South Mowich River
Camp and Shelter

South Mowich River

North Mowich
Glacier

Rushingwater Creek

Golden
Lakes

North Mowich
Glacier

Russell Glacier

5192000mN

Golden Lakes
Camp

Sunset Park

Mount
Rainier
National
Park

Edmunds
Glacier

5192000mN

**Wonderland
Trail**

North
Puyallup
Trail

North
Puyallup River

Puyallup River

South Mowich Glacier

MOUNT
RAINIER

Klapatche
Point

North
Puyallup
Camp

Puyallup Glacier

5188000mN

South Puyallup River

Klapatche Park
Camp

Aurora
Lake

St. Andrews
Lake

Tahoma Glacier

5188000mN

**St. Andrews
Trail**

St. Andrews Creek

St. Andrews
Ranger
Station

Park

St. Andrews

South Tahoma Glacier

**Mount Baker-
Snoqualmie
National Forest**

Westside Road

South
Puyallup
Trail

Emerald
Ridge

Kautz Glacier

5184000mN

**Round Pass
Trail**

South Puyallup
Camp

Tahoma Creek

Mirror
Lakes

Hunting Ground

Pyramid Peak
6,937 ft.

5184000mN

Gobbler's Knob
5,485 ft.

Lake
George

Indian Henry's

Copper Mountain

Iron Mountain
6,283 ft.

Devil's Dream
Camp

Van Trump
Park

to Paradise
Complex and Stevens
Canyon Road

Pyramid
Creek
Camp

Van Trump Park Trail

Elevation (feet)

6,000
5,500
5,000
4,500
4,000
3,500
3,000
2,500

**Wonderland
Trail**

Kautz Creek Trail

Pyramid Creek

Kautz Creek

Rampart
Ridge

to Ashford
706

Westside Road

**Rampart
Ridge
Trail**

5180000mN

Paradise River

Longmire-
Paradise Road

Longmire
Complex

Nisqually
Entrance
Station

Park Trail on your left heading west; continue south on the Wonderland Trail through beautiful forest. After you pass the Paul Peak Trail junction, the trail continues downhill all the way to the North Mowich River.

Two footlogs take you over the North Mowich River and put you on the North Mowich River Bar. You might still be able to see the remains of the North Mowich Shelter, which was torn down in 1993, atop this river bar. About 0.25 mile after you cross the North Mowich River, you come to South Mowich River Camp and its shelter. Depending on your itinerary, you may set up camp here. This is also the last place to filter water until Golden Lakes.

Beyond South Mowich River Camp, you cross the South Mowich River, 4.0 miles into your hike. The area around the South Mowich River is scattered with debris and crushed trees from previous glacial outburst floods from the ever-changing south fork of the Mowich River. When we hiked this trail, one of the three footlogs over the South Mowich River was washed out; it apparently washes out several times a year. Be aware that it is a tricky ford, and glacial boulders in the river are a possible hazard. It is a good idea to call ahead to the Wilkeson Wilderness Information Center to find out if the bridge is down so that you can prepare accordingly, but understand that washouts are unpredictable and the bridge may be gone on the day you arrive.

▶ Until 1952 mining was permitted in the park, but hunting and logging were not. The park allowed limited cattle grazing during World War I, but not during World War II.

After you leave the South Mowich River, the trail climbs uphill all the way to Golden Lakes, 6.1 miles away. At first the grade is slight, but after a mile or so the trail switches back and forth at a steep grade to the top of the ridge. At the top, the trail descends briefly and then sustains a slight pitch for almost a mile to Golden Lakes, 10.1 miles into your hike. The scattered pools you see around you are Golden Lakes. Wildflowers, such as shooting stars and avalanche lilies, line their banks in mid-July.

From Golden Lakes head south for Klapatche Park. A 0.5-mile ascent will bring you to Sunset Park in all its glory. Magenta paintbrushes and avalanche lilies fill the meadows of the park. At the edge of Sunset Park, the hillside is filled with ghost trees, the eerie remains of a fire from years ago. The trail is all downhill for about the next 5.0 miles to the North Puyallup River. Just before you cross the North Puyallup River, a spur trail leads to North Puyallup Camp to the left (north); the Wonderland Trail continues to the right (south). As you cross the river, make sure to look down at the raging white waters of the North Puyallup River and up at the Puyallup Glacier. If the bridghe makes you uneasy, you can enjoy the sights from a more grounded viewpoint on the other side of the river.

The junction with the North Puyallup Trail is also on the other side of the bridge. This trail forks right (west) and runs directly left of the group site and its toilet. Stay to the left, unless you are taking the side trip to Klapatche Point, and head up Klapatche Ridge.

Watch your step as you hike up this ridge; the trail is very steep and has an unstable ledge that drops straight off the side. At the top of the ridge, Klapatche Park unfolds before your eyes. Beautiful wildflowers fill the meadows and surround Aurora Lake in mid-July. Aurora Lake may technically be only a shallow pool of snowmelt, but it looks astonishing with Mount Rainier towering above it. If you are staying at Klapatche Park Camp, it is located at the west end of the lake.

From Aurora Lake, take off for St. Andrews Lake and St. Andrews Park. At the south end of Aurora Lake, the St. Andrews Trail forks off to the right (west). Stay to the left (south), unless you plan to take a side trip to Denman Falls. It is only 0.8 mile to St. Andrews Lake from this junction.

Previous hikers have greatly impacted St. Andrews Lake by creating numerous social trails along the fragile banks of this subalpine lake. Minimize your impact by admiring the lake from the designated trail. You can also see a west-side climbing route that many have used to attempt the summit. Fortunately the trails do not entirely take away from the deep-blue waters of St. Andrews Lake. As much as you will hate leaving the lake, do not worry— St. Andrews Park will soon stun you with its subalpine beauty. In mid-July avalanche lilies, lupine, and magenta paintbrush fill the meadows with their splendor.

▶ **Puyallup Valley, rich in volcanic soil, was once the daffodil capital of the world.**

From the end of St. Andrews Park, it is another 2.5 miles down to the South Puyallup River, 21.8 miles into your hike. The descent is steep, and the trail is surrounded by scratchy brush. At the end of your descent, you cross the silty waters of the South Puyallup River and come to the junction with the South Puyallup Trail. The South Puyallup Trail heads right (west) toward South Puyallup Camp, 0.1 mile away. Go left (east) toward Emerald Ridge on the Wonderland Trail, unless you had previously decided to stay at South Puyallup Camp.

It is 1.7 miles to the top of Emerald Ridge from the junction with the South Puyallup Trail. The Tahoma Glacier and its moraine are to your left (north) as you head east on the Wonderland Trail. If you look up at Mount Rainier, you will see the top of the Tahoma Glacier, accompanied by the South Tahoma Glacier to the right. The Tahoma Glaciers resides in a land scar carved out by a previous mud slide. To date, twenty-three glaciers have burst from South Tahoma Glacier. Between the two glaciers is Glacier Island. Mountain goats can often be seen grazing on Glacier Island, a green haven in a sea of glaciers. If you look closely, you can see fields of lupine.

The top of Emerald Ridge is an emerald-green meadow filled with wildflowers in mid-July. The scent of lupine fills hikers' nostrils with its sweet perfume. A plethora of hoary marmots live in the meadows. Do not feed these wild animals; they need to remain self-sufficient to survive in their natural habitat. The trail along the north side of Emerald Ridge has washed out many times and lines a steep, unstable ledge. Take the new trail that diagonally traverses the ridge.

After Emerald Ridge, you head down toward Indian Henry's Hunting Ground. The trail takes you on the other side of Emerald Ridge to the South Tahoma Moraine. Hike over the moraine and head back into the forest. From there it is more downhill switchbacks until you reach the suspension bridge over Tahoma Creek, 2.0 miles from the top of Emerald Ridge. Just before you reach the bridge, you will see a sign for the Tahoma Creek Trail on your right, which connects with Westside Road. As the sign indicates, using the unmaintained trail is not recommended.

From the suspension bridge there is an amazing view of Tahoma Creek. If it is not too windy, take the time to look up the creek. Tahoma Creek continually experiences glacial outburst floods; if you hear a loud, roaring sound, immediately proceed to higher ground.

Uphill switchbacks await you on the other side of the bridge. It is about a 1,000-foot climb to Indian Henry's Hunting Ground. When you arrive there, the trail winds through the picturesque meadows of Indian Henry's Hunting Ground, from which you have an excellent view of Mount Rainier and the Sunset Amphitheater. Just before the Kautz Creek Trail junction, you will pass Mount Rainier's oldest patrol cabin to your left. This rustic cabin is still in use. You should take a break in these pleasant meadows before heading off to Devil's Dream Camp.

The trail enters the forest and drops steadily in elevation to Devil's Dream Camp, which is 29.5 miles into your hike. You will pass Squaw Lake on your left before you reach the camp. This is the water source for Devil's Dream Camp when the stream below the camp dries up in late summer. As you will see, it is a little hike from the camp.

From Devil's Dream Camp the trail travels all downhill for less than 6 miles through beautiful forest to the Longmire Historic District. It is 2.1 miles to Pyramid Creek Camp and then under 0.7 mile to Kautz Creek.

During a hot spell, the waters of Kautz Creek can rise, washing out the footlogs. The trail gets routinely rerouted. If the Park Service has not yet repaired the trail, they will often flag a route for hikers to follow in the meantime. After you cross Kautz Creek, the trail is relatively flat to the intersection with the Rampart Ridge Trail, 1.8 miles from the end. The forest offers a cool respite for the remainder of your trip.

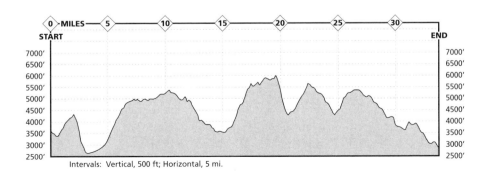

Intervals: Vertical, 500 ft; Horizontal, 5 mi.

Miles and Directions

0.0 Start at Mowich Lake Campground. Head south on the Wonderland Trail.

0.2 Stay to the right (south) as the Spray Park Trail veers off to the left, heading east.

3.1 The Paul Peak Trail splits off to the right (west). Stay on the Wonderland Trail heading south.

4.0 After crossing North Mowich River, you will also cross the South Mowich River. Continue on the trail to Golden Lakes.

10.1 Arrive at Golden Lakes Camp. Continue on the Wonderland Trail.

15.1 At the junction with North Puyallup Trail, stay to the left (south). (See Options for a possible side trip to Klapatche Point.)

17.8 Just after Klapatche Park Camp, St. Andrews Trail forks off to the right (west). Stay to the left heading south. (See Options for a possible side trip to Denman Falls.)

18.6 Reach St. Andrews Lake. Continue along the Wonderland Trail through St. Andrews Park.

21.8 At the junction with South Puyallup Trail, stay to the left, heading south.

23.5 Reach the highest point of Emerald Ridge.

25.5 Cross the suspension bridge over Tahoma Creek

27.0 The trail to Mirror Lakes forks off to the left (northeast). Stay to the right (south). (See Options for a possible side trip to Mirror Lakes.)

27.2 The Wonderland Trail intersects the Kautz Creek Trail on the right (southwest). Stay on the Wonderland Trail, traveling south.

28.3 Reach Devil's Dream Camp.

30.6 Arrive at Pyramid Creek Camp.

31.3 Cross Kautz Creek, which frequently washes out.

32.3 Reach the Rampart Ridge Trail on the right (west). Continue on the Wonderland Trail, heading south.

34.1 Arrive back at Longmire Historic District.

Options: If you cannot complete the whole hike as outlined, you can head out to Westside Road after spending the night at Klapatche Park. It is 2.5 miles down the St. Andrews Trail from Klapatche Park to reach Westside Road. If the road is still closed, it is another 7.8 miles to the closure, making your total trip 28.1 miles long.

Klapatche Point offers a panoramic view of the land bordering the west side of Mount Rainier National Park. From the junction with the North Puyallup Trail, go right (west) by the group site of North Puyallup Camp. The trail is flat all the way to Westside Road. Due to the closure of the road, this trail receives minimum use and has become overgrown with bushes, particularly salmonberries. This could explain the bear scat we saw everywhere. At the end of the North Puyallup Trail is Klapatche Point; you can see out of the park from here.

Another option is the refreshing Denman Falls. At the west end of Aurora Lake, you come to the junction with the St. Andrews Trail. Hike 2.5 miles down steep switchbacks to Westside Road. The Denman Falls Trail begins on the other side of the road a couple of steps north. Denman Falls is a little more than 0.1 mile from road. The first spur trail that forks off from the Denman Falls Trail takes you to St. Andrews Creek above the falls. The Denman Falls Trail continues and takes you below the falls.

You can also opt to take a side trip to Mirror Lakes, adding 1.8 miles to your hike. These small pools are surrounded by beautiful flower-filled meadows. Go left (north) at the junction with the Wonderland Trail and proceed northeast 0.6 mile to the lakes. Follow the Mirror Lakes Trail to its end, where there is a great view of Pyramid Peak and Mount Rainier.

Wilderness camping: Campfires are not permitted at any of the seven camps available.

South Mowich River Camp, the first camp, has four individual sites and a group site. (The South Mowich Shelter is considered one of the individual sites.) Sites 3 and 4 are closer to the South Mowich River. Sites 1 and 2, along with the group site, are crunched together and near the trail. There is an outhouse here.

North Puyallup Camp is along the North Puyallup River, although you do not see the river from any of the sites. The camp, tucked away in the forest, has three individual sites and one group site. Each individual site is flat, small, and directly next to the trail. The group site is rather spacious and open. It is separated from the three individual sites, located across the bridge over the North Puyallup River.

There are five individual campsites and one group site at Golden Lakes Camp. The camp also has a food storage pole to hang your food. Sites 1, 2, and 3 are near the outhouse. The group site (number 4) and Site 5 are near the lake. You have a fantastic view at Site 5, as well as a close water source. The group site is closest to the lake.

The campsites at Klapatche Park spoil you. There are four individual sites. The toilet is near all the sites, although the food storage pole is too close. Site 1 is closest to the lake and has an incomparable view. Watching the sun rise and reflect Mount Rainier in Aurora Lake will astound you. You cannot see Mount Rainier clearly from any of the other sites, but the view down the north side of Klapatche Ridge from Sites 2, 3, and 4 is very pleasant.

There are four individual sites and one group site at South Puyallup Camp. Site 1 is probably the best campsite. It is private, with a close water source. Be forewarned that the toilet is 0.1 mile from all the campsites. Site 2 also has its own water source and good tent sites. Sites 3 and 4 have just been improved; if seclusion is your primary concern, Site 4 is your best bet.

All seven campsites at Devil's Dream Camp, as well as the group site, provide hikers with a very nice, flat place to lay their heads. Sites 5 and 6 offer the most privacy. There are two pit toilets, and the camp is often filled with Wonderland Trail hikers. Be careful when you use the toilet near Site 4—it is likely that the residents there can see you! All the other sites are next to the trail, spacious, and flat. Usually the water source for Devil's Dream Camp is near Site 1, but it often dries up in late summer. If this is the case, you will have to hike about 0.25 mile to Squaw Lake or to the creek directly after Squaw Lake, depending on where you prefer to obtain your water.

Pyramid Creek Camp has only two sites. It has a pit toilet, and its water source is Pyramid Creek, less than 0.1 mile north on the Wonderland Trail. Both are flat and nice, Site 2 being more private and more spacious.

Hike Information

Local Information

Mount Rainier National Park Web site, www.nps.gov/mora; twenty-four-hour visitor information, (360) 569-2211.

Gifford Pinchot National Forest, www.fs.fed.us/gpnf.

Longmire Museum, (360) 569-2211, ext. 3314.

Lodging

National Park Inn, (360) 569-2275; Paradise Inn, (360) 569-2275. For a list of accommodations outside the park, visit www.nps.gov/mora/general/accom.htm.

Campgrounds

You can stay at a campground inside the park if you wish to day hike and car camp. Sunshine Point Campground is located in the southwest corner of the park, 0.25 mile inside the Nisqually Entrance. Register at the campground. Cougar Rock Campground is located in the southwest corner of the park, 2.3 miles north of the Longmire Historic District. Reserve a site at Cougar Rock Campground online at http://reservations.nps.gov, or call (800) 365-CAMP (2267) 7:00 A.M. to 7:00 P.M. PST.

Paradise

More people visit the Paradise region than any other area of Mount Rainier. Situated high on the south slope, the Paradise area affords close-up inspection of massive glacial formations, as well as panoramic views of the Tatoosh and Cascade Ranges. The Nisqually Glacier, a debris- and crevasse-ridden glacier, inches farther down the mountain each year into alpine rock fields. Subalpine meadows are full of wildlife emboldened by the high human traffic on the myriad trails that encircle Paradise.

Recent tourists were not the first to appreciate the wonders of Paradise. The name itself, taken from the native *Saghalie Illahe,* literally means "Land of Peace." For the surrounding Native American tribes, this area signified not only a wonderland of beauty but also a haven from violence. Fighting was prohibited in Paradise.

Today, with so many visitors yearly, this land of peace faces a new challenge. Incessant tromping on the fragile meadows has led to extreme erosion. Recent efforts at meadow restoration have shown promise, but without the cooperation of Paradise visitors, no improvements will last. Please, in this and all areas around Mount Rainier National Park, stay on the designated trails, do not feed the animals, and enjoy the splendors of conservation.

12 Nisqually Vista

This short hike travels through beautiful forest overlooking the Nisqually Glacier.

Start: Deadhorse Creek trailhead.
Distance: 1.2-mile out-and-back.
Approximate hiking time: 1 hour.
Difficulty: Easy.
Seasons: Early July through September.
Nearest towns: Ashford, Packwood.
Fees and permits: $10.00 vehicle or $5.00 individual entry fee (seven days); $30.00 annual entry fee.

Maps: USGS: Mount Rainier East; Trails Illustrated Mount Rainier National Park; Astronaut's Vista: Mount Rainier National Park, Washington; Earthwalk Press Hiking Map & Guide.
Trail contacts: Paradise Ranger Station, (360) 569-2211, ext. 2314.
Jackson Visitor Center—Paradise, (360) 569-6036.
Trail conditions: www.nps.gov/mora/trail/tr_cnd.htm; weather, www.nps.gov/mora/current/weather.htm.

Finding the trailhead: From the Nisqually Entrance Station (see Getting There), travel 16 miles east on Longmire-Paradise Road. Stay to the left (north) where the road forks, following the signs to Paradise. From the Stevens Canyon Entrance Station (see Getting There), travel nearly 19 miles on Stevens Canyon Road to the intersection with Longmire-Paradise Road. Turn right (north) and follow the signs to Paradise. Park in the lot by the Jackson Visitor Center, if possible. *DeLorme: Washington Atlas and Gazetteer:* Page 48 B2, B3.

Special considerations: Parking at the Paradise Complex can get really hectic. Watch for a flashing sign when you enter the park that indicates whether the parking lots at Paradise are full, a common scenario on weekends from 11:00 A.M. until early evening. You can hope for a vacant spot, but if one does not open up promptly, consider an alternative hike.

The Hike

This is a great hike for kids and adults alike. The trail takes you through beautiful forested areas and wonderful meadows to an overlook of the Nisqually Glacier. The Nisqually Vista Trail is a self-guiding trail, but the National Park Service offers a guided tour of this hike in summer and leads snowshoe walks throughout winter. Inquire at the Jackson Visitor Center for more information. It is downhill all the way to the lookout and then uphill back to the parking lot, but both gradients are gradual.

To begin the hike, head to the northwest end of the Jackson Visitor Center parking lot. Look for a trail sign for the Dead Horse Creek Trail. Stay toward the left

▶ **Five tribes revered Mount Rainier: Nisqually, Puyallup, Muckleshoot, Yakama, and Upper Cowlitz (Taidnapam). Today, members of the Nisqually Tribe enjoy free access to Mount Rainier National Park, with the privilege of collecting plants for traditional religious or ceremonial purposes.**

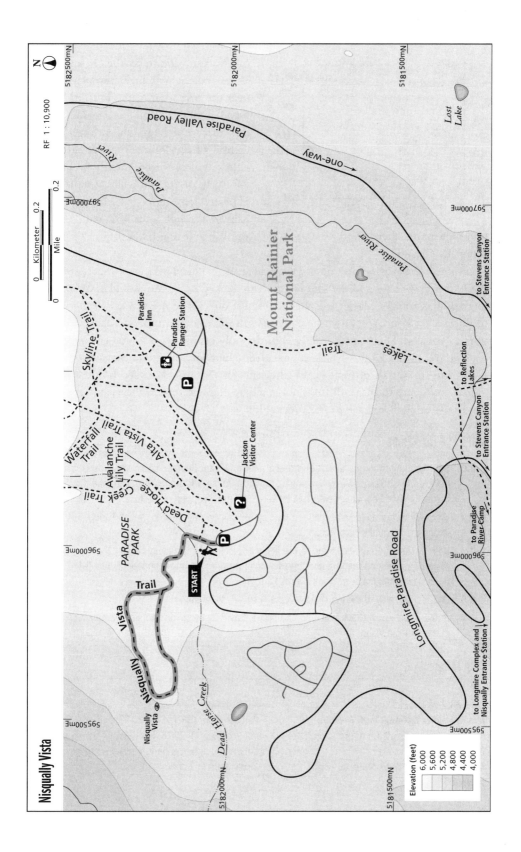

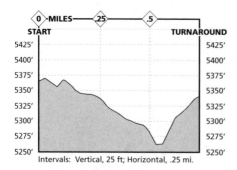

Intervals: Vertical, 25 ft; Horizontal, .25 mi.

(northwest), and take the Nisqually Vista Trail, which branches off very near the inception of the hike. In less than 0.3 mile the trail forks again. This fork marks the beginning of the loop section of the lollipop. You could go either way. We recommend heading left (west) on the Nisqually Vista Trail. Halfway through the loop, and halfway through your hike, you come to a viewpoint. There are three viewpoints, and the first one has a display on the Nisqually Glacier.

From all the viewpoints you can see where the Nisqually River originates from the Nisqually Glacier and the massive moraine kicked up by years of glacial movement. The Nisqually Glacier is a relatively active one. Once it extended all the way to Ricksecker Point. You might have seen Ricksecker Point on the way from Longmire to Paradise. The point is visible from the only bridge between the two areas.

The rest of the loop is a little over 0.3 mile long and takes you through quaint forest with meadows of lupine and pasqueflower (commonly called bottlebrush). When you come to the end of the loop, stay to the left, toward the visitor center. Enjoy a leisurely hike back to the parking lot.

Miles and Directions

0.0 Start heading to the northwest end of the Jackson Visitor Center parking lot. Look for a trail sign for the Dead Horse Creek Trail. Stay toward the left (northwest), and take the Nisqually Vista Trail, which branches off very near the inception of the hike.

0.3 Nisqually Vista Trail forks at the loop part of the lollipop trail. Stay to the left (west), following the Nisqually Vista Trail.

0.6 Halfway through the hike, come to the first viewpoint of the Nisqually Glacier, the Nisqually River, and the moraine; the viewpoint provides an informational display. Two more viewpoints follow in quick succession.

0.9 End of loop; stay to the left (east) on the Nisqually Vista Trail.

1.2 At the Dead Horse Creek trailhead, the hike is basically over; you can see the parking lot of the Jackson Visitor Center.

Hike Information

Local Information
Mount Rainier National Park Web site, www.nps.gov/mora; visitor information, (360) 569-2211, ext. 3314.
Jackson Visitor Center—Paradise, (360) 569-6036.

Lodging
Paradise Inn, (360) 569-2275; National Park Inn, (360) 569-2275. For a list of accommodations outside the park, visit www.nps.gov/mora/general/accom.htm.

Campgrounds

You can stay at a campground inside the park if you wish to day hike and car camp. Sunshine Point Campground is located in the southwest corner of the park, 0.25 mile inside the Nisqually Entrance. Register at the campground. Cougar Rock Campground is located in the southwest corner of the park, 2.3 miles north of Longmire. Ohanapecosh Campground is located in the southeast corner of the park, 11.0 miles north of Packwood off Highway 123. You can reserve a site at Ohanapecosh or Cougar Rock Campground online at http://reservations.nps.gov, or call (800) 365–CAMP (2267) 7:00 A.M. to 7:00 P.M. PST.

13 Alta Vista Summit

This short hike travels through beautiful forest overlooking the Nisqually Glacier.

Start: Jackson Visitor Center.
Distance: 1.6-mile out-and-back.
Approximate hiking time: 1 hour.
Difficulty: Easy.
Seasons: Early July through September.
Nearest towns: Ashford, Packwood.
Fees and permits: $10.00 vehicle or $5.00 individual entry fee (seven days); $30.00 annual entry fee.

Maps: USGS: Mount Rainier East; Trails Illustrated Mount Rainier National Park; Astronaut's Vista: Mount Rainier National Park, Washington; Earthwalk Press Hiking Map & Guide.
Trail contacts: Paradise Ranger Station, (360) 569–2211. ext. 2314.
Jackson Visitor Center–Paradise, (360) 569–6036.
Trail conditions: www.nps.gov/mora/trail/tr_cnd.htm; weather, www.nps.gov/mora/current/weather.htm.

Finding the trailhead: From the Nisqually Entrance Station (see Getting There), travel 16.0 miles east on Longmire-Paradise Road. Stay to the left (north) where the road forks, following the signs to Paradise. From the Stevens Canyon Entrance Station (see Getting There), travel nearly 19 miles on Stevens Canyon Road to the intersection with Longmire-Paradise Road. Turn right (north) and follow the signs to Paradise. Park in the lot by the Jackson Visitor Center, if possible. *DeLorme: Washington Atlas and Gazetteer:* Page 48 B2, B3.

Special considerations: Parking at the Paradise Complex can get really hectic. Watch for a flashing sign when you enter the park that indicates whether the parking lots at Paradise are full, a common scenario on weekends from 11:00 A.M. until early evening. You can hope for a vacant spot, but if one does not open up promptly, consider an alternative hike.

The Hike

This hike is excellent for children. It is short and scenic and gives you a little taste of Mount Rainier National Park. If you take this hike in July or August, an abundance of wildflowers will line the trails. Please preserve the fragile meadows where the flowers

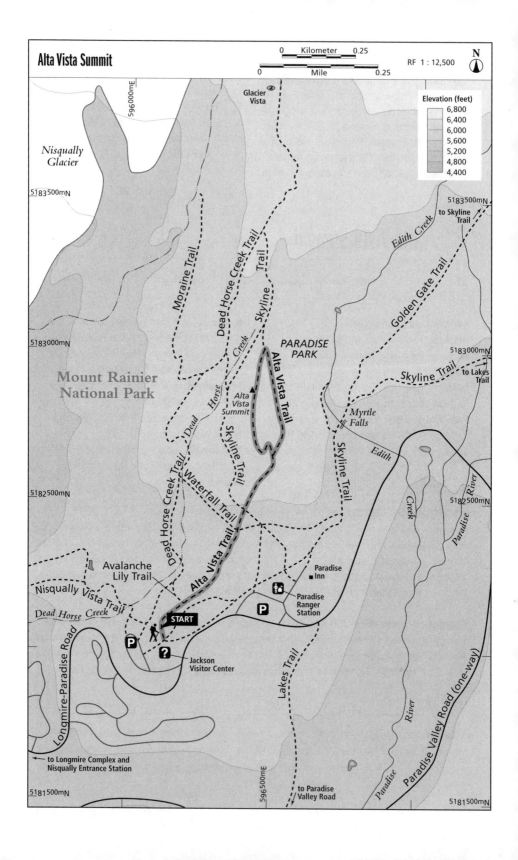

grow by staying on the trail. Expect to see a lot of people on this popular trail.

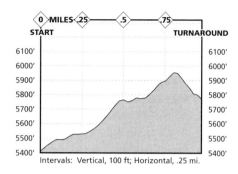

The trail, paved and well maintained, begins directly west of the Jackson Visitor Center. No trailhead sign marks the beginning of the Alta Vista Trail, but follow the paved steps that head north for just a few steps and you will come to a display of trails in the Paradise area. Do not take the spur trail heading to the right (east); it leads to the Paradise Ranger Station.

Continue 0.1 mile north on the Alta Vista Trail to the Avalanche Lily Trail, which runs west to the Dead Horse Creek Trail and east to the Paradise Ranger Station. Go straight and immediately pass another small spur trail that connects with the Avalanche Lily Trail on your left, heading southwest. Stay on the Alta Vista Trail, traveling north. There are detailed signs to help you continue on the Alta Vista Trail.

After another 0.1 mile the Waterfall Trail goes left (west) to connect with the Dead Horse Creek Trail or right (east) to the Skyline Trail. Again, stay on the Alta Vista Trail, heading north. Very soon after this junction, you come to the Skyline Trail. Again, stay on the Alta Vista Trail. At this point the trail grade turns markedly steep. Pace yourself.

About 0.5 mile into your hike, you come to the beginning of the loop to the Alta Vista summit. Go left (northwest) and uphill toward the summit with the help of a sign that points you in the correct direction. Below, Paradise Park is to the right (east). You can see tons of people milling about below you on other Paradise trails. Turn around and look to the south for a fabulous view of the jutting peaks of the Tatoosh Range.

If you need a rest, enjoy the view from one of the many rock benches along the trail. Please preserve the meadows by staying on the trail or in a designated rest area.

When you have enjoyed yourself to the fullest, complete the loop by continuing north on the Alta Vista Trail, or simply turn around and go back the way you came. If you decide to complete the loop, you reach the east side of the loop 0.1 mile from the summit, about 0.8 mile from the Jackson Visitor Center. Turn right and head south on the east side of the Alta Vista Trail until the loop rejoins itself, 1.1 miles into your hike. From this point, head back down the trail to the parking lot.

Miles and Directions

0.0 Start heading directly west of the Jackson Visitor Center. No trailhead sign marks the beginning of the Alta Vista Trail; follow the paved steps that head north for just a few steps and you will come to a display of trails.

0.1 At the junction with the Avalanche Lily Trail, which heads toward the Dead Horse Creek Trail to the west and Paradise ranger station to the right, stay straight ahead on the Alta Vista Trail.

0.2 Again, stay on the Alta Vista Trail, heading north when the Waterfall Trail crosses your path.

0.5 The loop of the lollipop begins. Take a left (west) at the fork, following the signs for Alta Vista Summit. Notice Paradise Park down below you to the northeast and the myriad hikers on other trails in the area.

1.1 Complete the loop; stay to the left (south) at the stem of the lollipop.

1.6 Reach the Jackson Visitor Center and the parking lot where you most likely left your car.

Hike Information

Local Information

Mount Rainier National Park Web site, www.nps.gov/mora; visitor information, (360) 569-2211, ext. 3314.
Jackson Visitor Center—Paradise, (360) 569-6036.

Lodging

Paradise Inn, (360) 569-2275; National Park Inn, (360) 569-2275. For a list of accommodations outside the park, visit www.nps.gov/mora/general/accom.htm.

Campgrounds

You can stay at a campground inside the park if you wish to day hike and car camp. Sunshine Point Campground is located in the southwest corner of the park, 0.25 mile inside the Nisqually Entrance. Register at the campground. Cougar Rock Campground is located in the southwest corner of the park, 2.3 miles north of Longmire. Ohanapecosh Campground is located in the southeast corner of the park, 11.0 miles north of Packwood off Highway 123. You can reserve a site at Ohanapecosh or Cougar Rock Campground online at http://reservations.nps.gov, or call (800) 365-CAMP (2267) 7:00 A.M. to 7:00 P.M. PST.

14 Camp Muir

A very steep hike through Paradise Snowfield up to Camp Muir, the most popular base camp used by climbers. From Camp Muir you can see Mount Adams, Mount St. Helens, and the Tatoosh Range in amazing panorama.

Start: Skyline trailhead.
Distance: 8.6-mile out-and-back.
Approximate hiking time: 4 to 6 hours.
Difficulty: Strenuous.
Seasons: Mid-July through September.
Nearest towns: Ashford, Packwood.
Fees and permits: $10.00 vehicle or $5.00 individual entry fee (seven days); $30.00 annual entry fee.

Maps: USGS: Mount Rainier East; Trails Illustrated Mount Rainier National Park; Astronaut's Vista: Mount Rainier National Park, Washington; Earthwalk Press Hiking Map & Guide.
Trail contacts: Paradise Ranger Station, (360) 569-2211, ext. 2314.
Jackson Visitor Center–Paradise, (360) 569-6036.
Trail conditions: www.nps.gov/mora/trail/tr_cnd.htm; weather, www.nps.gov/mora/current/weather.htm.

Finding the trailhead: From the Nisqually Entrance Station (see Getting There), travel 16 miles east on Longmire-Paradise Road. Stay to the left (north) where the road forks, following the signs to Paradise. From the Stevens Canyon Entrance Station (see Getting There), travel nearly 19 miles on Stevens Canyon Road to the intersection with Longmire-Paradise Road. Turn right (north) and follow the signs to Paradise. Park in the lot by the Paradise Ranger Station and the Paradise Inn, if possible. *DeLorme: Washington Atlas and Gazetteer:* Page 48 B2, B3.

Special considerations: Parking at the Paradise Complex can get really hectic. Watch for a flashing sign when you enter the park that indicates whether the parking lots at Paradise are full, a common scenario on weekends from 11:00 A.M. until early evening. You can hope for a vacant spot, but if one does not open up promptly, you may consider an alternative hike.

Bring plenty of water after the Pebble Creek area. The rest of the way to Camp Muir, you will be surrounded by water—in the form of snow—and not want to take the time to melt it on a stove.

The Hike

The hike with the greatest elevation gain included in this book, Camp Muir affords you views of other regal cascades, Mount Adams and Mount St. Helens, a panorama of the jagged Tatoosh Range, and an up-close look at the glaciers and ridges traversed by climbers on their way to the summit. This hike reaches an elevation of 10,080 feet, which feels like the top of the world. Expect an intense workout, because this hike gains 4,680 feet of elevation in 4.3 miles. Bring plenty of sunscreen, and apply it on all exposed skin. Make sure you apply some under your chin and nose and behind your knees to protect against the sun's rays reflected off the snow.

From the Paradise Inn parking lot, head up one of the two paved trails to the north. Both trails soon intersect with the Skyline Trail. Turn left (northwest) onto the Skyline Trail and continue northwest/north on the west side of the Skyline Trail loop for 1.6 miles until the Skyline Trail splits into the High and Low Skyline Trails. A maze of trails intersects the Skyline Trail before this point, but signs at every intersection keep you on the Skyline Trail. Remember to just continue traveling north. The Skyline Trail is relatively steep, gaining about 1,200 feet in the first 1.6 miles.

Go left (north) up the High Skyline Trail. In just 0.3 mile, turn left onto the Pebble Creek Trail, heading north toward the Muir Snowfield. Another 0.3 mile, 2.2 miles into your hike, and you reach the end of the Pebble Creek Trail. You stand below a steep snowfield. From this point on, the route is unmaintained. The National Park Service reminds you to travel safely and cause a minimal amount of impact beyond this point. Head up the snowfield, keeping to the snow. Do not walk on fragile alpine rock surfaces.

The rest of your ascent will be on snow, gaining 2,888 feet in the next 2.1 miles. By August, footprints cover the snowfield. You can choose to follow someone else's tracks or make your own. This decision may depend on the traction of your hiking boots and your sense of rugged individualism. The route passes over several false summits before reaching Camp Muir. The camp itself rests next to Cowlitz Cleaver, and if you strain your eyes you might be able to see it on the approach.

The view from the snowfield is amazing. As you rise higher and higher, the surrounding mountains grow more prominent. You also have a close-up view of the Nisqually Glacier.

At the top, the amount of development might be surprising. The buildings on the left are for those partaking in an RMI-guided climb. RMI (Rainier Mountaineering, Inc.) has a contract with the National Park Service to allow its operation within the park. The buildings to your right are National Park Service buildings. The first one is a bunkhouse open to climbers on a first-come, first-served basis. From the campsites to the left of the bunkhouse you can see a slice of the eastern portion of the park, and all other vantages provide a panorama of the southern end of the park. Find a place to rest and enjoy the view.

The trip back takes half the time as going up. You may want to glissade down in a sitting position. Some bring an ice ax, but it is largely unnecessary—the slopes aren't really steep enough to call for one. But if conditions prove particularly harsh or icy, you may consider an ax. We found ski poles very helpful for the trek up the mountain. Contact the Paradise Ranger Station for daily advice on conditions.

Miles and Directions

0.0　Start from the Paradise Inn parking lot, heading up one of the two paved trails to the north. Both trails soon intersect with the Skyline Trail. Turn left (northwest) onto the Skyline Trail.

◀ *Camp Muir.* JOHN CALDWELL

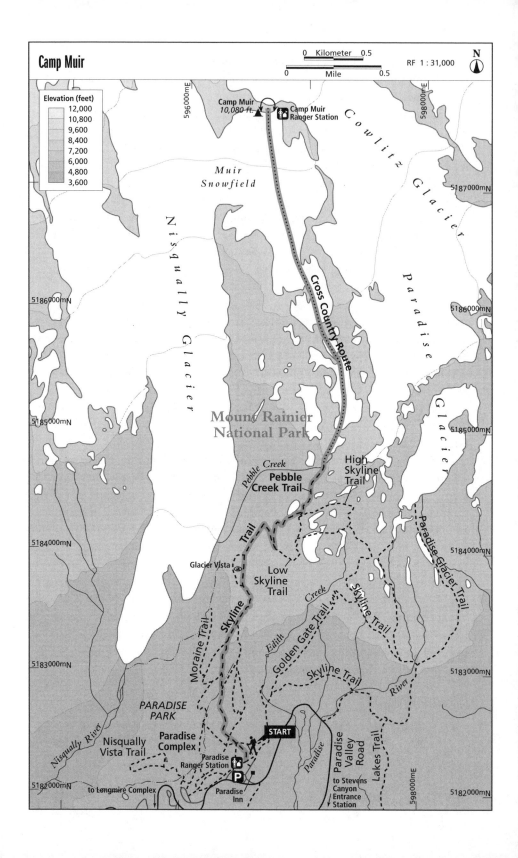

Camp Muir

0 Kilometer 0.5
0 Mile 0.5

RF 1 : 31,000

N

Elevation (feet)
12,000
10,800
9,600
8,400
7,200
6,000
4,800
3,600

596000mE

Camp Muir
10,080 ft.
▲ Camp Muir
Ranger Station

Cowlitz Glacier

598000mE

5187000mN

*Muir
Snowfield*

Nisqually Glacier

Cross Country Route

Paradise

5186000mN

5186000mN

Mount Rainier
National Park

Glacier

5185000mN

5185000mN

Pebble Creek

**Pebble
Creek Trail**

High
Skyline
Trail

Paradise Glacier Trail

5184000mN

Skyline Trail

Glacier Vista

Low
Skyline
Trail

Edith Creek

Skyline Trail

5184000mN

Moraine Trail

Skyline

Golden Gate Trail

Skyline Trail

River

5183000mN

5183000mN

*PARADISE
PARK*

START

Paradise Valley Road

Lakes Trail

Nisqually River

**Nisqually
Vista Trail**

**Paradise
Complex**

Paradise
Ranger Station

Paradise

598000mE

P

Paradise
Inn

to Longmire Complex

to Stevens
Canyon
Entrance
Station

5182000mN

5182000mN

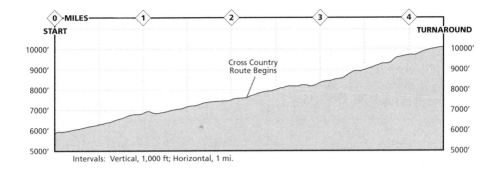

Intervals: Vertical, 1,000 ft; Horizontal, 1 mi.

1.6 After ascending the Skyline Trail for 1.6 miles, reach the point that the Skyline splits into the High and Low Skyline Trails. Stay to the left (northeast) on the High Skyline Trail.

1.9 In just 0.3 mile, the Pebble Creek Trail branches off to the left (north). Take the Pebble Creek Trail over Pebble Creek and toward the snow.

2.2 The Pebble Creek Trail terminates at the base of the Muir Snowfield. Camp Muir sits due north over several ridges. There should be tracks to follow from a constant stream of climbers.

4.3 You have reached the base camp for the south-side summit, Camp Muir. Catch your breath—only to lose it once again from the beauty of the scenery. Then retrace your path.

8.6 Arrive back at the parking lot.

Wilderness camping: You can camp at one of the sites at Camp Muir, whether or not you intend to summit the mountain. There are special regulations for base camps, especially pertaining to the disposal of human waste. The snowfield itself is your water source.

Hike Information

Local Information

Mount Rainier National Park Web site, www.nps.gov/mora; visitor information, (360) 569-2211, ext. 3314.

Jackson Visitor Center—Paradise, (360) 569-6036.

Lodging

Paradise Inn, (360) 569-2275; National Park Inn, (360) 569-2275. For a list of accommodations outside the park, visit www.nps.gov/mora/general/accom.htm.

Campgrounds

You can stay at a campground inside the park if you wish to day hike and car camp. Sunshine Point Campground is located in the southwest corner of the park, 0.25 mile inside the Nisqually Entrance. Register at the campground. Cougar Rock Campground is located in the southwest corner of the park, 2.3 miles north of Longmire. Ohanapecosh Campground is located in the southeast corner of the park, 11 miles north of Packwood off Highway 123. You can reserve a site at Ohanapecosh or Cougar Rock Campground online at http://reservations.nps.gov, or call (800) 365-CAMP (2267) 7:00 A.M. to 7:00 P.M. PST.

15 Lakes Trail

This popular three-hour loop descends from subalpine forest, through a mountain meadow, along Mazama Ridge to the aptly named Reflection Lakes, then up a steep pitch to the trailhead parking lot.

Start: Paradise Complex.
Distance: 5.1-mile loop.
Approximate hiking time: 2 to 3 hours.
Difficulty: Moderate.
Seasons: Mid-July through September
Nearest towns: Ashford, Packwood.
Fees and permits: $10.00 vehicle or $5.00 individual entry fee (seven days); $30.00 annual entry fee. Wilderness Camping Permits free—reservations recommended ($20 fee).

Maps: USGS: Mount Rainier East; Trails Illustrated Mount Rainier National Park; Astronaut's Vista: Mount Rainier National Park, Washington; Earthwalk Press Hiking Map & Guide.
Trail contacts: Paradise Ranger Station, (360) 569-2211, ext. 2314.
Jackson Visitor Center—Paradise, (360) 569-6036.
Trail conditions: www.nps.gov/mora/trail/tr_cnd.htm; weather, www.nps.gov/mora/current/weather.htm.

Finding the trailhead: From the Nisqually Entrance Station (see Getting There), travel 16 miles east on Longmire-Paradise Road. Stay to the left (north) where the road forks, following the signs to Paradise. From the Stevens Canyon Entrance Station (see Getting There), travel nearly 19 miles on Stevens Canyon Road to the intersection with Longmire-Paradise Road. Turn right (north) and follow the signs to Paradise. If possible, you may want to bypass the visitor center and park by the Paradise Ranger Station and the Paradise Inn. *DeLorme: Washington Atlas and Gazetteer:* Page 48 B2, B3

Special considerations: Parking at the Paradise Complex can get really hectic. Watch for a flashing sign when you enter the park that indicates whether the parking lots at Paradise are full, a common scenario on weekends from 11:00 A.M. until early evening. You can hope for a vacant spot, but if one does not open up promptly, consider an alternative hike.

The Hike

The Lakes Trail begins in the most popular tourist area of the park. After parking in the Paradise Inn lot, follow the well-marked trail from the northernmost part of the parking lot. Start hiking to the right (east), following the signs that read SKYLINE TRAIL. Wide and paved, the first 0.5 mile of the trail is barrier free and wheelchair accessible.

In 0.4 mile the trail comes to Myrtle Falls. A very short but steep walk down to the bottom of the spur trail gives you a view of a small, pretty waterfall. Back on the main trail, cross Edith Creek and come to a junction with the Golden Gate Trail. Once again, stay to the right along the Skyline Trail.

In 0.3 mile, the 4th Crossing Trail intersects the Skyline Trail to the right (south). Stay on the Skyline Trail heading east. For 0.4 mile the trail climbs, sometimes with

Mount Rainier as seen from the Lakes Trail.

switchbacks, until it intersects the Lakes Trail. Take a right (south) onto the Lakes Trail. The trail now descends gradually for 2.0 miles. This area is renowned for its subalpine forest and alpine scenery; catch a good look before descending into denser forest. About 1.6 miles from the junction with the Lakes Trail, a fork marks the High Lakes Trail junction. Stay to the left (south) for the best view of Reflection Lakes.

When you come to the Wonderland Trail junction, in 0.5 mile, stay to the right (south). Continue descending for another 0.2 mile, until you see Reflection Lakes to the right (east). The trail spits you out onto Stevens Canyon Road. Walk along the road toward the lakes for only 0.1 mile. When not socked in by clouds, Mount Rainier's image reflects on the surface of the lake.

Proceed along the road and by the lakes until you see the Lakes Trail heading north. Turn right (north) onto that trail. It skirts the lake for 0.25 mile, then moves away, climbing abruptly. Less than 0.5 mile after leaving Stevens Canyon Road, the Lakes Trail meets the High Lakes Trail once again. Stay to the left (west). The trail immediately begins to descend and continues the descent for 0.4 mile, at which point it crosses Paradise Valley Road. On the opposite side of the road, look for a small parking area. The trail continues from the northernmost corner of this lot.

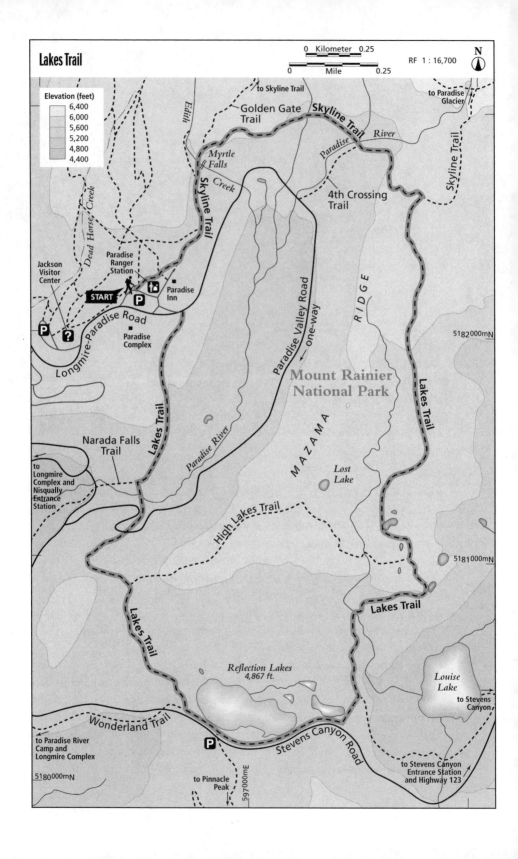

The trail quickly descends to the bank of the crystal-clear waters of the Paradise River. You follow along its banks, then cross the river. About 0.1 mile beyond Paradise Valley Road, the trail meets the Narada Falls Trail. Turn right (north). You have now come 4.5 miles and, with just over 0.5 mile remaining, have set out on the steepest section of the hike. Climb steadily and steeply until the trail leads into the southeastern corner of the Paradise Complex parking lot. Remember where you parked your car?

Miles and Directions

0.0 Start hiking to the right (east) at the well-marked trail in the northernmost part of the Paradise Inn parking lot.

0.3 Myrtle Falls Trail spurs off the Skyline Trail; you can shuffle down the hill a bit for a peek at the falls. Soon after, the Golden Gate Trail intersects the Skyline Trail. Stay to the right (east) along the Skyline Trail.

0.7 The 4th Crossing Trail intersects the Skyline Trail from the right (southwest). Stay to the left (southeast) on the Skyline Trail.

1.1 After several switchbacks, the Lakes Trail branches off the Skyline Trail. Take a right (south) onto the Lakes Trail, through meadow and toward Reflection Lakes.

2.7 At 2.7 miles come to the High Lakes Trail junction, which makes a smaller loop with the Lakes Trail. For this longer loop, stay to the left (south) on the Lakes Trail.

3.2 At the east end of Reflection Lakes, intersect the Wonderland Trail, which joins the Lakes Trail to the other side of the lake. Take a right (west) toward the center of Reflection Lakes, and the trail puts you onto Stevens Canyon Road. Stay along the sidewalk for a short while.

3.4 Reach a trail that heads north to the Reflection Lakes from the parking lot area. Resuming on the trail, you have a fantastic look at Mount Rainier mirrored in the still waters of the natural reflection pool. Hope for a day with no clouds!

3.5 After joining the Lakes Trail for a 0.3-mile stint, the Wonderland Trail once again branches out on its own, toward the left (southwest) and across the Stevens Canyon Road. Again stay on the Lakes Trail, as you will throughout your journey.

3.9 As expected, since it forms a loop with the Lakes Trail, you again come upon the High Lakes Trail. Again stay to the left (north) toward Paradise on the Lakes Trail.

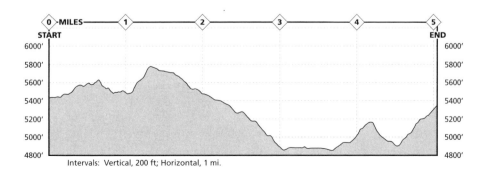

Intervals: Vertical, 200 ft; Horizontal, 1 mi.

4.4 The trail descends to Paradise Valley Road and continues from the northeast corner of the small parking lot on the other side of the road.

4.5 Not far from Paradise Valley Road, reach the Narada Falls Trail junction. Stay to the right (north) and climb the last steep section back to Paradise.

5.1 Reach the southeast corner of the Paradise Inn parking lot.

Hike Information

Local Information

Mount Rainier National Park Web site, www.nps.gov/mora; visitor information, (360) 569–2211, ext. 3314.
Jackson Visitor Center–Paradise, (360) 569–6036.

Lodging

Paradise Inn, (360) 569–2275; National Park Inn, (360) 569–2275. For a list of accommodations outside the park, visit www.nps.gov/mora/general/accom.htm.

Campgrounds

You can stay at a campground inside the park if you wish to day hike and car camp. Sunshine Point Campground is located in the southwest corner of the park, 0.25 mile inside the Nisqually Entrance. Register at the campground. Cougar Rock Campground is located in the southwest corner of the park, 2.3 miles north of Longmire. Ohanapecosh Campground is located in the southeast corner of the park, 11 miles north of Packwood off Highway 123. You can reserve a site at Ohanapecosh or Cougar Rock Campground online at http://reservations.nps.gov, or call (800) 365–CAMP (2267) 7:00 A.M. to 7:00 P.M. PST.

16 Dead Horse Creek

This short spur trail connects with the Skyline Trail and has great views of the Tatoosh Range, Mount Rainier, and the Nisqually Glacier.

Start: Jackson Visitor Center parking lot.
Distance: 2.3-mile out and back.
Approximate hiking time: 1 hour.
Difficulty: Easy.
Seasons: July through September.
Nearest towns: Ashford, Packwood.
Fees and permits: $10.00 vehicle or $5.00 individual entry fee (seven days); $30.00 annual entry fee. Wilderness Camping Permits free—reservations recommended ($20 fee).

Maps: USGS: Mount Rainier East; Trails Illustrated Mount Rainier National Park; Astronaut's Vista: Mount Rainier National Park, Washington; Earthwalk Press Hiking Map & Guide.
Trail contacts: Paradise Ranger Station, (360) 569-2211, ext. 2314. Jackson Visitor Center–Paradise, (360) 569-6036.
Trail conditions: www.nps.gov/mora/trail/ tr_cnd.htm; weather, www.nps.gov/mora/ current/weather.htm.

Finding the trailhead: From the Nisqually Entrance Station (see Getting There), drive nearly 16 miles east on Longmire-Paradise Road to the turnoff for the Ohanapecosh area. Stay to the left and continue on Longmire-Paradise Road for 2.1 miles. From the Stevens Canyon Entrance Station (see Getting There), travel nearly 19 miles on Stevens Canyon Road to the intersection with Longmire-Paradise Road. Turn right (north) and follow the signs to Paradise. If possible, park in the parking lot in front of the Jackson Visitor Center. *DeLorme: Washington Atlas and Gazetteer:* Page 48 B2, B3

Special considerations: Parking at the Paradise Complex can get really hectic. Watch for a flashing sign when you enter the park that indicates whether the parking lots at Paradise are full. Even if all the lots are not full, the lot in front of the visitor center is likely to be full. If it is, you can drive another 0.1 mile up the road to the parking lot in front of the Paradise Ranger Station and the Paradise Inn.

The Hike

If you want to hike the Skyline Trail but would prefer a shorter, more gradual ascent, consider the Dead Horse Creek Trail as an alternative. In August, wildflowers, including lupine and Lewis monkeyflower, line your path. Please preserve these flowers by staying on designated trails.

To start the hike, head to the west end of the parking lot. Look for a trail sign for the Dead Horse Creek Trail. Stay to the right, heading north on the Dead Horse Creek Trail. The trail first takes you through serene subalpine forest. Although the Paradise area is extremely high traffic, this trail receives less use than others in the area.

Wildlife is commonly seen along the trail. Deer, grouse, and marmots often venture into this area. Remember not to feed these wild animals; they need to remain

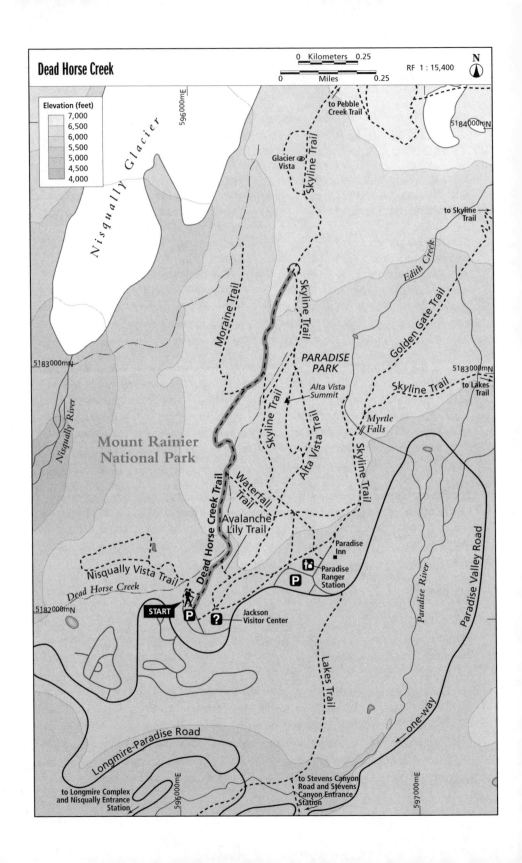

Dead Horse Creek

Elevation (feet)
7,000
6,500
6,000
5,500
5,000
4,500
4,000

0 Kilometers 0.25

0 Miles 0.25

RF 1 : 15,400

N

596000mE

to Pebble
Creek Trail

5184000mN

Skyline Trail

Glacier
Vista

to Skyline
Trail

Nisqually   Glacier

Moraine Trail

Skyline Trail

Edith Creek

Golden Gate Trail

5183000mN

*PARADISE
PARK*

Alta Vista
Summit

Skyline Trail

to Lakes
Trail

5183000mN

Skyline Trail

Skyline Trail

Nisqually River

**Mount Rainier
National Park**

Alta Vista Trail

*Myrtle
Falls*

Skyline Trail

Waterfall
Trail

Avalanche
Lily Trail

Dead Horse Creek Trail

Paradise River

Nisqually Vista Trail

Paradise
Inn

Paradise Valley Road

Dead Horse Creek

Paradise
Ranger
Station

P

5182000mN

START

P

?

Jackson
Visitor Center

Lakes Trail

one-way

Longmire-Paradise Road

596000mE

597000mE

to Longmire Complex
and Nisqually Entrance
Station

to Stevens Canyon
Road and Stevens
Canyon Entrance
Station

self-sufficient to survive in their natural habitat. Also, it is illegal to feed the wildlife in Mount Rainier National Park.

Continue going north on the Dead Horse Creek Trail, ignoring the two trails that come in from the right at 0.1 mile (the Avalanche Lily Trail) and 0.4 mile (the Waterfall Trail). Both of these trails travel to the Paradise Ranger Station and the Paradise Inn. At every intersection, a sign bears directions to help you stay on the Dead Horse Creek Trail. The Nisqually Glacier lies to the west. The National Park Service has set up several rock benches to help you enjoy this view. Please use the provided benches to minimize your impact on the fragile subalpine meadows.

The Moraine Trail intersects the Dead Horse Creek Trail from the left at 0.7 mile. Stay to the right (northeast), unless you plan to take the Moraine Trail option. Not far from the junction with the Moraine Trail, a small spur trail branches off to the right, connecting with the Skyline Trail. Stay on the main trail.

The trail is considerably steeper at this point, but you have only 0.4 mile to the end of the trail, over a mile into your hike. The end of Dead Horse Creek Trail is the Skyline Trail. You have the option of hiking back down the way you just came or making a loop by following the Skyline Trail. If you choose to take the Skyline Trail, follow the signs for it until you see a sign for the visitor center; follow the signs that point to the visitor center.

Miles and Directions

0.0   Start by heading to the west end of the Jackson Visitor Center parking lot. Look for a trail sign for the Dead Horse Creek Trail and stay to the right, heading north.

0.1   When the Avalanche Lily Trail comes in from the right (east), continue straight (north) on the Dead Horse Creek Trail.

0.4   Ignore the junction with the Waterfall Trail, which heads toward the Paradise Inn, and hike north on the Dead Horse Creek Trail.

0.7   The Moraine Trail spurs off to the left. If you want to see the Nisqually Glacier up-close and personal, you can take this option and add a mile of trail to your hike. Otherwise, stay to the right (northeast) along the Dead Horse Creek Trail. Also stay on the main trail when you encounter the connector to the Skyline Trail in just a few paces.

1.1   The Skyline Trail junction marks the end of the Dead Horse Creek Trail. You can turn around (south) or take a right (southeast) and follow signs to the visitor center.

2.2   Arrive back at the visitor center.

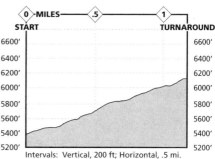

Option: More than halfway up the Dead Horse Creek Trail is the Moraine Trail. The park maintains this trail for less than 0.1 mile of its total 0.5-mile length. Taking this option adds 1.0 mile to your trip. The trail takes you down to the Nisqually Glacier Moraine, where the Nisqually River flows from its glacial source. People often hear and see chunks of ice falling from the end of the glacier. Be forewarned—the Moraine Trail is extremely steep.

Hike Information

Local Information
Mount Rainier National Park Web site, www.nps.gov/mora; visitor information, (360) 569-2211, ext. 3314.
Jackson Visitor Center—Paradise, (360) 569-6036.

Lodging
Paradise Inn, (360) 569-2275; National Park Inn, (360) 569-2275. For a list of accommodations outside the park, visit www.nps.gov/mora/general/accom.htm.

Campgrounds
You can stay at a campground inside the park if you wish to day hike and car camp. Sunshine Point Campground is located in the southwest corner of the park, 0.25 mile inside the Nisqually Entrance. Register at the campground. Cougar Rock Campground is located in the southwest corner of the park, 2.3 miles north of Longmire. Ohanapecosh Campground is located in the southeast corner of the park, 11 miles north of Packwood off Highway 123. You can reserve a site at Ohanapecosh or Cougar Rock Campground online at http://reservations.nps.gov, or call (800) 365-CAMP (2267) 7:00 A.M. to 7:00 P.M. PST.

17 High Lakes Trail

This short loop offers a great view of the Tatoosh Range and Reflection Lakes.

Start: Reflection Lakes.
Distance: 2.7-mile loop.
Approximate hiking time: 1 to 1.5 hours.
Difficulty: Easy.
Seasons: July through September.
Nearest towns: Ashford, Packwood.
Fees and permits: $10.00 vehicle or $5.00 individual entry fee (seven days); $30.00 annual entry fee. Wilderness Camping Permits free–reservations recommended ($20 fee).

Maps: USGS: Mount Rainier East; Trails Illustrated Mount Rainier National Park; Astronaut's Vista: Mount Rainier National Park, Washington; Earthwalk Press Hiking Map & Guide.
Trail contacts: Paradise Ranger Station, (360) 569-2211, ext. 2314.
Jackson Visitor Center—Paradise, (360) 569-6036.
Trail conditions: www.nps.gov/mora/trail/tr_cnd.htm; weather, www.nps.gov/mora/current/weather.htm.

Finding the trailhead: From Stevens Canyon Entrance Station (see Getting There), drive nearly 18 miles on Stevens Canyon Road to Reflection Lakes. From the Nisqually Entrance Station (see Getting There), travel nearly 16 miles east on Longmire-Paradise Road to the turnoff for the Ohanapecosh area. Turn right (southeast) onto Stevens Canyon Road and toward Ohanapecosh.

Reflection Lakes.

Stay on this road for just under a mile. Reflection Lakes has three parking lots. The High Lakes Trail starts from the center parking lot, though you can access the trail from the flanking parking lots as well. The trail loops the lakes. *DeLorme: Washington Atlas and Gazetteer:* Page 48 B3.

The Hike

This is an easy day hike that explores the area around Reflection Lakes, possibly the most photographed spot on Mount Rainier. Aptly named, on a clear day you can see the entire mountain mirrored in the still waters of Reflection Lakes. The High Lakes Trail leaves the lakeside and follows Mazama Ridge, gaining just enough elevation to afford a view of the Tatoosh Range.

We recommend hiking this loop counterclockwise to lessen the elevation gain, but that decision is yours alone. From the Reflection Lakes parking lot, walk east along Stevens Canyon Road until you reach the junction with the Wonderland Trail toward Louise Lake. Go left (northeast) onto the Lakes Trail, leaving the Wonderland Trail behind. Continue on the Lakes Trail up the south side of Mazama Ridge—a relatively steep but short section—to the High Lakes Trail, 0.7 mile into your hike.

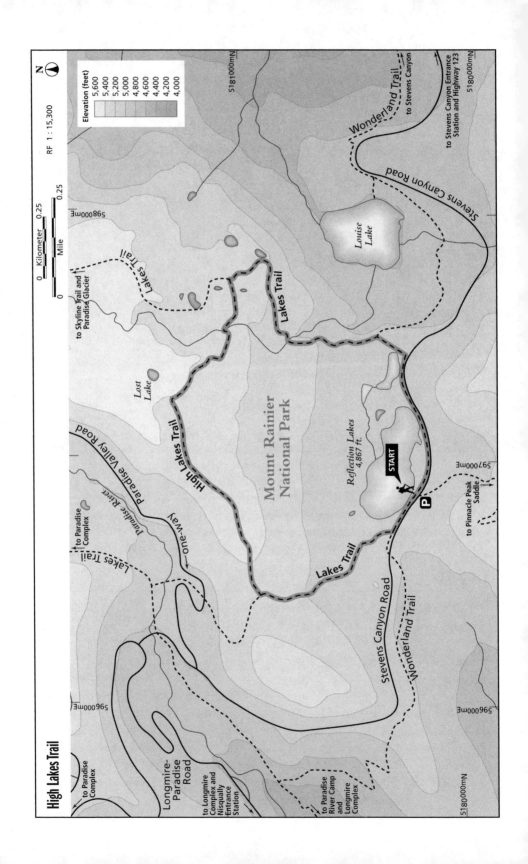

Turn left (west) onto the High Lakes Trail. This trail is mostly downhill or flat, with many opportunities to view the Tatoosh Range and three of its jagged pinnacles—Pinnacle, Plummer, and Unicorn Peaks—jutting above the horizon.

After 1.2 miles the High Lakes Trail rejoins the Lakes Trail. Go left (south) and downhill on the lower Lakes Trail for 0.5 mile to a junction with the Wonderland Trail. Stay to the left and head toward Reflection Lakes for the next 0.2 mile to Stevens Canyon Road. Walk 0.1 mile east along the road back to where you parked.

Miles and Directions

0.0 Start from the Reflection Lakes parking lot. Walk east along Stevens Canyon Road until you reach the junction with the Wonderland Trail toward Louise Lake.

0.3 The Wonderland Trail diverges from the Lakes Trail to head toward Louise Lake. Stay left (north) on the Lakes Trail and head up Mazama Ridge.

0.7 At the High Lakes Trail junction, make sure you take a left (west) onto High Lakes. Otherwise, you could follow the Lakes Trail all the way to Paradise.

1.9 When you reach the Lakes Trail junction, you have completed the top section of the loop known as the High Lakes Trail. Stay to the left (south) on the Lakes Trail to get back to your car.

2.4 Once again, the Wonderland Trail intersects the Lakes Trail. Stay to the left (southeast) toward the Reflection Lakes parking lot.

2.7 Arrive back at the Reflection Lakes trailhead.

Hike Information

Local Information

Mount Rainier National Park Web site, www.nps.gov/mora; visitor information, (360) 569-2211, ext. 3314.

Jackson Visitor Center–Paradise, (360) 569-6036.

Lodging

Paradise Inn, (360) 569-2275; National Park Inn, (360) 569-2275. For a list of accommodations outside the park, visit www.nps.gov/mora/general/accom.htm.

Campgrounds

You can stay at a campground inside the park if you wish to day hike and car camp. Sunshine Point Campground is located in the southwest corner of the park, 0.25 mile inside the Nisqually Entrance. Register at the campground. Cougar Rock Campground is located in the southwest corner of the park, 2.3 miles north of Longmire. Ohanapecosh Campground is located in the southeast corner of the park, 11 miles north of Packwood off Highway 123. You can reserve a site at Ohanapecosh or Cougar Rock Campground online at http://reservations.nps.gov, or call (800) 365-CAMP (2267) 7:00 A.M. to 7:00 P.M. PST.

18 Pinnacle Peak Saddle

This short climb up to the saddle between Pinnacle and Plummer Peaks offers great views of Mount Rainier along the trail and from the saddle.

Start: Pinnacle Peak trailhead, across from Reflection Lakes.
Distance: 2.6-mile out-and-back.
Approximate hiking time: 1 to 1.5 hours.
Difficulty: Easy.
Seasons: Late July through September.
Nearest towns: Ashford, Packwood.
Fees and permits: $10.00 vehicle or $5.00 individual entry fee (seven days); $30.00 annual entry fee. Wilderness Camping Permits free—reservations recommended ($20 fee).

Maps: USGS: Mount Rainier East; Trails Illustrated Mount Rainier National Park; Astronaut's Vista: Mount Rainier National Park, Washington; Earthwalk Press Hiking Map & Guide.
Trail contacts: Paradise Ranger Station, (360) 569-2211, ext. 2314.
Jackson Visitor Center—Paradise, (360) 569-6036.
Trail conditions: www.nps.gov/mora/trail/tr_cnd.htm; weather, www.nps.gov/mora/current/weather.htm.

Finding the trailhead: From Stevens Canyon Entrance Station (see Getting There), drive nearly 18 miles on Stevens Canyon Road to Reflection Lakes. From the Nisqually Entrance Station (see Getting There), travel nearly 16 miles east on Longmire-Paradise Road to the turnoff for the Ohanapecosh area. Turn right (southeast) onto Stevens Canyon Road and toward Ohanapecosh. Stay on this road for just under a mile. Reflection Lakes has three parking lots. The well-marked trailhead to Pinnacle Peak starts opposite the middle lot. *DeLorme: Washington Atlas and Gazetteer:* Page 48 B3.

The Hike

This hike is uphill all the way to the turnaround point. Wildflowers, such as lupine and magenta paintbrush, often grow along the trail in July and August. Pikas inhabit the rockfields along the trail, squeaking at passersby. The saddle offers an excellent view of Mount Rainier. Hope for a clear day.

There are no tricky turns or trail junctions on this hike. Simply start from the trailhead, directly across from the west end of Reflection Lakes, and hike all the way to the saddle. The first half of the trail is in the forest and climbs gradually, but keep in mind that once you hit the first rockfield, the trail becomes steep and rocky. Snow lingers on these rockfields late into summer—sturdy hiking boots are the footwear of choice here.

Once you reach the saddle, you can see to the south boundary of the park and all the way to Packwood. Plummer Peak rises to the right (west) and Pinnacle Peak to the left (east). Looking southeast you can see both Unicorn Peak and the Castle;

Pinnacle Peak.

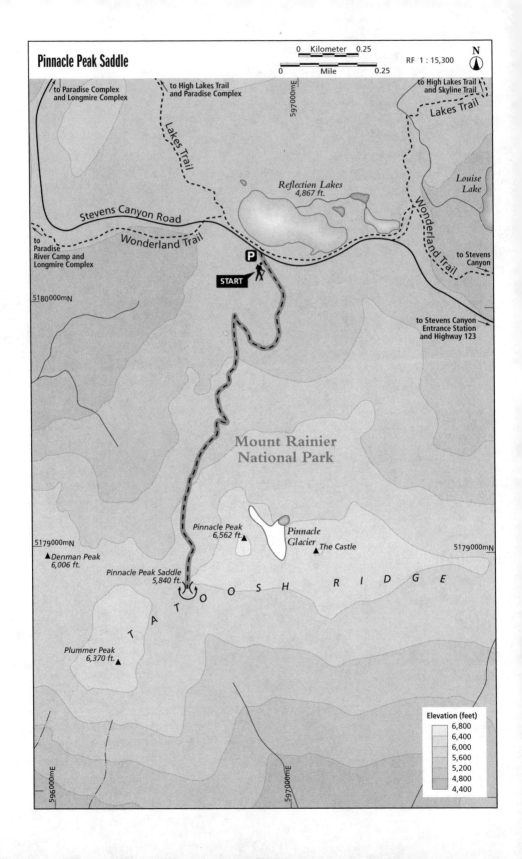

to the southwest, Wahpenayo Peak is visible. Enjoy the amazing view before heading back the way you came.

Miles and Directions

0.0 Start heading south from the Pinnacle Peak trailhead, across Stevens Canyon Road from Reflection Lakes.

1.3 Reach the Pinnacle Peak saddle. Head back the way you came, or opt for the scramble to the top. See Option.

2.6 Arrive back at the trailhead.

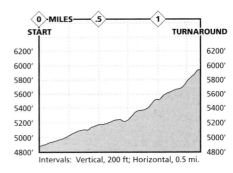

Intervals: Vertical, 200 ft; Horizontal, 0.5 mi.

Option: The maintained trail ends 1.3 miles into the hike, but there are unmaintained trails heading along the ridges of both Pinnacle and Plummer Peaks. The scramble up to Pinnacle Peak does not require technical climbing equipment, but it is hazardous and should be approached with caution.

Hike Information

Local Information

Mount Rainier National Park Web site, www.nps.gov/mora; visitor information, (360) 569-2211, ext. 3314.

Jackson Visitor Center–Paradise, (360)569-6036.

Lodging

Paradise Inn, (360) 569-2275; National Park Inn, (360) 569-2275. For a list of accommodations outside the park, visit www.nps.gov/mora/general/accom.htm.

Campgrounds

You can stay at a campground inside the park if you wish to day hike and car camp. Sunshine Point Campground is located in the southwest corner of the park, 0.25 mile inside the Nisqually Entrance. Register at the campground. Cougar Rock Campground is located in the southwest corner of the park, 2.3 miles north of Longmire. Ohanapecosh Campground is located in the southeast corner of the park, 11 miles north of Packwood off Highway 123. You can reserve a site at Ohanapecosh or Cougar Rock Campground online at http://reservations.nps.gov, or call (800) 365-CAMP (2267) 7:00 A.M. to 7:00 P.M. PST.

19 Skyline Trail

Quite possibly the most popular hike in Mount Rainier National Park, the Skyline Trail is very well maintained and partly paved, with a close-up view of the Nisqually Glacier.

Start: Skyline trailhead.
Distance: 5.2-mile loop.
Approximate hiking time: 2 to 3 hours.
Difficulty: Moderate.
Seasons: Mid-July through September.
Nearest towns: Ashford, Packwood.
Fees and permits: $10.00 vehicle or $5.00 individual entry fee (seven days); $30.00 annual entry fee. Wilderness Camping Permits free—reservations recommended ($20 fee).

Maps: USGS: Mount Rainier East; Trails Illustrated Mount Rainier National Park; Astronaut's Vista: Mount Rainier National Park, Washington; Earthwalk Press Hiking Map & Guide.
Trail contacts: Paradise Ranger Station, (360) 569-2211, ext. 2314.
Jackson Visitor Center—Paradise, (360) 569-6036.
Trail conditions: www.nps.gov/mora/trail/tr_cnd.htm; weather, www.nps.gov/mora/current/weather.htm.

Finding the trailhead: From the Nisqually Entrance Station (see Getting There), travel 16.0 miles east on Longmire-Paradise Road. Stay to the left (north) where the road forks, following the signs to Paradise. From the Stevens Canyon Entrance Station (see Getting There), travel nearly 19 miles on Stevens Canyon Road to the intersection with Longmire-Paradise Road. Turn right (north) and follow the signs to Paradise. If possible, bypass the visitor center and park by the Paradise Ranger Station and the Paradise Inn. *DeLorme: Washington Atlas and Gazetteer:* Page 48 B2, B3.

Special considerations: Parking at the Paradise Complex can get really hectic. Watch for a flashing sign when you enter the park that indicates whether or not the lots at Paradise are full, a common scenario on weekends from 11:00 A.M. until early evening. You can hope for a vacant spot, but if one does not open up promptly, consider an alternative hike.

The Hike

For good reason, more people visit Paradise than any other location on Mount Rainier. The views are spectacular, the services plentiful, and the trails many. Of all the trails in Paradise, Skyline is the most well known and frequently hiked. As you might guess by the name, the Skyline Trail goes above timberline into alpine terrain, with an awe-inspiring look at the Nisqually Glacier.

For the longest and best view of Mount Rainier, hike this trail clockwise. Start from the Skyline trailhead in the northwestern corner of the Paradise area parking lot. Rather than turning right (east), stay to the left (northwest), heading directly up the mountain. With so many intersecting trails, this area can get a bit confusing, but the Park Service has done a good job of putting up and maintaining clear, direct

Van Trump Monument on Skyline Trail.

signposts that explicitly point the way. Stay on the Skyline Trail through all the intersections. You will likely see deer and marmots on this hike. Please do not feed the wildlife. They have already grown bold from constant handouts.

The trail ascends rather steeply for the next 2.0 miles, so prepare for a workout. At 1.1 miles, the Glacier Vista Trail intersects the main trail. For a slightly closer view of the Nisqually Glacier and a few words on the wonders of glaciation, take the Glacier Vista Trail to your left (west). It parallels the Skyline Trail briefly and then rejoins it. Back on the main trail, continue north for 0.5 mile of switchbacks, at which point the Low Skyline Trail splits to the right toward Panorama Point. Turn left (northeast) to stay on the High Skyline Trail.

Rocky alpine terrain provides the foreground for a remarkable view of Mount Rainier for nearly 0.5 mile. At the junction with the Pebble Creek Trail, 2.0 miles into the hike, you reach the top of your ascent. This is the path many mountaineers take on their trek to the summit. To see the Camp Muir Snowfield, turn left (north) onto the Pebble Creek Trail. A good glimpse of the path to the top can be had less than 0.5 mile from the turnoff, where Pebble Creek makes a good lunch spot.

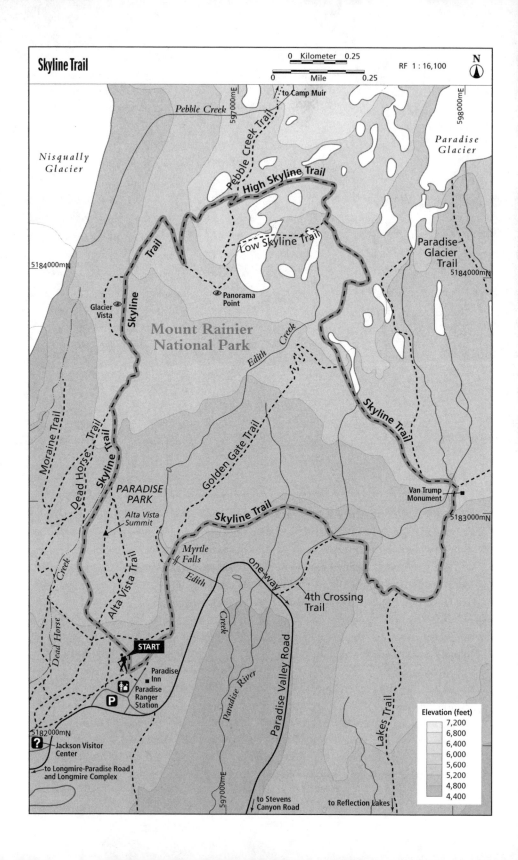

Otherwise, stay to the right (east), following the High Skyline Trail. You descend steeply along switchbacks in alpine terrain almost all the way to the Golden Gate Trail junction, about 0.8 mile. The Golden Gate Trail provides a shortcut back to Paradise, cutting about 2 miles off the hike length. To stay on the Skyline Trail, bear left.

In 0.7 mile a unique bench made of stone serves as a monument to P. B. Van Trump and Hazard Stevens, for the first recorded successful ascent of Mount Rainier. It also serves as a marker for the trailhead to the Paradise Glacier. Sit and relax on the stone slabs before continuing south on the Skyline Trail. Behind the monument, facing south, you have an excellent view of the Tatoosh Range on a sunny day.

Another 1.3 miles of descent with sporadic switchbacks leads to Myrtle Falls, a pretty little waterfall. You must walk to the bottom of the spur trail, a short side trip, to see it well. Return to the now-paved main trail. You should be able to see Paradise from the trail. Walk 0.4 mile back to the trailhead.

Miles and Directions

0.0 Start from the Skyline trailhead in the northwestern corner of the Paradise area parking lot. Stay to the left (northwest), heading directly up the mountain.

1.1 The Glacier Vista Trail spurs the main Skyline Trail, then rejoins just up the trail. Take the spur trail to see the display the park has erected on glaciation.

1.6 The Skyline Trail divides into the High and Low Skyline Trails. If the day is clear, take the Low Skyline Trail option to the right (southeast) and check out the vista at Panorama Point. (See Option.) Otherwise, go left (northeast) on the High Skyline Trail to view the Muir Snowfields and more alpine terrain.

2.0 Either way, in 0.4 mile you come upon Pebble Creek Trail. Stay on one of the Skyline Trails, which will converge in another 0.3 mile.

2.8 Unless you are in a time crunch, stay to the left (southeast) and remain on the Skyline Trail at the intersection with the Golden Gate Trail. If you need to shave a couple of miles off the hike, you can take the Golden Gate Trail back to Paradise.

3.4 Come to the Paradise Glacier Trail junction and, just beyond it, a surreal sort of rock loveseat in the trail known as the Van Trump Monument. Stay to the right (south) along the Skyline Trail.

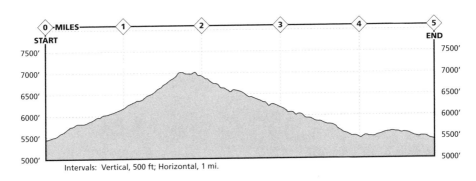

Intervals: Vertical, 500 ft; Horizontal, 1 mi.

4.8 Where the Golden Gate Trail rejoins the Skyline Trail on your right, there is also a spur trail to Myrtle Falls on your left. Take this short jog on your left (south) for a quick look at the falls.

5.2 Welcome back to Paradise.

Option: If the day is clear, follow the Low Skyline Trail detour to Panorama Point. Less than 0.25 mile of good trail leads to an excellent viewpoint. Here a panoramic picture of the Tatoosh Range and neighboring mountains is well labeled for your viewing pleasure and insight. A trail from Panorama Point joins the High Skyline Trail to the north, so you can easily jump back on the loop.

Hike Information

Local Information

Mount Rainier National Park Web site, www.nps.gov/mora; visitor information, (360) 569-2211, ext. 3314.
Jackson Visitor Center–Paradise, (360) 569-6036.

Lodging

Paradise Inn, (360) 569-2275; National Park Inn, (360) 569-2275. For a list of accommodations outside the park, visit www.nps.gov/mora/general/accom.htm.

Campgrounds

You can stay at a campground inside the park if you wish to day hike and car camp. Sunshine Point Campground is located in the southwest corner of the park, 0.25 mile inside the Nisqually Entrance. Register at the campground. Cougar Rock Campground is located in the southwest corner of the park, 2.3 miles north of Longmire. Ohanapecosh Campground is located in the southeast corner of the park, 11 miles north of Packwood off Highway 123. You can reserve a site at Ohanapecosh or Cougar Rock Campground online at http://reservations.nps.gov, or call (800) 365-CAMP (2267) 7:00 A.M. to 7:00 P.M. PST.

20 Paradise Glacier

A short day hike over a snowfield brings you to the foot of a small glacier.

Start: Skyline trailhead.
Distance: 6.4-mile out-and-back
Approximate hiking time: 3 to 4 hours.
Difficulty: Moderate.
Seasons: Mid-July through September.
Nearest towns: Ashford, Packwood.
Fees and permits: $10.00 vehicle or $5.00 individual entry fee (seven days); $30.00 annual entry fee. Wilderness Camping Permits free—reservations recommended ($20 fee).

Maps: USGS: Mount Rainier East; Trails Illustrated Mount Rainier National Park; Astronaut's Vista: Mount Rainier National Park, Washington; Earthwalk Press Hiking Map & Guide.
Trail contacts: Paradise Ranger Station, (360) 569–2211, ext. 2314.
Jackson Visitor Center—Paradise, (360) 569–6036.
Trail conditions: www.nps.gov/mora/trail/ tr_cnd.htm; weather, www.nps.gov/mora/ current/weather.htm.

Finding the trailhead: From the Nisqually Entrance Station (see Getting There), travel 16 miles east on Longmire-Paradise Road. Stay to the left (north) where the road forks, following the signs to Paradise. From the Stevens Canyon Entrance Station (see Getting There), travel nearly 19 miles on Stevens Canyon Road to the intersection with Longmire-Paradise Road. Turn right (north) and follow the signs to Paradise. If possible, bypass the visitor center and park by the Paradise Ranger Station and the Paradise Inn. *DeLorme: Washington Atlas and Gazetteer:* Page 48 B2, B3.

Special considerations: Parking at the Paradise Complex can get really hectic. Watch for a flashing sign when you enter the park that indicates whether the lots at Paradise are full, a common scenario on weekends from 11:00 A.M. until early evening. You can hope for a vacant spot, but if one does not open up promptly, consider an alternative hike.

The Paradise Glacier Trail is no longer maintained by the Park Service, but crews do check on the cairns once a year. Do not expect an immaculate trail beyond the Skyline Trail.

The Hike

The ice caves that once drew many to this trail have melted with the general increase in global temperature. This means a less sensational hike, but it also means fewer passersby and the same spectacular view as before.

Start hiking along the Skyline Trail in the northwestern corner of the parking lot; the trailhead is well marked. Proceed to the right (east), counterclockwise along the loop. Many trails congest this area, but just follow the Skyline Trail signs eastbound and you will reach your destination.

Hike gradually uphill along a wide, paved trail for 0.4 mile to arrive at Myrtle Falls. The path to the bottom of the falls is short but steep and offers a closer look.

View of Little Tahoma Peak along the Paradise Glacier Trail.

Back on the main trail, cross Edith Creek, the source of Myrtle Falls; stay to the right beyond the Golden Gate Trail junction.

Climb steadily, through occasional switchbacks, for 0.3 mile to the 4th Crossing Trail. Stay to the left, continuing east. Much like previous parts of the trail, this is a medium ascent through subalpine forest. You soon reach the Lakes Trail junction, 1.4 miles into the hike. Again, stay to the left, heading northeast.

The trail turns to head north; 0.4 mile after the Lakes Trail junction, look for a stone bench at a fork in the trail. This firm resting spot was erected by the Mountaineers and the Mazamas as a tribute to Hazard Stevens and Philemon Beecher Van Trump. The monument marks the campsite from which the two made the first recorded ascent of Mount Rainier. It also marks the Paradise Glacier Trail junction.

Turn right (east) onto the Paradise Glacier Trail. From here the ascent is gradual, but it leads into alpine terrain. Even in late summer expect to encounter quite a bit of snow; wear boots if you have them. The trail ends in a snowfield—hike only as far as you feel comfortable. No sign marks the end of the maintained trail. Cairns guide you to the snowfield, where the ice caves once were.

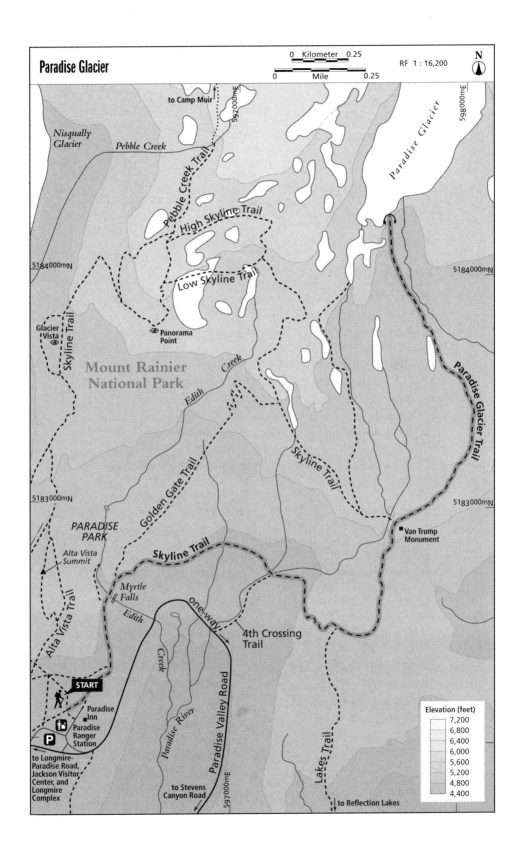

Paradise Glacier

0 — Kilometer — 0.25

0 — Mile — 0.25

RF 1 : 16,200

N

Nisqually Glacier

Pebble Creek

to Camp Muir

597000mE

Pebble Creek Trail

High Skyline Trail

Paradise Glacier

598000mE

5184000mN

Low Skyline Trail

Panorama Point

Glacier Vista

5184000mN

Skyline Trail

Mount Rainier National Park

Creek

Edith

Paradise Glacier Trail

Golden Gate Trail

Skyline Trail

5183000mN

5183000mN

PARADISE PARK

Alta Vista Summit

Van Trump Monument

Skyline Trail

Myrtle Falls

Edith

one-way

4th Crossing Trail

Alta Vista Trail

START

Paradise Inn

Paradise Ranger Station

Creek

Paradise River

Paradise Valley Road

P

to Longmire-Paradise Road, Jackson Visitor Center, and Longmire Complex

to Stevens Canyon Road

597000mE

Lakes Trail

to Reflection Lakes

Elevation (feet)

7,200
6,800
6,400
6,000
5,600
5,200
4,800
4,400

A good view of the Paradise Glacier is not the only reason to hike this trail. The snowfield, however, is a good place to play "name that glacier." Facing north up the trail, you have a close view of the glaciated mountain. To the east are the headwaters of Stevens Creek, and directly behind you (south) is an amazing view of the Tatoosh Range, the Goat Rocks, and Mount Adams. When you are ready, return to Paradise along the same trail.

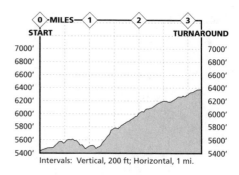

Intervals: Vertical, 200 ft; Horizontal, 1 mi.

Miles and Directions

0.0 Start hiking to the right (east) along the Skyline Trail in the northwestern corner of the parking lot.

0.4 Less than half a mile into your hike, come to a small trail to Myrtle Falls on your right (south) and the Golden Gate Trail junction on your left (north). You can take a peek at the falls, but come back to the Skyline Trail and continue east.

0.7 Reach the 4th Crossing Trail junction; stay to the left (east) along the Skyline Trail.

1.4 Stay to the left at the Lakes Trail junction.

1.8 When you spy a surreal rocky sofa in the middle of the trail, you know you have reached the Van Trump Monument junction and the Paradise Glacier Trail junction. Take the Paradise Glacier Trail to your right (northeast).

3.2 Arrive at Paradise Glacier. After exploring the snowfield, return the way you came.

6.4 Arrive back at the trailhead.

Hike Information

Local Information

Mount Rainier National Park Web site,
www.nps.gov/mora; visitor information, (360) 569-2211, ext. 3314.
Jackson Visitor Center–Paradise, (360) 569-6036.

Lodging

Paradise Inn, (360) 569-2275; National Park Inn, (360) 569-2275. For a list of accommodations outside the park, visit www.nps.gov/mora/general/accom.htm.

Campgrounds

You can stay at a campground inside the park if you wish to day hike and car camp. Sunshine Point Campground is located in the southwest corner of the park, 0.25 mile inside the Nisqually Entrance. Register at the campground. Cougar Rock Campground is located in the southwest corner of the park, 2.3 miles north of Longmire. Ohanapecosh Campground is located in the southeast corner of the park, 11.0 miles north of Packwood off Highway 123. You can reserve a site at Ohanapecosh or Cougar Rock Campground online at http://reservations.nps.gov, or call (800) 365-CAMP (2267) 7:00 A.M. to 7:00 P.M. PST.

21 Snow Lake

Perfect for children, this medium-length day hike passes one lake and ends at a lake in a glacial cirque.

Start: Snow Lake trailhead.
Distance: 2.6-mile out-and-back.
Approximate hiking time: 1 to 2 hours.
Difficulty: Easy.
Seasons: Mid-July through September.
Nearest towns: Ashford, Packwood.
Fees and permits: $10.00 vehicle or $5.00 individual entry fee (seven days); $30.00 annual entry fee. Wilderness Camping Permits free—reservations recommended ($20 fee).

Maps: USGS: Mount Rainier East; Trails Illustrated Mount Rainier National Park; Astronaut's Vista: Mount Rainier National Park, Washington; Earthwalk Press Hiking Map & Guide.
Trail contacts: Paradise Ranger Station, (360) 569-2211, ext. 2314. Jackson Visitor Center—Paradise, (360) 569-6036.
Trail conditions: www.nps.gov/mora/trail/ tr_cnd.htm; weather, www.nps.gov/mora/ current/weather.htm.

Finding the trailhead: From the Stevens Canyon Entrance Station (see Getting There), drive 16.4 miles west along the winding Stevens Canyon Road. A small parking lot on the left (south) marks the trailhead to Snow Lake. From the Nisqually Entrance Station (see Getting There), travel nearly 16 miles east on Longmire-Paradise Road to the turnoff for the Ohanapecosh area. Turn right (southeast) onto Stevens Canyon Road and toward Ohanapecosh; follow this road for 3.0 miles to the trailhead on your right (south). *DeLorme: Washington Atlas and Gazetteer:* Page 48 B3.

The Hike

Trees obscure the Snow Lake trailhead. When ready to hike, walk to the eastern corner of the parking lot to find the trail, heading south. The trail immediately begins to ascend rather steeply, but do not worry, it eventually levels off and descends, then crosses several ridges throughout the hike.

The trail leads 0.7 mile through silver subalpine forest to the junction with the path to Bench Lake on the left (east). The path down to the lake is steep, but the bank is worth the struggle, particularly if you fish. Though Bench Lake is cursed by the evasive fish common throughout Mount Rainier, they do rise here, so you may want to pack that pole. Fishing permits are not required, and there are no limits on fish caught. Of course you may not fish for the endangered bull trout. Similar to brook trout, but identified by the lack of black markings on its dorsal fin, the bull trout is a federally listed species under the Environmental Protection Act. Follow the motto "No Black, Throw It Back" when fishing in Mount Rainier National Park, or face a guilty conscience and hefty fines.

▶ **A tarn is the term for a lake that fills a cirque, a round valley carved by a glacier with sheer rock faces on three sides.**

Returning to the main trail, you only have 0.5 mile of hiking before you reach Snow Lake, named possibly because snow rings the lake nearly year-round. When you arrive at the mountain meadow, turn around. This area offers a beautiful view of Mount Rainier. And in the foreground, depending on the season, you can spy a variety of flowers, from glacier lilies to mountain bog gentian, beargrass, huckleberry bushes, and mountain ash.

The last 0.2 mile of trail slopes upward until you see the lovely tarn. In a glacial cirque, the peaks of the Tatoosh Range frame the lake, and glacial waters cascade down their flanks into the ice-cold aqua waters.

If you would like to camp here or see the marvelous view from the campsites, turn left (east) at the fork in the trail—a sign points the way. Descend for less than 0.2 mile until the trail crosses a stream out of Snow Lake. To cross this stream you must hop from log to log. Be careful—some of these logs are not quite as stable as they appear. As soon as you cross the stream, you reach Snow Lake Camp. The toilet is almost immediately to your left; the campsites are farther down (southeast) and along the lakeside. Site 1 sits on a small peninsula with a view of Unicorn Peak across the aqua waters. A jutting rock makes for a great place to jump in the freezing waters for a refreshing dunk or a painful swim. If you decide to stay at this idyllic spot, be sure to hang your food; black bears have been spotted here.

You can also follow the path to the right (southwest) at the fork before the lake. This path is 0.3 mile and ends in a small lake-access point. If you hike this trail, plan to spend some time at one of these places; they are lovely. When you're ready to return, just retrace your steps.

Miles and Directions

0.0 Start by walking to the eastern corner of the Snow Lake trailhead parking lot to find the trail, heading south.

0.7 A short trail heads to Bench Lake. If you want to see the lake or fish for a while, take the trail to the left (east). Otherwise, stay on the main trail to Snow Lake.

1.2 Reach the aqua glacial waters of Snow Lake. If you plan on visiting the camp, head left (east) for less than 0.2 mile .

1.3 After hopping carefully from log to log, arrive at Snow Lake Camp. Retrace your steps.

2.6 Arrive back at the trailhead.

Wilderness camping: Snow Lake Camp comes highly recommended. The campsites have excellent views of the spectacular beauty of the tarn.

◀ *The Tatoosh Peaks over Snow Lake.*

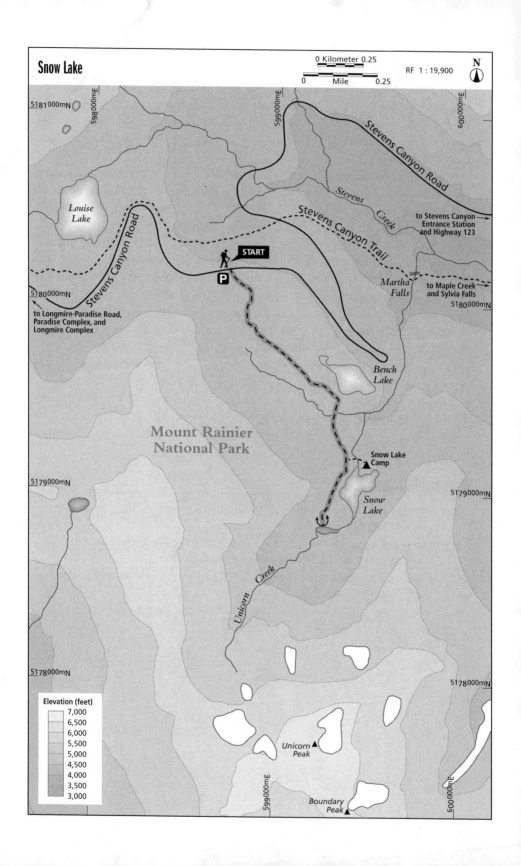

Snow Lake

0 Kilometer 0.25
0 Mile 0.25
RF 1 : 19,900
N

5181000mN
598000mE

Louise
Lake

Stevens Canyon Road

Stevens Canyon Road

Stevens Creek

599000mE

Stevens Canyon Trail

START

P

5180000mN

to Longmire-Paradise Road,
Paradise Complex, and
Longmire Complex

to Stevens Canyon
Entrance Station
and Highway 123

Martha
Falls

to Maple Creek
and Sylvia Falls

5180000mN

600000mE

Bench
Lake

Mount Rainier
National Park

Snow Lake
Camp

5179000mN

Snow
Lake

5179000mN

Unicorn Creek

5178000mN

599000mE

Unicorn
Peak

600000mE

Boundary
Peak

Elevation (feet)
7,000
6,500
6,000
5,500
5,000
4,500
4,000
3,500
3,000

Hike Information

Local Information

Mount Rainier National Park Web site, www.nps.gov/mora; visitor information, (360) 569-2211, ext. 3314.
Jackson Visitor Center—Paradise, (360) 569-6036.

Lodging

Paradise Inn, (360) 569-2275; National Park Inn, (360) 569-2275. For a list of accommodations outside the park, visit www.nps.gov/mora/general/accom.htm.

Campgrounds

You can stay at a campground inside the park if you wish to day hike and car camp. Sunshine Point Campground is located in the southwest corner of the park, 0.25 mile inside the Nisqually Entrance. Register at the campground. Cougar Rock Campground is located in the southwest corner of the park, 2.3 miles north of Longmire. Ohanapecosh Campground is located in the southeast corner of the park, 11.0 miles north of Packwood off Highway 123. You can reserve a site at Ohanapecosh or Cougar Rock Campground online at http://reservations.nps.gov, or call (800) 365-CAMP (2267) 7:00 A.M. to 7:00 P.M. PST.

22 Stevens Canyon

This half-day hike travels through a canyon strewn with wildflowers, wildlife, and waterfalls.

Start: Stevens Creek trailhead/Box Canyon Picnic Area.
Distance: 6.6-mile one-way shuttle.
Approximate hiking time: 3 to 5 hours
Difficulty: Strenuous.
Seasons: June through September.
Nearest towns: Ashford, Packwood.
Fees and permits: $10.00 vehicle or $5.00 individual entry fee (seven days); $30.00 annual entry fee. Wilderness Camping Permits free—reservations recommended ($20 fee).

Maps: USGS: Mount Rainier East; Trails Illustrated Mount Rainier National Park; Astronaut's Vista: Mount Rainier National Park, Washington; Earthwalk Press Hiking Map & Guide.
Trail contacts: Paradise Ranger Station, (360) 569-2211, ext. 2314.
Jackson Visitor Center—Paradise, (360) 569-6036.
Trail conditions: www.nps.gov/mora/trail/tr_cnd.htm; weather, www.nps.gov/mora/current/weather.htm.

Finding the trailhead: From the Stevens Canyon Entrance Station (see Getting There), drive 10.8 miles west on Stevens Canyon Road to the Box Canyon Picnic Area on the left, about 0.3 mile beyond the Box Canyon wayside exhibit. From the Nisqually Entrance Station (see Getting There), travel nearly 16 miles east on Longmire-Paradise Road to the turnoff for the Ohanapecosh area. Turn right (southeast) onto Stevens Canyon Road and toward Ohanapecosh. Stay

on this road for 8.6 miles until you reach the Box Canyon Picnic Area. The hike starts from the picnic area. *DeLorme: Washington Atlas and Gazetteer:* Page 48 B2, B3.

Special considerations: Since this hike is a shuttle, you must leave a bike or car at the trail's end at Reflection Lakes or face twice the hiking. If coming from Nisqually Entrance Station, you will pass Reflection Lakes on your way to the trailhead, 1.5 miles after you turn onto Stevens Canyon Road toward Ohanapecosh. To reach the Reflection Lakes trailhead from the Box Canyon Picnic Area, drive 7.0 miles west on Stevens Canyon Road. Look for a parking lot in front of a scenic lake on the right (north) side of the road. After leaving a bike or vehicle there, return to the Box Canyon Picnic Area to start hiking.

The Hike

If you enjoy crashing water, you will adore this hike. You pass five waterfalls while hiking through a canyon replete with wildflowers and wildlife. Do not let deer or snakes startle you; they are common in this area. Wildflowers such as phlox and glacier lilies line the trail in late spring, but Stevens Canyon is best known for its many waterfalls.

To begin hiking, follow the sign that points south from the Box Canyon Picnic Area. Two unnamed falls are visible in the first 0.6 mile of the hike alone. Just 0.5 mile from the trailhead, a sign points west to a river viewpoint, which offers a nice view of the first falls. Return to the trail and continue west 0.1 mile to the junction of the Stevens Creek Trail and the Wonderland Trail. Turn right (west) onto the Wonderland Trail. Cross the bridge where Stevens Creek falls in churning rapids over gray, black, and turquoise boulders.

After hiking on relatively flat terrain, you reach Maple Creek Camp, 2.1 miles into your hike. Unless you want to explore campsites or use the pit toilet, stay to the right (northwest) toward a deceptively narrow part of the trail. The trail, however, widens and crosses a stream on a small log. While crossing, look up and to your left to see Maple Falls in the distance.

Continue west to Sylvia Falls, 1.2 miles beyond Maple Falls. Sylvia Falls appears as though the water shoots directly out of the land from no source. A small clearing that looks out on Sylvia Falls makes a nice, cool lunch spot for summer hikers. A gradual ascent begins here and continues for 1.0 mile to Martha Falls, the most impressive of the five falls, if just for its size. The gradual ascent soon becomes a steep ascent for 0.7 mile of switchbacks. The sound of cars tells you that you are close to Stevens Canyon Road. The trail crosses Stevens Canyon Road and continues west.

The ascent continues for 1.0 mile before you catch sight of Louise Lake through the trees. If you would like a closer look, choose the marked and maintained trail to the sandy beaches of Louise Lake. Park rangers report decent fishing here. Permits are not required to fish in the national park and there are no limits on most fish. You

◀ Martha Falls.

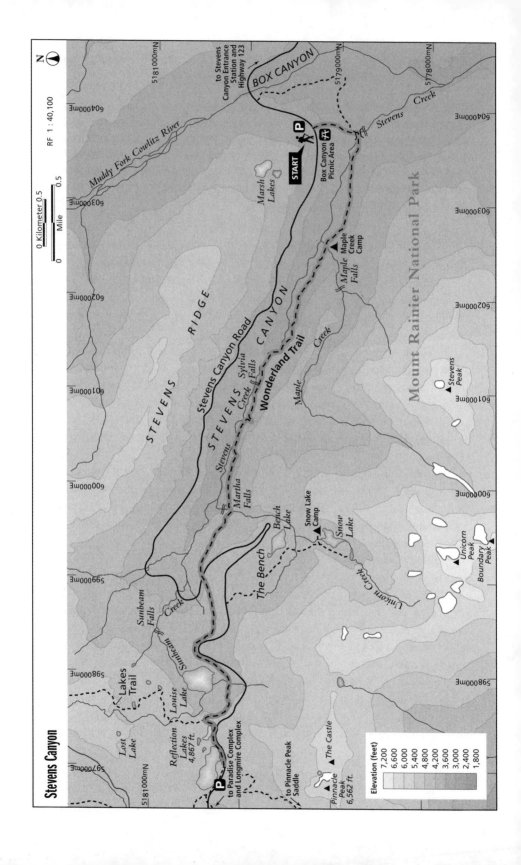

may not fish for bull trout, an endangered species listed by the Environmental Protection Agency.

After you've had your fill of the lake, continue along the main trail, which widens, a sign of more frequent use. A more gradual ascent heads to the junction with the Lakes Trail. Turn left (south) to once more encounter Stevens Canyon Road in 0.1 mile. The trail's end, Reflection Lakes, can be seen 0.1 mile up the road to your right (west). Bike or drive back to the Box Canyon Picnic Area to complete the hike.

Miles and Directions

0.0 Start by following the sign that points south from the Box Canyon Picnic Area.

0.5 A sign points to a vista overlooking an unnamed falls. Continue southwest on the main trail to the intersection with the Wonderland Trail.

0.6 At the junction with the Wonderland Trail, turn right (west) onto the Wonderland Trail. The rest of this hike will take place along a small section of this more than 90-mile trail that loops the entirety of Mount Rainier National Park.

0.7 Just after you get onto the Wonderland Trail, come to the Stevens Creek crossing. Continue over the bridge.

2.1 After hiking on relatively flat terrain, reach Maple Creek Camp, 2.1 miles into your hike. Unless you want to visit the camp, stay to the right (northwest) toward the hatched log over Maple Creek and a view of Maple Falls.

3.3 Crashing water tells you that you have reached Sylvia Falls. You can see it through the trees; continue west along the main trail.

4.3 You can't miss Martha Falls on your right (north). Continue along the main trail once again, as the gradual uphill turns into steep switchbacks.

5.0 The sound of cars probably turned you on to the fact that you would soon reach Stevens Canyon Road. The trail continues toward Louise and Reflection Lakes on the other side of the road.

6.0 Just 1.0 mile past Stevens Canyon Road, arrive at Louise Lake. A sign marks the trail to the lake on your right (north). This side trip to the lake is recommended, although you can still see the road from the lake. The tarn has sandy beaches and relatively decent fishing.

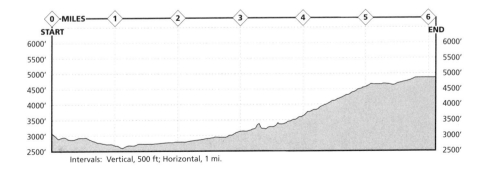

Intervals: Vertical, 500 ft; Horizontal, 1 mi.

6.4 At the Lakes Trail junction, stay to the left (east) on the Wonderland Trail toward the Reflection Lakes parking lot.

6.6 Reach Reflection Lakes and the trail's end.

Option: If you have two cars and your knees can handle the 6.0 miles of downhill, consider leaving your car at the Box Canyon Picnic Area and starting from Reflection Lakes.

Hike Information

Local Information

Mount Rainier National Park Web site, www.nps.gov/mora; visitor information, (360) 569-2211, ext. 3314.
Jackson Visitor Center—Paradise, (360) 569-6036.

Lodging

Paradise Inn, (360) 569-2275; National Park Inn, (360) 569-2275. For a list of accommodations outside the park, visit www.nps.gov/mora/general/accom.htm.

Campgrounds

You can stay at a campground inside the park if you wish to day hike and car camp. Sunshine Point Campground is located in the southwest corner of the park, 0.25 mile inside the Nisqually Entrance. Register at the campground. Cougar Rock Campground is located in the southwest corner of the park, 2.3 miles north of Longmire. Ohanapecosh Campground is located in the southeast corner of the park, 11.0 miles north of Packwood off Highway 123. You can reserve a site at Ohanapecosh or Cougar Rock Campground online at http://reservations.nps.gov, or call (800) 365-CAMP (2267) 7:00 A.M. to 7:00 P.M. PST.

23 Stevens Creek

A one-hour hike in the southern section of the park leads to two unamed waterfalls along the same river.

Start: Box Canyon Picnic Area.
Distance: 1.4-mile out-and-back.
Approximate hiking time: 1 hour.
Difficulty: Easy.
Seasons: Late May through September.
Nearest towns: Ashford, Packwood.
Fees and permits: $10.00 vehicle or $5.00 individual entry fee (seven days); $30.00 annual entry fee. Wilderness Camping Permits free—reservations recommended ($20 fee).

Maps: USGS: Mount Rainier East; Trails Illustrated Mount Rainier National Park; Astronaut's Vista: Mount Rainier National Park, Washington; Earthwalk Press Hiking Map & Guide.
Trail contacts: Paradise Ranger Station, (360) 569-2211, ext. 2314. Jackson Visitor Center—Paradise, (360) 569-6036.
Trail conditions: www.nps.gov/mora/trail/tr_cnd.htm; weather, www.nps.gov/mora/current/weather.htm.

Finding the trailhead: From the Stevens Canyon Entrance Station (see Getting There), drive 10.8 miles west on Stevens Canyon Road to the Box Canyon Picnic Area on the left, about 0.3 mile beyond the Box Canyon wayside exhibit. From the Nisqually Entrance Station (see Getting There), travel nearly 16 miles east on Longmire-Paradise Road to the turnoff for the Ohanapecosh area. Turn right (southeast) onto Stevens Canyon Road and toward Ohanapecosh. Stay on this road for 8.6 miles until you reach the Box Canyon Picnic Area. The hike heads south from the picnic area. *DeLorme: Washington Atlas and Gazetteer:* Page 48 B3.

The Hike

This trail descends rather steeply through woods full of wildlife to reach two unnamed waterfalls. Well marked and well maintained, the trail is easy to follow. The first point of interest comes after only 0.5 mile. A sign marks the river viewpoint to your right (west). Only a few paces more and you stand in a fenced clearing, admiring the first waterfall.

Return to the main trail and head right (south) to see the other nameless falls. Walk 0.1 mile beyond the river viewpoint, a total of 0.6 mile from the trailhead, to a junction with the famed Wonderland Trail. Stay to the right (southwest) for 0.1 mile more to reach the bridge over Stevens Creek.

This bridge marks an incredible meeting of stream and stone. Iceberg white water rushing from the glaciers above has rounded these boulders and shaped them into something out of a fairy tale.

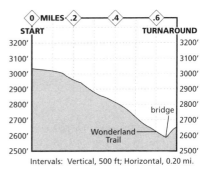

Stevens Creek.

When you have appreciated the falls to your content, turn around and follow the same path back to the picnic area. The returning trail is not long, but it is a rather steep ascent; do not be surprised if you are winded by the end.

Miles and Directions

0.0 Start by heading south from the Box Canyon Picnic Area.

0.5 A sign points to a vista overlooking an unnamed waterfall. Check out the falls, then continue southwest on the main trail to the intersection with the Wonderland Trail.

0.6 At the junction with the Wonderland Trail, turn right (west) onto the Wonderland Trail.

0.7 Just after you get onto the Wonderland Trail, come to the Stevens Creek crossing. The bridge offers a great look at the multicolored boulders carved and smoothed by the waters of Stevens Creek. Enjoy the view before retracing your steps.

1.4 Arrive back at the picnic area.

Hike Information

Local Information
Mount Rainier National Park Web site,
www.nps.gov/mora; visitor information, (360) 569-2211, ext. 3314.

Jackson Visitor Center—Paradise, (360) 569-6036.

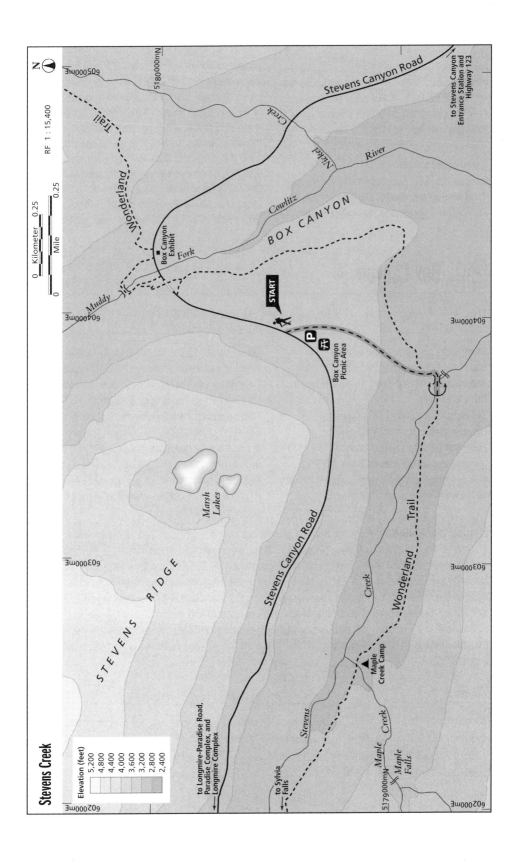

Stevens Creek

Elevation (feet)
5,200
4,800
4,400
4,000
3,600
3,200
2,800
2,400

RF 1 : 15,400

0   Kilometer   0.25

0   Mile   0.25

N

BOX CANYON

Box Canyon Exhibit

Wonderland Trail

Muddy Fork

Cowlitz

Nickel Creek

Creek

River

Stevens Canyon Road

to Stevens Canyon Entrance Station and Highway 123

START

P

Box Canyon Picnic Area

STEVENS RIDGE

Marsh Lakes

Stevens Canyon Road

to Longmire-Paradise Road, Paradise Complex, and Longmire Complex

Wonderland Trail

Maple Creek Camp

Stevens Creek

Maple Creek

Maple Falls

to Sylvia Falls

602000mE
603000mE
604000mE
6040000mE

5179000mN
5180000mN

605000mE

Lodging

Paradise Inn, (360) 569–2275; National Park Inn, (360) 569–2275. For a list of accommodations outside the park, visit www.nps.gov/mora/general/accom.htm.

Campgrounds

You can stay at a campground inside the park if you wish to day hike and car camp. Sunshine Point Campground is located in the southwest corner of the park, 0.25 mile inside the Nisqually Entrance. Register at the campground. Cougar Rock Campground is located in the southwest corner of the park, 2.3 miles north of Longmire. Ohanapecosh Campground is located in the southeast corner of the park, 11.0 miles north of Packwood off Highway 123. You can reserve a site at Ohanapecosh or Cougar Rock Campground online at http://reservations.nps.gov, or call (800) 365–CAMP (2267) 7:00 A.M. to 7:00 P.M. PST.

24 Box Canyon

This very short loop crosses a bridge over a canyon carved by a powerful glacier.

Start: Box Canyon wayside exhibit.
Distance: 0.3-mile loop.
Approximate hiking time: 15 to 30 minutes.
Difficulty: Easy.
Seasons: May through September
Nearest towns: Ashford, Packwood.
Fees and permits: $10.00 vehicle or $5.00 individual entry fee (seven days); $30.00 annual entry fee. Wilderness Camping Permits free—reservations recommended ($20 fee).

Maps: USGS: Mount Rainier East; Trails Illustrated Mount Rainier National Park; Astronaut's Vista: Mount Rainier National Park, Washington; Earthwalk Press Hiking Map & Guide.
Trail contacts: Paradise Ranger Station, (360) 569–2211, ext. 2314.
Jackson Visitor Center—Paradise, (360) 569–6036.
Trail conditions: www.nps.gov/mora/trail/tr_cnd.htm; weather, www.nps.gov/mora/current/weather.htm.

Finding the trailhead: From the Stevens Canyon Entrance Station (see Getting There), drive 10.5 miles west on Stevens Canyon Road to the Box Canyon wayside exhibit. Parking is on the left (south). If you pass the Box Canyon Picnic Area, you have gone 0.3 mile too far west. From the Nisqually Entrance Station (see Getting There), travel nearly 16 miles east on Longmire-Paradise Road to the turnoff for the Ohanapecosh area. Turn right (southeast) onto Stevens Canyon Road and toward Ohanapecosh. Stay on this road for 9.0 miles until you reach the Box Canyon wayside exhibit, 0.3 mile past the Box Canyon Picnic Area. The paved trail begins across the street from the parking lot to the right (east) of the bridge. *DeLorme: Washington Atlas and Gazetteer:* Page 48 B3.

The Hike

This hike is great for those interested in glaciers. Many years ago a glacier gouged dirt and boulders out of the mountainside to create Box Canyon. The paved trail takes you past wildflowers and the thundering canyon itself. For the first half of this hike, the paved trail is wide, smooth, and wheelchair accessible. The entirety of the

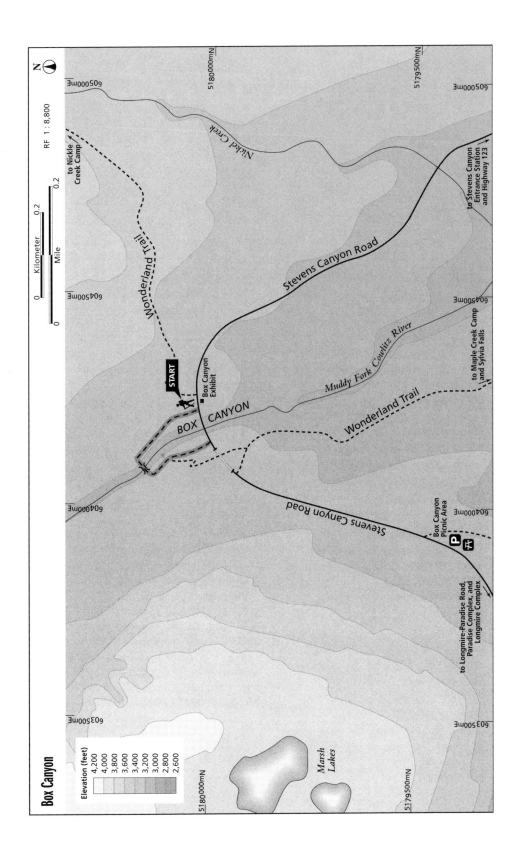

Box Canyon

Elevation (feet)
- 4,200
- 4,000
- 3,800
- 3,600
- 3,400
- 3,200
- 3,000
- 2,800
- 2,600

RF 1 : 8,800

Kilometer
0   0.2   0.2

Mile
0   0.2

N

to Nickle
Creek Camp

Wonderland Trail

Nickel Creek

Stevens Canyon Road

START

Box Canyon
Exhibit

BOX CANYON

Muddy Fork Cowlitz River

Wonderland Trail

to Maple Creek Camp
and Sylvia Falls

to Stevens Canyon
Entrance Station
and Highway 123

Stevens Canyon Road

Box Canyon
Picnic Area

to Longmire-Paradise Road,
Paradise Complex, and
Longmire Complex

Marsh
Lakes

5180000mN

5179500mN

604500mE

604000mE

603500mE

605000mE

5180000mN

5179500mN

hike is paved, but the second stretch is considerably rougher and would prove tumultuous travel for a wheelchair.

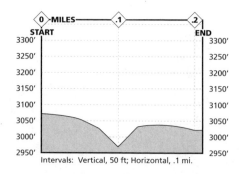

At the trailhead there is an informational sign about the hike. After reading it, head straight up the trail. The trail merging from the right (northeast) is the Wonderland Trail. Notice the bare rocks on the right side of the canyon, where a powerful glacier once wiped out the vegetation.

Less than 0.2 mile into your hike is a bridge over Muddy Fork. Take the time to look down and enjoy the unique canyon. After you cross the bridge the trail is paved, but less maintained, all the way to where it rejoins Stevens Canyon Road. Either retrace your steps or walk along the road to loop back to your car.

Miles and Directions

0.0 Head north across the Stevens Canyon Road from the Box Canyon Exhibit to the Box Canyon Trail, a short informative section of the Wonderland Trail.

0.1 You reach the bridge crossing the Muddy Fork of the Cowlitz River, continue across the bridge to the other side of the loop.

0.2 The Wonderland Trail splits off on its route around Mount Rainier. Stay to the left (southeast) back to the Box Canyon Exhibit.

0.3 You skirt the Stevens Canyon Road to reach the trailhead.

Hike Information

Local Information

Mount Rainier National Park Web site,
www.nps.gov/mora; visitor information, (360) 569-2211, ext. 3314.
Jackson Visitor Center—Paradise, (360) 569-6036.

Lodging

Paradise Inn, (360) 569-2275; National Park Inn, (360) 569-2275. For a list of accommodations outside the park, visit www.nps.gov/mora/general/accom.htm.

Campgrounds

You can stay at a campground inside the park if you wish to day hike and car camp. Sun-shine Point Campground is located in the southwest corner of the park, 0.25 mile inside the Nisqually Entrance. Register at the campground. Cougar Rock Campground is located in the southwest corner of the park, 2.3 miles north of Longmire. Ohanapecosh Campground is located in the southeast corner of the park, 11.0 miles north of Packwood off Highway 123. You can reserve a site at Ohanapecosh or Cougar Rock Campground online at http://reservations.nps.gov, or call (800) 365-CAMP (2267) 7:00 A.M. to 7:00 P.M. PST.

Ohanapecosh

The Ohanapecosh region is situated in the southeast corner of Mount Rainier National Park. Farther from the metropolitan areas of Seattle and Portland than other parts of the park, Ohanapecosh sees fewer visitors. Nestled in dense forest, the hikes in the Ohanapecosh region afford few views of Mount Rainier and the other Cascades. This region, however, does offer numerous waterfalls, old-growth trees, a crystal-clear glacial river, the Ohanapecosh, and freedom from the crowds that plague other regions of the park.

25 Silver Falls

This short, beautiful day hike takes you to spectacular Silver Falls.

Start: Silver Falls Loop
trailhead/Ohanapecosh Visitor Center.
Distance: 2.7-mile loop.
Approximate hiking time: 1 to 2 hours.
Difficulty: Easy.
Seasons: May through September.
Nearest town: Packwood.
Fees and permits: $10.00 vehicle or $5.00
individual entry fee (seven days); $30.00
annual entry fee. Wilderness Camping Permits
free—reservations recommended ($20 fee).

Maps: USGS: Ohanapecosh Hot Springs and
Chinook Pass; Trails Illustrated Mount Rainier
National Park; Astronaut's Vista: Mount Rainier
National Park, Washington; Earthwalk Press
Hiking Map & Guide.
Trail contacts: Ohanapecosh Visitor Center,
(360) 569-6046.
Trail conditions: www.nps.gov/mora/trail/
tr_cnd.htm; weather, www.nps.gov/mora/
current/weather.htm.

Finding the trailhead: From Packwood drive 7.0 miles northeast on U.S. Highway 12 to the junction with Highway 123. Turn left (north) onto Highway 123 and continue for 3.0 miles to the turnoff for Ohanapecosh Campground, just 1.8 miles south of the Stevens Canyon Entrance Station (see Getting There). Turn left (west) and immediately right again at the fork in the road toward the campground. Continue on this road as it winds past the visitor center. Go right (north) toward the day parking area. Loop around to enter the parking lot from the other (east) side. On the way you will see the Silver Falls trailhead to your left (north). Park and walk to the trailhead. *DeLorme: Washington Atlas and Gazetteer:* Page 48 B4, C4.

The Hike

Silver Falls opens early in the year due to its low elevation, and visitors can enjoy the falls as early as May. The trail wanders through a beautiful forest. Traffic can be very heavy on this trail, since the trailhead is located at Ohanapecosh Campground.

The first 0.1 mile of this hike is also part of an educational self-guided loop trail that explains the Mount Rainier ecosystem. The numbered posts along the trail correspond to text in an interpretive pamphlet available in the Ohanapecosh Visitor Center. Stay left (north) when the Hot Springs Trail forks off to the right.

The beginning of the trail runs through a thermal area. You will see hot springs and interpretive signs telling you more about the thermal features. The ground is fragile and easily damaged here, making it especially important that you stay on the trail. Walking off the trail in this area is illegal, and park officials may cite violators. Remember that water originating from hot springs is unsafe for human consumption.

The trail gains a bit of elevation in the beginning. You will cross two bridges before you reach the bridge over Laughingwater Creek. The first bridge is more

Silver Falls.

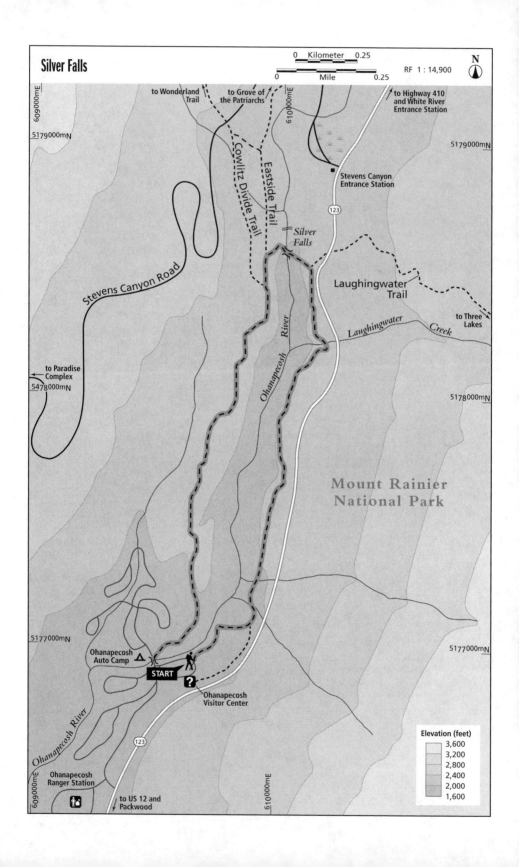

than 0.1 mile into your hike; the second bridge is a little less than 0.8 mile. Both of these bridges cross streams that empty into the Ohanapecosh River, which is to your left (west). At 0.9 mile you reach Laughingwater Creek, aptly named as the water bounces and frolics over the rocks. Cross Laughingwater Creek and walk 0.1 mile to the Laughingwater Trail junction. Stay to the left and on the Silver Falls Loop.

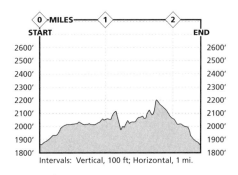

Intervals: Vertical, 100 ft; Horizontal, 1 mi.

Silver Falls is 0.2 mile from the Laughingwater Trail junction, 1.2 miles into your hike. An overlook, 0.1 mile from where you first see the falls, faces the shining waters of Silver Falls. Take your time and enjoy the marvelous view until you are ready to move on. We must emphasize that the rocks at Silver Falls are moss covered and slippery. People have lost their lives as a result of disregarding the warning signs posted by the falls. Please stay behind the guardrails.

The second half of the loop is not as eventful as the first half, but the trail winds through a pleasant mixture of western hemlock, Douglas fir, and western red cedar. The trail exits at a different location than where it began; simply walk over the bridge and head back to the day parking lot.

Miles and Directions

0.0 Start at the trailhead near the Ohanapecosh Visitor Center.

0.1 Hot Springs Trail forks to the right; stay to the left (north) on the Silver Falls Trail.

1.0 At the Laughingwater Trail junction, stay to the left (north). Again, head toward Silver Falls.

1.2 Enjoy Silver Falls, but stay behind the barricades.

1.4 Just 0.2 mile beyond Silver Falls and the Silver Falls overlook, reach the Eastside Trail. Take a sharp left (south), heading back toward the Ohanapecosh Visitor Center and Campground.

1.5 Stay to the left (south) at the Cowlitz Divide Trail junction.

2.7 The end of the loop drops you off at the Ohanapecosh Campground, just north of the trailhead.

Hike Information

Local Information
Mount Rainier National Park Web site,
www.nps.gov/mora; visitor information, (360) 569-2211, ext. 3314.

Lodging
Paradise Inn, (360) 569-2275; National Park Inn, (360) 569-2275. For a list of accommodations outside the park, visit www.nps.gov/mora/general/accom.htm.

Campgrounds

Silver Falls Trail basically terminates at the Ohanapecosh Campground, a large car camping area by the clear-flowing Ohanapecosh River that allows campfires. You can reserve a site at Ohanapecosh Campground online at http://reservations.nps.gov, or call (800) 365-CAMP (2267) 7:00 A.M. to 7:00 P.M. PST.

Hike Tours

Park employees at the Ohanapecosh Visitor Center (see Trail Contacts) often lead interactive tours of this hike on weekend mornings. Times may vary; contact the visitor center for further information.

26 Grove of the Patriarchs

This short interpretive hike takes you through magnificent old-growth forest.

Start: Grove of the Patriarchs parking lot.
Distance: 1.1-mile lollipop.
Approximate hiking time: 1 hour.
Difficulty: Easy.
Seasons: May through September.
Nearest town: Packwood.
Fees and permits: $10.00 vehicle or $5.00 individual entry fee (seven days); $30.00 annual entry fee. Wilderness Camping Permits free—reservations recommended ($20 fee).

Maps: USGS: Chinook Pass; Trails' Illustrated Mount Rainier National Park; Astronaut's Vista: Mount Rainier National Park, Washington; Earthwalk Press Hiking Map & Guide.
Trail contacts: Ohanapecosh Visitor Center, (360) 569-6046.
Trail conditions: www.nps.gov/mora/trail/tr_cnd.htm; weather, www.nps.gov/mora/current/weather.htm.

Finding the trailhead: From Stevens Canyon Entrance Station (see Getting There), go west 0.2 mile on Stevens Canyon Road to a parking lot on your right (north), marked by a sign that reads GROVE OF THE PATRIARCHS. The trailhead is to the right (west) of the restrooms. *DeLorme: Washington Atlas and Gazetteer:* Page 48 B4.

The Hike

The trail is very well maintained but often muddy, due to its low elevation and proximity to the Ohanapecosh River. Wear your hiking boots, and remember to step through the mud instead of around it to avoid widening the trails. Interpretive signs line the trail, helping you discern differences between the western hemlock, Douglas fir, and western red cedar. This is a great trail to take if you are interested in learning more about the life cycles and species of old-growth forests.

The Ohanapecosh River flows on your right for the first 0.3 mile as the trail meanders through old-growth forest. The waters flow abnormally clearly for a glacial river; the inactivity of the Ohanapecosh Glacier reduces the amount of suspended glacial flour.

The trail forks 0.3 mile into the hike. The Eastside Trail continues heading north;

The Grove of the Patriarchs Trail.

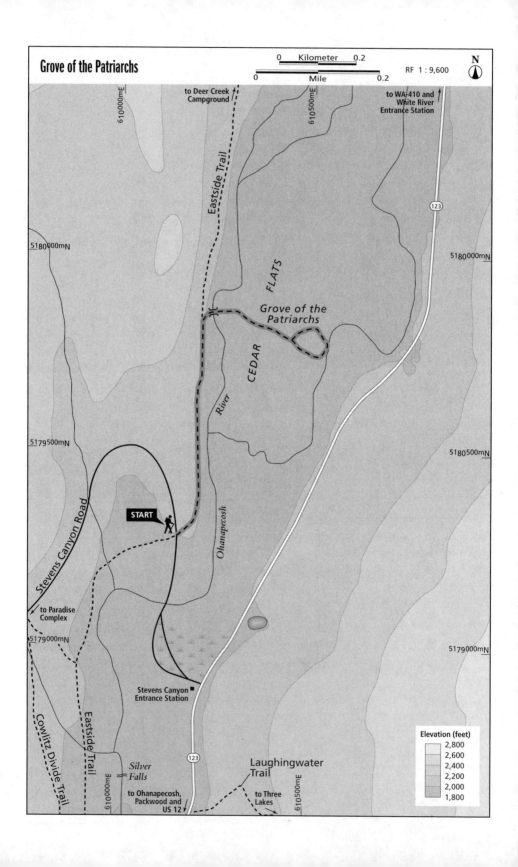

Grove of the Patriarchs

0 Kilometer 0.2
0 Mile 0.2

RF 1 : 9,600

N

to Deer Creek
Campground

to WA-410 and
White River
Entrance Station

Eastside Trail

123

5180000mN

610000mE

610500mE

5180000mN

FLATS

*Grove of the
Patriarchs*

CEDAR

River

5179500mN

5180500mN

START

Ohanapecosh

Stevens Canyon Road

to Paradise
Complex

5179000mN

5179000mN

Stevens Canyon
Entrance Station

Eastside Trail

610000mE

123

610500mE

Cowlitz Divide Trail

*Silver
Falls*

Laughingwater
Trail

to Ohanapecosh,
Packwood and
US 12

to Three
Lakes

Elevation (feet)
2,800
2,600
2,400
2,200
2,000
1,800

the Grove of the Patriarchs Trail veers off to the right (southeast) toward a steel suspension bridge over the Ohanapecosh River. The bridge links to an island rich with old-growth forest. Some of the trees towering over the forest floor are more than 1,000 years old.

Around 0.1 mile past the Grove of the Patriarchs junction, the trail splits to form a loop. Go left (northeast) around the loop. Make sure to check out the humbling height of the red cedar about halfway through the loop. Continue along the loop until you are back to the stem of the lollipop. The return trip gives you a chance to apply your newfound tree identification skills.

Miles and Directions

0.0 Follow the signs to the Grove of the Patriarchs and the Eastside Trail, heading east on the right side of the bathrooms. The trail quickly turns north to parallel the crystal clear Ohanapecosh River.

0.3 The Grove of the Patriarchs Trail splinters off the Eastside Trail to cross the Ohanapecosh River.

0.4 The stem of the lollipop trail splits in two, we recommend going left around this loop section.

1.1 Return the way you came to reach the parking lot.

Hike Information

Local Information

Mount Rainier National Park Web site, www.nps.gov/mora; visitor information, (360) 569-2211, ext. 3314.

Lodging

Paradise Inn, (360) 569-2275; National Park Inn, (360) 569-2275. For a list of accommodations outside the park, visit www.nps.gov/mora/general/accom.htm.

Campgrounds

You can stay at the Ohanapecosh Campground, a large car camping area by the clear-flowing Ohanapecosh River that allows campfires. You can reserve a site at Ohanapecosh Campground online at http://reservations.nps.gov, or call (800) 365-CAMP (2267) 7:00 A.M. to 7:00 P.M. PST.

Hike Tours

Park rangers lead an interactive tour of this hike throughout the week. Contact the Ohanapecosh Visitor Center (see Trail Contacts) to confirm times and availability.

27 Three Lakes

A long day hike or moderate overnighter ends at three marshy lakes on the eastern border of the park near the Pacific Crest Trail.

Start: Laughingwater trailhead.
Distance: 12.0-mile out-and-back.
Approximate hiking time: 5 to 7 hours.
Difficulty: Strenuous day hike or moderate overnighter.
Seasons: Mid-July through September.
Nearest town: Packwood.
Fees and permits: $10.00 vehicle or $5.00 individual entry fee (seven days); $30.00 annual entry fee. Wilderness Camping Permits free-reservations recommended ($20 fee).

Maps: USGS: Chinook Pass; Trails Illustrated Mount Rainier National Park; Astronaut's Vista: Mount Rainier National Park, Washington; Earthwalk Press Hiking Map & Guide.
Trail contacts: Ohanapecosh Visitor Center, (360) 569-6046.
Trail conditions: www.nps.gov/mora/trail/ tr_cnd.htm; weather, www.nps.gov/mora/ current/weather.htm.

Finding the trailhead: From Packwood, drive 7.0 miles northeast on U.S. Highway 12 to where it intersects Highway 123. Turn left (north) onto Highway 123 and travel 4.5 miles to the Laughingwater trailhead, just 0.5 mile south of the Stevens Canyon Entrance Station (see Getting There). A hiking sign and small parking lot mark the trailhead. If you reach the junction with the Stevens Canyon Road, you have gone too far. *DeLorme: Washington Atlas and Gazetteer:* Page 48 B4, C4.

The Hike

The Three Lakes trail lacks the kind of magnificent mountain views or copious trail junctions found in other regions of the park. The path constantly ascends through little-changing forest until it reaches the lakes. You will see little wildlife, few people, no waterfalls, and no views of Mount Rainier on this trail—that is, not until you reach your destination.

From the small parking lot, cross to the east side of the road and walk north along Highway 123 a few paces to the Laughingwater trailhead to your right (east). The trail starts uphill and does not relent until 0.25 mile from the lakes.

Winding switchbacks characterize the first 2.0 miles of trail. When you see a marshy pool to your left (north), you know the switchbacks have ended. The rest of the route heads almost directly east for nearly 4 miles.

Beyond the marsh, the trail flattens out a bit for 1.5 miles. The crossing of the last of three streams marks the end of this more gradual stretch. By late August these streams have dried up, so carry adequate water for the entire 6.0 miles. From this point the trail begins to ascend steeply and continues for nearly 2 miles. It contours

Pensive by the last of the Three Lakes.

along a ridge and nears the top but never quite reaches it. About 0.5 mile from Three Lakes, the trail passes through a small meadow and begins to descend. When you see a small patrol cabin to your left (north) and two lakes beyond it, you have reached your destination.

A small peninsula that separates the two lakes has a campsite that would make a nice place to lunch and relax, as long as the sometimes ferocious bugs do not bother you. Watch for herons flying into the lakes area for respite.

If you have chosen to do this hike in one day, follow the same trail back to the parking lot. Otherwise, see the campsite information below.

Option: The last of the three lakes is located 0.1 mile east of the two lakes and just outside the park's boundary. To visit this lake, continue along the same trail. This side trip increases your total hike length to 12.2 miles, but the sight of the many newts cavorting in the water is worthwhile. Watch your step! These newts like to meditate on the trail and are in great danger from hiking boots.

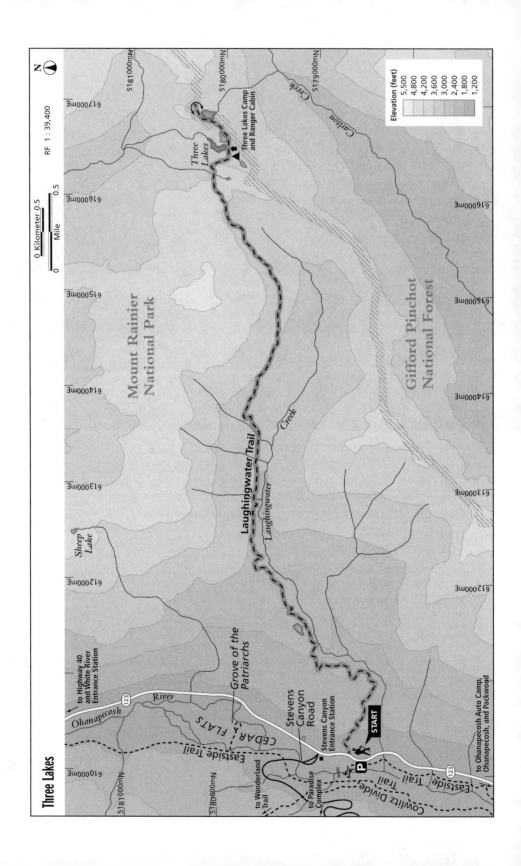

Three Lakes

RF 1 : 39,400

N

Elevation (feet)
5,500
4,800
4,200
3,600
3,000
2,400
1,800
1,200

0 Kilometer 0.5
0   0.5 Mile

Mount Rainier National Park

Gifford Pinchot National Forest

Three Lakes

Three Lakes Camp and Ranger Cabin

Carlton Creek

Laughingwater Trail

Laughingwater Creek

Sheep Lake

Grove of the Patriarchs

Ohanapecosh River

CEDAR FLATS

Eastside Trail

Stevens Canyon Road

Stevens Canyon Entrance Station

to Highway 40 and White River Entrance Station

to Wonderland Trail

to Paradise Complex

Cowlitz Divide Trail

Eastside Trail

START

to Ohanapecosh Auto Camp, Ohanapecosh, and Packwood

P

123

123

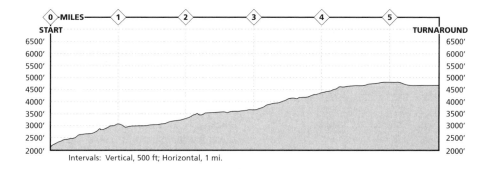

Intervals: Vertical, 500 ft; Horizontal, 1 mi.

Wilderness camping: Three Lakes has three campsites to choose from. Site 1 offers the best view of the lake.

Miles and Directions

0.0 Head east along the Laughingwater Trailhead across the street from the small parking lot.

6.0 With no trail junctions to mislead you, you have reached Three Lakes. Grab a site or a lunch spot and enjoy.

12.0 After simply retracing your steps, you arrive back at the trailhead.

Hike Information

Local Information

Mount Rainier National Park Web site, www.nps.gov/mora; visitor information, (360) 569-2211, ext. 3314.

Lodging

Paradise Inn, (360) 569-2275; National Park Inn, (360) 569-2275. For a list of accommodations outside the park, visit www.nps.gov/mora/general/accom.htm.

Campgrounds

Day hikers can stay at the Ohanapecosh Campground, a large car camping area by the clear-flowing Ohanapecosh River that allows campfires. You can reserve a site at Ohanapecosh Campground online at http://reservations.nps.gov, or call (800) 365-CAMP (2267) 7:00 A.M. to 7:00 P.M. PST.

28 Pacific Crest Trail

A three-night backpacking trip mostly through forest; a portion of the Pacific Crest Trail follows a ridge and passes many lakes.

Start: Laughingwater trailhead.
Distance: 29.3-mile loop.
Approximate hiking time: 4 days.
Difficulty: Moderate.
Seasons: Late June through September.
Nearest town: Packwood.
Fees and permits: $10.00 vehicle or $5.00 individual entry fee (seven days); $30.00 annual entry fee. Wilderness Camping Permits free—reservations recommended ($20 fee).

Maps: USGS: Chinook Pass; Trails Illustrated Mount Rainier National Park; Astronaut's Vista: Mount Rainier National Park, Washington; Earthwalk Press Hiking Map & Guide.
Trail contacts: Ohanapecosh Visitor Center, (360) 569-6046.
Trail conditions: www.nps.gov/mora/trail/tr_cnd.htm; weather, www.nps.gov/mora/current/weather.htm.

Finding the trailhead: From Packwood drive 7.0 miles northeast on U.S. Highway 12 to where it intersects Highway 123. Turn left (north) onto Highway 123 and continue on it for 4.5 miles to the Laughingwater trailhead, just 0.5 mile south of the Stevens Canyon Entrance Station (see Getting There). A hiking sign and small parking lot mark the trailhead. If you reach the junction with the Stevens Canyon Road, you have overshot the trailhead. *DeLorme: Washington Atlas and Gazetteer:* Page 48 B4, C4.

Special considerations: As noted in the hike description, potential water sources between the trailhead and Three Lakes dry up by late summer. Bring enough water to make it through the first 6.0 miles of uphill hiking.

The Hike

From the small parking lot, cross to the east side of the road and walk north along Highway 123 a few paces to the Laughingwater trailhead to the right (east). The trail starts uphill and does not relent until 0.25 mile from the lakes. A marshy pool about 2 miles into the hike marks the end of the switchbacks. From this point the trail heads due east until you reach Three Lakes. The last 2.0 miles before the lakes are at a steep pitch, and the sources for water on this section of the hike are nil in late summer. If you hike this trail in those months, bring plenty of water.

Three Lakes Camp makes a nice place to stay—and after 2,800 feet of ascent, you might need the rest. There also are many places to camp along the Pacific Crest Trail. To reach the Pacific Crest Trail, continue east along the Laughingwater Trail. A few spur trails might lead you astray here; stay on the better-maintained trail, and you should be fine.

You pass one well-marked county trail, but stay to the left and head north. The Laughingwater Trail intersects the Pacific Crest Trail less than a mile beyond the

Small falls on Chinook Creek. JOHN CALDWELL

county trail. Because the Pacific Crest Trail is not a part of Mount Rainier National Park and falls under different management, it is not as well maintained as trails within the park boundaries. This means a few more jutting rocks and downed trees in the way.

After 3.0 miles, the Pacific Crest Trail intersects the American Lake Trail to your right (east). Look at the options, below for more details on this day hike, but otherwise proceed north on the Pacific Crest Trail. The trail ascends steeply until you reach the top of a ridge with a few sites for camping. A very short descent on the other side of the ridge leads you to the banks of Anderson Lake. Because it rests within park boundaries, no camping is permitted around Anderson Lake, but you can stay in the sites on the ridge just above the lake.

Dewey Lake provides many good campsites as well. About 14 miles into the hike, 2.7 miles beyond the Anderson Lake Trail junction, the trail forks. Both trails encircle Dewey Lake. For the best luck in campsite grabbing, stay to the left, north along the Pacific Crest Trail. Most of the good sites are on the northern part of the lake. If you stay here, set camp at least 100 feet from the lake, keep stock animals at least 200 feet from water, and do not set campfires. Otherwise, enjoy one of the few lakes on this loop that is clear, warm, and large enough for taking a dip.

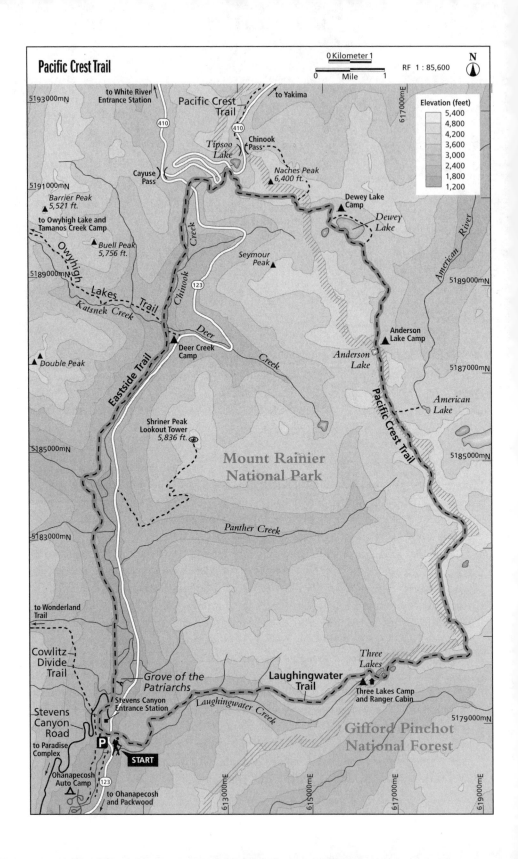

When you leave Dewey Lake, you also leave behind the privacy of the first part of the hike. Only 1.0 mile from Dewey Lake, the trail comes to the Naches Peak Loop. Many visitors come to this area, particularly on weekends. At this intersection you have a choice to round the loop to the left (northwest) or the right (northeast). We suggest going left. On a clear day this hike provides you awesome views of Little Tahoma, the Cowlitz Chimneys, Governors Ridge, Seymour Peak, and a spectacular look on Mount Rainier itself. This direction also intersects sooner with the Eastside Trail.

If you would like to picnic on the Naches Peak Picnic Area tables, cross Highway 410 and follow the path to the left (west) of Tipsoo Lake. If you would rather avoid the masses of people and cars, when you reach the intersection, just before Highway 410, turn left (west) onto the Eastside Trail. In 1.5 miles, after a gradual downhill, you come to Highway 123. Cross the road and look for the continuation of the trail a bit to the right (north).

From this point on the trail proceeds downhill very near Highway 123. The first mile of the 3.0 miles to Deer Creek can feel dangerously steep. You may need to grab onto trees for support. The pitch then levels out. Stay to the left (south) past the Owyhigh Lakes Trail junction. Only 0.1 mile beyond the junction, 22.0 miles into the trip, you come to Deer Creek Camp. If you do not want to stay here, you must hike 7.4 more miles before reaching your car. If you decide to stay at Deer Creek Camp, mind the rodents and be sure to hang your food!

The rest of the trip is much the same. You are surrounded by forest, but you occasionally cross very pretty streams. The forest grows denser and wetter on your way to the Grove of the Patriarchs Trail junction, 6.3 miles beyond Deer Creek. (See Options for details on this possible side trip). If you choose not to enter the Grove of the Patriarchs, stay to the right (south) and hike for 0.3 mile to Stevens Canyon Road. The trail continues on the south side of the road.

You now have only 0.8 mile of trail left to hike. The Eastside Trail intersects the Silver Falls Loop in 0.5 mile. Turn onto the Silver Falls Loop, and cross the Ohanapecosh River to the left (east). Enjoy Silver Falls for a while, and then continue east about 0.1 mile. A sign points the way to the Laughingwater Trail and your car, both on your left (east).

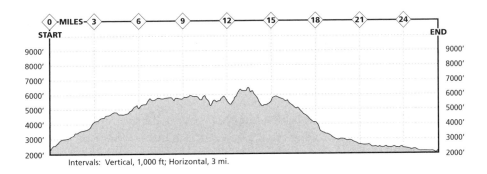

Intervals: Vertical, 1,000 ft; Horizontal, 3 mi.

Miles and Directions

6.0   Three Lakes appears after 6.0 miles and 2,800 feet elevation gain. You may choose to stay at the Three Lakes Camp before continuing on the Laughingwater Trail to the Pacific Crest Trail.

7.3   Stay on the main trail, Laughingwater Trail, past several way trails until it feeds into the Pacific Crest Trail.

10.3   American Lake Trail heads off to the right (east), a good side trip of 1.0 mile.

11.3   The trail leads to the banks of Anderson Lake on your left (west). You may want to camp at the sites on the ridge to your right (east).

14.0   The trail forks; each direction encircles Dewey Lake. Stay to the left for better luck with campsites and a nice shot of the lake.

15.0   Naches Peak Loop intersects the Pacific Crest Trail. For better views and a shorter trip, stay to the left (west) around Naches Peak.

17.5   Unless you want to stop at Tipsoo Lake, turn left (southwest) onto the Eastside Trail before you reach Highway 410.

19.0   After just 1.5 mile, arrive at Highway 123. This time, cross the road and resume your trek on the other side.

21.8   Owyhigh Lakes Trail junction arises after a very steep descent. Stay to the left (south), bypassing the Owyhigh Lakes Trail and heading toward Deer Creek.

21.9   Arrive at Deer Creek Camp. Unless you're ready to hike more than 7 miles to your car, you'll be spending the night here.

28.3   Grove of the Patriarchs junction comes after a long stint in the forest. If you want to take this side trip option, head left (east). Otherwise, continue south on the Eastside Trail.

28.6   Reach Stevens Canyon Road. Cross to the south side of the road and resume your hike on the Eastside Trail.

29.1   At the Silver Falls Loop junction, stay to the left (east) to view the crashing falls. Then continue on over the bridge.

29.2   Laughingwater Trail intersects the Silver Falls Loop; turn left (east) onto the short, steep trail that takes you to your car.

29.3   Reach your car and the end of your backpack at Highway 123.

Options: Consider two easy side trips along this long backpack. The trail to American Lake intersects the Pacific Crest Trail 3.0 miles north of the junction with the Laughingwater Trail. The hike to American Lake is only 0.5 mile, adding 1.0 mile to the total hiking distance. Innumerable trails, a result of careless use, circle this pretty lake. It has good swimming potential but small fish for anglers.

The second recommended side trip is to the Grove of the Patriarchs. (See Hike 26: Grove of the Patriarchs.) The trip adds less than 0.3 mile to your hike, and the massive trees make quite an impression.

Wilderness camping: Three Lakes Camp has three available campsites. You may camp for free at any place along the Pacific Crest Trail that is outside the park. We suggest Dewey or American Lake. Deer Creek is a below-average campground with two individual sites. Hang your packs and your food very carefully—when we were here, an onslaught of mice ate through one pack and the food bag. The Park Service has begun experimenting with rodent guards on the bear poles. If the guards work, you may see them at each site.

Hike Information

Local Information

Mount Rainier National Park Web site, www.nps.gov/mora; visitor information, (360) 569–2211, ext. 3314.

Lodging

Paradise Inn, (360) 569–2275; National Park Inn, (360) 569–2275. For a list of accommodations outside the park, visit www.nps.gov/mora/general/accom.htm.

Campgrounds

You can stay at the Ohanapecosh Campground, a large car camping area by the clear-flowing Ohanapecosh River that allows campfires. You can reserve a site at Ohanapecosh Campground online at http://reservations.nps.gov, or call (800) 365-CAMP (2267) 7:00 A.M. to 7:00 P.M. PST.

29 Shriner Peak

A steep climb to a lookout offers spectacular views of the "Four Sisters": Mount Rainier, Mount Adams, Mount Hood, and Mount St. Helens.

Start: Shriner Peak trailhead.
Distance: 8.4-mile out-and-back.
Approximate hiking time: 5 to 6 hours.
Difficulty: Strenuous.
Seasons: Early July through September.
Nearest town: Packwood.
Fees and permits: $10.00 vehicle or $5.00 individual entry fee (seven days); $30.00 annual entry fee. Wilderness Camping Permits free—reservations recommended ($20 fee).

Maps: USGS: Ohanapecosh Chinook Pass; Trails Illustrated Mount Rainier National Park; Astronaut's Vista: Mount Rainier National Park, Washington; Earthwalk Press Hiking Map & Guide.
Trail contacts: Ohanapecosh Visitor Center, (360) 569-6046.
Trail conditions: www.nps.gov/mora/trail/tr_cnd.htm; weather, www.nps.gov/mora/current/weather.htm.

Finding the trailhead: From the Stevens Canyon Entrance Station (see Getting There), turn left onto Highway 123 and drive 3.6 miles north. If you are coming from Packwood, drive 7.0 miles northeast on U.S. Highway 12 to where it intersects Highway 123. Turn left (north) onto Highway 123 and follow it for nearly 9 miles to the Shriner Peak trailhead, 3.6 miles past the junction with Stevens Canyon Road and the Stevens Canyon Entrance Station. You will pass the trailhead on your right. Continue driving to the pullout just past the trailhead on your left. *DeLorme: Washington Atlas and Gazetteer:* Page 48 B4.

Special considerations: Water sources along the trail to Shriner Peak dry up early in the year. Bring enough water for a very steep ascent in sometimes blistering sun.

Shriner Peak Lookout.

The Hike

This is a very tough, steep hike. The steepness, combined with little shade and limited water sources, might make this hike seem undesirable, but we can not emphasize enough how incredible the view is from the top of Shriner Peak. You can see the whole east side of Mount Rainier National Park and many other Cascades rising in the distance. Just remember to bring plenty of water, and start early in the morning.

The first 1.4 miles of the trail wander through a forest, but then the trail enters an area that was burned by a fire several years ago and is currently in the beginning stages of the forest cycle. A switchbacked trail leads through open meadows, created by the fire, all the way to the top. Wildflowers and wild strawberries line these switchbacks.

At the top, you have an amazing view. On a clear day you can see the "Four Sisters": Mount Rainier, Mount Adams, Mount Hood, and Mount St. Helens. A spur trail to Shriner Peak Camp heads southeast from the lookout area. Panoramic photos propped up in the lookout help you identify the surrounding landmarks. The

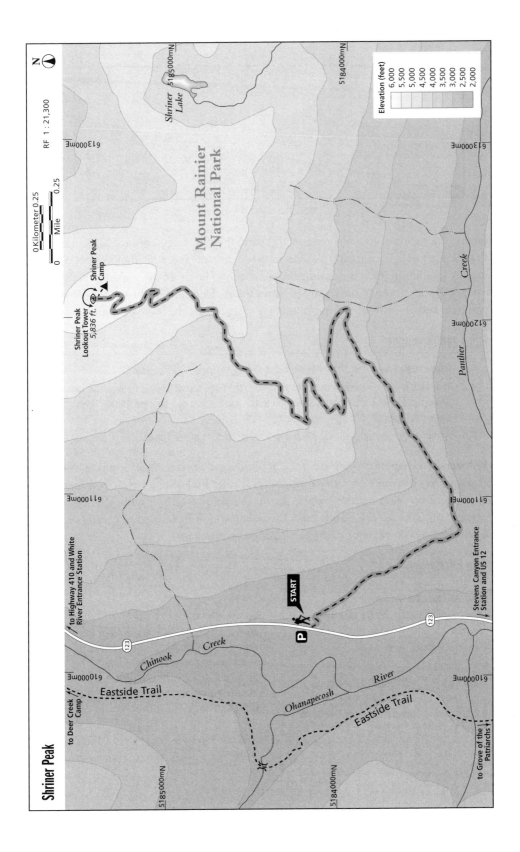

Shriner Peak

Mount Rainier National Park

RF 1 : 21,300

N

Shriner Lake

5185000mN

6130000mE

0 Kilometer 0.25

0   Mile   0.25

Shriner Peak
Lookout Tower
5,836 ft.

Shriner Peak
Camp

Elevation (feet)
6,000
5,500
5,000
4,500
4,000
3,500
3,000
2,500
2,000

6130000mE

5184000mN

6112000mE

Panther   Creek

6111000mE

to Highway 410 and White
River Entrance Station

123

START

P

Stevens Canyon Entrance
Station and US 12

123

6111000mE

Chinook   Creek

6110000mE

to Deer Creek
Camp

Eastside Trail

Ohanapecosh   River

Eastside Trail

5185000mN

6110000mE

5184000mN

to Grove of the
Patriarchs

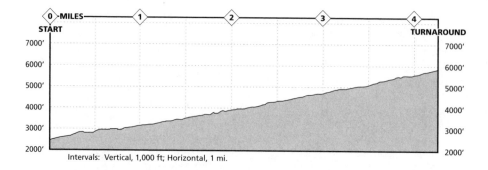
Intervals: Vertical, 1,000 ft; Horizontal, 1 mi.

oldest of four lookouts remaining in the park, this fire cabin epitomizes National Park Service design for such structures in the 1930s; the park still employs it in critical fire conditions. Hikers cannot gain access to the inside of the building, but you can peek inside at the photography or gain a bit of elevation for a better view. When you have had your fill of the spectacular view, head back the way you came.

Miles and Directions

0.0 Follow the signs to the Shriner Peak Trail, heading southeast off Highway 123.

4.2 Your struggle is rewarded with panoramic views from the top of Shriner Peak and a look at the old fire lookout. On your approach to the lookout you can see the Shriner Peak Camp Trail spur to your right (southeast).

8.4 A much quicker trek down the hill and you arrive back at the trailhead.

Wilderness camping: Campfires are not allowed at Shriner Peak Camp, as is the case for every backcountry camp in the park. Shriner Peak Camp has two campsites, but there is no reliable water source. Snowmelt can be used as a water source early in the season, but after the snow melts the only water source is a small stream a mile from camp. This small stream often dries up in midsummer.

Hike Information

Local Information

Mount Rainier National Park Web site, www.nps.gov/mora; visitor information, (360) 569-2211, ext. 3314.

Lodging

Paradise Inn, (360) 569-2275; National Park Inn, (360) 569-2275. For a list of accommodations outside the park, visit www.nps.gov/mora/general/accom.htm.

Campgrounds

You can stay at the Ohanapecosh Campground, a large car camping area by the clear-flowing Ohanapecosh River that allows campfires. You can reserve a site at Ohanapecosh Campground online at http://reservations.nps.gov, or call (800) 365-CAMP (2267) 7:00 A.M. to 7:00 P.M. PST.

30 Ohanapecosh Park

Touted as one of the most spectacular hikes in Mount Rainier National Park, Ohanapecosh Park does not disappoint as an amazing four-day backpacking trip.

Start: Fryingpan Creek trailhead.
Distance: 34.1-mile loop.
Approximate hiking time: 4 to 5 days.
Difficulty: Strenuous.
Seasons: Late July through September.
Nearest town: Greenwater.
Fees and permits: $10.00 vehicle or $5.00 individual entry fee (seven days); $30.00 annual entry fee. Wilderness Camping Permits free—reservations recommended ($20 fee).

Maps: USGS: White River, East and Chinook Pass; Trails Illustrated Mount Rainier National Park; Astronaut's Vista: Mount Rainier National Park, Washington; Earthwalk Press Hiking Map & Guide.
Trail contacts: White River Wilderness Information Center, (360) 569-6030.
Trail conditions: www.nps.gov/mora/trail/ tr_cnd.htm; weather, www.nps.gov/mora/ current/weather.htm.

Finding the trailhead: From the White River Ranger Station (see Getting There), drive 2.8 miles west on White River Road. Adequate parking becomes visible just after you cross Fryingpan Creek. The trailhead is well marked on the left (south) side of the road. *DeLorme: Washington Atlas and Gazetteer:* Page 48 A4.

The Hike

Many have trumpeted Ohanapecosh Park and Indian Bar as the best hike in the park. It very well might live up to its reputation. The trail begins in dense forest and ascends into subalpine forest, then alpine terrain, even crossing snowfields. The hike affords awesome views of Mount Rainier, fields of wildflowers, alpine lakes, and small ice caves.

Heading south from the Fryingpan Creek trailhead, the trail climbs moderately through woods. A few switchbacks indicate that you are nearing the Fryingpan Creek crossing, about 2.0 miles into the hike. Just beyond the creek, you enter a gap in the forest that allows for a good glimpse of Mount Rainier. The trail gets steeper. When the trail turns south, you have only 1.0 mile of switchbacks to go until you reach Summerland, 4.2 miles into the hike.

After crossing the creek that provides water for Summerland campers, the fields of subalpine flowers turn into rockfields as you enter alpine terrain. The mountain looms over you as you pass an iceberg lake and Panhandle Gap, a saddle between two rocky rises. At this point you have reached the zenith of the hike.

In this area snow is a constant. Prepare to cross several steep and slippery snowfields, even in the heat of late summer. As you descend along a ridge flanked by cliffs and waterfalls on one side and a flowered valley on the other, you have only 1.5 miles to Indian Bar. The gnarled cliffs rise above the inception of the Ohanapecosh

Approaching Panhandle Gap.

River, a unique glacial stream characterized by clear water that stems from the inactive Ohanapecosh Glaciers.

Switchbacks take you down to a mountain meadow dappled with lupine and magenta paintbrush. The Indian Bar Shelter sits just across the meadow, the group camp that doubles as a refuge for frostbitten victims of the elements. If you are camping here, follow the sign that points left (east) to an available site. Otherwise, continue south along the main trail.

From Indian Bar the trail heads steadily uphill. Make sure you turn around for another great view of the mountain. The top of a nearby knoll makes for a great photo opportunity if the weather is nice. The descent from the top leads to a wooded ridge. The mountain disappears. Walk along this ridge for 3.0 miles until you reach a fork in the trail.

Head left (southeast) toward Olallie Creek Camp and Ohanapecosh. After descending abruptly for 1.3 miles, cross Olallie Creek. Immediately after the crossing, a trail spurs to the left (north). Keep an eye out for it if you plan to stay at the camp.

The main trail keeps descending steeply until highway noises indicate that you are approaching Stevens Canyon Road, 17.1 miles from the trailhead. Cross the road and look for the other side of the trail a bit to the right (west). You reach the intersection with the Eastside Trail only 0.2 mile from the road. Take a sharp left (north) onto the Eastside Trail. Stevens Canyon Road bisects the 1.2-mile path to the junction with the Grove of the Patriarchs Trail. Walk along the small lollipop loop and admire massive trees if you have the time for the extra 0.3 mile, or else stay to the left (north).

Six miles of trail through woods and over a few gurgling streams lead to Deer Creek Camp near the merging of three rivers. Only 0.1 mile beyond Deer Creek Camp, the path forks again. Stay to the left (west) toward Owyhigh Lakes. Nearly 2 miles from the intersection, the trail takes you just west enough to glimpse a sliding falls along a tributary to Needle Creek. Now the ascent begins. Gradual but numerous switchbacks lead you to a meadow below Barrier Peak.

When you enter the woods again, you know that the lakes are only 1.0 mile away. Like in the Panhandle Gap and Indian Bar areas, snow lingers here into late summer. You might need some orienteering skills to reach Owyhigh Lakes if you attempt this hike before August. From the lakes you do not have a view of Mount Rainier because it is obscured by the Cowlitz Chimneys, but the view of Governors Ridge and the Cowlitz Chimneys makes up for the lack of mountain view.

Less than a mile beyond the lakes, you reach Tamanos Creek Camp, then Tamanos Creek. Cross the prepared log and descend through the forest for 3.0 miles to reach White River Road. Head left (west) along the road for 0.5 mile to find your car.

Miles and Directions

0.0   Start heading south from White River Road at the well-marked Fryingpan Creek trailhead.

4.2   The trail to Summerland Camp appears on your left (east). If you do not plan to stay in Summerland, continue south on the Wonderland Trail toward Indian Bar.

8.2   You can see Indian Bar shelter across the meadow to the right (west) of the trail. The spur trail to Indian Bar camp goes left (east).

12.8   At the Cowlitz Divide Trail junction, take a left (east) onto the Cowlitz Divide Trail, leaving behind the Wonderland Trail.

14.1   A sign to the Olallie Creek Camp points left (north), if you plan to camp there. Otherwise, stay on the Cowlitz Divide Trail toward Stevens Canyon Road.

17.1   Cross the Stevens Canyon Road and continue heading south on the other side.

17.3   At the Eastside Trail junction, make a sharp left (north) back to Stevens Canyon Road.

18.5   After you cross Stevens Canyon Road for the second time, arrive at the junction with the Grove of the Patriarchs Trail. Unless you want to take this quick, informative lollipop side trip, stay on the Eastside Trail heading north.

25.0   Deer Creek Camp presents an option for camping.

25.1   At the Owyhigh Lakes Trail junction, head left (west) onto the Owyhigh Lakes Trail.

29.8   After more than 4 miles of ascent, reach Owyhigh Lakes, the reflective foreground to Governors Ridge.

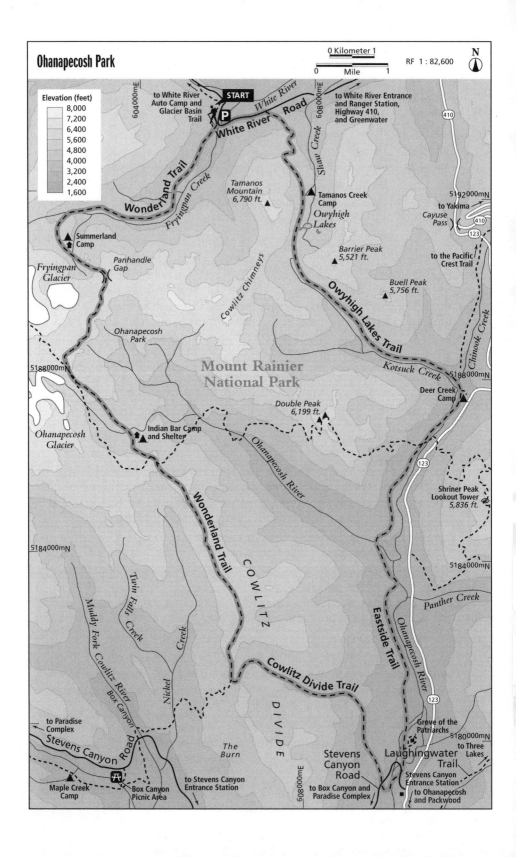

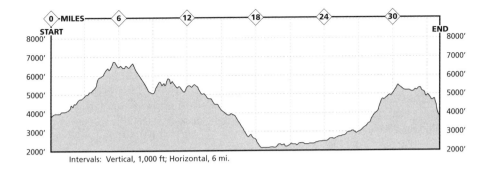

Intervals: Vertical, 1,000 ft; Horizontal, 6 mi.

30.6 You may choose to spend your last night on this hike at Tamanos Creek Camp.

33.6 The sound of traffic means you have reached the White River Road. Take a left (west) and walk along the road to complete the loop.

34.1 Arrive back at Fryingpan trailhead.

Option: If you have two cars and less time, see Hike 48: Indian Bar for a shuttle option.

Wilderness camping: You have five options for backcountry camps along this loop. We highly recommend both Summerland and Indian Bar. If the campsites are full, which is very possible on this popular section of the Wonderland Trail, select another hike.

Summerland Camp has five individual campsites and one group site. We recommend camping at either Site 3 or 4, even though they are farther from the toilet than the other sites (except Site 5, which has no view). Sites 3 and 4 have the best views. The water source for all sites is a stream south along the main trail.

Indian Bar Camp, nestled at the end of a meadow teaming with wildflowers and abutting an awesome glacial valley, has three private individual sites and one group site with bunks within the shelter. Olallie Creek Camp has less spectacular views with two individual sites and one group site.

Deer Creek Camp is a below-average campground with two individual sites. Hang your packs and your food very carefully—when we were here, an onslaught of mice ate through one pack and the food bag. The Park Service has begun experimenting with rodent guards on the bear poles. If the guards work, you may see them at each site. Tamanos Creek Camp has four individual sites and one group site.

Hike Information

Local Information

Ohanapecosh Visitor Center, (360) 569-6046.

Mount Rainier National Park Web site, www.nps.gov/mora; visitor information, (360) 569-2211, ext. 3314.

Lodging

Paradise Inn, (360) 569–2275; National Park Inn, (360) 569–2275. For a list of accommodations outside the park, visit www.nps.gov/mora/general/accom.htm.

Campgrounds

If you plan to car camp, you can stay at the White River or Ohanapecosh Campgrounds. White River Campground is located 5.0 miles beyond the White River Entrance Station. You can claim one of the 112 sites on a first-come, first-served basis. Ohanapecosh Campground is located by the Ohanapecosh Visitor Center, 1.8 miles south of the junction with Stevens Canyon Road and the Stevens Canyon Entrance Station on Highway 123. You can reserve a site at Ohanapecosh Campground online at http://reservations.nps.gov, or call (800) 365–CAMP (2267) 7:00 A.M. to 7:00 P.M. PST.

Sunrise

S unrise, the northeastern section of Mount Rainier National Park, is home to many natural wonders and scenic treasures. As the name implies, the morning light rises dramatically on Mount Rainier, accentuating the massive glaciers, sliced crevasses, and jagged ridges. The radiant Mount Rainier is visible from almost all the hikes in this section, along with the jutting peak of Little Tahoma rising from the east flank of Mount Rainier. In Native American legends, Little Tahoma is said to be Mount Rainier's son sitting on her shoulder. Rising into the alpine zones, most of the hikes around Sunrise enter terrain similar to that found in arctic tundra, though the difficulty of the trails varies drastically.

The Sunrise Complex, the highest point in the park accessible by car, consists of the Sunrise Ranger Station, the Sunrise Visitor Center, and a snack bar and gift shop. Besides Mount Rainier, several other dormant Cascade volcanoes are visible from the Sunrise Complex, including Mount Hood, Mount Adams, and Mount Baker, as well as two massive glaciers, Emmons and Winthrop.

31 Owyhigh Lakes

This hike is a steep then gradual ascent to mountain lakes surrounded by a meadow of wildflowers and the majestic, jutting Governors Ridge.

Start: Owyhigh Lakes trailhead
Distance: 7.0-mile out-and-back; 8.8-mile shuttle.
Approximate hiking time: 4 to 5 hours
Difficulty: Moderate.
Seasons: Mid-July through September
Nearest town: Greenwater.
Fees and permits: $10.00 vehicle or $5.00 individual entry fee (seven days); $30.00 annual entry fee. Wilderness Camping Permits free—reservations recommended ($20 fee).

Maps: USGS: White River Park and Chinook Pass; Trails Illustrated Mount Rainier National Park; Astronaut's Vista: Mount Rainier National Park, Washington; Earthwalk Press Hiking Map & Guide.
Trail contacts: White River Wilderness Information Center, (360) 569-6030.
Trail conditions: www.nps.gov/mora/trail/tr_cnd.htm; weather, www.nps.gov/mora/current/weather.htm.

Finding the trailhead: From the White River Entrance Station (see Getting There), drive 2.1 miles west on White River Road. A small parking area to the right (north) and a hiking sign to the left (south) mark the Owyhigh Lakes trailhead. *DeLorme: Washington Atlas and Gazetteer:* Page 48 A4.

Special considerations: To hike one-way along the Owyhigh Lakes Trail to Highway 123, you must first leave a shuttle car at the Deer Creek trailhead. From the northern entrance to the park, drive south on Highway 410 to the junction with Highway 123. Stay to the right (southbound), turning onto Highway 123. Follow this road for 5.1 miles. Watch for a sign for Deer Creek just before a widening of the road and a hiking sign. Leave your car in the pulloff on the left (east), and drive to the Owyhigh Lakes trailhead to begin the hike.

The Hike

The trail to Owyhigh Lakes sees fewer hikers than many other hikes in the park, perhaps because it offers an uneventful first 3.0 miles of uphill and no view of Mount Rainier. However, those who forego the Owyhigh Lakes Trail are missing out. An extensive field of assorted wildflowers separates the well-maintained trail from the picturesque lakes, and the jutting bluffs of Governors Ridge frame the lakes beautifully.

The hike begins with a 3.0-mile moderate ascent through forest to the top of the hill. The eastern edge of a few long switchbacks gives you a glimpse of Shaw Creek, but beyond that obscured view the only scenery to be found lies in the surrounding forest. A prepared log stretching across Tamanos Creek marks the end of

View of Governors Ridge from
Owyhigh Lakes.

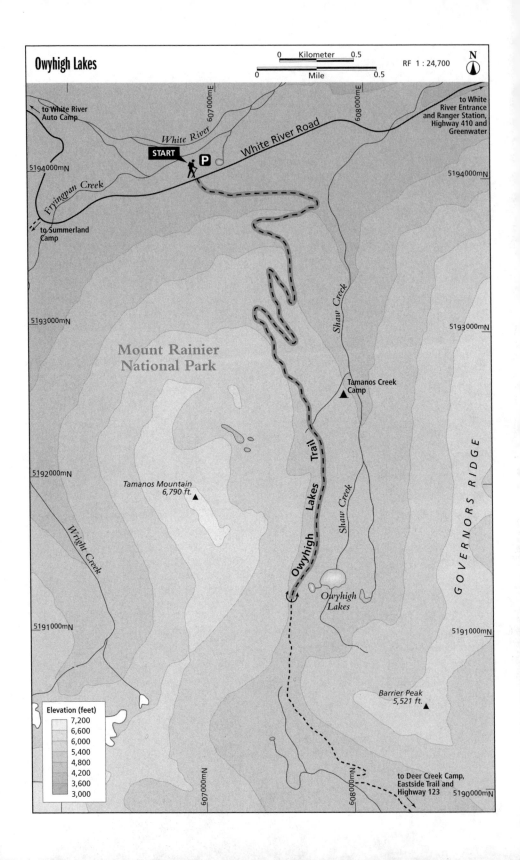

Owyhigh Lakes

Kilometer 0 0.5

Mile 0 0.5

RF 1 : 24,700

N

to White River Auto Camp

White River

to White River Entrance and Ranger Station, Highway 410 and Greenwater

White River Road

607000mE

608000mE

5194000mN

5194000mN

START

P

Fryingpan Creek

to Summerland Camp

Shaw Creek

5193000mN

5193000mN

Mount Rainier National Park

Tamanos Creek Camp

5192000mN

Owyhigh Lakes Trail

Shaw Creek

Tamanos Mountain 6,790 ft.

Wright Creek

GOVERNORS RIDGE

Owyhigh Lakes

5191000mN

5191000mN

Barrier Peak 5,521 ft.

5190000mN

607000mE

608000mE

5190000mN

to Deer Creek Camp, Eastside Trail and Highway 123

Elevation (feet)
7,200
6,600
6,000
5,400
4,800
4,200
3,600
3,000

the ascent. Immediately after Tamanos Creek crossing, a trail splits left to Tamanos Creek Camp. Unless you need to visit the pit toilet, stay on the main trail, walking south for 0.5 mile. Just before reaching the lakes, the trees become sparser and are replaced by wildflowers. No maintained trail leads to the lakes, only casual-use trails. Please stay on the main Owyhigh Lakes Trail—these mountain meadows are very fragile and susceptible to damage from tromping humans.

From the lakes you do not have a view of Mount Rainier because it is obscured by the Cowlitz Chimneys, but the view of Governors Ridge and the Cowlitz Chimneys is quite lovely. After you have rested, snacked, or admired long enough on a nearby boulder, return along the same path to your vehicle.

Miles and Directions

0.0 Start heading south at the Owyhigh Lakes trailhead, across from the small parking area.

3.0 The trail to Tamanos Creek Camp appears on your left (east). If you plan to camp here, you may want to leave your packs before moving on to the lakes, just 0.5 mile up the trail.

3.5 Reach Owyhigh Lakes, with fields of flowers in the foreground and Governors Ridge as a backdrop. Retrace your steps back to Tamanos Creek Camp or back to the trailhead.

7.0 Arrive back at the trailhead.

Highway 123/Eastside Trail Option:

6.9 If you choose the shuttle option, you will reach an unnamed falls along the trail at 6.9 miles.

8.3 Come to the confluence of three streams; cross Boundary Creek and then Deer Creek.

8.4 At the Eastside Trail junction, turn left (east), following the signs to Highway 123.

8.8 A steep 0.4 mile puts you on Highway 123 and near your car.

Option: Rather than turning around at Owyhigh Lakes, you can continue along the trail heading southeast. For nearly 3 miles, the trail drops gently through flowered meadows, then dense forest. Then 0.5 mile of switchbacks takes you down to a falls made unique by volcanic rock and sliding water. Only 1.4 more miles of a mild descent, and you reach a place where three creeks merge. Cross Boundary Creek,

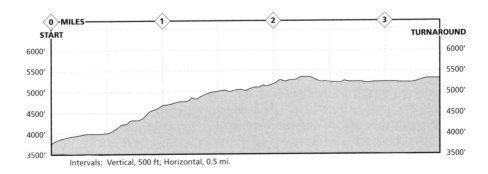

Intervals: Vertical, 500 ft; Horizontal, 0.5 mi.

then Deer Creek. A sign points east toward Highway 123. The last 0.4 mile to Highway 123 is very steep, but the sound of traffic tells you that you are near the end.

Wilderness camping: If you want to backcountry camp, Tamanos Creek Camp is only 0.5 mile north of Owyhigh Lakes.

Hike Information

Local Information
Sunrise Visitor Center, Sunrise (no contact information).
Mount Rainier National Park Web site, www.nps.gov/mora; visitor information, (360) 569-2211, ext. 3314.

Lodging
Paradise Inn, (360) 569-2275; National Park Inn, (360) 569-2275. For a list of accommodations outside the park, visit www.nps.gov/mora/general/accom.htm.

Campgrounds
If you plan to car camp, the nearest facility is White River Campgrounds, located 5.0 miles beyond the White River Entrance Station, just 3.0 miles beyond the Owyhigh Lakes trailhead. You can claim one of the 112 sites on a first-come, first-served basis. You can reserve sites at other campgrounds throughout the park online at http://reservations.nps.gov, or call (800) 365-CAMP (2267) 7:00 A.M. to 7:00 P.M. PST.

32 Naches Peak

A popular loop in summer, Naches Peak Trail offers small mountain lakes, subalpine forest, good views of Mount Rainier, and a worthwhile side trip to Dewey Lake.

Start: Naches Peak trailhead.
Distance: 5.0-mile loop.
Approximate hiking time: 2 hours.
Difficulty: Easy.
Seasons: Late July through September.
Nearest town: Greenwater.
Fees and permits: Possible fee for use of the national forest (Dewey Lake).

Maps: USGS: Chinook Pass; Trails Illustrated Mount Rainier National Park; Astronaut's Vista: Mount Rainier National Park, Washington; Earthwalk Press Hiking Map & Guide.
Trail contacts: White River Wilderness Information Center, (360) 569-6030.
Trail conditions: www.nps.gov/mora/trail/tr_cnd.htm; weather, www.nps.gov/mora/current/weather.htm.

Finding the trailhead: From the junction of Highways 410 and 123 on the eastern edge of the park, drive east on Highway 410 to Chinook Pass. Continue east, out of the park, and park in the Tipsoo Lake parking lot on the right (south) side of the road just west of Chinook Pass. Walk west along the highway for less than 0.5 mile to the large park entrance sign above the road. The top of the sign doubles as a bridge; the trailhead sign is on the north side of the bridge. *DeLorme: Washington Atlas and Gazetteer: Page 48 A4.*

View from the Naches Peak Loop. JOHN CALDWELL

The Hike

For good reason, the loop around Naches Peak is a very popular hike. The first 2.0 miles of trail are outside the park and along the Pacific Crest Trail. Because this part of the Naches Peak loop is pet-friendly, you may see many hikers with leashed dogs and the occasional horseback rider. If you have a pet you would like to walk, however, you cannot complete the loop. Because pets are not allowed on the section of trail inside park boundaries, you must turn around at the park entrance signs where the Naches Peak Trail intersects the Pacific Crest Trail.

From the Naches Peak trailhead, cross the bridge to the southeast side of Highway 410. The trail ascends steadily, passing a few small subalpine lakes. Trails lead to the lakes, but they are not maintained, and trekking through such fragile meadow is discouraged. Stay on the trail.

The trail reaches its highest point just before entering the park and curves eastward. Soon, 2.2 miles into the hike, the Pacific Crest Trail branches left (south) toward Dewey Lake; the Naches Peak Loop continues straight ahead (west). If you

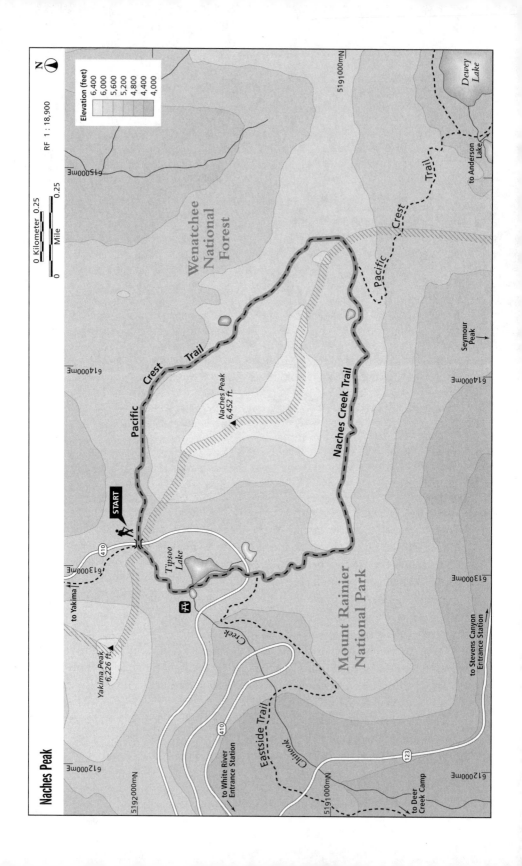

Naches Peak

RF 1 : 18,900

Elevation (feet)
6,400
6,000
5,600
5,200
4,800
4,400
4,000

0 Kilometer 0.25
0 Mile 0.25

N

to Yakima

410

Yakima Peak
6,226 ft.

START

Tipsoo Lake

Pacific

Crest

Trail

Naches Peak
6,452 ft.

Wenatchee
National
Forest

Pacific

Crest

Trail

to Anderson Lake

Dewey Lake

Seymour Peak

Naches Creek Trail

Mount Rainier
National Park

Creek

Chinook

Eastside Trail

to White River
Entrance Station

410

123

to Stevens Canyon
Entrance Station

to Deer
Creek Camp

5192000mN

5191000mN

612000mE

613000mE

614000mE

615000mE

5191000mN

612000mE

613000mE

614000mE

want to see Dewey Lake up close, take the Pacific Crest Trail down the hill. (See Option.)

Continuing along the Naches Peak Trail, you round the bend to catch a great view of Mount Rainier. In fact, this part of the hike boasts some of the most spectacular views of the entire eastern slope. If you have a map, you can try to identify Little Tahoma, the Cowlitz Chimneys, Governors Ridge, and Seymour Peak to the west.

The trail wraps to the right, around Naches Peak. Wildflowers blanket the meadows in midsummer; huckleberries do the same in late summer. The trail also passes a small mountain lake on this side of the peak. As the trail turns north, you can see Tipsoo Lake, with its parking lot and picnic tables.

To reach the picnic area, 4.6 miles into the hike, you must cross Highway 410. The continuing trail is visible across the road. A maintained trail loops around Tipsoo Lake, if you are up for a casual stroll.

The steepest incline on the hike is left for the end. The trail passes just north of the picnic area, switches back a few times, then sets you back at the trailhead. Walk east along Highway 410 to return to your car.

Miles and Directions

0.0 Start heading east on the Pacific Crest Trail/Naches Peak Trail on the path that goes over the MOUNT RAINIER NATIONAL PARK ENTRANCE sign that straddles Highway 410 at the park boundary.

2.2 Almost halfway through the loop, the Pacific Crest Trail spurs off to the left (south) and heads toward Dewey Lake, a side trip option for this hike.

4.6 Reach Highway 410; the trail continues on the other side.

4.7 Arrive at the banks of Tipsoo Lake just after crossing the road.

5.0 After skirting the lake and climbing in forest, you have come full circle back to Highway 410.

Option: If you have the time and the energy, a side trip to Dewey Lake is worthwhile. Halfway through the hike described above (milepoint 2.2), follow the signs for Dewey Lake leading southeast. The path down to the lake is a bit steep, but in warm weather the lake is perfect for swimming, fishing, and admiring. This side trip adds almost 2.0 miles to the total trip distance.

Wilderness camping: Campsites are available at Dewey Lake free of charge. Since the lake rests outside park boundaries, wilderness permits are not required, but you need to register with the national forest at the junction of the Naches Peak Loop and the Pacific Crest Trail.

Hike Information

Local Information

Sunrise Visitor Center, Sunrise (no contact information).

Mount Rainier National Park Web site, www.nps.gov/mora; visitor information, (360) 569–2211, ext. 3314.

Lodging

Paradise Inn, (360) 569–2275; National Park Inn, (360) 569–2275. For a list of accommodations outside the park, visit www.nps.gov/mora/general/accom.htm.

Campgrounds

If you plan to car camp, the nearest facility is White River Campgrounds, located 5.0 miles beyond the White River Entrance Station. You can claim one of the 112 sites on a first-come, first-served basis. You can reserve sites at other campgrounds throughout the park online at http://reservations.nps.gov, or call (800) 365–CAMP (2267) 7:00 A.M. to 7:00 P.M. PST.

33 Crystal Lakes

A steep climb to two beautiful mountain lakes tucked away in meadows abounding with glacier lilies beneath an impressive ridge.

Start: Crystal Lakes trailhead.
Distance: 6.0-mile out-and-back.
Approximate hiking time: 3 to 4 hours.
Difficulty: Moderate.
Seasons: Mid-July through September.
Nearest town: Greenwater.
Fees and permits: If you are staying overnight, the following information applies: $10.00 vehicle or $5.00 individual entry fee (seven days); $30.00 annual entry fee. Wilderness Camping Permits free—reservations recommended ($20 fee).

Maps: USGS: White River Park; Trails Illustrated Mount Rainier National Park; Astronaut's Vista: Mount Rainier National Park, Washington; Earthwalk Press Hiking Map & Guide.
Trail contacts: White River Wilderness Information Center, (360) 569–6030.
Trail conditions: www.nps.gov/mora/trail/tr_cnd.htm; weather, www.nps.gov/mora/current/weather.htm.

Upper Crystal Lake.

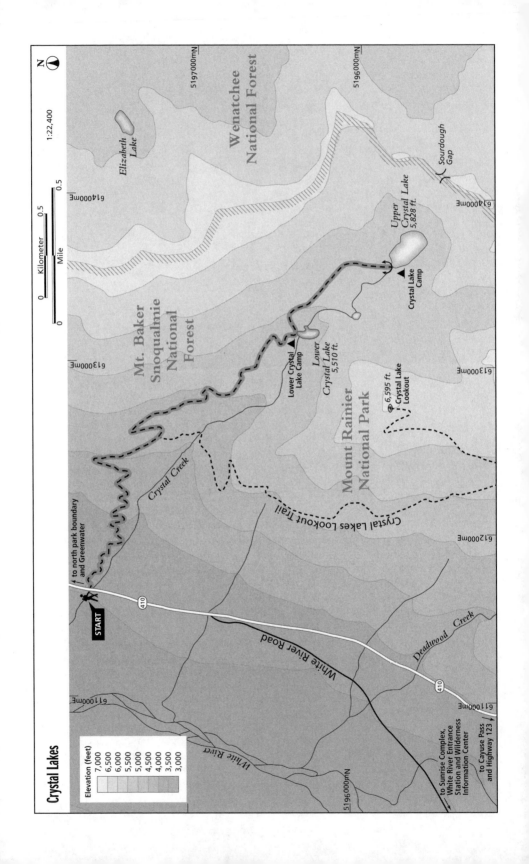

Crystal Lakes

1:22,400

Elevation (feet)
7,000
6,500
6,000
5,500
5,000
4,500
4,000
3,500
3,000

N

0   Kilometer   0.5
0   Mile   0.5

Wenatchee
National Forest

Elizabeth
Lake

5197000mN

5196000mN

Mt. Baker
Snoqualmie
National
Forest

Upper
Crystal Lake
5,828 ft.

Sourdough
Gap

6140000mE

Crystal Lake
Camp

Lower Crystal
Lake Camp

Lower
Crystal Lake
5,510 ft.

6,595 ft.
Crystal Lake
Lookout

Mount Rainier
National Park

6139000mE

Crystal Creek

Crystal Lakes Lookout Trail

6138000mE

6137000mE

to north park boundary
and Greenwater

START

410

White River Road

Deadwood Creek

410

6136000mE

White River

5196000mN

to Sunrise Complex,
White River Entrance
Station and Wilderness
Information Center

to Cayuse Pass
and Highway 123

Finding the trailhead: Since there are no entrance stations on Highway 410, you can access this trailhead without paying the park entrance fee. (You still need a backcountry permit to camp at Lower or Upper Crystal Lake, which for the White River Wilderness Information Center would necessitate passing through the White River Entrance Station. Many people have been asked by rangers to leave because they failed to obtain permits in an attempt to avoid the entrance fee.)

If you are coming from the north, drive south on Highway 410 for 4.0 miles past signs that mark your entrance into Mount Rainier National Park. A hiking sign marks the trailhead. You can park in the lots on either side of the road.

If you are coming from the south or from the White River Wilderness Information Center (see Getting There), drive north on Highway 410 0.5 mile past its intersection with White River Road. Look for a hiking sign on the left pointing east across the street. The parking lot is on the right (east). *DeLorme: Washington Atlas and Gazetteer:* Page 48 A4.

The Hike

This steep hike climbs through serene forest into flower-filled meadows, ending at two lovely mountain lakes. Elk are often seen grazing around the lakes, and mountain goats gambol along the ridges lining Upper Crystal Lake. This is a very popular hike, so plan on seeing a lot of fellow hikers.

The first 2.3 miles of switchbacks climb up to Lower Crystal Lake. This part of the trail is heavily forested, except where it crosses an avalanche slope. The avalanche slope ends just before you reach the Crystal Lakes Lookout Trail, 1.3 miles into your hike. This unmaintained trail takes you to Crystal Lakes Lookout, more than 2.7 miles away. From the avalanche slope you have a great view of Mount Rainier and White River.

At Lower Crystal Lake a trail goes down to the lake and to the campsites. No designated trail leads around the lake, and there are limited viewing opportunities. Take only a short break here, and save your time for Upper Crystal Lake.

The real treat begins as you head up to Upper Crystal Lake. A variety of wildflowers line the trail in July, from phlox to avalanche lilies. Lupine, paintbrush, and valeria arrive in August. Despite the showy blossoms, the 0.7 mile to Upper Crystal Lake seems much longer.

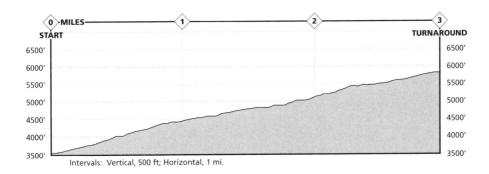

When you reach Upper Crystal Lake, take the time to walk around the lake. Don't be surprised if a snowbank or two lies in the way. Glacier lilies are often seen in midsummer along the shores, and Sourdough Gap towers above the lake. When you have enjoyed yourself to the fullest, head back the way you came. The steep downhill really does a job on your knees, so take the necessary breaks.

Miles and Directions

0.0   Start heading east on the Crystal Lakes trailhead on the same side of the road as the small parking lot.

1.3   At the end of a long switchback, the unmaintained Crystal Lakes Lookout Trail branches off to your right (south). Stay on the main trail toward Crystal Lakes.

2.3   The trail to Lower Crystal Lake Camp heads off to your right (south). If you're not staying here, continue on the main trail toward Upper Crystal Lake.

3.0   You can see Upper Crystal Lake nestled in its spot below the ridge. The trail divides and circles the lake. Enjoy your time here, and then retrace your steps.

6.0   Arrive back at the trailhead.

Wilderness camping: If you want to stay overnight, there are camps at both Crystal Lakes. Fires are not permitted, as in all the backcountry campgrounds. The lakes are the water source for both campgrounds. Lower Crystal Lake has two flat tent sites, but limited scenery. The two campsites at Upper Crystal Lake are on the south side of the lake and are considerably more scenic.

Hike Information

Local Information

Sunrise Visitor Center, Sunrise (no contact information).
Mount Rainier National Park Web site, www.nps.gov/mora; visitor information, (360) 569-2211, ext. 3314.

Lodging

Paradise Inn, (360) 569-2275; National Park Inn, (360) 569-2275. For a list of accommodations outside the park, visit www.nps.gov/mora/general/accom.htm.

Campgrounds

If you plan to car camp, the nearest facility is White River Campgrounds, located 5.0 miles beyond the White River Entrance Station. You can claim one of the 112 sites on a first-come, first-served basis. You can reserve sites at other campgrounds throughout the park online at http://reservations.nps.gov, or call (800) 365-CAMP (2267) 7:00 A.M. to 7:00 P.M. PST.

34 Palisades Lakes

A sharp descent leads down into a valley with many lakes.

Start: Palisades trailhead.
Distance: 7.0-mile out-and-back.
Approximate hiking time: 4 to 5 hours.
Difficulty: Moderate.
Seasons: Mid-July through September.
Nearest town: Greenwater.
Fees and permits: $10.00 vehicle or $5.00 individual entry fee (seven days); $30.00 annual entry fee. Wilderness Camping Permits free—reservations recommended ($20 fee).

Maps: USGS: White River Park; Trails Illustrated Mount Rainier National Park; Astronaut's Vista: Mount Rainier National Park, Washington; Earthwalk Press Hiking Map & Guide.
Trail contacts: White River Wilderness Information Center, (360) 569-6030.
Trail conditions: www.nps.gov/mora/trail/tr_cnd.htm; weather, www.nps.gov/mora/current/weather.htm.

Finding the trailhead: From the White River Ranger Station (see Getting There), continue 11.0 miles on White River Road to well-marked Sunrise Point. *DeLorme: Washington Atlas and Gazetteer:* Page 48 A4.

The Hike

After parking at Sunrise Point, cross White River Road to the east. The trail begins at the easternmost corner of the point beyond a few informational displays. At first the trail descends gradually, but the slight grade soon gives way to a steep, rocky trail. Wear shoes with good traction. We saw more than one person in inadequate footwear slip on the dusty trail. The steep switchbacks end in 0.5 mile at a junction. The westbound trail heads to Sunrise Lake, a pretty lake that unfortunately lies close to a busy road.

To continue toward Palisades Lakes, stay to the right (north). The next mile to Clover Lake is almost completely flat. You walk alternately through forest and meadow. When the forest opens to reveal a lake, you have reached Clover Lake. You cannot camp here, but it makes a lovely spot for a break. Stay on the maintained trails—the terrain encircling Clover Lake is very fragile.

Immediately north of Clover Lake, the trail climbs a low ridge. The ascent is not long, but it is steep. From the top of the ridge, it's all downhill or flat to the junction with the Hidden Lake Trail, 2.6 miles into the hike. (See Option.)

If you do not plan to take the Hidden Lake option, stay to the right (north) on the main trail. Another 0.3 mile of trail takes you to Tom, Dick, and Harry Lakes and to Dick Lake Camp. If you plan to stay at Dick Lake Camp, follow signs for Dick Lake, a short trek through the woods. Situated in forest, these green lakes are filled with grass. In midsummer beware of the bugs; mosquitoes thrive here.

A troop descending to Sunrise Lake.

Mosquitoes are also abundant at Upper Palisades Lake. When we were here, one of the backpacking groups abandoned camp because of the bug infestation. Infestations vary by year and depend on seasonal factors as well, but be forewarned. To get to Palisades Lakes, stay to the north on the main trail. A very slight ascent leads you first through forest, then field. When you reach a large emerald meadow that "resembles a golf course," as a ranger told us, turn around. From this spot you have a nice view of the Cowlitz Chimneys over rolling green hills.

Beyond this meadow, it is less than 0.5 mile to Upper Palisades Lake. The trail stays relatively flat until you reach the fork to Upper Palisades Camp. To head toward the camp, take the trail to the left (southwest). To filter water from the lake, take the path straight down to the lake (west). To see Lower Palisades Lake from a distance, stay on the main trail (north).

Upper Palisades Lake is beautiful. From the direction you approach, a field of flowers leads all the way to the water's edge. Striated rock formations, the Palisades, provide the backdrop for the deep-blue and aqua waters of the lake. If you planned only a day hike, retrace your steps along the main trail.

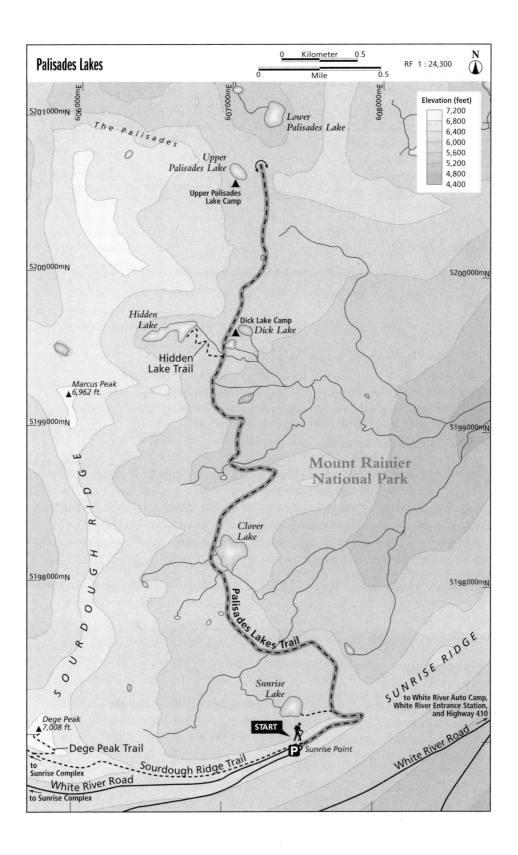

Palisades Lakes

0   Kilometer   0.5

0   Mile   0.5

RF 1 : 24,300

N

Elevation (feet)

| 7,200 |
| 6,800 |
| 6,400 |
| 6,000 |
| 5,600 |
| 5,200 |
| 4,800 |
| 4,400 |

5201000mN

606000mE

607000mE

608000mE

The Palisades

Lower Palisades Lake

Upper Palisades Lake

▲ **Upper Palisades Lake Camp**

5200000mN

5200000mN

Hidden Lake

Dick Lake Camp
▲ *Dick Lake*

Hidden Lake Trail

Marcus Peak
▲ *6,962 ft.*

5199000mN

5199000mN

Mount Rainier National Park

S O U R D O U G H   R I D G E

Clover Lake

5198000mN

5198000mN

Palisades Lakes Trail

Sunrise Lake

S U N R I S E   R I D G E

to White River Auto Camp,
White River Entrance Station,
and Highway 410

Dege Peak
▲ *7,008 ft.*

START

P *Sunrise Point*

Dege Peak Trail

Sourdough Ridge Trail

White River Road

to
Sunrise Complex

White River Road

to Sunrise Complex

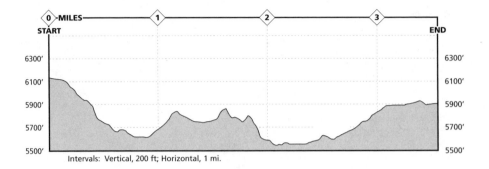

Intervals: Vertical, 200 ft; Horizontal, 1 mi.

Miles and Directions

0.0   Start heading east on the Palisades Lakes Trail from the easternmost tip of Sunrise Point.

0.5   At the spur trail to Sunrise Lake, stay to the right (north) toward the more private Palisades.

1.5   Clover Lake appears on your right (east). Stay on the main trail, and mind the fragility of the meadow.

2.6   Reach the Hidden Lake Trail junction. Be sure to take this side trip!

2.9   Tom, Dick, and Harry Lakes rest to your right; Dick Lake has a camp to offer.

3.5   Whether or not you plan to camp there, take the trail to the lovely Upper Palisades Lake. Though rather anticlimactic, you can stay on the main trail for less than a mile to catch a glimpse at Lower Palisades Lake before returning the way you came.

7.0   Arrive back at the trailhead.

Option: Don't miss the side trip to Hidden Lake. At the junction, 2.6 miles into the hike, turn left (west). A steep, dusty 0.6-mile ascent with a few switchbacks leads to a lovely lake. In a glacial cirque, the cool waters of the lake are surrounded on three sides by jutting rocks. A maintained trail runs around a large peninsula and stops abruptly. Although some social trails have been created around Hidden Lake, stay on the main trail. The Park Service is working to restore the soil and vegetation in this area.

Wilderness camping: You have two options for backcountry camping: Dick and Upper Palisades Camps. Dick Camp, the less desirable of the two, is situated in a place that requires a hike to reach both the toilet and the lake. Upper Palisades Lake has two very nice sites.

Hike Information

Local Information

Sunrise Visitor Center, Sunrise (no contact information).

Mount Rainier National Park Web site, www.nps.gov/mora; visitor information, (360) 569-2211, ext. 3314.

Lodging

Paradise Inn, (360) 569-2275; National Park Inn, (360) 569-2275. For a list of accommodations outside the park, visit www.nps.gov/mora/general/accom.htm.

Campgrounds

If you plan to car camp, the nearest facility is White River Campgrounds, located 5.0 miles beyond the White River Entrance Station. You can claim one of the 112 sites on a first-come, first-served basis. You can reserve sites at other campgrounds throughout the park online at http://reservations.nps.gov, or call (800) 365-CAMP (2267) 7:00 A.M. to 7:00 P.M. PST.

35 Dege Peak

A short climb to the top of Dege Peak affords views of Mount Rainier, the North Cascades, Mount Adams, Mount Baker, and Sunrise Lake.

Start: Sunrise Point.
Distance: 2.8-mile out-and-back.
Approximate hiking time: 1 to 2 hours.
Difficulty: Easy.
Seasons: Mid-July through September.
Nearest town: Greenwater.
Fees and permits: $10.00 vehicle or $5.00 individual entry fee (seven days); $30.00 annual entry fee.

Maps: USGS: White River Park; Trails Illustrated Mount Rainier National Park; Astronaut's Vista: Mount Rainier National Park, Washington; Earthwalk Press Hiking Map & Guide.
Trail contacts: White River Wilderness Information Center, (360) 569-6030.
Trail conditions: www.nps.gov/mora/trail/tr_cnd.htm; weather, www.nps.gov/mora/current/weather.htm.

Finding the trailhead: From the White River Ranger Station (see Getting There), continue 11.0 miles on White River Road to the well-marked Sunrise Point. *DeLorme: Washington Atlas and Gazetteer:* Page 48 A4.

Special considerations: There is a sizable parking lot at Sunrise Point, but it is often busy. If the parking lot is full, parking along the road is not an option. Instead, consider climbing Dege Peak from the west side. (See Option.)

The Hike

Although this hike is only 2.8 miles long, you climb uphill for the entire 1.4-mile trip to Dege Peak. Make sure to bring plenty of water, and pace yourself throughout the climb. From the top of Dege Peak, jaw-dropping scenery surrounds you in every direction.

The Sourdough Ridge Trail begins from the west end of the parking lot; head west. Subalpine wildflowers, such as lupine and magenta paintbrush, often line the trail in midsummer, and trees provide much-needed shade on a hot day. Marcus Peak rises on the right (north), and when you have gained enough elevation, Mount Rainier comes into view to the west.

Sunrise and Clover Lakes from the Sourdough Ridge Trail.

After hiking 1.1 miles, you come to the junction with the Dege Peak Trail. Turn right (northeast) onto this trail. It is only 0.3 mile to the summit from this point, but the trail follows steep switchbacks all the way to the top. At the top of Dege Peak you have entered the alpine zone. The peak consists of rock; little vegetation grows on the rocky surface. You can see two dormant volcanoes, Mount Baker and Mount Adams, and enjoy an impressive view of majestic Mount Rainier.

When you decide to head back, it is all downhill! Relish the view of Clover and Sunrise Lakes as you descend the peak. Sunrise Lake is closest to Sunrise Point, where you began your hike; Clover Lake is farther north, near Marcus Peak.

Miles and Directions

0.0 Start heading west on the Sourdough Ridge Trail from the west end of the Sunrise Point parking lot.

1.1 At the junction with the Dege Peak Trail, turn right (north) and begin the steep climb to Dege Peak.

1.4 Reach Dege Peak summit. Enjoy the view and then begin your descent.

2.8 Arrive back at the trailhead.

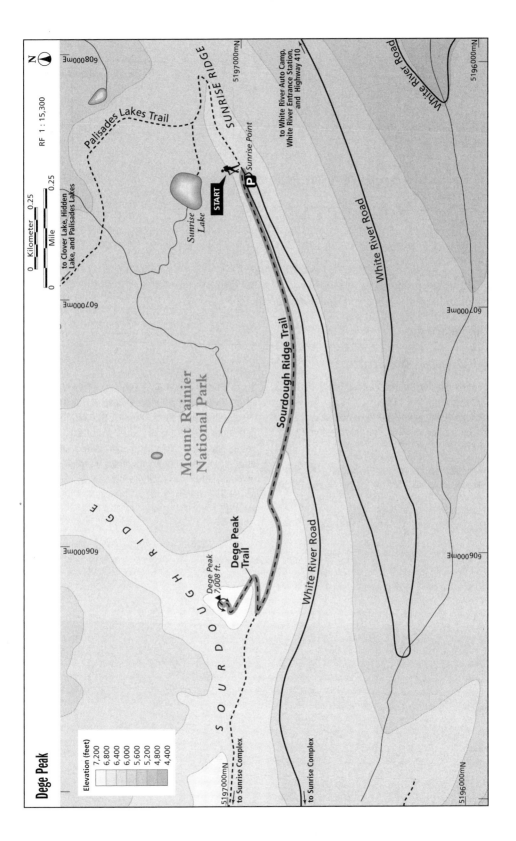

Dege Peak

RF 1 : 15,300

N

Elevation (feet)
7,200
6,800
6,400
6,000
5,600
5,200
4,800
4,400

Palisades Lakes Trail

SUNRISE RIDGE

Sunrise Point

to White River Auto Camp,
White River Entrance Station,
and Highway 410

White River Road

White River Road

START

Sunrise Lake

to Clover Lake, Hidden
Lake, and Palisades Lakes

P

Mount Rainier
National Park

Sourdough Ridge Trail

S O U R D O U G H   R I D G E

Dege Peak
7,008 ft.

Dege Peak
Trail

White River Road

to Sunrise Complex

to Sunrise Complex

0   Kilometer   0.25

0   Mile   0.25

6080000mE

607000mE

606000mE

607000mE

606000mE

5197000mN

5196000mN

5197000mN

5196000mN

Option: If the parking lot is full, or if you want to start from the Sunrise Complex, park in the Sunrise parking lot, 2.6 miles west from Sunrise Point on White River Road. There is a huge parking lot there, but on a sunny weekend it, too, might be full. If it is, you might have to choose an alternative hike.

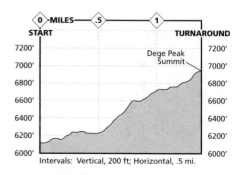

Intervals: Vertical, 200 ft; Horizontal, .5 mi.

From the Sunrise Complex, head up the paved path to the right of the restrooms leading to the Sourdough Ridge Nature Trail. Turn right (northeast) up the nature trail and stay on it for a little over 0.3 mile to the junction with the Sourdough Ridge Trail. Turn right (east) onto the Sourdough Ridge Trail and head east toward Dege Peak, which is 1.5 miles away. This option has a total out-and-back distance of 3.8 miles.

Hike Information

Local Information

Sunrise Visitor Center, Sunrise (no contact information).
Mount Rainier National Park Web site, www.nps.gov/mora; visitor information, (360) 569-2211, ext. 3314.

Lodging

Paradise Inn, (360) 569-2275; National Park Inn, (360) 569-2275. For a list of accommodations outside the park, visit www.nps.gov/mora/general/accom.htm.

Campgrounds

If you plan to car camp, the nearest facility is White River Campgrounds, located 5.0 miles beyond the White River Entrance Station. You can claim one of the 112 sites on a first-come, first-served basis. You can reserve sites at other campgrounds throughout the park online at http://reservations.nps.gov, or call (800) 365-CAMP (2267) 7:00 A.M. to 7:00 P.M. PST.

36 Sourdough Ridge Nature Trail

This is a one-hour self-guiding informative stroll along Sourdough Ridge.

Start: Sunrise Complex
Distance: 1.5-mile lollipop.
Approximate hiking time: 1 hour.
Difficulty: Easy.
Seasons: Mid-July through September
Nearest town: Greenwater.
Fees and permits: $10.00 vehicle or $5.00 individual entry fee (seven days); $30.00 annual entry fee.

Maps: USGS: Sunrise; Trails Illustrated Mount Rainier National Park; Astronaut's Vista: Mount Rainier National Park, Washington; Earthwalk Press Hiking Map & Guide.
Trail contacts: White River Wilderness Information Center, (360) 569-6030.
Trail conditions: www.nps.gov/mora/trail/tr_cnd.htm; weather, www.nps.gov/mora/current/weather.htm.

Finding the trailhead: From the White River Entrance Station (see Getting There), drive 13.8 miles west on the White River Road to the Sunrise Complex parking lot. Park and walk to the trailhead on the northwestern end of the lot, to the right of the restrooms. *DeLorme: Washington Atlas and Gazetteer:* Page 48 A3.

The Hike

To begin this hike, go to the northwestern part of the parking lot. Follow the wide trail running north beyond the restrooms. About 0.1 mile into the hike, a map and display on the right (east) delineate some of the trails in the Sunrise area, including elevation charts and short descriptions. Left (north) of the map, a small box holds the accompanying pamphlet to Sourdough Ridge Nature Trail, entitled *Sourdough Ridge: Subalpine Meadow Ecology.* If you plan to keep this pamphlet, put 50 cents in the fee box. Otherwise, return the pamphlet upon completion of the hike.

Continue north on this trail until it forks. Follow the sign pointing right (east). For Stations 1 through 7, you walk along the south slope of Sourdough Ridge. You have a fantastic view of the grandeur of Mount Rainier, while the stations inform you about the small but crucial parts of the ecosystem.

After Station 7, the path forks. Take the left (west) fork. From Stations 8 to 13, you walk along the top of Sourdough Ridge with views off both sides of the ridge. On a clear day you can see Mount Baker, Mount Adams, and Glacier Peak.

After Station 13, turn left (south). The Sunrise Complex comes into sight as the lollipop reaches its end. As

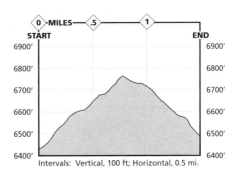

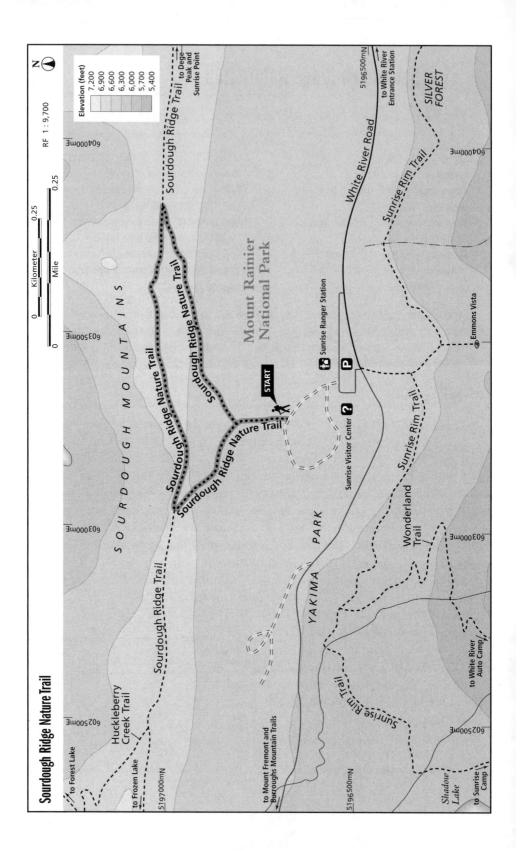

Sourdough Ridge Nature Trail

RF 1 : 9,700

N

Elevation (feet)
7,200
6,900
6,600
6,300
6,000
5,700
5,400

Kilometer
0   0.25   0.25

Mile
0

SOURDOUGH MOUNTAINS

Sourdough Ridge Nature Trail

Sourdough Ridge Nature Trail

Sourdough Ridge Nature Trail

Sourdough Ridge Trail
to Dege Peak and Sunrise Point

Sourdough Ridge Trail

Huckleberry Creek Trail

to Forest Lake

to Frozen Lake

Mount Rainier National Park

START

Sunrise Ranger Station

Sunrise Visitor Center

P

White River Road

to White River Entrance Station

Sunrise Rim Trail

SILVER FOREST

Emmons Vista

Sunrise Rim Trail

Wonderland Trail

YAKIMA PARK

to Mount Fremont and Burroughs Mountain Trails

Sunrise Rim Trail

Shadow Lake

to White River Auto Camp

to Sunrise Camp

5197000mN

5196500mN

5196500mN

602500mE

603000mE

603500mE

604000mE

602500mE

603000mE

604000mE

the pamphlet says, "We hope this walk has given you a look behind the scenery, into the ever changing environmental forces that influence this subalpine community."

Hike Information

Local Information
Sunrise Visitor Center, Sunrise (no contact information).
Mount Rainier National Park Web site, www.nps.gov/mora; visitor information, (360) 569-2211, ext. 3314.

Lodging
Paradise Inn, (360) 569-2275; National Park Inn, (360) 569-2275. For a list of accommodations outside the park, visit www.nps.gov/mora/general/accom.htm.

Campgrounds
If you plan to car camp, the nearest facility is White River Campgrounds, located 5.0 miles beyond the White River Entrance Station. You can claim one of the 112 sites on a first-come, first-served basis. You can reserve sites at other campgrounds throughout the park online at http://reservations.nps.gov, or call (800) 365-CAMP (2267) 7:00 A.M. to 7:00 P.M. PST.

37 Silver Forest

Enjoy an easy one-hour walk to informative viewpoints along a flowery subalpine meadow.

Start: Sunrise Complex.
Distance: 2.0-mile out-and-back.
Approximate hiking time: 1 hour.
Difficulty: Easy.
Seasons: Mid-July through September.
Nearest town: Greenwater.
Fees and permits: $10.00 vehicle or $5.00 individual entry fee (seven days); $30.00 annual entry fee.

Maps: USGS: Sunrise and White River Park; Trails Illustrated Mount Rainier National Park; Astronaut's Vista: Mount Rainier National Park, Washington; Earthwalk Press Hiking Map & Guide.
Trail contacts: White River Wilderness Information Center, (360) 569-6030.
Trail conditions: www.nps.gov/mora/trail/tr_cnd.htm; weather, www.nps.gov/mora/current/weather.htm.

Finding the trailhead: From the White River Entrance Station (see Getting There), drive 13.8 miles west on White River Road to the Sunrise Complex parking lot. Park in one of the many spaces provided. The trailhead is south of the parking lot. *DeLorme: Washington Atlas and Gazetteer:* Page 48 A3.

The Hike

The Silver Forest Trail involves two parts. First, a short descent leads to two informative exhibits with great views of Mount Rainier. Then the trail continues east through subalpine forest and meadow.

Mount Rainier from Emmons Vista.

To find the trailhead, park in the Sunrise parking lot. From the south side of the lot, directly across from the ranger station and cafeteria, a trail heads south and a dirt road heads west. As the sign directs, follow the southbound trail, the Emmons Vista Nature Trail.

In only 0.1 mile you reach the junction with the Sunrise Rim Trail. Stay to the left (south). The path curves east, and a sign points south to the first Emmons Vista exhibit. Walk down to the viewpoint and admire the tree-framed view of the Emmons and Winthrop Glaciers. The exhibit explains the various features of a glaciated mountain and how they were formed.

Return to the main trail and continue east. You soon come upon the second exhibit, again immediately south of the trail. This vista point has a nice, sheltered seating area and two more informative signs. The first, SNOW SHADOW, includes climatic information about the winds and snow of Paradise. The other, ROCKS RIDING ON AIR, gives a historical account of the Little Tahoma Peak rockslide of 1963.

Back on the main trail, head east once again. In less than 0.1 mile you come to a sign indicating that you have reached the Silver Forest portion of the trail. A fire of unknown origins incinerated this area long ago. Today the only remnants of the

Silver Forest

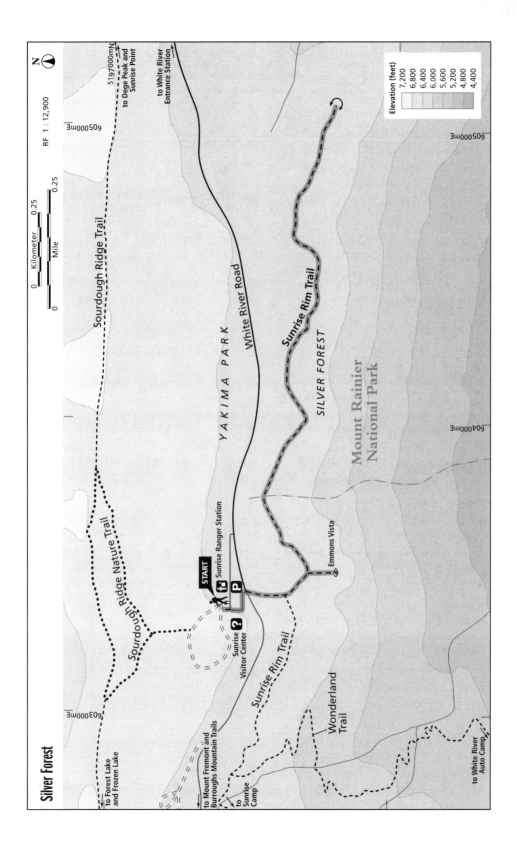

RF 1 : 12,900

N

Elevation (feet)
7,200
6,800
6,400
6,000
5,600
5,200
4,800
4,400

Sourdough Ridge Trail

to Dege Peak and
Sunrise Point

to White River
Entrance Station

White River Road

YAKIMA PARK

Sunrise Rim Trail

SILVER FOREST

Mount Rainier
National Park

Sourdough Ridge Nature Trail

to Forest Lake
and Frozen Lake

Sunrise Ranger Station

START

Sunrise
Visitor Center

Sunrise Rim Trail

Emmons Vista

Wonderland
Trail

to Mount Fremont and
Burroughs Mountain Trails

to Sunrise
Camp

to White River
Auto Camp

old forest are "silver sentinels," long-dead but standing trees. In the fire's wake, subalpine trees and wildflowers have grown, making this forest particularly intriguing. Small, gnarled trees are dispersed throughout this meadow, along with blankets of violet flowers in midsummer. Walk along this trail for 0.8 mile before reaching a sign that indicates the end of the maintained

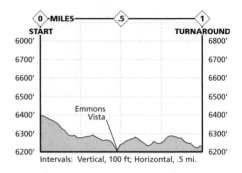

Intervals: Vertical, 100 ft; Horizontal, .5 mi.

trail, 1.0 mile from the trailhead. The trail continues for quite some distance beyond this sign, so venture farther if you want an extended hike. Otherwise, turn around and walk back to the Sunrise Complex.

Miles and Directions

0.0 Start heading south on the trail across the parking lot from the snack bar and gift shop.

0.1 In just a short while, reach the juncture of the Emmons Vista and Sunrise Rim Trails. Stay to the left (east) toward the Emmons Vista exhibits.

0.2 There are two Emmons Vista exhibits, one with information on glaciation and one on climatic conditions. Both have viewpoints.

1.0 The trail heads through silver forest and peters out. Retrace your steps.

2.0 Arrive back at the trailhead.

Hike Information

Local Information

Sunrise Visitor Center, Sunrise (no contact information).
Mount Rainier National Park Web site, www.nps.gov/mora; visitor information, (360) 569-2211, ext. 3314.

Lodging

Paradise Inn, (360) 569-2275; National Park Inn, (360) 569-2275. For a list of accommodations outside the park, visit www.nps.gov/mora/general/accom.htm.

Campgrounds

If you plan to car camp, the nearest facility is White River Campgrounds, located 5.0 miles beyond the White River Entrance Station. You can claim one of the 112 sites on a first-come, first-served basis. You can reserve sites at other campgrounds throughout the park online at http://reservations.nps.gov, or call (800) 365-CAMP (2267) 7:00 A.M. to 7:00 P.M. PST.

38 Emmons Moraine

A short hike up to the Emmons Moraine provides an excellent view of the Emmons Glacier, the largest glacier in the contiguous United States.

Start: Glacier Basin trailhead.
Distance: 2.8-mile out-and-back.
Approximate hiking time: 1 to 2 hours.
Difficulty: Easy.
Seasons: Early July through September
Nearest town: Greenwater.
Fees and permits: $10.00 vehicle or $5.00 individual entry fee (seven days); $30.00 annual entry fee.

Maps: USGS: Sunrise; Trails Illustrated Mount Rainier National Park; Astronaut's Vista: Mount Rainier National Park, Washington; Earthwalk Press Hiking Map & Guide.
Trail contacts: White River Wilderness Information Center, (360) 569-6030.
Trail conditions: www.nps.gov/mora/trail/ tr_cnd.htm; weather, www.nps.gov/mora/ current/weather.htm.

Finding the trailhead: From the White River Entrance Station (see Getting There), drive 4.0 miles west on White River Road to the White River Campground turnoff. Turn left (northwest) toward the campground, and drive another mile to the parking area on the left. A sign indicates that the parking lot is for backpackers and climbers. Park here and walk to the Glacier Basin trailhead on the west side of Loop D, one of the many loops that make up White River Campground. *DeLorme: Washington Atlas and Gazetteer:* Page 48 A3.

The Hike

This short, gradual uphill hike is great for children. Hike along the Emmons Moraine for a close-up view of the Emmons Glacier. At one time the Emmons Glacier filled the whole valley here, carving an amazingly flat and expansive section out of the earth.

Head west along the Glacier Basin Trail. Very near the beginning of the trail, you come to an informational billboard about this hike and other hikes in the immediate area. From here, hike 0.9 mile through tranquil forest to the junction with the Emmons Moraine Trail. At the junction go left (southwest), up the Emmons Moraine Trail.

Travel slightly uphill for another 0.5 mile to the end of the maintained trail. Your feet sink into the sandy trail formed from silt deposits by the

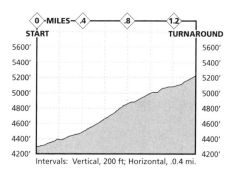

Intervals: Vertical, 200 ft; Horizontal, .0.4 mi.

Emmons Glacier. On a hot day the sand soaks up the sun, adding to the scorching heat, and the small trees along the Emmons Moraine provide little or no shade. Be sure to bring sunscreen. When you have marveled at the Emmons Glacier long enough, head back the same way you came.

Miles and Directions

0.0 Start heading west on the Glacier Basin Trail from Loop D of the White River Campground.

0.9 Emmons Moraine Trail separates from the Glacier Basin Trail toward the left (southwest); take the Emmons Moraine spur trail.

1.4 Emmons Moraine Trail ends with a view of the glacial wake. See Option if you chose to continue on to Glacier Basin. Otherwise, head back the way you came.

2.8 Arrive back at the trailhead.

Option: At the junction with Emmons Moraine Trail, you can head up to Glacier Basin. It will be another 2.2 miles from the junction to the end of the maintained trail, adding 4.4 miles to your hike. (See Hike 44: Glacier Basin.) From the lovely Glacier Basin mountain meadow, you can see the Inter Glacier, the hiking route for climbers to reach the Camp Schurman base camp, and St. Elmo's Pass.

Hike Information

Local Information
Sunrise Visitor Center, Sunrise (no contact information).
Mount Rainier National Park Web site, www.nps.gov/mora; visitor information, (360) 569-2211, ext. 3314.

Lodging
Paradise Inn, (360) 569-2275; National Park Inn, (360) 569-2275. For a list of accommodations outside the park, visit www.nps.gov/mora/general/accom.htm.

Campgrounds
If you plan to car camp, the nearest facility is White River Campgrounds, located 5.0 miles beyond the White River Entrance Station. You can claim one of the 112 sites on a first-come, first-served basis. You can reserve sites at other campgrounds throughout the park online at http://reservations.nps.gov, or call (800) 365-CAMP (2267) 7:00 A.M. to 7:00 P.M. PST.

◀ *The Wedge between Emmons and Winthrop Glaciers.* JOHN CALDWELL

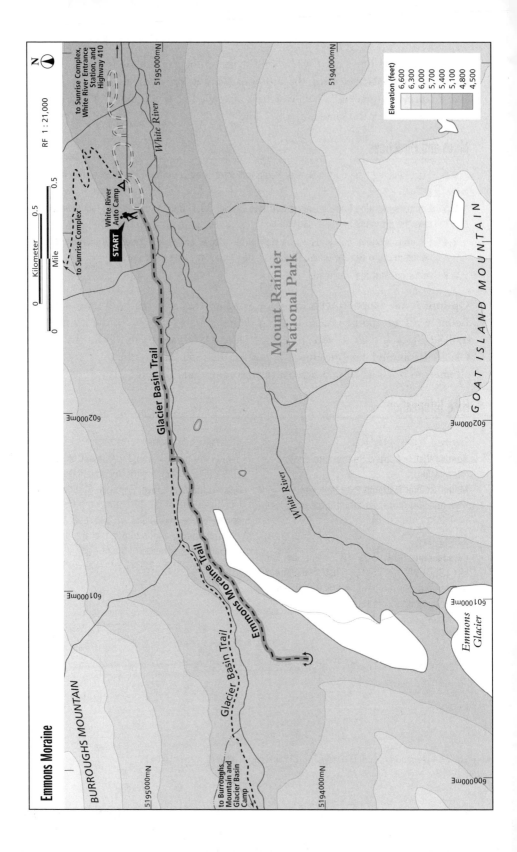

Emmons Moraine

BURROUGHS MOUNTAIN

to Burroughs Mountain and Glacier Basin Camp

Glacier Basin Trail

Emmons Moraine Trail

Glacier Basin Trail

Emmons Glacier

Mount Rainier National Park

White River

GOAT ISLAND MOUNTAIN

White River

to Sunrise Complex

START

White River Auto Camp

to Sunrise Complex, White River Entrance Station, and Highway 410

N

RF 1 : 21,000

Kilometer
0   0.5

Mile
0   0.5

Elevation (feet)
6,600
6,300
6,000
5,700
5,400
5,100
4,800
4,500

5195000mN

5194000mN

600000mE

601000mE

602000mE

5195000mN

5194000mN

39 Mount Fremont Lookout

This hike makes a short ascent to a fire lookout on Mount Fremont that towers over the north side of the park. The lookout affords great views of Mount Rainier, Skyscraper Mountain, Grand Park, and Sourdough Ridge.

Start: Sunrise Complex.
Distance: 5.4-mile out-and-back.
Approximate hiking time: 2 to 4 hours.
Difficulty: Easy.
Seasons: Early July through September.
Nearest town: Greenwater.
Fees and permits: $10.00 vehicle or $5.00 individual entry fee (seven days); $30.00 annual entry fee.

Maps: USGS: Sunrise; Trails Illustrated Mount Rainier National Park; Astronaut's Vista: Mount Rainier National Park, Washington; Earthwalk Press Hiking Map & Guide.
Trail contacts: White River Wilderness Information Center, (360) 569-6030.
Trail conditions: www.nps.gov/mora/trail/tr_cnd.htm; weather, www.nps.gov/mora/current/weather.htm.

Finding the trailhead: From the White River Entrance Station (see Getting There), drive 13.8 miles west on the White River Road to the Sunrise Complex parking lot. Park and walk to the trailhead on the northwestern end of the lot, to the right of the restrooms. *DeLorme: Washington Atlas and Gazetteer:* Page 48 A3.

The Hike

Walk up the paved path to the right (east) of the restrooms until you see a dirt trail on your right (north). Get on that trail and travel north until you come to the junction with the Sourdough Ridge Nature Trail. Turn left (northwest) onto the nature trail, and walk 0.2 mile to the Sourdough Ridge Trail. Turn left (west) onto the Sourdough Ridge Trail.

While you are walking along this trail, you can see the North Cascades to your right. Mount Rainier looms magnificent from Sourdough Ridge. After 0.3 mile you pass the Huckleberry Creek Trail on your right, heading northwest. Keep going west (left) another 0.8 mile to a five-way junction, immediately after Frozen Lake and 1.4 miles from the trailhead. At this junction the Mount Fremont Trail is the first trail on your right; follow it, heading north. The trail runs above timberline for the remainder of the hike. Fat marmots inhabit the green meadows along the trail. Keep in mind that it is illegal to feed animals and detrimental to their natural survival skills.

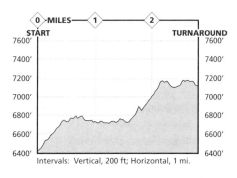

View from Mount Fremont.

Soon the trail threads along the rocky side of Mount Fremont. Watch your step—the ledge drops straight off the ridge! Low-growing subalpine wildflowers line the trail in late July. Walk along the ridge until you reach the lookout, 2.7 miles from the Sunrise Complex. From the lookout you can see all the way to the north end of the park, where clear-cuts begin to shave indiscriminate splotches in the forest. Skyscraper Mountain is to your left, just beyond the deep green and flower fields of Berkeley Park. North of Berkeley Park you can easily identify Grand Park, a massive plateau dappled with ghost trees. Mount Rainier towers above it all. Take the time to get out your map and identify the landmarks around you.

Miles and Directions

0.0 Start from the Sunrise parking lot and follow the paved path to the right (east) of the restrooms, heading north. Don't let the road heading off to the left (west) tempt you; stay on the main trail, heading north past the informative display.

0.1 The Sourdough Ridge Nature Trail forks; stay to the left (northwest) toward Frozen Lake and Mount Fremont.

0.3 Reach the top of Sourdough Ridge and the junction with the Sourdough Ridge Nature Trail. Take a left (west) onto the trail.

0.6 Bypass the steep Huckleberry Creek Trail on your right (north).

Mount Fremont Lookout

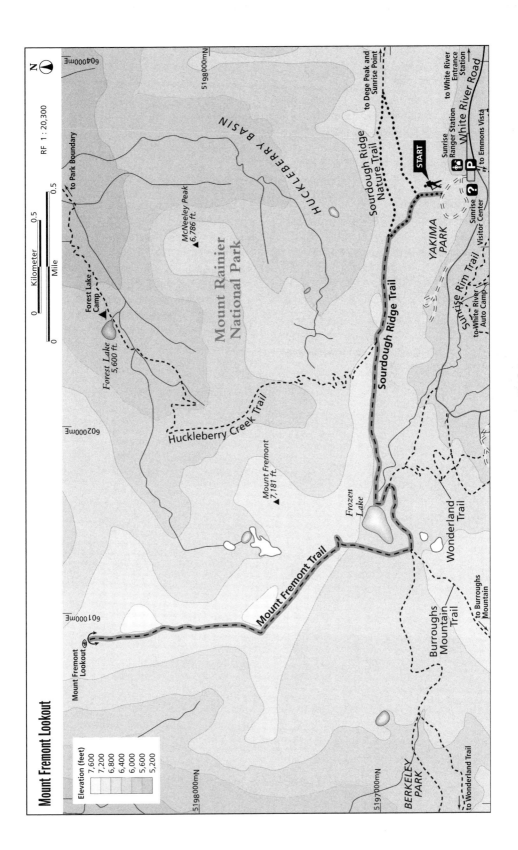

Elevation (feet)
7,600
7,200
6,800
6,400
6,000
5,600
5,200

RF 1 : 20,300

N

Kilometer
0   0.5

Mile
0   0.5

to Park Boundary

Forest Lake Camp

Forest Lake
5,600 ft.

Huckleberry Creek Trail

HUCKLEBERRY BASIN

McNeeley Peak
6,786 ft.

Mount Rainier
National Park

Mount Fremont
7,181 ft.

Mount Fremont Trail

Frozen Lake

Mount Fremont
Lookout

Burroughs
Mountain
Trail

to Burroughs
Mountain

BERKELEY
PARK

to Wonderland Trail

Sourdough Ridge Nature Trail

Sourdough Ridge Trail

START

to Dege Peak and
Sunrise Point

to White River
Entrance Station

White River Road

Sunrise
Ranger Station

Sunrise Station

to Emmons Vista

Sunrise
Visitor Center

YAKIMA
PARK

Sunrise Rim Trail

to White River
Auto Camp

Wonderland
Trail

604000mE

5198000mN

602000mE

601000mE

5198000mN

5197000mN

1.4 Just beyond Frozen Lake, come to the Mount Fremont Trail junction. Follow the trail to the right (north).

2.7 Just over a mile of uphill along a rocky mountain slope and you can see Mount Fremont Lookout. Enjoy the view, and then retrace your steps.

5.4 Arrive back at the trailhead.

Hike Information

Local Information

Sunrise Visitor Center, Sunrise (no contact info).
Mount Rainier National Park Web site, www.nps.gov/mora; visitor information, (360) 569-2211, ext. 3314.

Lodging

Paradise Inn, (360) 569-2275; National Park Inn, (360) 569-2275. For a list of accommodations outside the park, visit www.nps.gov/mora/general/accom.htm.

Campgrounds

If you plan to car camp, the nearest facility is White River Campgrounds, located 5.0 miles beyond the White River Entrance Station. You can claim one of the 112 sites on a first-come, first-served basis. You can reserve sites at other campgrounds throughout the park online at http://reservations.nps.gov, or call (800) 365-CAMP (2267) 7:00 A.M. to 7:00 P.M. PST.

40 Forest Lake

A short descent over rocky alpine terrain travels through subalpine meadows to a quaint mountain lake.

Start: Sunrise Complex.
Distance: 5.0-mile out-and-back.
Approximate hiking time: 2 to 3 hours.
Difficulty: Easy.
Seasons: Mid-July through September.
Nearest town: Greenwater.
Fees and permits: $10.00 vehicle or $5.00 individual entry fee (seven days); $30.00 annual entry fee. Wilderness Camping Permits free—reservations recommended ($20 fee).

Maps: USGS: Sunrise; Trails Illustrated Mount Rainier National Park; Astronaut's Vista: Mount Rainier National Park, Washington; Earthwalk Press Hiking Map & Guide.
Trail contacts: White River Wilderness Information Center, (360) 569-6030.
Trail conditions: www.nps.gov/mora/trail/tr_cnd.htm; weather, www.nps.gov/mora/current/weather.htm.

Finding the trailhead: From the White River Entrance Station (see Getting There), drive 13.8 miles west on White River Road to the Sunrise Complex parking lot. Park and walk to the trailhead on the north end of the lot, to the right of the restrooms. *DeLorme: Washington Atlas and Gazetteer:* Page 48 A4.

The Hike

If you want to escape the crowd at Sunrise and experience a variety of different ecosystems, this is the hike for you. From the tundra on the north side of Sourdough Ridge to the deciduous forest that surrounds Forest Lake, you will have a taste of everything.

Walk up the paved path to the right (east) of the restrooms until the trail forks. Take the dirt trail on your right (north). Walk up that trail until you come to the junction with the Sourdough Ridge Nature Trail. Turn left (northwest) onto the nature trail and walk 0.2 mile to the Sourdough Ridge Trail. Turn left (west) onto the Sourdough Ridge Trail.

While you are walking along this trail, you can see the Cascades to the north, and Mount Rainier looks magnificent from here. Soon the Huckleberry Creek Trail splits right. Take the Huckleberry Creek Trail, 0.6 mile into your hike. The trail briefly ascends and then begins a long descent to Forest Lake. The first part of the trail is in the alpine zone and relatively rocky. There are low-growing wildflowers, such as red mountain heather, all around. Patches of snow might linger on the trail until August, but the trail is usually easy to follow.

Keep your eyes open for wildlife on both Mount Fremont, to your left, and McNeeley Peak, to your right. Visible from Sourdough Ridge, the lush Huckleberry Basin lies between the two peaks.

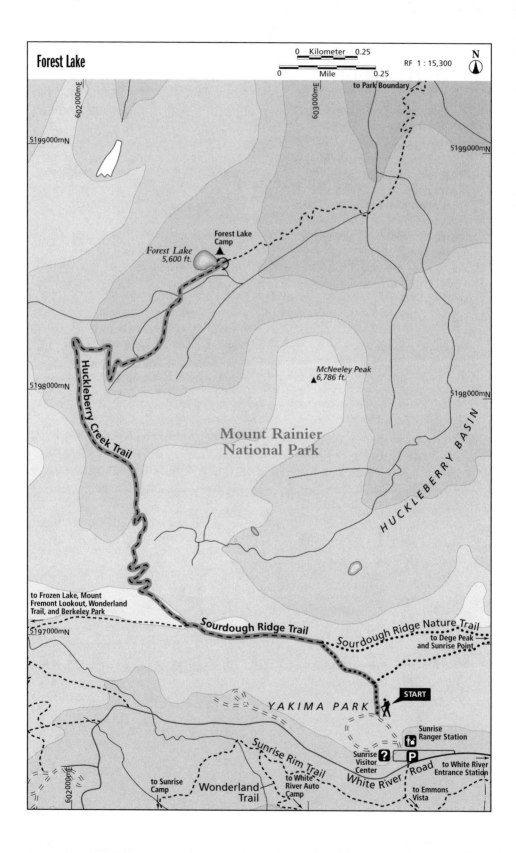

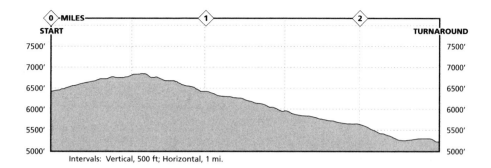

Intervals: Vertical, 500 ft; Horizontal, 1 mi.

Soon the trail heads into the trees and wanders through forest and meadows, overflowing with wildflowers in late July, all the way to Forest Lake. Forest Lake is small but charming. There is a great place right next to the campsite to take a break and enjoy the lake.

Miles and Directions

0.0 Start from the Sunrise parking lot; follow the paved path to the right (east) of the restrooms heading north. Don't let the road heading off to the left (west) tempt you, stay on the main trail, heading north past the informative display.

0.1 The Sourdough Ridge Nature Trail forks; stay to the left (northwest) toward Frozen Lake and Mount Fremont.

0.3 Reach the top of Sourdough Ridge and the junction with the Sourdough Ridge Nature Trail. Take a left (west) onto the trail.

0.6 Turn right (north) onto the Huckleberry Creek Trail, heading sharply down the hillside.

2.5 At Forest Lake and the Forest Lake Camp, you have reached your destination. Enjoy! Then head back the way you came.

5.0 Arrive back at the trailhead.

Wilderness camping: Forest Lake Camp has one individual campsite with slightly slanted tent sites and an incredible view.

Hike Information

Local Information

Sunrise Visitor Center, Sunrise (no contact information).
Mount Rainier National Park Web site, www.nps.gov/mora; visitor information, (360) 569–2211, ext. 3314.

Lodging

Paradise Inn, (360) 569–2275; National Park Inn, (360) 569–2275. For a list of accommodations outside the park, visit www.nps.gov/mora/general/accom.htm.

Campgrounds

If you plan to car camp, the nearest facility is White River Campgrounds, located 5.0 miles beyond the White River Entrance Station. You can claim one of the 112 sites on a first-come, first-served basis. You can reserve sites at other campgrounds throughout the park online at http://reservations.nps.gov, or call (800) 365–CAMP (2267) 7:00 A.M. to 7:00 P.M. PST.

41 Berkeley Park

A mild descent leads to a lovely mountain meadow brimming with wildflowers and clear streams.

Start: Sunrise Complex.
Distance: 7.8-mile out-and-back.
Approximate hiking time: 3 to 5 hours.
Difficulty: Moderate.
Seasons: Mid-July through September.
Nearest town: Greenwater.
Fees and permits: $10.00 vehicle or $5.00 individual entry fee (seven days); $30.00 annual entry fee. Wilderness Camping Permits free—reservations recommended ($20 fee).

Maps: USGS: Sunrise; Trails Illustrated Mount Rainier National Park; Astronaut's Vista: Mount Rainier National Park, Washington; Earthwalk Press Hiking Map & Guide.
Trail contacts: White River Wilderness Information Center, (360) 569-6030.
Trail conditions: www.nps.gov/mora/trail/tr_cnd.htm; weather, www.nps.gov/mora/current/weather.htm.

Finding the trailhead: From the White River Entrance Station (see Getting There), drive 13.8 miles west on White River Road to the Sunrise parking lot. Park and walk to the trailhead on the north end of the lot, to the right of the restrooms. *DeLorme: Washington Atlas and Gazetteer:* Page 48 A4.

The Hike

To begin this hike, go to the northwestern part of the parking lot. Follow the wide trail north beyond the restrooms. After about 0.1 mile, a map and display on the right (east) delineate some of the trails in the Sunrise area, including elevation charts and short descriptions. Continue 0.1 mile north of this sign to the junction with the Sourdough Ridge Trail. Turn left (west) onto this trail. This wide, dusty path runs along Sourdough Ridge, providing various opportunities to admire the awesome views on both sides. In 1.1 miles you descend from the ridge, only to rise again to a junction of five trails.

Follow the Wonderland Trail, heading directly west. The trail goes down a hill and toward a valley for 1.1 miles. At this point the Northern Loop Trail goes right (north). Take this trail, entering the meadow below. This gap between Skyscraper Mountain to the west and Mount Fremont to the east is named Berkeley Park. Pink flowers line the creek that meanders beside you. If you look behind you (south), you can see Burroughs Mountain and Mount Rainier. Take your time appreciating the beauty of a subalpine meadow, because you soon leave it and enter the woods.

If Berkeley Camp, 3.9 miles into the hike, is your destination, continue to descend beyond the meadow and into a forested area. The camp rests right next to the trail. Day hikers can filter water from Lodi Creek before beginning the 1,400-foot ascent back to the top of Sourdough Ridge.

Berkeley Park

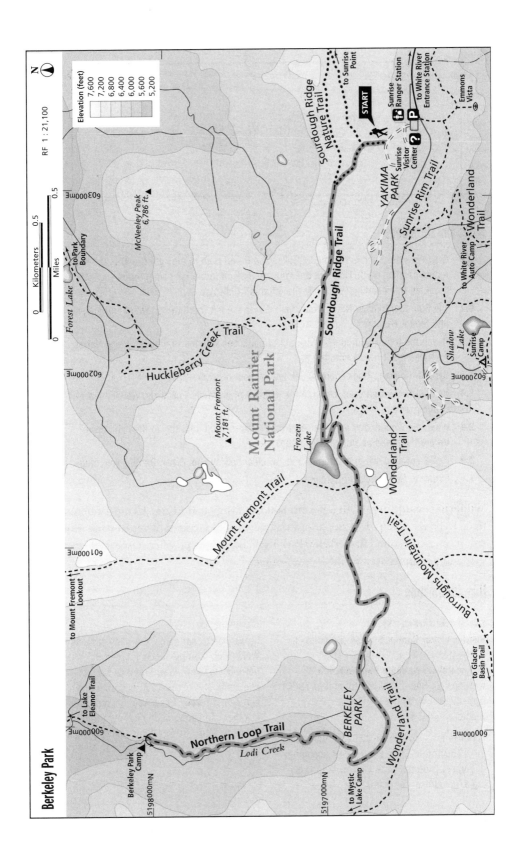

RF 1 : 21,100

Elevation (feet)
7,600
7,200
6,800
6,400
6,000
5,600
5,200

N

Kilometers
0   0.5

Miles
0   0.5

Mount Rainier National Park

Mount Fremont
▲ 7,181 ft.

McNeeley Peak
6,786 ft. ▲

Forest Lake

to Park Boundary

Huckleberry Creek Trail

Frozen Lake

Sourdough Ridge Trail

Sourdough Ridge Nature Trail

to Sunrise Point

START

Sunrise Ranger Station
to White River Entrance Station

Sunrise Visitor Center
?
P

YAKIMA PARK

Emmons Vista

Sunrise Rim Trail

Wonderland Trail

to White River Auto Camp

Shadow Lake

Sunrise Camp
△

Wonderland Trail

Mount Fremont Trail

to Mount Fremont Lookout

Burroughs Mountain Trail

to Glacier Basin Trail

Northern Loop Trail

Berkeley Park Camp
▲

to Lake Eleanor Trail

Lodi Creek

BERKELEY PARK

Wonderland Trail

to Mystic Lake Camp

5198000mN

5197000mN

600000mE

601000mE

602000mE

603000mE

602000mE

600000mE

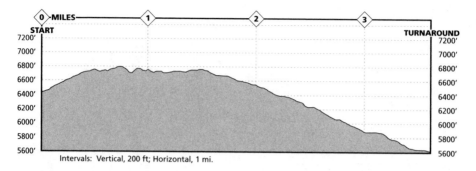

Intervals: Vertical, 200 ft; Horizontal, 1 mi.

Miles and Directions

0.0 Start from the Sunrise parking lot; follow the paved path to the right (east) of the restrooms heading north. Don't let the road heading off to the left (west) tempt you; stay on the main trail heading north past the informative display.

0.1 The Sourdough Ridge Nature Trail forks; stay to the left (northwest) toward Frozen Lake and Mount Fremont.

0.3 Reach the top of Sourdough Ridge and the junction with the Sourdough Ridge Nature Trail. Take a left (west) onto the trail.

0.6 Bypass the steep Huckleberry Creek Trail on your right (north).

1.4 Just beyond Frozen Lake, come to the junction of five trails. Follow the Wonderland Trail heading west.

2.4 When the Wonderland Trail intersects the Northern Loop Trail, stay to the right, down toward the meadow along the Northern Loop.

3.9 Berkeley Camp sits in a stand of trees by clear-flowing Lodi Creek. Retrace your steps.

7.8 Return to Sunrise Visitor Center.

Wilderness camping: With a permit you can camp at Berkeley Camp. Buffered by trees, Berkeley Camp does not afford the views of Skyscraper Mountain and mountain meadows featured in Berkeley Park itself, but the camp offers respectable campsites and proximity to a quality water source.

Hike Information

Local Information
Sunrise Visitor Center, Sunrise (no contact information).
Mount Rainier National Park Web site, www.nps.gov/mora; visitor information, (360) 569-2211, ext. 3314.

Lodging
Paradise Inn, (360) 569-2275; National Park Inn, (360) 569-2275. For a list of accommodations outside the park, visit www.nps.gov/mora/general/accom.htm.

Campgrounds
If you plan to car camp, the nearest facility is White River Campgrounds, located 5.0 miles beyond the White River Entrance Station. You can claim one of the 112 sites on a first-come, first-served basis. You can reserve sites at other campgrounds throughout the park online at http://reservations.nps.gov, or call (800) 365-CAMP (2267) 7:00 A.M. to 7:00 P.M. PST.

42 Grand Park

A mild descent to a lovely mountain meadow brimming with wildflowers and clear streams becomes a relatively flat hike to a massive expanse of subalpine park atop a plateau.

Start: Sunrise Complex.
Distance: 12.2-mile out-and-back.
Approximate hiking time: 6 to 8 hours.
Difficulty: Strenuous day hike, moderate overnighter.
Seasons: Mid-July through September.
Nearest town: Greenwater.
Fees and permits: $10.00 vehicle or $5.00 individual entry fee (seven days); $30.00 annual entry fee. Wilderness Camping Permits free—reservations recommended ($20 fee).

Maps: USGS: Sunrise; Trails Illustrated Mount Rainier National Park; Astronaut's Vista: Mount Rainier National Park, Washington; Earthwalk Press Hiking Map & Guide.
Trail contacts: White River Wilderness Information Center, (360) 569-6030.
Trail conditions: www.nps.gov/mora/trail/ tr_cnd.htm; weather, www.nps.gov/mora/ current/weather.htm.

Finding the trailhead: From the White River Entrance Station (see Getting There), drive 13.8 miles west on White River Road to the Sunrise parking lot. Park and walk to the trailhead on the north end of the lot, to the right of the restrooms. *DeLorme: Washington Atlas and Gazetteer:* Page 48 A3.

The Hike

To begin this hike, go to the northwestern part of the parking lot and follow the wide trail north beyond the restrooms. After about 0.1 mile, a map and display on the right (east) delineate some of the trails in the Sunrise area, including elevation charts and short descriptions. Continue 0.1 mile north of this sign to the junction with the Sourdough Ridge Trail. Turn left (west) onto this trail. This wide, dusty path runs along Sourdough Ridge, giving you various opportunities to admire the awesome views on both sides. In 1.1 miles you descend from the ridge, only to rise again to a junction of five trails.

Follow the Wonderland Trail heading directly west. The trail goes down a hill and toward a valley for 1.1 miles. At this point the Northern Loop Trail heads right (north). Take this trail, entering the meadow below. This gap between Skyscraper Mountain to the west and Mount Fremont to the east is known as Berkeley Park. If you look behind you (south), you can see Burroughs Mountain and Mount Rainier.

Lewis and mountain monkeyflowers line the creek that meanders beside you, adorning it with pink and yellow highlights. Depending on the season, Berkeley Park boasts most varieties of subalpine flowers. Bring a guide to decode if you have the flower bug. We identified lupine, hellebore, spirea, aster, columbine, gentian,

Mount Rainier from Grand Park.

lousewort, and an abundance of pasqueflower seedhead—otherwise known as bottlebrush and most likely the inspiration for the Lorax of Dr. Seuss.

Take your time appreciating the beauty of a subalpine meadow, because you soon leave it and enter the woods. Continue to descend beyond the meadow and into a forested area. Berkeley Camp, 3.9 miles into the hike, is a possible camp for an overnight stay. The camp rests right next to the trail. If you plan to stay here, you can leave your packs before venturing to Grand Park.

Continue north on the main trail 2.2 miles to Grand Park. You can divide this trip into three sections. First, the trail climbs, then it descends, and finally it levels off for the final approach to Grand Park. The crest of the uphill affords a nice view of Mount Rainier behind you, so be sure to turn around once in a while. The trail eventually leaves the sparse subalpine forest for an expansive meadow. The signs posted at the Lake Eleanor Trail junction indicate that you have traveled 3.0 miles from Berkeley Park Camp. Our internal odometer and a mileage disc from the park confirmed otherwise. Grand Park is just over 2 miles from Berkeley. But we encourage you to go farther.

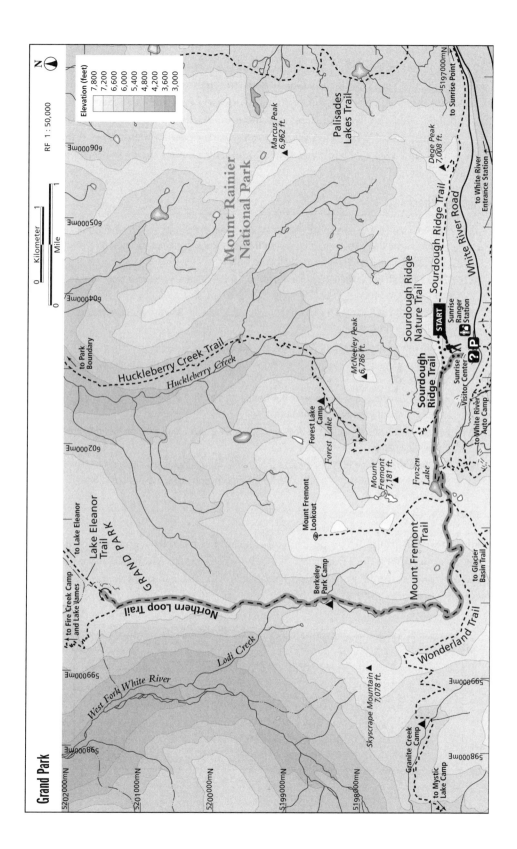

Grand Park

RF 1 : 50,000

Mount Rainier
National Park

GRAND PARK

Elevation (feet)
7,800
7,200
6,600
6,600
5,400
4,800
4,200
3,600
3,000

N

Kilometer 1

Mile 1

6060000mE
6050000mE
6040000mE
6020000mE
5990000mE
5980000mE

5202000mN
5201000mN
5200000mN
5199000mN
5198000mN
5197000mN

Marcus Peak
6,962 ft.

Palisades
Lakes Trail

Dege Peak
7,008 ft.

Sourdough Ridge Trail

Sourdough Ridge Trail

White River Road

to Sunrise Point

to White River
Entrance Station

Sunrise
Ranger Station

START

Sourdough Ridge Nature Trail

Sunrise
Visitor Center

Sourdough Ridge Trail

McNeeley Peak
6,786 ft.

to White River
Auto Camp

Huckleberry Creek Trail

to Park
Boundary

Huckleberry Creek

Forest Lake
Camp

Forest Lake

Mount Fremont
Lookout

Mount Fremont
7,181 ft.

Frozen
Lake

Mount Fremont
Trail

to Glacier
Basin Trail

Wonderland Trail

Lake Eleanor
Trail

to Lake Eleanor

to Fire Creek Camp
and Lake James

Northern Loop Trail

Lodi Creek

West Fork White River

Berkeley
Park Camp

Skyscrape Mountain
7,078 ft.

Granite Creek
Camp

to Mystic
Lake Camp

At the junction with the Lake Eleanor Trail, 6.1 miles from the trailhead, turn right (northeast). You cannot miss Grand Park, the massive plateau with numerous wildflowers directly in front of you. Aptly named, Grand Park is about 1.5 miles long and 0.5 mile wide, the flattest ground anywhere on or around Mount Rainier. It is absolutely spectacular. Walk along the Lake Eleanor Trail for a mile or so, and then turn around. Few places in Mount Rainier National Park offer such a majestic view of Mount Rainier.

Miles and Directions

0.0 Start from the Sunrise parking lot; follow the paved path to the right (east) of the restrooms heading north. Don't let the road heading off to the left (west) tempt you, stay on the main trail, heading north past the informative display.

0.1 The Sourdough Ridge Nature Trail forks; stay to the left (northwest) toward Frozen Lake and Mount Fremont.

0.3 Reach the top of Sourdough Ridge and the junction with the Sourdough Ridge Nature Trail. Take a left (west) onto the trail.

0.6 Bypass the steep Huckleberry Creek Trail on your right (north).

1.4 Just beyond Frozen Lake, come to the junction of five trails. Follow the Wonderland Trail heading west.

2.4 When the Wonderland Trail intersects the Northern Loop, stay to the right down toward the meadow along the Northern Loop.

3.9 Berkeley Camp sits in a stand of trees by clear-flowing Lodi Creek. Stay on the main trail through the camp.

6.1 You can't mistake the huge expanse of Grand Park—a signpost marks the junction with the Lake Eleanor Trail. Head back to Berkeley Camp for the night, or head back to the trailhead.

12.2 Arrive back at the trailhead.

Wilderness camping: With a permit you can camp at Berkeley Camp. Buffered by trees, Berkeley Camp does not afford the views of Skyscraper Mountain and mountain meadows featured in Berkeley Park itself, but the camp offers respectable campsites and proximity to a quality water source. If you want to travel through

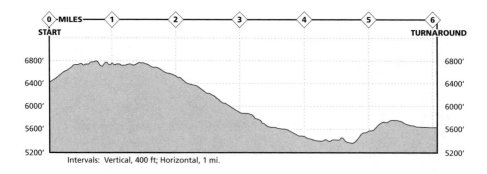

Intervals: Vertical, 400 ft; Horizontal, 1 mi.

Grand Park and camp, you may consider overnighting at Lake Eleanor. (See Hike 46: Lake Eleanor.)

Hike Information

Local Information

Sunrise Visitor Center, Sunrise (no contact information).
Mount Rainier National Park Web site, www.nps.gov/mora; visitor information, (360) 569-2211, ext. 3314.

Lodging

Paradise Inn, (360) 569-2275; National Park Inn, (360) 569-2275. For a list of accommodations outside the park, visit www.nps.gov/mora/general/accom.htm.

Campgrounds

If you plan to car camp, the nearest facility is White River Campgrounds, located 5.0 miles beyond the White River Entrance Station. You can claim one of the 112 sites on a first-come, first-served basis. You can reserve sites at other campgrounds throughout the park online at http://reservations.nps.gov, or call (800) 365-CAMP (2267) 7:00 A.M. to 7:00 P.M. PST.

43 Burroughs Mountain

Make a gentle ascent from the Sunrise Complex to the top of a long mountain with the tundralike terrain of alpine areas.

Start: Sunrise Complex.
Distance: 6.2-mile out-and-back.
Approximate hiking time: 2 to 3 hours.
Difficulty: Moderate.
Seasons: Late July through September.
Nearest town: Greenwater.
Fees and permits: $10.00 vehicle or $5.00 individual entry fee (seven days); $30.00 annual entry fee. Wilderness Camping Permits free—reservations recommended ($20 fee).

Maps: USGS: Sunrise; Trails Illustrated Mount Rainier National Park; Astronaut's Vista: Mount Rainier National Park, Washington; Earthwalk Press Hiking Map & Guide.
Trail contacts: White River Wilderness Information Center, (360) 569-6030.
Trail conditions: www.nps.gov/mora/trail/tr_cnd.htm; weather, www.nps.gov/mora/current/weather.htm.

Finding the trailhead: From the White River Entrance Station (see Getting There), drive 13.8 miles west on White River Road to the Sunrise parking lot. Park and walk to the trailhead on the north end of the lot, to the right of the restrooms. *DeLorme: Washington Atlas and Gazetteer:* Page 48 A3.

The Hike

To begin this hike, go to the northwestern part of the parking lot. Follow the wide trail north beyond the restrooms. After about 0.1 mile, a map and display on the right

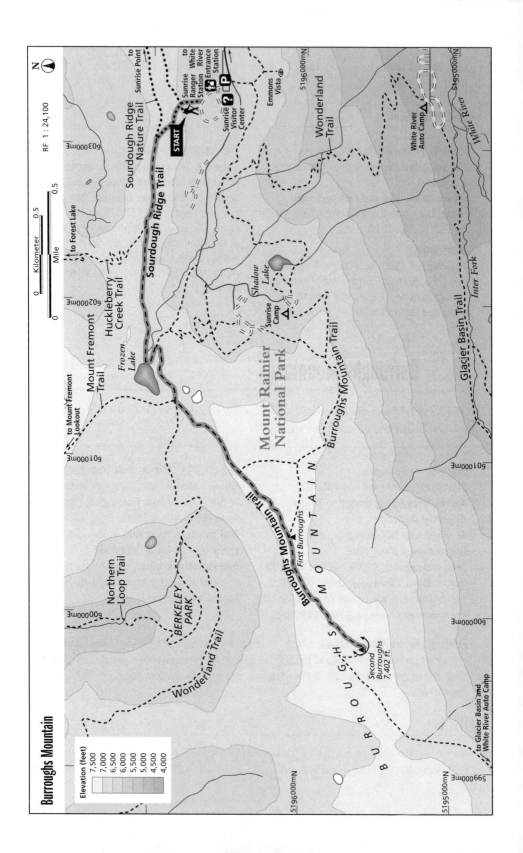

Burroughs Mountain

RF 1 : 24,100

N

Elevation (feet)
7,500
7,000
6,500
6,000
5,500
5,000
4,500
4,000

Kilometer

Mile

0   0.5

Sourdough Ridge Nature Trail

to Sunrise Point

Sourdough Ridge Trail

START

Sunrise Ranger Station

to White River Entrance Station

Sunrise Visitor Center

Emmons Vista

Wonderland Trail

White River Auto Camp

White River

to Forest Lake

Huckleberry Creek Trail

Mount Fremont Trail

to Mount Fremont Lookout

Frozen Lake

Shadow Lake

Sunrise Camp

Burroughs Mountain Trail

Mount Rainier National Park

Glacier Basin Trail

Inter Fork

Northern Loop Trail

BERKELEY PARK

Wonderland Trail

B U R R O U G H S   M O U N T A I N

First Burroughs

Burroughs Mountain Trail

Second Burroughs 7,402 ft.

to Glacier Basin and White River Auto Camp

(east) delineate some of the trails in the Sunrise area, including elevation charts and short descriptions. Continue 0.1 mile north of this sign to the Sourdough Ridge Nature Trail. Turn left (west) onto this trail. This wide, dusty path runs to and along Sourdough Ridge, giving you various opportunities to admire the awesome views of mountains and valleys on each side. In 1.1 miles you descend from the ridge, only to rise again to a junction of five trails.

Follow the signs that point toward Burroughs Mountain (southwest). The trail follows Burroughs Mountain uphill with no switchbacks. The path is steep but fairly short. As you approach the top of the mountain, the turf on both sides of the trail has fewer and fewer plants. This region has terrain and fauna similar to that found in arctic regions. Stay on the trail; although this terrain looks rough and tumble, it is very susceptible to the damage caused by human tromping.

From the five-way intersection, you ascend 1.0 mile before reaching the top of First Burroughs Mountain. As you walk southwest, you have a view of Mount Rainier throughout the first half of the hike. Take the time to identify the major glaciers and landforms in front of you: Emmons Glacier, Winthrop Glacier, Inter Glacier, and Little Tahoma Peak.

From the crest of First Burroughs Mountain, you have only 0.7 mile to the zenith of Second Burroughs Mountain. The trail drops at first and then climbs again. The top of Second Burroughs Mountain offers you much the same view as the first. When you're finished, retrace your steps to the trailhead.

Miles and Directions

0.0   Start from the Sunrise parking lot; follow the paved path to the right (east) of the restrooms heading north. Don't let the road heading off to the left (west) tempt you; stay on the main trail heading north past the informative display.

0.1   The Sourdough Ridge Nature Trail forks; stay to the left (northwest) toward Frozen Lake and Mount Fremont.

0.3   Reach the top of Sourdough Ridge and the junction with the Sourdough Ridge Nature Trail. Take a left (west) onto the trail.

0.6   Bypass the steep Huckleberry Creek Trail on your right (north).

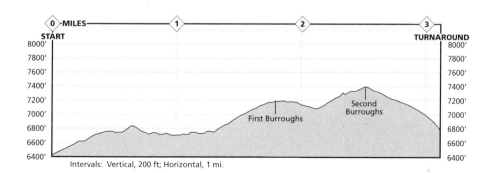

1.4 Just beyond Frozen Lake, come to the junction of five trails. Take the Burroughs Mountain Trail, heading southwest.

2.4 In just 1.0 mile, reach First Burroughs Mountain and the junction with the south part of the loop toward Shadow Lake and Sunrise Camp. Stay to the right (west) along the Burroughs Mountain Trail.

3.1 Second Burroughs Mountain attains an elevation of 7,402 feet. Take in the great view before heading back to the trailhead.

6.2 Arrive back at the trailhead.

Option: If you want to return along a different route, take the south loop to Shadow Lake and back to Sunrise. When returning east toward Sunrise, rather than heading back toward Frozen Lake at the junction atop First Burroughs Mountain, stay to the right (southeast). This trail descends steeply past Sunrise Camp to Shadow Lake. Stay to the right (east) at the junction with the Wonderland Trail, then to the left (east) toward the Emmons Vista Trail. This alternate route increases the total miles hiked by 0.5 mile. (See Hike 49: Sunrise Rim.)

Wilderness camping: If you want to camp in the backcountry, you can stay at Sunrise Camp, although its proximity to the Sunrise Complex increases the traffic and lessens the wilderness experience. There are eight sites available. None of the sites are very private, but Site 8 is the most secluded. Try to snag Sites 5 or 6, which have a great view of Shadow Lake.

Hike Information

Local Information

Sunrise Visitor Center, Sunrise (no contact information).
Mount Rainier National Park Web site, www.nps.gov/mora; visitor information, (360) 569-2211, ext. 3314.

Lodging

Paradise Inn, (360) 569-2275; National Park Inn, (360) 569-2275. For a list of accommodations outside the park, visit www.nps.gov/mora/general/accom.htm.

Campgrounds

If you plan to car camp, the nearest facility is White River Campgrounds, located 5.0 miles beyond the White River Entrance Station. You can claim one of the 112 sites on a first-come, first-served basis. You can reserve sites at other campgrounds throughout the park online at http://reservations.nps.gov, or call (800) 365-CAMP (2267) 7:00 A.M. to 7:00 P.M. PST.

44 Glacier Basin

A moderate ascent skirts the Emmons Glacier Moraine to a camp at the foot of the Inter Glacier, the icy path crossed by climbers summiting Mount Rainier from Camp Schurman.

Start: Glacier Basin trailhead
Distance: 7.0-mile out-and-back.
Approximate hiking time: 3 to 5 hours.
Difficulty: Moderate.
Seasons: Early July through September
Nearest town: Greenwater.
Fees and permits: $10.00 vehicle or $5.00 individual entry fee (seven days); $30.00 annual entry fee. Wilderness Camping Permits free—reservations recommended ($20 fee).

Maps: USGS: Sunrise; Trails Illustrated Mount Rainier National Park; Astronaut's Vista: Mount Rainier National Park, Washington; Earthwalk Press Hiking Map & Guide.
Trail contacts: White River Wilderness Information Center, (360) 569-6030.
Trail conditions: www.nps.gov/mora/trail/ tr_cnd.htm; weather, www.nps.gov/mora/ current/weather.htm.

Finding the trailhead: From the White River Entrance Station (see Getting There), drive west 3.9 miles to the White River Campground turnoff. Turn left (west) toward the campground and drive 1.2 miles to the parking area on the left. A sign indicates that the parking lot is for backpackers and climbers. Park here and walk to the Glacier Basin trailhead heading west from the middle of Loop D, one of the many loops that make up White River Campground. *DeLorme: Washington Atlas and Gazetteer:* Page 48 A3.

The Hike

Head west along the Glacier Basin Trail. Immediately after the trailhead, an informational board describes this and other hikes near White River Campground. From here continue 1.0 mile through tranquil forest to the junction with the Emmons Moraine Trail. At this junction stay to the right (west) along the main trail.

In about 0.1 mile, a small, bubbling falls crosses the path. The trail ascends gradually but steadily for 2.0 miles. Only 0.5 mile from Glacier Basin Camp, the trail gets steeper. A sign marks your entrance into the camp.

The maintained trail ends soon after the camp, but a number of way-trails continue up the mountain. Just beyond the camp to the west, you can see a small, marshy lake and the Inter River. A very steep path leads down the bank to the river below. The main trail, although unmaintained here, goes nearly to the mouth of the Inter River from the Inter Glacier. Camp Schurman, a possible base camp for the final ascent to the summit, sits beyond the Inter Glacier, beneath the protruding bow of Steamboat Prow, a triangular nautical rock wedge that seems to float atop the frozen waters of Winthrop and Emmons Glaciers.

Glacier Basin from Burroughs Mountain.

When you have finished glacier spotting, turn around and follow the same path back to the White River Campground.

Miles and Directions

0.0 Start heading west on the Glacier Basin Trail from Loop D of the White River Campground.

0.9 Stay to the right (west) on the main Glacier Basin Trail when the Emmons Moraine Trail separates toward the left (southwest). (See Option for a possible side trip along Emmons Moraine.)

3.5 Your destination, Glacier Basin Camp, is on your right. Enjoy the views, then retrace your steps.

7.0 Arrive back at the trailhead.

Option: The Emmons Moraine Trail proves a worthwhile side trip along this day hike. It ascends gradually along the Emmons Moraine, a collection of dirt and debris from glacial movement. The trail offers great views of the Emmons Glacier, and visitors may hear the crashing of falling rocks on ice. This trip adds 1.0 mile total to

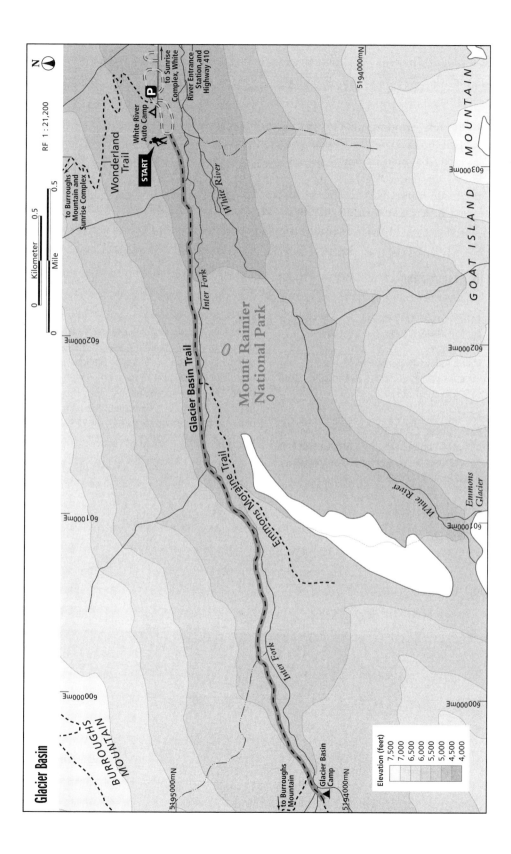

Glacier Basin

RF 1 : 21,200

N

Kilometer
0   0.5

Mile
0   0.5

to Burroughs
Mountain and
Sunrise Complex

Wonderland
Trail

White River
Auto Camp

START

P

to Sunrise
Complex, White
River Entrance
Station, and
Highway 410

Glacier Basin Trail

White River

Inter Fork

Mount Rainier
National Park

Emmons Moraine Trail

White River

Emmons Glacier

GOAT ISLAND MOUNTAIN

Inter Fork

to Burroughs
Mountain

Glacier Basin
Camp

BURROUGHS
MOUNTAIN

Elevation (feet)
7,500
7,000
6,500
6,000
5,500
5,000
4,500
4,000

5194000mN
5193000mN
5195000mN
600000mE
601000mE
602000mE
603000mE

your hike, raising the total to 8.0 miles round-trip. (See Hike 38: Emmons Moraine.)

Wilderness camping: If you want to camp in the backcountry, you can stay at Glacier Basin Camp with a permit. There are five individual and one group site from which to choose. An overnight stay would change the difficulty rating of this hike from moderate to easy.

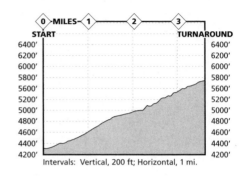

Intervals: Vertical, 200 ft; Horizontal, 1 mi.

Hike Information

Local Information

Sunrise Visitor Center, Sunrise (no contact information).
Mount Rainier National Park Web site, www.nps.gov/mora; visitor information, (360) 569-2211, ext. 3314.

Lodging

Paradise Inn, (360) 569-2275; National Park Inn, (360) 569-2275. For a list of accommodations outside the park, visit www.nps.gov/mora/general/accom.htm.

Campgrounds

If you plan to car camp, the nearest facility is White River Campgrounds, located 5.0 miles beyond the White River Entrance Station. You can claim one of the 112 sites on a first-come, first-served basis. You can reserve sites at other campgrounds throughout the park online at http://reservations.nps.gov, or call (800) 365-CAMP (2267) 7:00 A.M. to 7:00 P.M. PST.

45 Northern Loop

This wondrous loop around the roadless northern section of Mount Rainier National Park involves intense ascents and descents and offers spectacular views of mountain meadows, massive parks, numerous lakes, glaciers and glacial moraines, abundant wildlife, and of course, Mount Rainier.

Start: Sunrise Complex.
Distance: 33.3-mile loop.
Approximate hiking time: 3 to 5 days.
Difficulty: Strenuous.
Seasons: Mid-July through September.
Nearest town: Greenwater.
Fees and permits: $10.00 vehicle or $5.00 individual entry fee (seven days); $30.00 annual entry fee. Wilderness Camping Permits free—reservations strongly recommended for the Northern Loop ($20 fee).

Maps: USGS: Sunrise and Mowich Lake; Trails Illustrated Mount Rainier National Park; Astronaut's Vista: Mount Rainier National Park, Washington; Earthwalk Press Hiking Map & Guide.
Trail contacts: White River Wilderness Information Center, (360) 569-6030.
Trail conditions: www.nps.gov/mora/trail/tr_cnd.htm; weather, www.nps.gov/mora/current/weather.htm.

Finding the trailhead: From the White River Entrance Station (see Getting There), drive 13.8 miles west on White River Road to the Sunrise Complex parking lot. Park and walk to the trailhead on the north end of the lot, to the right of the restrooms. *DeLorme: Washington Atlas and Gazetteer:* Page 48 A3.

The Hike

Quite possibly our favorite backpacking trip in Mount Rainier National Park, the Northern Loop offers all anyone could want in the way of scenery. From a massive expanse of mountain meadow to an even more massive expanse of nearby glaciers, this hike traverses nearly all the climatic zones in the park. It also produced the greatest number of wildlife sightings for the authors.

To begin this hike, go to the northwestern part of the parking lot. Follow the wide trail that runs north beyond the restrooms. After about 0.1 mile, a map and display on the right (east) delineate some of the trails in the Sunrise area, including elevation charts and short descriptions. Continue 0.1 mile north of this sign to the Sourdough Ridge Nature Trail. Turn left (west) onto this trail. This wide, dusty path runs to and along Sourdough Ridge, giving you various opportunities to admire the awesome views on both sides. In 1.1 miles you descend from the ridge, only to rise again to a junction of five trails.

Follow the Wonderland Trail heading directly west. The trail goes downhill and toward a valley for 1.1 miles. At this point the Northern Loop Trail splits right (north). Take this trail, entering the meadow below. This gap between Skyscraper

Mountain to the west and Mount Fremont to the east is named Berkeley Park. Pink flowers line the creek that meanders beside you. If you look behind you (south), you can see Burroughs Mountain and Mount Rainier. Take your time appreciating the beauty of a subalpine meadow, because you soon leave it and enter the woods.

Continue to descend beyond the meadow and into a forested area. Berkeley Park Camp, 3.9 miles into the hike, is a possible camp for an overnight stay. The camp rests right next to the trail.

Continuing north on the main trail, the next 2.2 miles to Grand Park are divided into three sections. First the trail climbs, then descends, and finally levels off for the final approach to Grand Park. The crest of the uphill gives you a nice view of Mount Rainier to the rear, so be sure to turn around for a look. The trail eventually leaves the sparse subalpine forest for an expanse of meadow. At the junction with the Lake Eleanor Trail, 6.1 miles from the trailhead, Grand Park is to the right (northeast). You cannot miss the massive plateau with numerous wildflowers directly in front of you.

If you do not plan to stay at Lake Eleanor (see Options), turn left (northwest) following the sign to Fire Creek Camp. The trail quickly takes a downhill turn with switchbacks into forest for 1.3 miles. At this point the trail forks. To the right (north) Fire Creek Camp is only 0.4 mile off the main trail. To the left (west) more than 2 miles of descending switchbacks lead to the West Fork of the White River. You may need to ford this river. Fed by the Winthrop Glacier, the West Fork of the White River is riddled with silt and debris. Do not count on this water as a good source from which to filter drinking water. Clearer streams can be found up the trail just on the other side of the river. In fact, just after crossing the West Fork and before turning the first switchback of your ascent to Lake James, you hear pounding waters on the north side of the trail. Though difficult to see from the main trail, Van Horn Falls throws clear mountain water into a nice stream. Felled logs over a potential path would dissuade travelers from walking near and further eroding the streambed, but if you are in a pinch and need a water source, know that the stream is there.

From the river valley, the trail once again starts up a steep incline. Many switchbacks through dense forest lead to several false summits, deceptive clearings you may believe to be Lake James. Nearly 5 miles from Fire Creek Camp, the stirring of fellow campers may indicate that you have come upon Lake James Camp. Due to severe erosion and overuse, the park has moved this regional camp several times. Once moved 0.5 mile up the trail near the Redstone Ranger Cabin, the Lake James Camp has resumed its position near the lake; the sites sit above the lake, distanced from its fragile shores to prevent further damage. From the camp you cross small, clear streams (both good for filtering water) and reach the trail to Lake James, the once popular fishing and recreational lake. If you would like to fish Lake James, turn right (north). The lake appears soon after leaving the main trail.

◀ *Little Tahoma above the Wonderland Trail.*

If you plan to move on toward Windy Gap and Yellowstone Cliffs, stay to the left (south). Another 0.6-mile climb and you reach the trail to the Redstone Ranger Cabin. Follow this trail 0.25 mile to the Redstone Ranger Cabin to learn more of the history of Lake James. Bulletins outside the cabin offer historical accounts, and the location offers a look at Redstone Peak.

Continuing along the Northern Loop from the Redstone area, less than a mile of uphill switchbacks through a forest and a pika-filled rockfield open up to a clearing known as Windy Gap. The trail crosses Van Horn Creek and threads through Windy Gap. Surrounded by Independence Ridge, Crescent Mountain, and Sluiskin Mountain, Windy Gap is a haven. Apparently cougars think so, too—we saw many cat prints in this area.

From the western part of Windy Gap, a possible side trip beckons to Independence Ridge and a natural land bridge. (See Options.) From here the trail runs flat and straight. It passes a small lake, a decent source of water, 0.1 mile beyond the Independence Ridge Trail. Another spur trail leaves the main trail 0.2 mile beyond the junction with the Independence Ridge Trail. This trail, destination Tyee Peak and the Yellowstone Cliffs, is unmaintained, so tread carefully if you choose to hike it.

From this spur the trail begins to head downhill. Less than 1.5 miles from the western end of Windy Gap you reach the junction to Yellowstone Cliffs Camp. Towering above you and a meadow of flowers are the Yellowstone Cliffs, an impressive striated rock formation. The trail to Yellowstone Cliffs Camp, a very scenic place to stay, heads southeast for 0.2 mile. If you do not plan to stay here, keep to the right (west).

For nearly 3 miles the trail heads dramatically downhill. Your feet will hurt and your knees will ache by the time you reach the junction with the trail to Ipsut Creek Campground. Stay to the left (south). You will find the next mile of flatness a relief. Three cool streams provide excellent water before you once again begin to ascend steeply.

About 1 mile beyond the trail to Ipsut Creek Campground, the trail joins the Wonderland Trail. To the right (west), a suspension bridge crosses the Carbon River. The Northern Loop Trail continues to the left (south). Less than 0.5 mile from the bridge, the trail provides a close-up view of the Carbon Glacier, a massive glacial formation blackened by rocks and debris. Mount Rainier rises imposingly above the glacier. The trail grows steeper and remains steep for the next 0.7 mile to Dick Creek Camp.

If the clanking of rocks falling from the glacier's face deters you from staying at Dick Creek Camp, bypass the camp, continuing south. The next 2.0 miles of ascent switchbacks through a forest. The grade lessens when the path begins to run along Moraine Creek. Keep in mind that this is bear country. In fact, a fellow hiker told us that she has never come here without seeing a bear. When we were here, we saw a small black bear that was not easily deterred by loud voices, banging pots, and shrill singing.

Beyond the streambed, the trail passes a rockfield, then a large mountain meadow. At this point you have only two small hills to climb before beginning your descent to

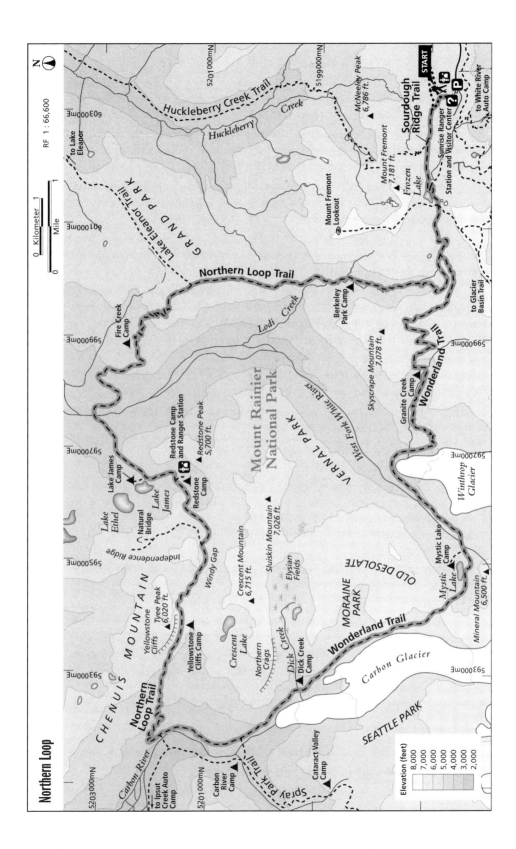

Northern Loop

RF 1 : 66,600

Mystic Lake, nearly 24 miles from the hike's beginning. The lake rests in a valley between Mineral Mountain and the appropriately named Old Desolate. The view is beautiful, but it cannot be seen from Mystic Lake Camp, 0.2 mile down the trail.

The next established camp, Granite Creek Camp, is only 4.0 miles beyond Mystic Lake Camp, but you must circumvent the Winthrop Glacier to get there. After leaving the cozy, subalpine forest near Mystic Lake, an easy 1.0-mile descent skirts the Winthrop Glacier, leading to Winthrop Creek. Cross the prepared log to the other side.

You now begin to climb your final big hill. Hike 2.0 miles uphill, with a few sporadic switchbacks, to Granite Creek Camp. These 2.0 miles run along the Winthrop Moraine, providing an excellent glimpse of the glacier, before turning west toward forest. More than 28 miles from the trailhead, Granite Creek Camp is your last camping option. If you plan to pass the camp to finish the loop and go out for a big meal, stay on the Wonderland Trail heading east through camp.

Less than 2 miles of nicely graded, long switchbacks lead to the highest point along the entire loop, a peak just below Skyscraper Mountain. From this peak you have great views in all directions, and you know that the worst is over. You can see the trail on which you started, and Sunrise seems deceptively close. More than 30 miles into your hike, you come to a familiar place, where the Wonderland Trail intersects the Northern Loop in the Sunrise area. Stay on the Wonderland Trail toward Sunrise. In almost a mile, you reach the junction of five trails near Frozen Lake. You may feel that you're home, but the last 1.4 miles to Sunrise along the Sourdough Ridge seem to go on forever. What a great trip!

Miles and Directions

0.0 Start from the Sunrise parking lot; follow the paved path to the right (east) of the restrooms heading north. Don't let the road heading off to the left (west) tempt you, stay on the main trail heading north past the informative display.

0.1 The Sourdough Ridge Nature Trail forks; stay to the left (northwest) toward Frozen Lake and Mount Fremont.

0.3 Reach the top of Sourdough Ridge and the junction with the Sourdough Ridge Nature Trail. Take a left (west) onto the trail.

0.6 Bypass the steep Huckleberry Creek Trail on your right (north).

1.4 Just beyond Frozen Lake, come to the junction of five trails. Follow the Wonderland Trail, heading west.

2.4 When the Wonderland Trail intersects the Northern Loop, stay to the right, down toward the meadow along the Northern Loop.

▶ Sluiskin Mountain is named in honor of Sluiskin, the Native American guide who in 1870 guided Hazard Stevens and P. B. Van Trump on the first recorded summit of Mount Rainier. Due to the extreme reverence that Native Americans held for the mountain, Sluiskin did not summit with them but led them only to the now aptly named Sluiskin Falls.

3.9 Berkeley Park Camp sits in a stand of trees by the clear-flowing Lodi Creek. Stay on the main trail through the camp.

6.1 You can't mistake the huge expanse of Grand Park; a signpost marks the junction with the Lake Eleanor Trail. Unless you choose the Lake Eleanor side trip (see Options), stay to the left (northwest) along the Northern Loop.

7.4 The spur trail to Fire Creek Camp heads off to the right (north). If you're not camping here, stay on the main trail. There's not much to look at for the extra 0.8 mile of round-trip hike to the camp, but the camp does provide a good water source.

12.0 After a series of false summits, come to a sign that points you to Lake James Camp on your right (north). Continue along the Northern Loop if not staying at Lake James.

12.1 A sign points the way to Lake James, a beautiful mountain lake highly eroded by over-use. If not visiting the lake, stay along the main trail.

12.7 The trail to a Ranger Cabin intersects from your left. Again, stay to the right (west) on the Northern Loop.

13.4 Leave the trees and enter the meadow known as Windy Gap.

14.1 Independence Ridge Trail, a possible side trip along the loop, separates off toward the right (north) and to a natural bridge.

15.5 Yellowstone Cliffs Camp Trail emerges on your left (south), with the cliffs themselves stationed proudly to your right (north).

18.3 When you hear the rushing waters of Carbon River, you soon come to a trail that heads off to the right (southwest) toward the Wonderland Trail and Ipsut Creek Campground. Stay to the left (southeast) along the Northern Loop.

19.4 Come to an intersection of another trail that crosses the Carbon River. This time it is the Wonderland Trail junction, and it crosses Carbon River by way of a suspension bridge on your right (west). You may want to take a look, but return to the Northern Loop–Wonderland Trail toward Dick Creek Camp and Mystic Lake.

19.7 Just beyond the suspension bridge, the Carbon Glacier comes into view.

20.4 Dick Creek Camp, overlooking Carbon Glacier, is a great place to stay. If you don't have a site, bypass the camp on the main trail.

24.0 Beyond Moraine Park, come over a rise to see Mystic Lake. You may consider taking the side trip to Mystic Lake Ranger Station. If you follow the signs, in just 0.2 mile you can observe one of the best views of Mount Rainier—right from the porch! Continuing on the main trail, at 24.0 miles you come to the far end of the lake and begin to descend.

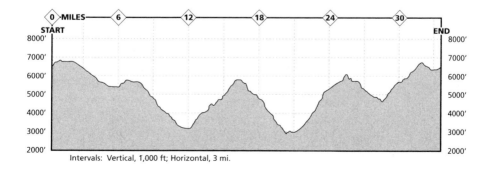

Intervals: Vertical, 1,000 ft; Horizontal, 3 mi.

24.2 Mystic Lake Camp trail turns left off the main trail, direction northeast.

25.6 Begin to skirt the Winthrop Glacier.

28.3 Reach your last camping option, Granite Creek Camp. If not staying here, continue on the Wonderland Trail through the camp.

30.9 The junction with the Northern Loop Trail should look familiar. You have come full circle. Stay along the Wonderland Trail toward Sunrise.

31.9 At the five trail junction, follow the signs for Sunrise Ridge.

33.3 Welcome back to the Sunrise Complex. What a trip!

Options: The Lake Eleanor Trail makes a nice addition to the Northern Loop Trail. At the intersection with the Lake Eleanor Trail, turn right (northeast). The trail leads through Grand Park and descends to the lake. This option adds 6.6 miles to the total hiking distance—and most likely another night's stay at Lake Eleanor Camp. (See Hike 46: Lake Eleanor.)

If you have the time and energy, take the side trip along Independence Ridge to the natural bridge in the Windy Gap area. Do not continue on the unmaintained trail beyond the spur trail to the natural bridge, but do descend to the natural bridge. The arching rocks are a wonder of nature. This side trip adds 1.8 miles to your hike.

Wilderness camping: There are several options for backcountry camps.

Berkeley Camp has four sites, the first three clustered at the southern end of camp. To find Site 4, walk farther north along the trail; a sign will point you there. Sites 3 and 4 are best for privacy, although Site 4 is farther from water and the toilet.

If you take the option to Lake Eleanor, the camp rests 3.0 miles northeast of Grand Park and has three individual sites. The camp was built on a very pretty lake that has reasonably good fishing. The tent sites leave something to be desired and the path back to Grand Park is rather steep, but the location is nice.

Fire Creek Camp, 1.6 miles beyond the Lake Eleanor Trail junction, has four mediocre sites with surprisingly good cooking areas.

The reopened Lake James Camp perches above Lake James, 0.1 mile northeast of the lake access trail, to avoid the erosion problems of years past. You can find water on the main trail from a stream that flows under a footbridge between the camps and the lake. The group site provides a view over the canyon below, and you can hear the harsh cracks of tumbling rocks thrusted down the West Fork of the White River. If you plan to check out the lake, please tread lightly. It is still in the fragile stages of recovery.

Yellowstone Cliffs Camp has a fantastic view of, what else, the Yellowstone Cliffs. It also has two nice campsites, Site 1 having the best view, and proximity to water.

Dick Creek Camp, one of our favorite backcountry camps, has two nice sites as well. Site 1 sits atop a precipice with an unbelievable view of the Carbon Glacier. Dick Creek, its water source, is also only a short walk away.

Mystic Lake Camp is unfortunately situated quite a distance from the lake. An established camp along the Wonderland Trail, this camp has a whopping five individual sites and two group sites, all with good tent sites but little privacy.

The two individual campsites and one group site at Granite Creek have no view, but quite a bit of privacy. Granite Creek makes a nice water source.

Hike Information

Local Information

Sunrise Visitor Center, Sunrise (no contact information).
Mount Rainier National Park Web site, www.nps.gov/mora; visitor information, (360) 569–2211, ext. 3314.

Lodging

Paradise Inn, (360) 569–2275; National Park Inn, (360) 569–2275. For a list of accommodations outside the park, visit www.nps.gov/mora/general/accom.htm.

Campgrounds

If you plan to car camp, the nearest facility is White River Campgrounds, located 5.0 miles beyond the White River Entrance Station. You can claim one of the 112 sites on a first-come, first-served basis. You can reserve sites at other campgrounds throughout the park online at http://reservations.nps.gov, or call (800) 365–CAMP (2267) 7:00 A.M. to 7:00 P.M. PST.

46 Lake Eleanor

A mild descent takes you to a lovely mountain meadow brimming with wildflowers and clear streams. Then enjoy a relatively flat hike through an expanse before a downhill to a forest lake.

Start: Sunrise Complex.
Distance: 18.8-mile out-and-back.
Approximate hiking time: 1 to 3 days.
Difficulty: Strenuous day hike; moderate overnighter.
Seasons: Mid-July through September.
Nearest town: Greenwater.
Fees and permits: $10.00 vehicle or $5.00 individual entry fee (seven days); $30.00 annual entry fee. Wilderness Camping Permits free—reservations recommended ($20 fee).

Maps: USGS: Sunrise; Trails Illustrated Mount Rainier National Park; Astronaut's Vista: Mount Rainier National Park, Washington; Earthwalk Press Hiking Map & Guide.
Trail contacts: White River Wilderness Information Center, (360) 569–6030.
Trail conditions: www.nps.gov/mora/trail/tr_cnd.htm; weather, www.nps.gov/mora/current/weather.htm.

Finding the trailhead: From the White River Entrance Station (see Getting There), drive 13.8 miles west on White River Road to the Sunrise Complex parking lot. Park and walk to the trailhead on the north end of the lot, to the right of the restrooms. *DeLorme: Washington Atlas and Gazetteer:* Page 48 A3.

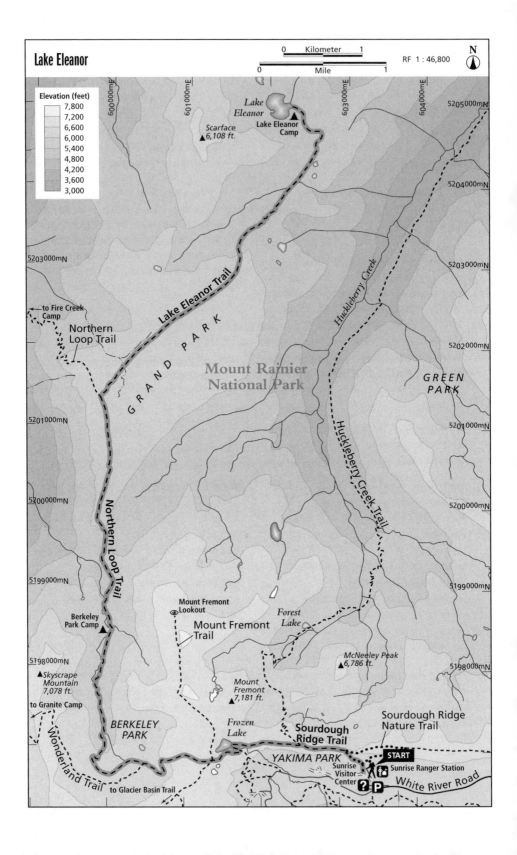

Lake Eleanor

Elevation (feet)
7,800
7,200
6,600
6,000
5,400
4,800
4,200
3,600
3,000

0   Kilometer   1
0   Mile   1

RF 1 : 46,800

N

Lake Eleanor

Scarface ▲ 6,108 ft.

Lake Eleanor Camp ▲

Lake Eleanor Trail

Huckleberry Creek

to Fire Creek Camp

Northern Loop Trail

G R A N D   P A R K

Mount Rainier National Park

GREEN PARK

Huckleberry Creek Trail

Northern Loop Trail

Berkeley Park Camp ▲

Mount Fremont Lookout

Mount Fremont Trail

Forest Lake

McNeeley Peak ▲ 6,786 ft.

▲ *Skyscrape Mountain 7,078 ft.*

to Granite Camp

BERKELEY PARK

Mount Fremont ▲ 7,181 ft.

Frozen Lake

Sourdough Ridge Trail

Sourdough Ridge Nature Trail

Wonderland Trail

to Glacier Basin Trail

YAKIMA PARK

Sunrise Visitor Center

START

Sunrise Ranger Station

White River Road

The Hike

To begin this hike, go to the northwestern part of the parking lot. Follow the wide trail that runs north beyond the restrooms. After about 0.1 mile, a map and display on the right (east) delineate some of the trails in the Sunrise area, with elevation charts and short descriptions. Continue 0.1 mile north of this sign to the Sourdough Ridge Trail. Turn left (west) onto this trail. This wide, dusty path runs to and along Sourdough Ridge, giving you various opportunities to admire the awesome views on both sides. Just over a mile into the hike, you descend from the ridge, only to rise again to a junction of five trails.

Follow the Wonderland Trail, heading directly west. The trail goes downhill and toward a valley for another mile. At this point the Northern Loop Trail splits right (north). Take this trail, entering the meadow below. This gap between Skyscraper Mountain to the west and Mount Fremont to the east is named Berkeley Park. Pink flowers line the creek that meanders beside you. If you look behind you (south), you can see Burroughs Mountain and Mount Rainier. Take your time appreciating the beauty of a subalpine meadow, because you soon leave it and enter the woods.

Continue to descend beyond the meadow and into a forested area. You reach Berkeley Park Camp 3.9 miles into the hike. Unless you plan to make this hike a multiple-nighter, bypass the camp, heading north toward Lake Eleanor.

Continue north on the main trail 3.0 miles to the Lake Eleanor Trail. The 3.0 miles is divided into three sections—first ascending, then descending, and finally leveling off for the final approach to Grand Park. The crest of the uphill gives you a nice view of Mount Rainier to the rear, so be sure to turn around at least once. The trail leaves the sparse subalpine forest and enters an expanse of meadow. At the junction with the Lake Eleanor Trail, 6.1 miles from the trailhead, Grand Park is to the right (northeast); you cannot miss the massive plateau with numerous wildflowers.

Aptly named, Grand Park is about 1.5 miles long and 0.5 mile wide, the largest area of flat ground on or around Mount Rainier. It is absolutely spectacular. Walk along the Lake Eleanor Trail about 1 mile, then turn around. Few places in Mount Rainier National Park offer such a majestic view of Mount Rainier, with a foreground of ridges extending their limbs into the surrounding parks and river valleys.

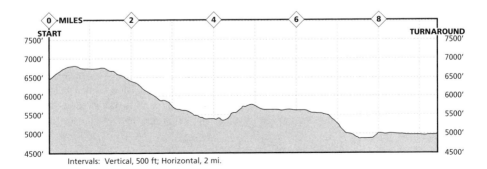

Intervals: Vertical, 500 ft; Horizontal, 2 mi.

The trail runs through Grand Park and descends steeply through woods. A little over 3 miles from the Lake Eleanor Trail junction, you reach the lake. Set up camp and fish to your heart's content (there are few restrictions on fishing in Mount Rainier National Park). This medium-size lake is greenish; dense forest surrounds it, preventing remarkable views. However, from some spots along an unmaintained trail encircling the lake you can catch a glimpse of Scarface (a rock formation) on the southwestern side of the lake. When you are ready to return to civilization, retrace your tracks to the Sunrise Complex.

Miles and Directions

0.0 Start from the Sunrise parking lot, follow the paved path to the right (east) of the restrooms, heading north. Don't let the road heading off to the left (west) tempt you; stay on the main trail heading north past the informative display.

0.1 The Sourdough Ridge Nature Trail forks; stay to the left (northwest) toward Frozen Lake and Mount Fremont.

0.3 Reach the top of Sourdough Ridge and the junction with the Sourdough Ridge Nature Trail. Take a left (west) onto the trail.

0.6 Bypass the steep Huckleberry Creek Trail on your right (north).

1.4 Just beyond Frozen Lake, come to the junction of five trails. Follow the Wonderland Trail, heading west.

2.4 When the Wonderland Trail intersects the Northern Loop, stay to the right, down toward the meadow along the Northern Loop.

3.9 Berkeley Park Camp sits in a stand of trees by the clear-flowing Lodi Creek. Stay on the main trail through the camp.

6.1 You can't mistake the huge expanse of Grand Park; a signpost marks the junction with the Lake Eleanor Trail. Take a right (northeast) as indicated.

9.4 Arrive at Lake Eleanor, nestled amid trees. Return the way you came.

18.8 Arrive back at the trailhead.

Wilderness camping: Lake Eleanor Camp has three mediocre individual sites and one nice group site. Of the three individual sites, Site 2 has the nicest view. You can also stay at Berkeley Park Camp, just beyond the flower-filled meadow of the same name.

Hike Information

Local Information

Sunrise Visitor Center, Sunrise (no contact information).
Mount Rainier National Park Web site, www.nps.gov/mora; visitor information, (360) 569-2211, ext. 3314.

Lodging

Paradise Inn, (360) 569-2275; National Park Inn, (360) 569-2275. For a list of accommodations outside the park, visit www.nps.gov/mora/general/accom.htm.

Campgrounds

If you plan to car camp, the nearest facility is White River Campgrounds, located 5.0 miles beyond the White River Entrance Station. You can claim one of the 112 sites on a first-come, first-served basis. You can reserve sites at other campgrounds throughout the park online at http://reservations.nps.gov, or call (800) 365-CAMP (2267) 7:00 A.M. to 7:00 P.M. PST.

47 Summerland

This is a moderate five-hour day hike to one of the most spectacular subalpine and alpine regions within the park.

Start: Fryingpan Creek trailhead.
Distance: 8.4-mile out-and-back.
Approximate hiking time: 4 to 6 hours.
Difficulty: Moderate.
Seasons: Mid-July through September.
Nearest town: Greenwater.
Fees and permits: $10.00 vehicle or $5.00 individual entry fee (seven days); $30.00 annual entry fee. Wilderness Camping Permits free—reservations recommended ($20 fee).

Maps: USGS: White River Park and Mt. Rainier East; Trails Illustrated Mount Rainier National Park; Astronaut's Vista: Mount Rainier National Park, Washington; Earthwalk Press Hiking Map & Guide.
Trail contacts: White River Wilderness Information Center, (360) 569-6030.
Trail conditions: www.nps.gov/mora/trail/tr_cnd.htm; weather, www.nps.gov/mora/current/weather.htm.

Finding the trailhead: From the White River Entrance Station (see Getting There), drive 2.8 miles west on White River Road. Adequate parking becomes visible just after you cross Fryingpan Creek. The Fryingpan Creek Trail, part of the Wonderland Trail that loops the entire mountain, is well marked on the left (south) side of the road. *DeLorme: Washington Atlas and Gazetteer:* Page 48 A4.

The Hike

Heading south from Fryingpan trailhead, the trail climbs gradually to moderately through woods. The path heads straight, with only a gradual incline for the first 1.5

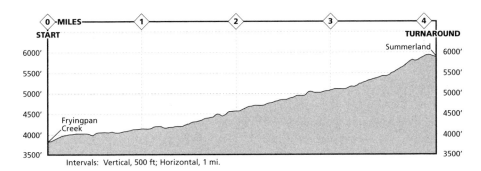

Summerland.

miles. The trail then steepens and starts to switchback. The southernmost end of two long switchbacks provides a good look at Fryingpan Creek below. The grade remains moderately steep for another mile, at which point you cross Fryingpan Creek.

Just beyond the creek, a gap in the forest allows a good glimpse of Mount Rainier. The trail then gets steeper. When the trail turns south, there is only 1.0 mile of switchbacks to go until you reach Summerland, 4.2 miles from the trailhead.

Summerland sits just below timberline, and we strongly recommend exploring farther along the trail into alpine regions. Less than 0.5 mile beyond Summerland, the abundant flora of subapline meadows retreat to reveal rocky terrain covered with snowfields.

If you do not plan to stay at Summerland Camp, return to the trailhead. Otherwise, see the section below for a description of the camp.

Wilderness camping: Summerland Camp has five individual campsites and one group site. Although they are farther from the toilet than the other sites (except Site 5, which has no view), we recommend camping at either Site 3 or 4. These sites have the better views. The water source for all sites is a stream that runs south along the main trail.

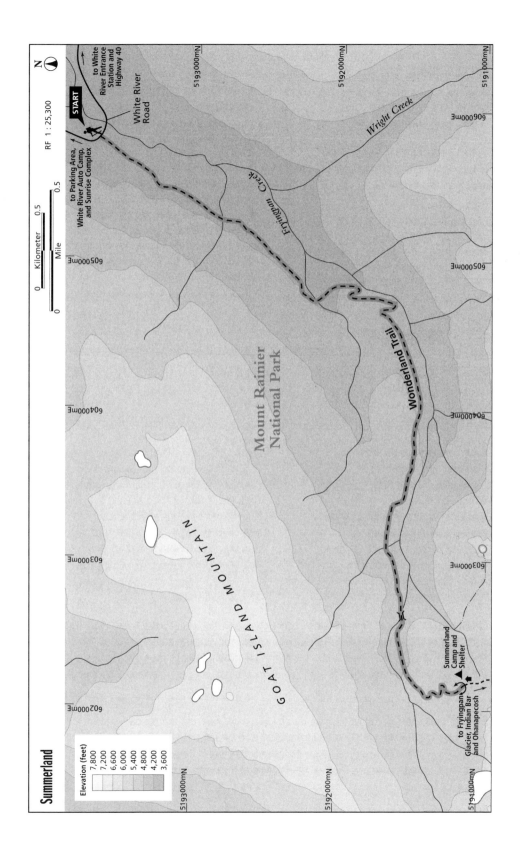

Summerland

Elevation (feet)
7,800
7,200
6,600
6,000
5,400
4,800
4,200
3,600

RF 1 : 25,300

N

0   Kilometer   0.5   0.5

0   Mile   0.5

START

to White
River Entrance
Station and
Highway 40

White River
Road

to Parking Area,
White River Auto Camp,
and Sunrise Complex

Wright Creek

Fryingpan Creek

Mount Rainier
National Park

GOAT ISLAND MOUNTAIN

Wonderland Trail

Summerland
Camp and
Shelter

to Fryingpan
Glacier, Indian Bar
and Ohanapecosh

5193000mN

5192000mN

5191000mN

602000mE

603000mE

604000mE

605000mE

606000mE

Hike Information

Local Information

Sunrise Visitor Center, Sunrise (no contact information).
Mount Rainier National Park Web site, www.nps.gov/mora; visitor information, (360) 569-2211, ext. 3314.

Lodging

Paradise Inn, (360) 569-2275; National Park Inn, (360) 569-2275. For a list of accommodations outside the park, visit www.nps.gov/mora/general/accom.htm.

Campgrounds

If you plan to car camp, the nearest facility is White River Campgrounds, located 5.0 miles beyond the White River Entrance Station. The turnoff intersects the road to Sunrise just 1.0 mile beyond the Fryingpan Creek trailhead. You can claim one of the 112 sites on a first-come, first-served basis. You can reserve sites at other campgrounds throughout the park online at http://reservations.nps.gov, or call (800) 365-CAMP (2267) 7:00 A.M. to 7:00 P.M. PST.

48 Indian Bar

Trumpeted as one of the most spectacular hikes in Mount Rainier National Park, the trail from White River to Ohanapecosh does not disappoint. It's an amazing overnight trip.

Start: Fryingpan Creek trailhead.
Distance: 17.7-mile shuttle.
Approximate hiking time: 2 days.
Difficulty: Strenuous.
Seasons: Mid-July through September.
Nearest town: Greenwater.
Fees and permits: $10.00 vehicle or $5.00 individual entry fee (seven days); $30.00 annual entry fee. Wilderness Camping Permits free—reservations recommended ($20 fee).

Maps: USGS: White River Park, Mount Rainier East, and Ohanapecosh Hot Springs; Trails Illustrated Mount Rainier National Park; Astronaut's Vista: Mount Rainier National Park, Washington; Earthwalk Press Hiking Map & Guide.
Trail contacts: White River Wilderness Information Center, (360) 569-6030.
Trail conditions: www.nps.gov/mora/trail/tr_cnd.htm; weather, www.nps.gov/mora/current/weather.htm.

Finding the trailhead: From the White River Entrance Station (see Getting There), drive 2.8 miles west on White River Road. Adequate parking becomes visible just after you cross Fryingpan Creek. The Fryingpan Creek Trail, part of the Wonderland Trail that loops the entire mountain, is well marked on the left (south) side of the road. *DeLorme: Washington Atlas and Gazetteer:* Page 48 A4.

Special considerations: As this hike requires a shuttle, you must first park a vehicle at the trail's end. From the Stevens Canyon Entrance Station (see Getting There), drive 0.8 mile south on Highway 123. A pullout on the right (west) side of the road is the trail's end. Check the nearby trail signs to make sure that you have parked at the Laughingwater trailhead.

Indian Bar.

To begin the hike, drive the second vehicle north on Highway 123 to the junction with Highway 410. Continue north on Highway 410 about 2 miles, and turn left (west) onto White River Road. From the White River Station Entrance, continue 2.8 miles west on White River Road. Adequate parking becomes visible just after you cross Fryingpan Creek. The trailhead is well marked on the left (south) side of the road.

The Hike

Heading south from Fryingpan trailhead, the trail climbs gradually to moderately through woods. A few switchbacks indicate that you are nearing the Fryingpan Creek crossing, about 2 miles into the hike. Just beyond the creek, a gap in the forest allows a good glimpse of Mount Rainier. The trail then gets steeper. When the trail turns south, you have only 1.0 mile of switchbacks to go until you reach Summerland, 4.2 miles into the hike. From the Summerland area, standing in fields of wildflowers, you have a fantastic view of Mount Rainier and the alpine land leading up to it.

After crossing the creek that provides water for the Summerland campers, the trail leaves fields of subalpine flowers and crosses rockfields as it enters alpine terrain.

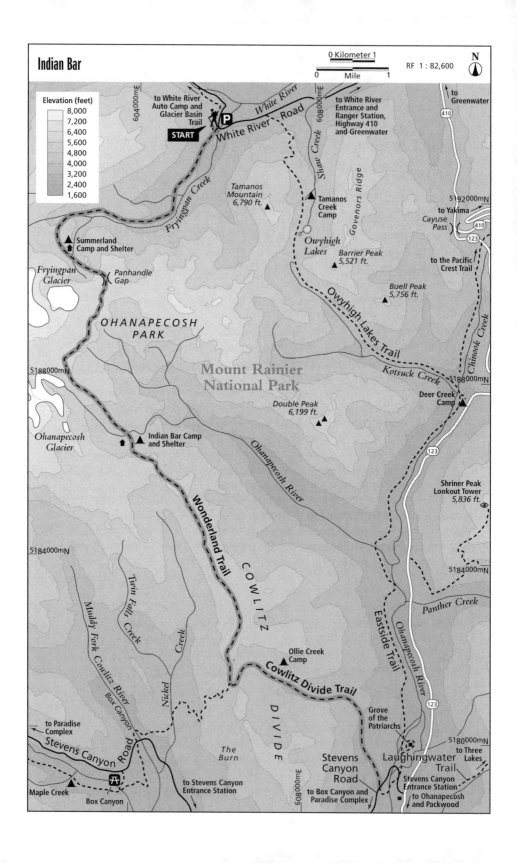

Indian Bar

0 Kilometer 1
0 Mile 1
RF 1 : 82,600

N

Elevation (feet)
8,000
7,200
6,400
5,600
4,800
4,000
3,200
2,400
1,600

to White River
Auto Camp and
Glacier Basin
Trail

P

START

White River Road

White River

604000mE

608000mE

Shaw Creek

to White River
Entrance and
Ranger Station,
Highway 410
and Greenwater

to
Greenwater

410

Fryingpan Creek

Tamanos
Mountain
6,790 ft.

Tamanos
Creek
Camp

Govenors Ridge

5192000mN

to Yakima
Cayuse
Pass

410

123

Owyhigh
Lakes

Barrier Peak
5,521 ft.

to the Pacific
Crest Trail

Summerland
Camp and Shelter

Buell Peak
5,756 ft.

Chinook Creek

Fryingpan
Glacier

Panhandle
Gap

OHANAPECOSH
PARK

Owyhigh Lakes Trail

Kotsuck Creek

5188000mN

Mount Rainier
National Park

Double Peak
6,199 ft.

Deer Creek
Camp

5188000mN

Ohanapecosh
Glacier

Indian Bar Camp
and Shelter

Ohanapecosh River

123

Shriner Peak
Lookout Tower
5,836 ft.

5184000mN

Wonderland Trail

C O W L I T Z

5184000mN

Panther Creek

Twin Falls Creek

Nickel Creek

Muddy Fork Cowlitz River

Ollie Creek
Camp

Eastside Trail

Ohanapecosh River

Box Canyon

Cowlitz Divide Trail

D I V I D E

Grove
of the
Patriarchs

123

to Paradise
Complex

Stevens Canyon Road

The
Burn

608000mE

Stevens
Canyon
Road

Laughingwater
Trail

5180000mN

to Three
Lakes

Maple Creek

Box Canyon

to Stevens Canyon
Entrance Station

Stevens Canyon
Entrance Station

to Box Canyon and
Paradise Complex

to Ohanapecosh
and Packwood

The mountain looms over you as you pass an iceberg lake and Panhandle Gap, a saddle between two rocky rises. At this point you have reached the zenith of the hike.

In this area snow is a constant. Prepare to cross several steep and slippery snowfields, even in the heat of late summer. As you begin to descend along a ridge flanked by cliffs and falls on one side and a flowered valley on the other, you have only 1.5 miles to go to reach Indian Bar. Numerous switchbacks snake down to a mountain meadow covered with lupine and magenta paintbrush. You can see the Indian Bar Shelter across the meadow. If you are group camping here, you can set up camp in the Indian Bar Shelter. If you plan to stay at one of the nongroup sites, follow the sign that points left (east). Otherwise, continue south along the main trail.

From Indian Bar, the trail heads uphill steadily. Be sure to turn around to enjoy another great view of Mount Rainier. The top of a nearby knoll makes for a great picture spot if the weather is nice. The descent from the top leads to a wooded ridge. Mount Rainier disappears. Follow this ridge 3.0 miles to a fork in the trail.

At the fork, head left (southeast) toward Olallie Creek Camp and Ohanapecosh. After descending abruptly for 1.3 miles, you cross Olallie Creek. Immediately after the crossing, a trail spurs to the left (north). If you plan to stay at Olallie Creek Camp, take this spur trail to the sites.

The main trail keeps descending steeply until highway noises indicate that you are approaching Stevens Canyon Road, 17.1 miles from the trailhead. Cross the road and look for the trail a bit to the right (west). You reach the intersection with the Eastside Trail shortly after crossing the road. Rather than turning sharply left (north) onto the Eastside Trail, continue south toward Silver Falls.

Stay on the Silver Falls Trail and cross the Ohanapecosh River to traveling east. Enjoy Silver Falls, then continue east about 0.1 mile. A sign points the way to the Laughingwater Trail; your car should be parked up the slope to your left.

Miles and Directions

0.0 Start heading south from the Fryingpan Creek trailhead.

4.2 The trail to Summerland Camp and Shelter appears on your left (east). If you do not plan to stay in Summerland, continue south on the Wonderland Trail toward Indian Bar.

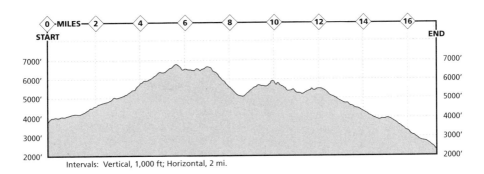

Intervals: Vertical, 1,000 ft; Horizontal, 2 mi.

8.2 You can see Indian Bar Shelter across the meadow to the right (west) of the trail. The spur trail to Indian Bar Camp goes left (east).

12.8 At the Cowlitz Divide Trail junction, take a left (east) onto the Cowlitz Divide Trail, leaving behind the Wonderland Trail.

14.1 A sign to the Olallie Creek Camp points left (north), if you plan to camp there. Otherwise, stay on the Cowlitz Divide Trail toward Stevens Canyon Road.

17.1 At Stevens Canyon Road, continue across the street toward Ohanapecosh and Silver Falls.

17.3 At the junction with the Eastside Trail, continue south to Silver Falls rather than taking a sharp left (north) onto the Eastside Trail.

17.5 Silver Falls comes up on your left if you follow the signs there.

17.6 At the Laughingwater Trail junction, just beyond the falls, take a left toward Highway 123 and your car.

Wilderness camping: Summerland Camp has five individual campsites and one group site. Although they are farther from the toilet than the other sites (except Site 5, which has no view), we recommend camping at either Site 3 or 4. Both have the best views. The water source for all sites is a stream that runs south along the main trail.

Indian Bar, nestled at the end of a meadow teaming with wildflowers and abutting an awesome glacial valley, has three private individual sites and one group site with bunks within the shelter.

If these two camps are full, you may want to reserve a site at Olallie Creek Camp. This camp has less spectacular views and sits just over 3.0 miles from the end of the hike.

Hike Information

Local Information
Sunrise Visitor Center, Sunrise (no contact information).
Mount Rainier National Park Web site, www.nps.gov/mora; visitor information, (360) 569-2211, ext. 3314.

Lodging
Paradise Inn, (360) 569-2275; National Park Inn, (360) 569-2275. For a list of accommodations outside the park, visit www.nps.gov/mora/general/accom.htm.

Campgrounds
If you plan to car camp, the nearest facility is White River Campgrounds, located 5.0 miles beyond the White River Entrance Station. The turnoff intersects the road to Sunrise just 1.0 mile beyond the Fryingpan Creek trailhead. You can claim one of the 112 sites on a first-come, first-served basis. You can reserve sites at other campgrounds throughout the park online at http://reservations.nps.gov, or call (800) 365-CAMP (2267) 7:00 A.M. to 7:00 P.M. PST.

49 Sunrise Rim

This loop travels past Shadow Lake, over the first hump of Burroughs Mountain, to an overlook of the Emmons Glacier.

Start: Sunrise Complex.
Distance: 4.9-mile loop.
Approximate hiking time: 2 hours.
Difficulty: Easy.
Seasons: August through September.
Nearest town: Greenwater.
Fees and permits: $10.00 vehicle or $5.00 individual entry fee (seven days); $30.00 annual entry fee. Wilderness Camping Permits free—reservations recommended ($20 fee).

Maps: USGS: Sunrise and White River Park, Mount Rainier East, and Ohanapecosh Hot Springs; Trails Illustrated Mount Rainier National Park; Astronaut's Vista: Mount Rainier National Park, Washington; Earthwalk Press Hiking Map & Guide.
Trail contacts: White River Wilderness Information Center, (360) 569-6030.
Trail conditions: www.nps.gov/mora/trail/tr_cnd.htm; weather, www.nps.gov/mora/current/weather.htm.

Finding the trailhead: From the White River Entrance Station (see Getting There), drive 13.8 miles west on White River Road to the Sunrise Complex parking lot. Park and walk to the trailhead on the north end of the lot, to the right of the restrooms. *DeLorme: Washington Atlas and Gazetteer:* Page 48 A4.

The Hike

Great for kids and adults alike, this hike explores the scenic area around the Sunrise Complex. You walk along Sourdough Ridge, climb to the first hump of Burroughs Mountain, and look over the Emmons Glacier. It is rare to cover such a wide range of landscapes and see such incredible views in such a short hike.

Walk up the paved path to the right (east) of the restrooms until you see a dirt trail on your right heading north. Get on the trail and walk until you come to the junction with the Sourdough Ridge Nature Trail. Turn left (northwest) onto the nature trail and walk 0.2 mile to the Sourdough Ridge Trail. Turn left (west) onto the Sourdough Ridge Trail.

While you are walking along this trail, you can see the Cascades to your right; on really clear days you can even see Mount Baker. Mount Rainier also looks magnificent from Sourdough Ridge. You will walk a total of 0.3 mile along the ridge, 0.6 mile from the Sunrise Complex, to the Huckleberry Creek Trail on your right, heading northwest. Stay to the left and on the Sourdough Ridge Trail for another 0.8 mile to the junction with Burroughs Mountain Trail. Directly before the junction, you pass Frozen Lake to your right (north). As the signs tell you, Frozen Lake is a domestic water supply; the National Park Service has fenced

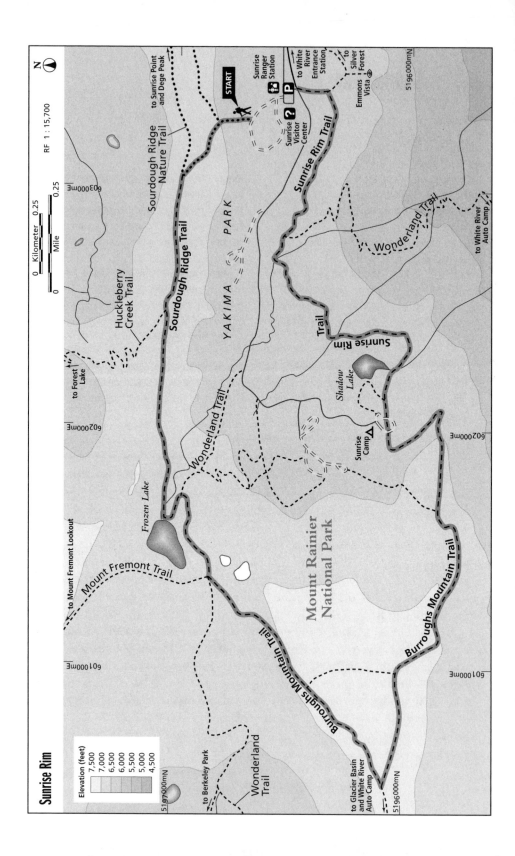

Sunrise Rim

RF 1 : 15,700

N

Elevation (feet)
7,500
7,000
6,500
6,000
5,500
5,000
4,500

0   Kilometer   0.25
0   Mile   0.25

6030000mE
6020000mE
6010000mE
5197000mN
5196000mN

to Sunrise Point and Dege Peak
Sourdough Ridge Nature Trail
START
Sunrise Ranger Station
to White River Entrance Station
to Silver Forest
P
Sunrise Visitor Center
Emmons Vista
Sourdough Ridge Trail
Huckleberry Creek Trail
YAKIMA PARK
Sunrise Rim Trail
Wonderland Trail
to White River Auto Camp
to Forest Lake
Wonderland Trail
Sunrise Rim Trail
Shadow Lake
Sunrise Camp
Frozen Lake
to Mount Fremont Lookout
Mount Fremont Trail
Mount Rainier National Park
Burroughs Mountain Trail
Burroughs Mountain Trail
Wonderland Trail
to Berkeley Park
to Glacier Basin and White River Auto Camp

in the lake to avoid possible human contamination. The fence is not very aesthetically pleasing, but it is necessary.

Once you have reached the five-trail junction, take the Burroughs Mountain Trail, which heads southwest. Steep snowfields cover this trail into August in some years. Sturdy boots and an ice ax are recommended. The trail up to the first hump of Burroughs Mountain gains about 200 feet and travels through alpine terrain. The vegetation in this area is very fragile and susceptible to human impact. Please stay on the trail to avoid damaging the delicate ecosystem.

From Burroughs Mountain, you can see Old Desolate to the northwest and Berkeley Park to the north. Old Desolate is a barren plateau that sticks out among forested hills. It is quite a contrast to the bright wildflowers that fill Berkeley Park.

When you reach the first hump of Burroughs Mountain, 0.7 mile from Frozen Lake, turn left (east). To the south is the Emmons Glacier, the largest glacier in the contiguous United States. A better view of the glacier comes from the glacier overlook, 1.0 mile away. It is all downhill to the overlook and to Sunrise Camp.

You can see the entire Emmons Glacier and the beginning of the White River from the glacial overlook. Goat Island Mountain towers above both these natural wonders. The White River originates from the Emmons Glacier and is filled with sediment and glacial flour. Notice that there are several pools in the valley below. These pools appear sea-foam green due to the large concentration of sediment suspended in their waters. The sun reflects light off the cloudy waters to produce this gorgeous color. It is amazing to imagine that the Emmons Glacier once filled the valley below. Global warming has reduced the glacier to its present size, but all glaciers in the park are currently advancing.

From the glacial overlook, continue heading downhill to Sunrise Camp until you intersect the Sunrise Rim Trail. To your left, an administrative road heads north and passes Sunrise Camp. Continue going east, but on the Sunrise Rim Trail instead of the Burroughs Mountain Trail.

After hiking 0.2 mile east on the Sunrise Rim Trail, a total of 3.6 miles into your hike, Shadow Lake appears to the left. Previous hikers have greatly damaged the area

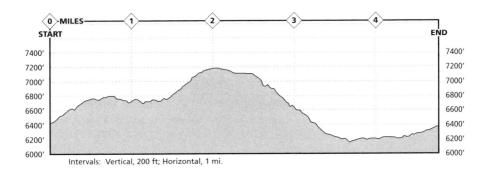

Intervals: Vertical, 200 ft; Horizontal, 1 mi.

around Shadow Lake, the water source for Sunrise Camp. Again, please stay on the trail to reduce your personal impact on the lake.

The remainder of the loop travels through the subalpine meadows of Yakima Park. In July and early August, Yakima Park is filled with a variety of wildflowers. At times you can see Goat Island Mountain and the Emmons Glacier from the trail. The trail is flat until you intersect the Wonderland Trail, and then it travels gradually uphill all the way to the Sunrise Complex parking lot.

Miles and Directions

0.0 Start from the Sunrise parking lot; follow the paved path to the right (east) of the restrooms, heading north. Don't let the road heading off to the left (west) tempt you; stay on the main trail, heading north past the informative display.

0.1 The Sourdough Ridge Nature Trail forks; stay to the left (northwest) toward Frozen Lake and Mount Fremont.

0.3 Reach the top of Sourdough Ridge and the junction with the Sourdough Ridge Nature Trail. Take a left (west) onto the trail.

0.6 Bypass the steep Huckleberry Creek Trail on your right (north). (See Options for a side trip to Forest Lake.)

1.4 Just beyond Frozen Lake, come to the junction of five trails. Take the Burroughs Mountain Trail, heading southwest. (See Options for a side trip to Mount Fremont Lookout.)

2.4 In just 1.0 mile, go over the First Burroughs Mountain and reach the junction with the southern section of the Sunrise Loop. At the junction take a left (east) toward Sunrise Camp.

3.4 At the junction with the Sunrise Rim Trail, continue east, ignoring the administrative road on your left.

3.6 Just beyond Sunrise Camp, come to Shadow Lake.

4.4 Beyond Shadow Lake, reach another trail junction. This time, the Wonderland Trail is splitting off to your right (south). Continue east toward Sunrise.

4.9 Arrive back at the Sunrise parking lot.

Options: This hike has myriad options. Almost every trail junction offers a desirable side trip. We recommend taking the Huckleberry Creek Trail to Forest Lake, a total of 2.6 miles out of your way. Another short side trip is to the Mount Fremont Lookout. At the Burroughs Mountain Trail junction, you come to the Mount Fremont Trail. This side trip is also a total of 2.6 miles long.

Wilderness camping: If you want to stay in the backcountry, you can stay at Sunrise Camp. There are eight sites available. None of the sites are very private, but Site 8 is the most secluded. Try to snag Site 5 or 6; both sites have a great view of Shadow Lake.

Hike Information

Local Information

Sunrise Visitor Center, Sunrise (no contact information).

Mount Rainier National Park Web site, www.nps.gov/mora; visitor information, (360) 569-2211, ext. 3314.

Lodging

Paradise Inn, (360) 569-2275; National Park Inn, (360) 569-2275. For a list of accommodations outside the park, visit www.nps.gov/mora/general/accom.htm.

Campgrounds

If you plan to car camp, the nearest facility is White River Campgrounds, located 5.0 miles beyond the White River Entrance Station. You can claim one of the 112 sites on a first-come, first-served basis. You can reserve sites at other campgrounds throughout the park online at http://reservations.nps.gov, or call (800) 365-CAMP (2267) 7:00 A.M. to 7:00 P.M. PST.

Carbon River

Carbon River, tucked away in the northwestern corner of Mount Rainier National Park, is the closest section to the Seattle and Tacoma, Washington area. Even so, actually getting to the trailheads in Carbon River can involve traveling slowly on winding dirt roads. The area houses Mount Rainier's only rain forest, rich in old-growth trees and a product of abundant rainfall and mild weather.

The Carbon River area, named for the coal found there, contains Carbon Glacier. This glacier extends to a lower elevation than any other glacier in the contiguous United States, making it available for ample viewing. It produces the silty Carbon River, whose unyielding, vigorous force shapes the landscape during glacial outburst floods. The sheer potency of these floods, referred to by the Icelandic term *jokulhlaups,* often washes out pieces of the Carbon River Road. This road provides access to numerous trailheads in the Carbon River Area. Due to the unpredictability of glacial outburst floods, the Carbon River Road may close on occasion or be open only to high-clearance vehicles, necessitating either a longer hike or an alternative hike.

Currently, glacial outburst floods pose the greatest threat to visitors, making landslides a potential concern. In the past, colossal mudflows greatly reshaped the land in and around the Carbon River area. Triggered by the collapse of Mount Rainier's summit 5,700 years ago, the Osceola Mudflow flowed through this area pouring across the Enumclaw Plateau and onto the present-day Seattle. This massive mudflow, the largest known to Mount Rainier, reduced the mountain's summit from 16,000 to 14,410 feet. Little Tahoma stands as a formidable remnant of the original slope.

Native Americans testify that another mudflow, coined the Electron Mudflow, rapidly covered Puget Sound as recently as 500 years ago. Within three hours, the foothills were buried 100 feet deep. It is postulated that debris was 30 feet deep at Orting, Washington. The volume of Mount St. Helen's mudflow was only a small fraction of the Electron Mudflow.

50 Yellowstone Cliffs and Windy Gap

A long, steep climb takes you through a beautiful forest, by the impressive rock formations of Yellowstone Cliffs, and over a subalpine meadow pass. The hike ends in the openness of boulder-strewn Windy Gap, a prime location for viewing the northeastern portion of Mount Rainier National Park.

Start: Ipsut Creek Campground.
Distance: 13.0-mile out-and-back.
Approximate hiking time: 5 to 8.5 hours.
Difficulty: Strenuous.
Seasons: Mid-July through September.
Nearest town: Wilkeson.
Fees and permits: $10.00 vehicle or $5.00 individual entry fee (seven days); $30.00 annual entry fee. Wilderness Camping Permits free—reservations recommended ($20 fee).

Maps: USGS: Mowich Lake and Sunrise; Trails Illustrated Mount Rainier National Park; Astronaut's Vista: Mount Rainier National Park, Washington; Earthwalk Press Hiking Map & Guide.
Trail contacts: Wilkeson Wilderness Information Center, (360) 829-5127.
Trail conditions: www.nps.gov/mora/trail/tr_cnd.htm; weather, www.nps.gov/mora/current/weather.htm.

Finding the trailhead: From the Carbon River Entrance Station (see Getting There), drive 5.0 miles east on Carbon River Road to Ipsut Creek Campground. This is the end of the road, and the trailhead. If the many spaces at Ipsut Creek Campground are full, you can park along the road in permitted areas. *DeLorme: Washington Atlas and Gazetteer:* Page 48 A2.

Special considerations: The Carbon River Road may be open only to high-clearance vehicles after washouts have eaten up portions of the road. This road often washes out and has been known to close all together. The footlogs over Carbon River may also wash out. Call ahead, or check the Mount Rainier Web site for current conditions.

The Hike

Although it offers little in the way of views of Mount Rainier, the hike to Windy Gap, a lovely high-mountain meadow, increases elevation dramatically, allowing you to explore the scenic northwestern portion of the park. From Ipsut Creek Campground follow the small connector trail south to the Wonderland Trail. The Ipsut Falls spur trail intersects to the right (west) shortly after you leave Ipsut Falls Campground. If you desire, take this spur trail to gently cascading Ipsut Falls. From the spur trail, continue traveling south to the Wonderland Trail. The trail ascends very gently for the first couple of miles and crosses the silty waters of the Carbon River. Once on the east bank of the river, you will be on the Northern Loop Trail.

The footlogs over Carbon River frequently washes out and sometimes remains washed out for weeks at a time. If fording the Carbon River seems too dangerous, follow the Wonderland Trail (southeast) for another mile, cross the Carbon River

over the suspension bridge, and then follow the Northern Loop Trail left (north) a little over a mile to reach the spot where you would have otherwise crossed.

Stay to the left (north) at the junction with the Northern Loop Trail, heading toward Yellowstone Cliffs and Windy Gap. The trail now takes a turn toward the sky. In about 3 miles, it climbs more than 3,000 feet, making this a long and very steep ridge. There are no views along the climb, save for the cooling foliage of the tall trees and lush low bushes, to distract you from the effort.

When the trees open up to reveal a steep mountain meadow covered with a variety of wildflowers, you know that you are near Yellowstone Cliffs. Almost immediately after entering the meadow, the trail forks. To your right (south), a small trail descends to Yellowstone Cliffs Camp. To your left (northeast), the main trail ascends toward Windy Gap. As you continue to switch back and forth through fields of flowers, look to the north to admire Yellowstone Cliffs, a columned rock formation topped by Tyee Peak.

▶ **Tyee is a Chinook word meaning "anyone of superior status," or more literally "chief."**

The switchbacks soon end in a subalpine clearing between two mountains and a ridge. About a mile beyond the junction to Yellowstone Cliffs Camp, an unmaintained trail spurs off to the left (north). If you want to explore Yellowstone Cliffs, this trail travels over Tyee Peak to Bee Flat. Tread lightly, though: The subalpine meadow is fragile and susceptible to damage.

Back on the Northern Loop Trail, you enter Windy Gap less than 1.0 mile beyond the unmaintained spur trail. Nestled between Sluiskin Mountain and Independence Ridge, Windy Gap is a green meadow strewn with boulders. As you reach Windy Gap, you also come to the intersection with the Independence Ridge Trail, 6.5 miles into the hike. A clear stream, perfect for filtering water, bisects the gap. A great view of the northeastern section of the park awaits you. Explore the meadows of Windy Gap, and then retrace your footsteps back to Ipsut Creek Campground.

Miles and Directions

0.0 Start at the Ipsut Creek Campground. Follow the small connector trail to the Wonderland Trail.

0.2 A less than 0.1 mile spur trail to Ipsut Falls presents itself on the right (west). Continue south (left) on the trail to the junction with Wonderland Trail. At the junction go southeast on the Wonderland Trail.

2.0 Turn left (northeast) onto the spur trail that crosses Carbon River to connect with the Northern Loop Trail.

◀ *Windy Gap.*

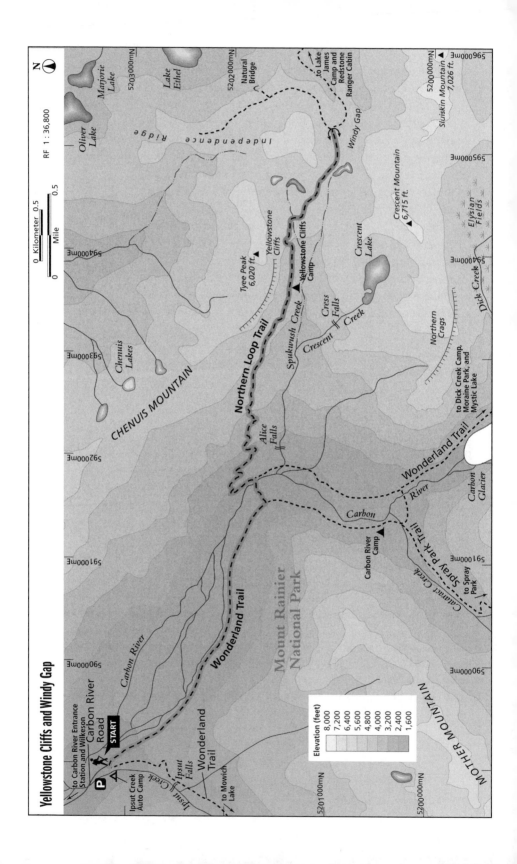

Yellowstone Cliffs and Windy Gap

RF 1 : 36,800

N

0 Kilometer 0.5

0 Mile 0.5

Marjorie Lake

Oliver Lake

Lake Ethel

5203000mN

5202000mN

Natural Bridge

to Lake James Camp and Redstone Ranger Cabin

Independence Ridge

Windy Gap

5200000mN

Sluiskin Mountain 7,026 ft.

596000mE

Chenuis Lakes

593000mE

594000mE

Tyee Peak 6,020 ft.

Yellowstone Cliffs

Yellowstone Cliffs Camp

595000mE

Crescent Mountain 6,715 ft.

Crescent Lake

Elysian Fields

594000mE

CHENUIS MOUNTAIN

Northern Loop Trail

Spukwush Creek

Cress Falls

Crescent Creek

Crescent Creek

Northern Crags

592000mE

Alice Falls

to Dick Creek Camp, Moraine Park, and Mystic Lake

Dick Creek

Wonderland Trail

Carbon River

Carbon Glacier

591000mE

Carbon River Camp

Spray Park Trail

to Spray Park

Cataract Creek

591000mE

Mount Rainier National Park

Wonderland Trail

to Carbon River Entrance Station and Wilkeson

Carbon River Road

590000mE

590000mE

START

Ipsut Creek Auto Camp

P

Ipsut Creek

Ipsut Falls

Wonderland Trail

to Mowich Lake

5201000mN

5200000mN

MOTHER MOUNTAIN

Elevation (feet)	
8,000	
7,200	
6,400	
5,600	
4,800	
4,000	
3,200	
2,400	
1,600	

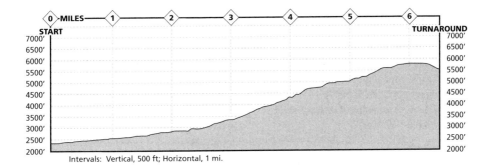

Intervals: Vertical, 500 ft; Horizontal, 1 mi.

2.3 Stay left (north) at the junction with the Northern Loop Trail, and begin climbing up the steep ridge toward Yellowstone Cliffs.

5.1 A trail forks downhill (south) to Yellowstone Cliffs Camp. Stay to left (northeast), traveling through the meadow.

6.1 To the left (north), an unmaintained trail goes over Tyee Peak to Bee Flat. Stay to the right toward Windy Gap.

6.5 A trail to Independence Ridge forks off to the north; you have reached the beginning of the Windy Gap area. Retrace your steps back to the trailhead. (See Options for a possible side trip to Independence Ridge or Lake James.)

13.0 Arrive back at the trailhead.

Options: If you have the time and energy, take the side trip along Independence Ridge to the natural bridge. Do not continue on the unmaintained trail beyond the spur trail to the natural bridge, but do descend to the natural bridge. The arching rocks are a wonder of nature. It's only 0.9 mile to the natural bridge, adding 1.8 miles to your hike.

If you would like to fish at Lake James or stay at Lake James Camp, continue east along the Northern Loop Trail. The trail leads through the boulder fields of Windy Gap and then through forest for about another 2.0 miles. A mileage sign in the middle of the trail to the lake attempts to dissuade people from trampling the banks of Lake James. Overuse in the 1970s led to the destruction of the land around Lake James, but recent restoration efforts are proving successful. Practice zero-impact principles to minimize your impact. Take the trail to the left (northwest) and encounter Lake James in less than 0.2 mile. If you go to Lake James to fish, you add about 4.0 miles round-trip to your hike.

Wilderness camping: Yellowstone Cliffs Camp has a fantastic view of, what else, Yellowstone Cliffs, and has two nice campsites. Site 1 has a better view and proximity to water. Lake James Camp has three individual sites and one group site located far from the banks of Lake James. The water source is Van Horn Creek, a short trek back on the Northern Loop Trail toward Lake James.

Hike Information

Local Information

Mount Rainier National Park Web site, www.nps.gov/mora; twenty-four-hour visitor information, (360) 569-2211.
Mount Baker Snoqualmie National Forest, www.fs.fed.us/r6/mbs/.

Lodging

For a list of accommodations outside the park, visit www.nps.gov/mora/general/accom.htm.

Campgrounds

Ipsut Creek Campground, located 5.0 miles east of the Carbon River Entrance, issues campsites on a first-come, first-served basis. For no fee, Mowich Lake Campground, at the end of Mowich Lake Road, also offers walk-in campsites on a first-come, first-served basis. Campfires are prohibited.

51 Carbon Glacier and Moraine

A moderate ascent to the foot of the Carbon Glacier, the lowest-elevation glacier in the contiguous United States, this hike travels along the glacier, allowing you to witness many of the geological processes associated with glaciers. Among other things, you will see the rock debris that has been shattered from the rock walls surrounding the glacier and deposited atop the massive river of ice, coloring the glacier brown and black.

Start: Ipsut Creek Campground.
Distance: 8.2-mile out-and-back.
Approximate hiking time: 3 to 5 hours.
Difficulty: Moderate
Seasons: Mid-July through September.
Nearest town: Wilkeson.
Fees and permits: $10.00 vehicle or $5.00 individual entry fee (seven days); $30.00 annual entry fee. Wilderness Camping Permits free—reservations recommended ($20 fee).

Maps: USGS: Mowich Lake; Trails Illustrated Mount Rainier National Park; Astronaut's Vista: Mount Rainier National Park, Washington; Earthwalk Press Hiking Map & Guide.
Trail contacts: Wilkeson Wilderness Information Center, (360) 829-5127.
Trail conditions: www.nps.gov/mora/trail/tr_cnd.htm; weather, www.nps.gov/mora/current/weather.htm.

Finding the trailhead: From the Carbon River Entrance Station (see Getting There), drive 5.0 miles east on Carbon River Road to Ipsut Creek Campground. This is the end of the road, and the trailhead. If the many spaces at Ipsut Creek Campground are full, you can park along the road in permitted areas. *DeLorme: Washington Atlas and Gazetteer: Page 48 A2.*

Special considerations: The Carbon River Road may be open only to high-clearance vehicles after washouts have eaten up portions of the road. This road often washes out and has

Suspension bridge over the Carbon River.

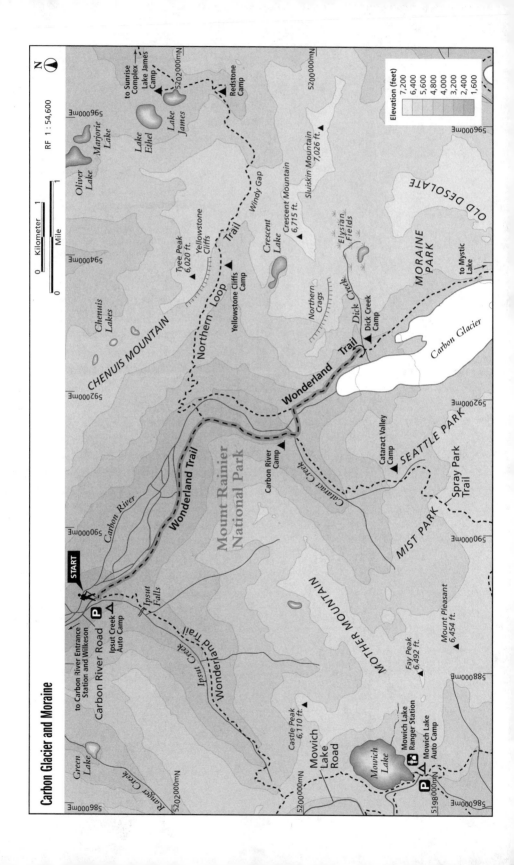

Carbon Glacier and Moraine

RF 1 : 54,600

N

Elevation (feet)

7,200
6,400
5,600
4,800
4,000
3,200
2,400
1,600

0   Kilometer   1

0   Mile   1

Green Lake

Ranger Creek

Oliver Lake

Marjorie Lake

Lake Ethel

Lake James

Lake James Camp

to Sunrise Complex

Redstone Camp

5202000mN

5200000mN

596000mE

Chenuis Lakes

CHENUIS MOUNTAIN

Tyee Peak 6,020 ft.

Yellowstone Cliffs

Northern Loop Trail

Windy Gap

Crescent Mountain 6,715 ft.

Sluiskin Mountain 7,026 ft.

594000mE

Yellowstone Cliffs Camp

Crescent Lake

Northern Crags

Elysian Fields

OLD DESOLATE

596000mE

Carbon River

START

Carbon River Road

to Carbon River Entrance Station: and Wilkeson

P

Ipsut Creek Auto Camp

Ipsut Falls

Wonderland Trail

Carbon River Camp

Mount Rainier National Park

Wonderland Trail

Cataract Creek

Dick Creek

Dick Creek Camp

Wonderland Trail

MORAINE PARK

to Mystic Lake

Carbon Glacier

592000mE

Cataract Valley Camp

SEATTLE PARK

Spray Park Trail

MIST PARK

590000mE

592000mN

Ipsut Creek

Wonderland Trail

MOTHER MOUNTAIN

Fay Peak 6,492 ft.

Mount Pleasant 6,454 ft.

588000mE

Castle Peak 6,110 ft.

Mowich Lake Road

Mowich Lake Ranger Station

Mowich Lake

Mowich Lake Auto Camp

P

5200000mN

5198000mN

586000mE

5202000mN

592000mE

590000mE

▶ Glaciers, like Carbon Glacier, are really moving rivers of ice. They advance when snow accumulates faster than it melts. The weight of the snow squeezes the air out, packs down the snow, and compresses the glacier into ice. Even when the summer snowmelt exceeds the winter snowfall, causing the terminus of a glacier to recede, the main body of the glacier always continues moving downhill. As glaciers travel, they displace rock debris and carve out U-shaped canyons. Frequent frosts burst the waterlogged rock walls along the glacier. These bursts cause large rocks to break away and join the glacier.

been known to close all together. Call ahead, or check the Mount Rainier Web site for current conditions.

The Hike

From Ipsut Creek Campground, follow the small connector trail south to the Wonderland Trail. The Ipsut Falls spur trail intersects to the right (southwest) shortly after you leave Ipsut Creek Campground. If you desire, take this spur trail to gently cascading Ipsut Falls. From the spur trail, continue traveling southeast to the Wonderland Trail. The trail ascends very gently for the first couple of miles through brushy forest, with an occasional view of the Carbon River. After the junction with the Northern Loop connector trail, the trail hugs the banks of the silty Carbon River until you reach the junction with Spray Park Trail and the suspension bridge over Carbon River.

This bridge offers a fantastic view of the Carbon River below. Its source, the massive, black Carbon Glacier, rests only 0.4 mile upstream. On the other side of the Carbon River, stay to the right (southeast), ascending toward the glacier and Dick Creek Camp. The easy grade gives way to a steep pitch. The trees open up to reveal the Carbon Glacier, nestled in shrubbery with Mount Rainier towering above it. Rubble and debris litter the blue ice of Carbon Glacier. Do not be surprised to hear the echoing crashes of falling rocks.

Carbon Glacier is currently undergoing a minor retreat, yet the glacier has experienced a total retreat of only 0.6 mile since the last ice age. With a thickness of 700 feet and a volume of 0.2 cubic mile, this glacier claims the greatest measured thickness and volume of any glacier in the contiguous United States. In the 1970s park visitors saw the glacier actively advancing and witnessed it crushing vegetation caught in its path.

For the rest of the way to Dick Creek Camp, the trail climbs steeply parallel to the Carbon Glacier. If you plan on camping, Dick Creek Camp has spectacular views and nice sites. Regardless of your camping plans, spend some time here admiring the Northern Crags over the Carbon Glacier. The main trail leads directly by the

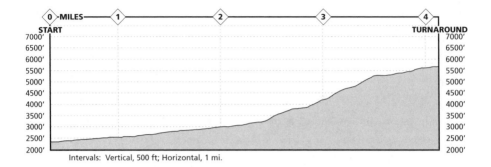

Intervals: Vertical, 500 ft; Horizontal, 1 mi.

camp. If you have time, we strongly recommend venturing to Moraine Park. If you're short on time, follow the same trail back to Ipsut Creek Campground.

Miles and Directions

0.0 Start at the Ipsut Creek Campground. Follow the small connector trail to the Wonderland Trail.

0.2 A less than 0.1-mile spur trail to Ipsut Falls presents itself on the right (southwest). Continue southeast on the trail to the junction with Wonderland Trail. At the junction go southeast on the Wonderland Trail.

2.0 A connector trail that crosses the Carbon River to meet with the Northern Loop Trail forks off to the left. Stay to the right (south) on the Wonderland Trail toward Carbon Glacier.

2.8 A trail to Carbon River Camp heads off to the right. Stay to the left, traveling south on the Wonderland Trail.

2.9 The Spray Park Trail forks off to the right (southwest). Continue on the Wonderland Trail over the Carbon River suspension bridge.

3.1 After crossing this bridge, the Northern Loop Trail presents itself on your left, traveling north. Again, stay on the Wonderland Trail and travel southeast.

3.5 Begin to see Carbon Glacier.

4.1 The trail heads back into the forest, ending the view of Carbon Glacier. Dick Creek Camp also forks off to the left. Return the way you came. (See Option for a possible side trip to Moraine Park.)

8.2 Arrive back at the trailhead.

Option: From Dick Creek Camp the trail climbs steadily, switching back and forth through a forest. The grade lessens when the path begins to run along Moraine Creek. Keep in mind that this is bear country. In fact, a fellow hiker said that she has not come to this area without seeing a bear. When we were here, we came across a small black bear that was not easily deterred by loud voices, banging pots, and shrill singing. Beyond the streambed you come to a boulder-strewn meadow and then a larger mountain meadow dotted with subalpine wildflowers below Mount Rainier. From here you can either move on to Mystic Lake or return the way you came. The trip from Dick Creek Camp to the beginning of Moraine Park increases your total hike by 3.4 miles round-trip.

Wilderness camping: If you plan to backpack, you have two options in the way of camps: Carbon River and Dick Creek. We suggest camping at Dick Creek Camp. The sites are few (two), but it has an amazing view of the Carbon Glacier and a great water source (Dick Creek).

Carbon River Camp is located just off the Carbon River, nestled in old-growth forest. There are four individual sites and one group site. The first two have excellent tent sites but are not very private. Sites 3 and 4 are more secluded with slanted tent sites; Site 4 is the most remote. The water source for this camp is Cataract Creek, a good 0.1 mile from all the sites.

Hike Information

Local Information

Mount Rainier National Park Web site,
www.nps.gov/mora; twenty-four-hour visitor information, (360) 569-2211.
Mount Baker Snoqualmie National Forest,
www.fs.fed.us/r6/mbs/.

Lodging

For a list of accommodations outside the park, visit www.nps.gov/mora/general/accom.htm.

Campgrounds

Ipsut Creek Campground, located 5.0 miles east of the Carbon River Entrance, issues campsites on a first-come, first-served basis. For no fee, Mowich Lake Campground, at the end of Mowich Lake Road, also offers walk-in campsites on a first-come, first-served basis. Campfires are prohibited.

52 Mystic Lake

A difficult ascent to the serene waters of Mystic Lake that traverses a variety of landscapes. At first the trail takes you through a low-elevation forest that opens up when the trail skirts the silty Carbon River in its rocky riverbed. The trail continues, taking you along the magnificent Carbon Glacier and through a high-mountain meadow.

Start: Ipsut Creek Campground.
Distance: 15.6-mile out-and-back.
Approximate hiking time: 2-day backpack.
Difficulty: Strenuous.
Seasons: Mid-July through September.
Nearest town: Wilkeson.
Fees and permits: $10.00 vehicle or $5.00 individual entry fee (seven days); $30.00 annual entry fee. Wilderness Camping Permits free—reservations recommended ($20 fee).

Maps: USGS: Mowich Lake and Sunrise; Trails Illustrated Mount Rainier National Park; Astronaut's Vista: Mount Rainier National Park, Washington; Earthwalk Press Hiking Map & Guide.
Trail contacts: Wilkeson Wilderness Information Center, (360) 829-5127.
Trail conditions: www.nps.gov/mora/trail/tr_cnd.htm; weather, www.nps.gov/mora/current/weather.htm.

Finding the trailhead: From the Carbon River Entrance Station (see Getting There), drive 5.0 miles east on Carbon River Road to Ipsut Creek Campground. This is the end of the road, and the trailhead. If the many spaces at Ipsut Creek Campground are full, you can park along the road in permitted areas. *DeLorme: Washington Atlas and Gazetteer:* Page 48 A2.
Special considerations: The Carbon River Road may be open only to high-clearance vehicles after washouts have eaten up portions of the road. This road often washes out and has been known to close all together. Call ahead, or check the Mount Rainier Web site for current conditions.

The Hike

From Ipsut Creek Campground, follow the small connector trail south to the Wonderland Trail. The Ipsut Falls spur trail intersects to the right (southwest) shortly after you leave Ipsut Creek Campground. If you desire, take this spur trail to gently cascading Ipsut Falls. From the spur trail, continue traveling southeast to the Wonderland Trail. The trail ascends very gently for the first couple of miles through brushy forest, with an occasional view of the Carbon River. After the junction with the Northern Loop connector trail, the trail hugs the banks of the silty Carbon River until you reach the junction with Spray Park Trail and the suspension bridge over Carbon River.

This bridge offers a fantastic view of the Carbon River below. Its source, the massive, black Carbon Glacier, rests only 0.4 mile upstream. On the other side of the Carbon River, stay to the right (southeast), ascending toward the glacier and Dick Creek Camp. The easy grade gives way to a steep pitch. The trees open up to reveal the Carbon Glacier, nestled in shrubbery with Mount Rainier towering above it.

Carbon Glacier. ▶

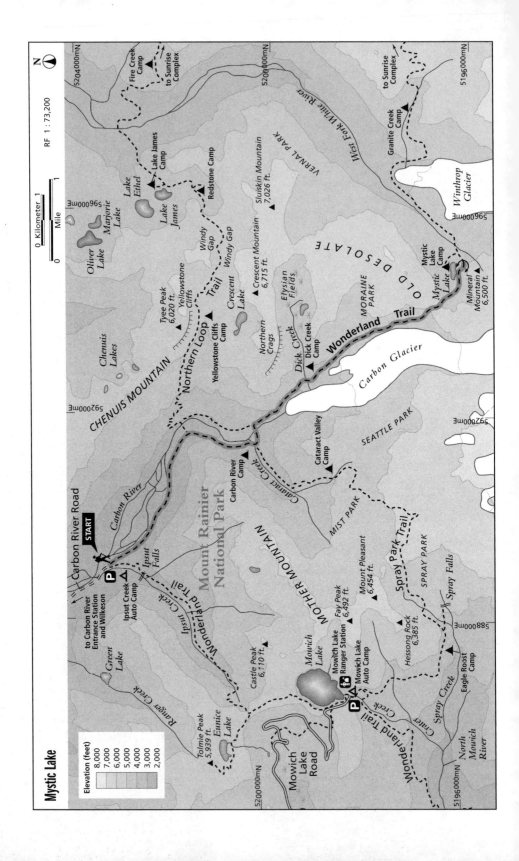

Mystic Lake

RF 1 : 73,200

N

Elevation (feet)

8,000
7,000
6,000
5,000
4,000
3,000
2,000

0   Kilometer   1

0   Mile   1

Rubble and debris litter the blue ice of the Carbon Glacier. Do not be surprised to hear the echoing crashes of falling rocks.

Carbon Glacier is currently undergoing a minor retreat, yet the glacier has experienced a total retreat of only 0.6 mile since the last ice age. With a thickness of 700 feet and a volume of 0.2 cubic mile, this glacier claims the greatest measured thickness and volume of any glacier in the contiguous United States. In the 1970s park visitors saw the glacier actively advancing and witnessed it crushing vegetation caught in its path.

For the rest of the way to Dick Creek Camp, the trail climbs steeply parallel to the Carbon Glacier. If you plan on camping, Dick Creek Camp has spectacular views and nice sites. Regardless of your camping plans, spend some time here admiring the Northern Crags over the Carbon Glacier. The main trail leads directly by the camp. The next couple of miles of trail climb steadily, switching back and forth through a forest. The grade lessens when the path begins to run along Moraine Creek. Keep in mind that this is bear country. In fact, a fellow hiker said that she has not come to this area without seeing a bear. When we were here, we came across a small black bear that was not easily deterred by loud voices, banging pots, and shrill singing.

▶ Mystic Lake was named by visiting professors J. B. Fleet and H. H. Garrelson. They saw a mysterious swirling whirlpool in one of the lake's outlets, giving the lake a certain mystique.

Beyond the streambed you come to a rockfield, then a large mountain meadow. This subalpine meadow, Moraine Park, is filled with colorful wildflowers and offers glorious views of Mount Rainier. At this point, you have only two small hills to climb before beginning your descent to Mystic Lake. The lake rests in a valley between Mineral Mountain and the appropriately named Old Desolate mountain. The view at the lake is beautiful, but it cannot be seen from Mystic Lake Camp, 0.2 mile down the trail. You can either stay at this camp or return to Ipsut Creek Campground.

Miles and Directions

0.0 Start at the Ipsut Creek Campground. Follow the small connector trail to the Wonderland Trail.

0.2 A less than 0.1-mile spur trail to Ipsut Falls presents itself on the right (southwest). Continue southeast on the trail to the junction with Wonderland Trail. At the junction go southeast on the Wonderland Trail.

2.0 A connector trail that crosses the Carbon River to meet with the Northern Loop Trail forks off to the left. Stay to the right (south) on the Wonderland Trail toward Carbon Glacier.

2.5 A trail to Carbon River Camp heads off to the right. Stay to the left, traveling south on the Wonderland Trail.

2.6 The Spray Park Trail forks off to the right (southwest). Continue on the Wonderland Trail over the Carbon River suspension bridge.

2.8 After crossing this bridge, the Northern Loop Trail diverges left, traveling north. Again, stay on the Wonderland Trail and travel southeast. You will begin to see Carbon Glacier in about 0.25 mile.

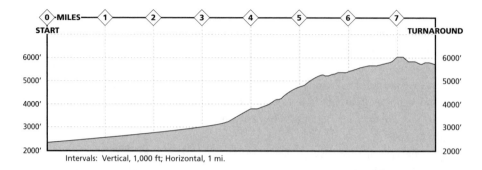

Intervals: Vertical, 1,000 ft; Horizontal, 1 mi.

3.8 When you reach Dick Creek Camp, the trail heads back into the forest, ending the view of Carbon Glacier. Continue traveling southeast on the Wonderland Trail into the forest. You will continue in the forest until the forest gives way to meadow as you enter Moraine Park in 1.7 miles.

7.8 Arrive at Mystic Lake. Enjoy your overnight, or head back to Ipsut Creek Campground.

15.6 Arrive back at Ipsut Creek Campground.

Wilderness camping: You can stay at one of three backcountry camps along the way: Carbon River, Dick Creek, or Mystic Lake. We recommend either Dick Creek or Mystic Lake. One of our favorite camps, Dick Creek Camp has two nice sites that overlook Carbon Glacier. Dick Creek, its water source, is only a short walk away.

Carbon River Camp is located just off the Carbon River, nestled in old-growth forest. There are four individual sites and one group site. The first two have excellent tent sites but are not very private. Sites 3 and 4 are more secluded, with slanted tent sites; Site 4 is the most remote. The water source for this camp is Cataract Creek, a good 0.1 mile from all the sites.

Mystic Lake Camp is unfortunately located quite a distance from the lake. An established camp along the Wonderland Trail, this camp has a whopping seven individual sites and two group sites, all with good tent sites but little privacy. Two food storage poles offer protection from a bear that apparently frequents this camp, as well as from mice and chipmunks, which are more of a nuisance.

Hike Information

Local Information
Mount Rainier National Park Web site, www.nps.gov/mora; twenty-four-hour visitor information, (360) 569-2211.
Mount Baker Snoqualmie National Forest, www.fs.fed.us/r6/mbs/.

Lodging
For a list of accommodations outside the park, visit www.nps.gov/mora/general/accom.htm.

Campgrounds
Ipsut Creek Campground, located 5.0 miles east of the Carbon River Entrance, issues campsites on a first-come, first-served basis. For no fee, Mowich Lake Campground, at the end of Mowich Lake Road, also offers walk-in campsites on a first-come, first-served basis. Campfires are prohibited.

53 Green Lake and Ranger Falls

An easy hike through old-growth forest travels past the gushing waters of Ranger Falls to a small, quaint emerald-green lake in the northwestern region of the park.

Start: Green Lake trailhead.
Distance: 3.6-mile out-and-back.
Approximate hiking time: 2 to 2.5 hours
Difficulty: Easy.
Seasons: May through October.
Nearest town: Wilkeson.
Fees and permits: $10.00 vehicle or $5.00 individual entry fee (seven days); $30.00 annual entry fee.

Maps: USGS: Mowich Lake; Trails Illustrated Mount Rainier National Park; Astronaut's Vista: Mount Rainier National Park, Washington; Earthwalk Press Hiking Map & Guide.
Trail contacts: Wilkeson Wilderness Information Center, (360) 829-5127.
Trail conditions: www.nps.gov/mora/trail/tr_cnd.htm; weather, www.nps.gov/mora/current/weather.htm.

Finding the trailhead: From the Carbon River Entrance Station (see Getting There), drive 3.0 miles east on Carbon River Road. The Green Lake trailhead is well marked by Ranger Creek to the right (south) and a small parking lot to the left (north). The Green Lake trailhead has few available spaces. Cars often line the road, parked on either side. *DeLorme: Washington Atlas and Gazetteer:* Page 48 A2.

Special considerations: The Carbon River Road may be open only to high-clearance vehicles after washouts have eaten up portions of the road. This road often washes out and has been known to close all together. Call ahead, or check the Mount Rainier Web site for current conditions.

The Hike

The hike to Green Lake attracts many late-spring hikers because the snow clears earlier on this trail than most others in the park. Its traffic may lessen as the other trails open, but the trail's charm does not.

Dense, green rain forest and the gurgling sound of streams surround you as you ascend this moderate hill. After only 1.0 mile the gurgling becomes churning. A very short jaunt to the left (east) leads you to a close-up view of Ranger Falls; the right takes you to Green Lake.

Only 0.5 mile beyond Ranger Falls on the way to Green Lake, you must cross Ranger Creek. No fording is necessary, but the footlog with only wire for a grip gets a bit slippery when wet, so cross carefully.

Less than 0.3 mile beyond the bridge, you come upon Green Lake. One glance, and the inspiration for the

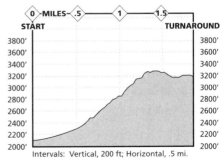

Green Lake.

name becomes apparent. Surrounded by evergreens, the water reflects their emerald hue. The surrounding mountains shelter the water, keeping it placid. From a small clearing at the trail's end, a nice view of Tolmie Peak can be seen across the lake. No trails run around the lake for further exploration, but the small clearing is a good place to picnic or just rest before descending along the same path.

Miles and Directions

0.0 Start at the Green Lake trailhead. Follow the trail uphill until you reach Ranger Falls.

1.0 A small spur trail to Ranger Falls heads left (east). Continue right (south) on the Green Lake Trail.

1.5 Cross the footlog over Ranger Creek.

1.8 Reach Green Lake. Rest a bit or enjoy a picnic before retracing your steps.

3.6 Arrive back at the trailhead.

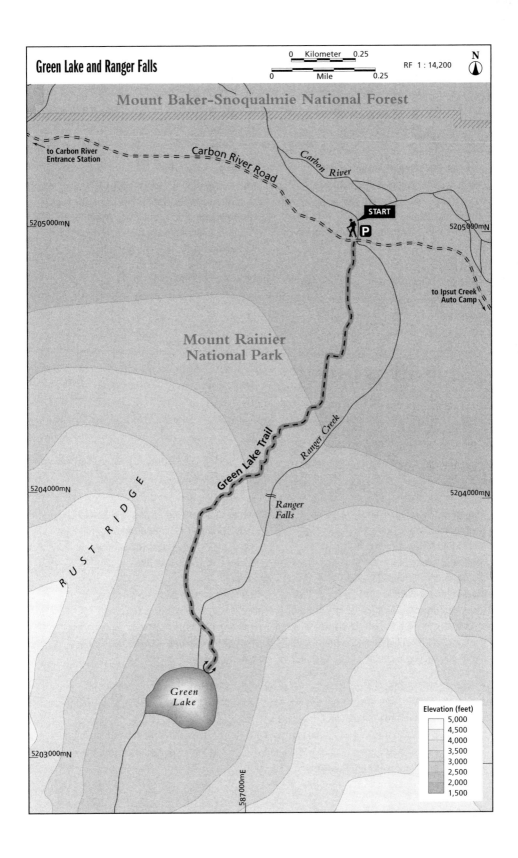

Green Lake and Ranger Falls

0   Kilometer   0.25
0   Mile   0.25

RF 1 : 14,200

N

Mount Baker-Snoqualmie National Forest

to Carbon River
Entrance Station

Carbon River Road

Carbon River

START

P

5205000mN

5205000mN

to Ipsut Creek
Auto Camp

Mount Rainier
National Park

Green Lake Trail

Ranger Creek

5204000mN

5204000mN

Ranger
Falls

R U S T   R I D G E

Green
Lake

5203000mN

587000mE

Elevation (feet)

5,000
4,500
4,000
3,500
3,000
2,500
2,000
1,500

Option: If you would rather not hike the full 3.6 miles, turning back at Ranger Falls shortens the hike to only 2.0 miles round-trip. The falls still make the effort worthwhile.

Hike Information

Local Information

Mount Rainier National Park Web site, www.nps.gov/mora; twenty-four-hour visitor information, (360) 569-2211.
Mount Baker Snoqualmie National Forest, www.fs.fed.us/r6/mbs/.

Lodging

For a list of accommodations outside the park, visit www.nps.gov/mora/general/accom.htm.

Campgrounds

Ipsut Creek Campground, located 5.0 miles east of the Carbon River Entrance, issues campsites on a first-come, first-served basis. For no fee, Mowich Lake Campground, at the end of Mowich Lake Road, also offers walk-in campsites on a first-come, first-served basis. Campfires are prohibited.

54 Paul Peak Trail

This is a relatively short descent along the side of Paul Peak. The trail, one of the few that may be snow-free in May, travels through lush forest and across the clear waters of Meadow Creek before descending to the pebbly banks of the North Mowich River.

Start: Paul Peak trailhead.
Distance: 8.0-mile out-and-back.
Approximate hiking time: 3 to 5 hours.
Difficulty: Moderate.
Seasons: May through October.
Nearest town: Wilkeson.
Fees and permits: $10.00 vehicle or $5.00 individual entry fee (seven days); $30.00 annual entry fee. Wilderness Camping Permits free—reservations recommended ($20 fee).

Maps: USGS: Golden Lakes and Mowich Lake; Trails Illustrated Mount Rainier National Park; Astronaut's Vista: Mount Rainier National Park, Washington; Earthwalk Press Hiking Map & Guide.
Trail contacts: Wilkeson Wilderness Information Center, (360) 829-5127.
Trail conditions: www.nps.gov/mora/trail/tr_cnd.htm; weather, www.nps.gov/mora/current/weather.htm.

Finding the trailhead: From Wilkeson, stay on Highway 165 for 9.0 miles until the road forks. Stay to the right (south) at this fork, the way to Mowich Lake. After 3.2 miles the road becomes a well-maintained dirt road, although it can be very slippery when muddy. Follow this road for another 8.8 miles to the Paul Peak trailhead on the right (south) side of the road. There is a fee station at the trailhead; make sure to pay the entrance fee before heading off on your trip. *DeLorme: Washington Atlas and Gazetteer:* Page 48 A1.

Bridge over Meadow Creek.

The Hike

The Paul Peak Trail is one of the few park trails that can be snow-free in May, although patches of snow can remain into mid-June. For this reason, the traffic on this trail is heavy in May and dwindles further into the summer. The trail takes you over a pleasant creek and through a beautiful forest, and the North Mowich River offers a destination worth the distance.

The first 0.6 mile of the trail is steep down to Meadow Creek. At the bottom of the hill, a wide sturdy bridge crosses the clear waters of Meadow Creek. It is worth spending a little time at Meadow Creek, which originates from Eunice Lake.

After Meadow Creek, the trail gradually climbs uphill through the forest until you reach a set of steep switchbacks that drop to the Wonderland Trail. On a foggy morning, the hazy sunlight shines through the trees and makes the forest seem magical.

At the junction with the Wonderland Trail, turn right (south) on the Wonderland Trail and continue for a little under a mile to the North Mowich River. The North

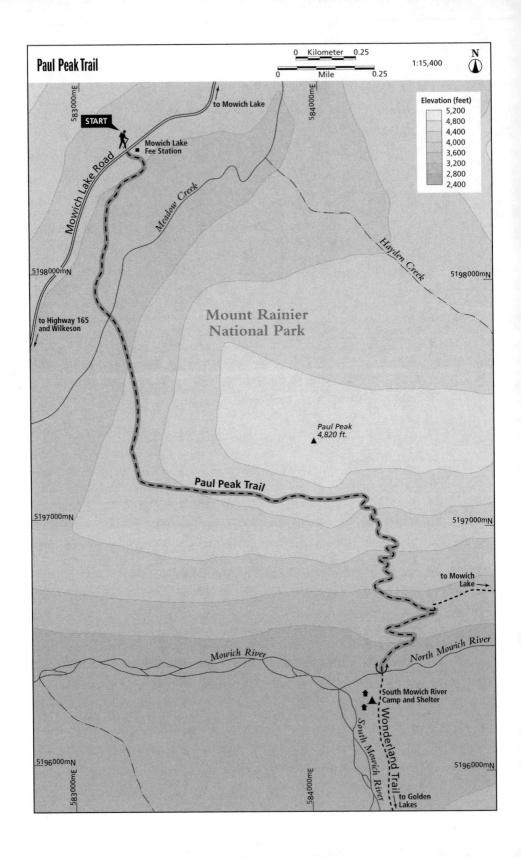

Paul Peak Trail

0   Kilometer   0.25

0   Mile   0.25

1:15,400

N

Elevation (feet)
5,200
4,800
4,400
4,000
3,600
3,200
2,800
2,400

to Mowich Lake

START

Mowich Lake
Fee Station

583000mE

584000mE

Mowich Lake Road

Meadow Creek

Hayden Creek

5198000mN

5198000mN

to Highway 165
and Wilkeson

Mount Rainier
National Park

Paul Peak
4,820 ft.

Paul Peak Trail

5197000mN

5197000mN

to Mowich
Lake

North Mowich River

Mowich River

South Mowich River
Camp and Shelter

Wonderland Trail

South Mowich River

583000mE

584000mE

5196000mN

5196000mN

to Golden
Lakes

Mowich Glacier, the origin of the North Mowich River, often sends debris and chunks of ice down its waters, downing trees, moving boulders, and washing out the footlogs that cross it. Evidence of these glacial outburst floods litter the riverbed. After enjoying the river's environs, turn around and retrace your steps to the Paul Peak trailhead.

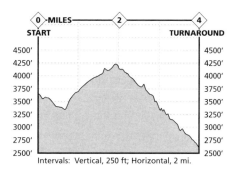

Intervals: Vertical, 250 ft; Horizontal, 2 mi.

Miles and Directions

0.0 Start at Paul Peak trailhead. Continue on the Paul Peak Trail until you reach Meadow Creek.

0.6 Cross Meadow Creek and continue on the Paul Peak Trail until you reach the Wonderland Trail.

3.1 At the junction stay right (south), heading on the Wonderland Trail toward the North Mowich River. (See Option for a possible side trip to Mowich Lake.)

4.0 Arrive at the North Mowich River. Enjoy the river and then retrace your path.

8.0 Arrive back at the trailhead.

Option: If it is at least mid-July, you can hike from the Paul Peak trailhead to Mowich Lake. At the junction with the Wonderland Trail, go left (northwest) for 3.2 miles to Mowich Lake. This 6.2-mile one-way hike requires a two-car shuttle.

Wilderness camping: To extend this hike into an overnighter, consider staying at the South Mowich River Camp. This camp has four individual sites and a group site. (The South Mowich Shelter is considered one of the individual sites.) Sites 3 and 4 are closer to the South Mowich River; Sites 1 and 2, along with the group site, are crunched together and near the trail. There is an outhouse.

Hike Information

Local Information

Mount Rainier National Park Web site, www.nps.gov/mora; twenty-four-hour visitor information, (360) 569-2211.

Mount Baker Snoqualmie National Forest, www.fs.fed.us/r6/mbs/.

Lodging

For a list of accommodations outside the park, visit www.nps.gov/mora/general/accom.htm.

Campgrounds

Ipsut Creek Campground, located 5.0 miles east of the Carbon River Entrance, issues campsites on a first-come, first-served basis. For no fee, Mowich Lake Campground, at the end of Mowich Lake Road, also offers walk-in campsites on a first-come, first-served basis. Campfires are prohibited.

55 Tolmie Peak

This very popular hike travels through forest and meadow to a fire lookout atop Tolmie Peak, which offers a spectacular view of the northwestern side of Mount Rainier. The trail also takes you by serene Eunice Lake, a mountain lake surrounded by jutting peaks and subalpine forest.

Start: Mowich Lake.
Distance: 6.4-mile out-and-back.
Approximate hiking time: 2.5 to 4.5 hours.
Difficulty: Moderate.
Seasons: Mid-July through September.
Nearest town: Wilkeson.
Fees and permits: $10.00 vehicle or $5.00 individual entry fee (seven days); $30.00 annual entry fee.

Maps: USGS: Golden Lakes and Mowich Lake; Trails Illustrated Mount Rainier National Park; Astronaut's Vista: Mount Rainier National Park, Washington; Earthwalk Press Hiking Map & Guide.
Trail contacts: Wilkeson Wilderness Information Center, (360) 829-5127.
Mowich Ranger Station, (360) 829-2127.
Trail conditions: www.nps.gov/mora/trail/tr_cnd.htm; weather, www.nps.gov/mora/current/weather.htm.

Finding the trailhead: From Wilkeson drive 9.0 miles south on Highway 165. Where Carbon River Road joins in, stay to the right on Highway 165. The pavement ends 3.2 miles beyond the intersection. Drive along a dirt road for 8.8 miles to reach the park boundary; pause here to pay the entry fee at the fee station. Continue another 5.3 miles to Mowich Lake Campground, which has a small parking lot. Many trails originate here; the trail to Tolmie Peak (Wonderland Trail) will be to your immediate left. *DeLorme: Washington Atlas and Gazetteer:* Page 48 A1.

The Hike

The hike to Tolmie Peak is one of the most popular in the park for many reasons. Neither too long nor too rigorous, it provides the opportunity to explore subalpine forests and a serene lake, as well as the opportunity to catch a breathtaking panorama of Mount Rainier.

Tolmie Peak and Tolmie Peak Trail are named for Dr. William Fraser Tolmie. This doctor, led by Nisqually headman Lahalet, was the first recorded non–Native American to approach Mount Rainier. Unlike others to follow him, he desired not to summit Mount Rainier but rather to collect herbs for medicinal purposes and simply to enjoy the captivating scenery. Records indicate that he ascended all the way to Hessong Rock.

From the Mowich Lake parking lot, go to the Wonderland Trail, which runs along the west side of Mowich Lake. There are several paths down to this trail, but the only trail that runs north–south along Mowich Lake is the Wonderland Trail.

View of Mount Rainier from Tolmie Peak.

Head north on the Wonderland Trail. The trail hugs the west side of Mowich Lake for about 0.5 mile before leaving the lake and heading north. After reaching the top of a small hill, continue on flat terrain to the junction with the Tolmie Peak Trail. At the junction turn left (northwest).

After turning, you immediately begin to descend steeply. At the bottom of this hill, the trail forks. The trail to the left is an unmaintained social trail created by those eager to see a small waterfall only a few paces off the beaten path. Stay to the right (north) to continue the journey to Eunice Lake and Tolmie Peak.

At this point the trail begins a steep climb via switchbacks. As you approach Eunice Lake, you may step into a field blanketed by avalanche lilies, as we did in mid-July. Jutting peaks and subalpine forest surround the lake's aqua-blue waters.

A sign points the way to Tolmie Peak. Stay to the left (west) on the marked trail around the lake. Those who have ventured off have spoiled the land, killing the fragile meadow plants and creating an array of ugly paths to the lake.

The trail reaches the northwestern part of the lake and then begins to ascend by means of long switchbacks to the Tolmie Peak Lookout. The view from the look-

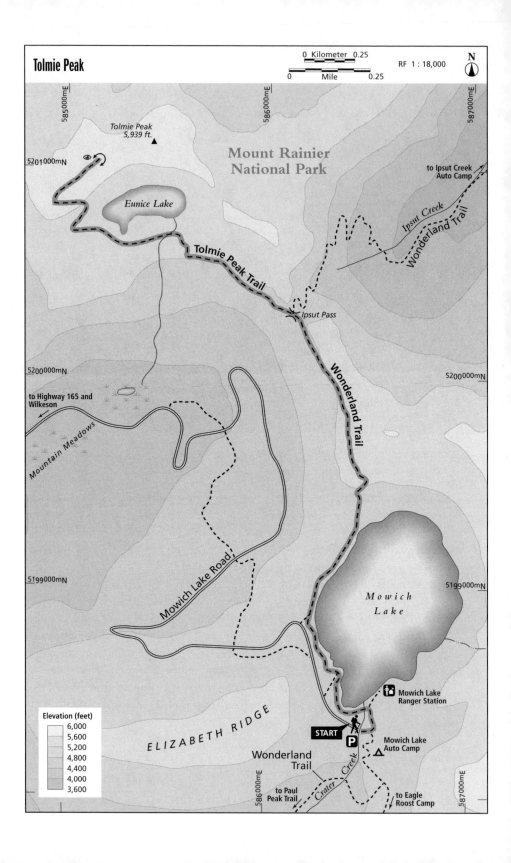

Tolmie Peak

0 Kilometer 0.25

0 Mile 0.25

RF 1 : 18,000

N

585000mE

586000mE

587000mE

5201000mN

Tolmie Peak
5,939 ft. ▲

Mount Rainier
National Park

Eunice Lake

Tolmie Peak Trail

to Ipsut Creek
Auto Camp

Ipsut Creek

Wonderland Trail

Ipsut Pass

5200000mN

5200000mN

to Highway 165 and
Wilkeson

Wonderland Trail

Mountain Meadows

Mowich Lake Road

5199000mN

Mowich
Lake

5199000mN

Mowich Lake
Ranger Station

ELIZABETH RIDGE

START

P

Wonderland
Trail

Mowich Lake
Auto Camp

Crater Creek

to Paul
Peak Trail

to Eagle
Roost Camp

586000mE

587000mE

Elevation (feet)

6,000
5,600
5,200
4,800
4,400
4,000
3,600

out is spectacular. To the north you see an expanse of rolling mountains. To the south is one of the best panoramic views of Mount Rainier available in the park.

The more adventurous can carefully walk the unmaintained trail along a ridge for 0.1 mile to the true Tolmie Peak. The trail is not steep, but it is rocky and a bit tricky at points.

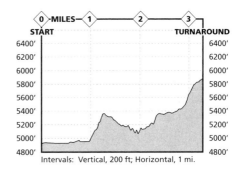

Intervals: Vertical, 200 ft; Horizontal, 1 mi.

Miles and Directions

0.0 Start at the Mowich Lake parking lot. Find the Wonderland Trail, which runs along the west side of Mowich Lake. There are several paths down to this trail, but the only trail that runs north-south along Mowich Lake is the Wonderland Trail. Head north on the Wonderland Trail.

1.5 At the Tolmie Peak Trail junction, turn left (northwest).

2.4 Stay to the left (west) on the marked trail around Eunice Lake.

3.1 Reach the Tolmie Peak Lookout and the end of the maintained trail.

3.2 A steep and rocky unmaintained trail takes you to the top of Tolmie Peak. Carefully make your way back to the main trail, and then head back to the trailhead.

6.4 Arrive back at the parking lot.

Option: Rather than hiking all the way to the top of Tolmie Peak, go only as far as Eunice Lake. This option cuts 1.6 miles off the total distance. Eunice Lake is absolutely delightful, as are the fields of avalanche lilies that bloom in July.

Hike Information

Local Information
Mount Rainier National Park Web site, www.nps.gov/mora; twenty-four-hour visitor information number, (360) 569-2211.
Mount Baker Snoqualmie National Forest, www.fs.fed.us/r6/mbs/.

Lodging
For a list of accommodations outside the park, visit www.nps.gov/mora/general/accom.htm.

Campgrounds
Ipsut Creek Campground, located 5.0 miles east of the Carbon River Entrance, issues campsites on a first-come, first-served basis. For no fee, Mowich Lake Campground, at the end of Mowich Lake Road, also offers walk-in campsites on a first-come, first-served basis. Campfires are prohibited.

56 Mother Mountain

A strenuous loop travels through the scenic meadows of Spray and Seattle Parks and around monolithic Mother Mountain. The flower-filled meadows of Spray Park offer mesmerizing views of Mount Rainier, as do the bright green boulder-strewn meadows of Seattle Park. The view from Ipsut Pass provides a view of the lands surrounding Mount Rainier National Park.

Start: Mowich Lake.
Distance: 16.0-mile loop.
Approximate hiking time: 2-day backpack.
Difficulty: Strenuous.
Seasons: Late-July through September.
Nearest town: Wilkeson.
Fees and permits: $10.00 vehicle or $5.00 individual entry fee (seven days); $30.00 annual entry fee. Wilderness Camping Permits free—reservations recommended ($20 fee).

Maps: USGS: Mowich Lake; Trails Illustrated Mount Rainier National Park; Astronaut's Vista: Mount Rainier National Park, Washington; Earthwalk Press Hiking Map & Guide.
Trail contacts: Wilkeson Wilderness Information Center, (360) 829-5127.
Trail conditions: www.nps.gov/mora/trail/tr_cnd.htm; weather, www.nps.gov/mora/current/weather.htm.

Finding the trailhead: From Wilkeson drive 9.0 miles south on Highway 165 to where the road forks. Stay to the right (south) at this fork, the way to Mowich Lake. After 3.2 miles the road becomes a well-maintained dirt road, although it can be very slippery when muddy. Follow this road another 8.8 miles to the Paul Peak trailhead on the right (south) side of the road. Pause here to pay the entry fee at the fee station, then continue south and east another 5.3 miles to Mowich Lake, a total of 26.3 miles from Wilkeson. The parking lot is fairly big, although on weekends you might have to park along the road. *DeLorme: Washington Atlas and Gazetteer:* Page 48 A1.

Special considerations: We recommend waiting until August to attempt this hike, unless you have well-tuned compass and navigational skills. Many hikers have lost their way in the snowfields of Seattle Park, especially under foggy conditions.

The Hike

Named for the impressive mountain it encircles, this loop affords excellent views of Mount Rainier and travels through Spray and Seattle Parks. Note that the second day of your hike contains most of the scenery and uphill hiking. There is one difficult hill, from the Spray Park Trail junction to Spray Park; break it up by staying at Cataract Valley Camp the first night.

▶ **Glacial silt can ruin your water filter. If you absolutely must filter such water, let the silt settle in a container before filtering.**

Some hikers prefer to do this loop counterclockwise, which means climbing the steep side of Ipsut Pass (a 3,000-foot climb). Weather may dictate which direction to hike the loop—go counterclockwise if the day you start on is

Mount Rainier from Spray Park.

clear and the following day is forecast to be cloudy. This way you will not miss the spectacular scenery in Spray Park.

From the Mowich Lake parking lot, go to the Wonderland Trail, which runs along the west side of Mowich Lake. There are several paths down to this trail, but the only trail that runs north-south along Mowich Lake is the Wonderland Trail. Head north on the Wonderland Trail. The first 0.5 mile continues along Mowich Lake, and then the trail slopes gently uphill to the top of Ipsut Pass. Just before the top of Ipsut Pass, the Tolmie Peak Trail splits left (northwest). Stay right (north), traveling on the Wonderland Trail.

The first 0.5 mile of the descent down Ipsut Pass is very steep and open. If it is a hot day, be sure to drink plenty of water—and be thankful you are not hiking up the pass! You can see Castle Peak to your right (east), towering above the valley. After this steep downhill, the trail levels out slightly and dives into the forest; the trail continues downhill for the next 3.1 miles. You will cross several clear streams on the descent, all pristine locations to filter cold mountain water.

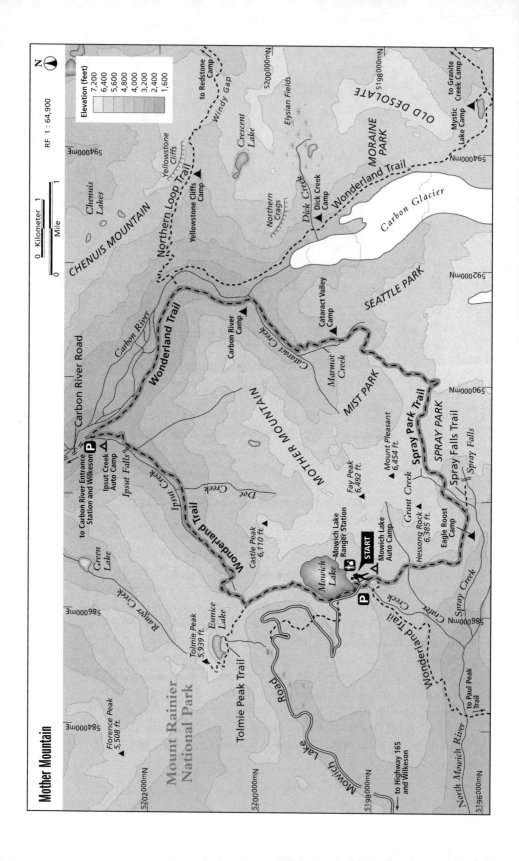

Mother Mountain

RF 1 : 64,900

Elevation (feet)

7,200
6,400
5,600
4,800
4,000
3,200
2,400
1,600

0 Kilometer 1

0 Mile 1

N

Mount Rainier National Park

to Carbon River Entrance Station and Wilkeson

Carbon River Road

Carbon River

Wonderland Trail

Northern Loop Trail

CHENUIS MOUNTAIN

Chenuis Lakes

Yellowstone Cliffs

Yellowstone Cliffs Camp

Crescent Lake

Windy Gap

to Redstone Camp

Northern Crags

Elysian Fields

Dick Creek

Dick Creek Camp

Wonderland Trail

OLD DESOLATE

MORAINE PARK

Mystic Lake Camp

to Granite Creek Camp

Carbon Glacier

SEATTLE PARK

Carbon River Camp

Cataract Creek

Cataract Valley Camp

Marmot Creek

MIST PARK

Spray Park Trail

SPRAY PARK

Spray Falls Trail

Spray Falls

Mount Pleasant 6,454 ft.

Grant Creek

Hessong Rock 6,385 ft.

Eagle Roost Camp

Spray Creek

Crater Creek

Wonderland Trail

to Paul Peak Trail

North Mowich River

Florence Peak 5,508 ft.

Ranger Creek

Green Lake

Ipsut Falls

Ipsut Creek

Ipsut Creek Auto Camp

Wonderland Trail

Doe Creek

Castle Peak 6,110 ft.

MOTHER MOUNTAIN

Fay Peak 6,492 ft.

Mowich Lake Ranger Station

Mowich Lake

Mowich Lake Auto Camp

START

Tolmie Peak 5,939 ft.

Eunice Lake

Tolmie Peak Trail

Mowich Lake Road

to Highway 165 and Wilkeson

The next couple of miles to the Spray Park Trail climb easily along the Carbon River, whose waters run brown from an abundance of glacier silt. Thimbleberry bushes line the trail. These berries ripen in August. You can see the north side of Mother Mountain at times, but the more impressive view of the south side awaits you.

At the junction with the Spray Park Trail, head west (right), unless you are taking the option to the Carbon Glacier. Steep switchbacks lead up to Cataract Valley Camp. Keep in mind that you have to gain 1,600 feet before reaching camp. If you are a berry lover, look for the salmonberries and blueberries that line the trail to Cataract Camp in August.

On the second day, you will continue up the hill, gaining another 1,700 feet. The trail travels through forest initially, but when the trail opens up, you know you have reached Seattle Park. Even though you travel through only a corner of Seattle Park, the green grass of the park is breathtaking, as are the charming little streams that wind through the meadows. From Seattle Park you can see Mother Mountain's jagged peaks.

▶ **Tillicum is from** *tilakum,* **a Chinook word meaning friend.**

Continuing uphill, you come to several snowfields. The number of snowfields you encounter depends on the time of year, although at least one lingers year-round. Flags, painted rocks, and cairns help you through the snowfields, but we recommend waiting until August unless you have well-tuned compass and navigational skills to prevent you from losing your way, especially under foggy conditions.

When you start heading downhill, you have entered Spray Park. Mount Rainier towers majestically above, with Tillicum Point jutting out its side. Marmots and lupine fill the meadows of Spray Park. As you head downhill you will see Hessong Rock and Mount Pleasant in front of you.

It is downhill to the end of Spray Park, with more downhill to the junction with Spray Falls Trail. Take the side trip to Spray Falls when you reach this junction. (See Options.) A viewpoint from Eagle Cliff, which has a great view of the North Mowich Glacier, is located less than 0.5 mile after the junction with the Spray Falls Trail. This home stretch takes you over gentlly rolling hills, a relief after the previous elevation gains and losses.

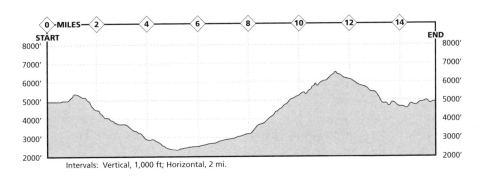

Intervals: Vertical, 1,000 ft; Horizontal, 2 mi.

Miles and Directions

0.0 Start at the Mowich Lake parking lot. Find the Wonderland Trail, which runs along the west side of Mowich Lake. There are several paths down to this trail, but the only trail that runs north-south along Mowich Lake is the Wonderland Trail. Head north on the Wonderland Trail.

1.5 The Tolmie Peak Trail forks off to the left. Stay to the right, heading north over Ipsut Pass.

5.1 A spur trail to Ipsut Creek Campground diverges left (north); stay to the right (east).

6.8 A trail that connects with the Northern Loop Trail heads off to the left, crossing the Carbon River. Stay to the right, heading south.

7.7 Take the Spray Park Trail to your right (south), heading uphill to Cataract Valley Camp. (See Options for a possible side trip to Carbon Glacier.)

9.3 A spur trail to Cataract Valley Camp travels off to the left (east).

11.9 After crossing the snowfields at the top of Seattle Park, enter the meadows of Spray Park.

14.0 At the junction with Spray Falls Trail, stay to the right (west), unless you want to take the short 0.1-mile jaunt to the falls. (See Options for a possible side trip to Spray Falls.)

14.1 A spur trail to Eagle's Roost Camp heads south; stay to the right, heading west.

15.8 At the junction with the Wonderland Trail, stay right, heading northwest toward Mowich Lake.

16.0 Return to Mowich Lake.

Options: A side trip to the Carbon Glacier is definitely worth your time. It is only about 1.0 mile round-trip from the junction with the Spray Park Trail. (See Hike 51: Carbon Glacier and Moraine.) The side trip to Spray Falls, only 0.1 mile one-way from the junction with the main trail, is also worthwhile.

Wilderness camping: Both Carbon River and Cataract Valley Camps allow stoves only, as is the case in all backcountry camps. You can stay at either Carbon River Camp or Cataract Valley Camp, depending on availability and your itinerary.

Carbon River Camp has four individual sites, and the Park Service is in the process of adding a group site. The first two sites have excellent tent sites, although they present little privacy. Sites 3 and 4 are more secluded but have slanted tent sites; Site 4 is the most remote. The water source for this camp is Cataract Creek, a good 0.1 mile from all the sites.

Cataract Valley Camp has seven individual sites and a group site for parties with more than five persons. The most reliable water source is located in the center of the camp. There are normally two small streams in early summer, but one dries up later in the season. Sites 3, 4, and 5 are located in the center of camp and are all very flat and spacious. The group site is much bigger and has the same attractive qualities. Sites 6 and 7 are tucked away at the end of camp next to a rockfield. The tent site at Site 6 is definitely lacking, but 7 is very flat and spacious. Sites 1 and 2 are at the beginning of camp, next to the outhouse. Avoid Site 1 if possible; Site 2 fits one tent without too much difficulty.

Hike Information

Local Information
Mount Rainier National Park Web site,
www.nps.gov/mora; twenty-four-hour visitor
information, (360) 569–2211.
Mount Baker Snoqualmie National Forest,
www.fs.fed.us/r6/mbs/.

Lodging
For a list of accommodations outside the
park, visit www.nps.gov/mora/general/
accom.htm.

Campgrounds
Ipsut Creek Campground, located 5.0 miles
east of the Carbon River Entrance, issues
campsites on a first-come, first-served basis.
For no fee, Mowich Lake Campground, at the
end of Mowich Lake Road, also offers walk-in
campsites on a first-come, first-served basis.
Campfires are prohibited.

57 Lake James

A long, steep climb takes you through a beautiful forest and to impressive rock formations of Yellowstone Cliffs. The trail continues over a subalpine meadow pass to
the boulder-strewn meadows of Windy Gap, an opportune location for viewing the
northeastern portion of Mount Rainier National Park. The hike ends at Lake James,
a tranquil mountain lake that is a popular fishing destination.

Start: Ipsut Creek Campground.
Distance: 16.8-mile out-and-back.
Approximate hiking time: 2-day backpack.
Difficulty: Strenuous.
Seasons: Mid-July through September.
Nearest town: Wilkeson.
Fees and permits: $10.00 vehicle or $5.00
individual entry fee (seven days); $30.00
annual entry fee. Wilderness Camping Permits
free—reservations recommended ($20 fee).

Maps: USGS: Mowich Lake and Sunrise; Trails
Illustrated Mount Rainier National Park; Astro-
naut's Vista: Mount Rainier National Park,
Washington; Earthwalk Press Hiking Map &
Guide.
Trail contacts: Wilkeson Wilderness Informa-
tion Center, (360) 829–5127.
Trail conditions: www.nps.gov/mora/trail/
tr_cnd.htm; weather, www.nps.gov/mora/
current/weather.htm.

Finding the trailhead: From the Carbon River Entrance Station (see Getting There), drive 5.0
miles east on Carbon River Road to Ipsut Creek Campground. This is the end of the road, and
the trailhead. If the many spaces at Ipsut Creek Campground are full, you can park along the
road in permitted areas. *DeLorme: Washington Atlas and Gazetteer:* Page 48 A2.

Special considerations: The Carbon River Road may be open only to high-clearance vehicles
after washouts have eaten up portions of the road. This road often washes out and has been
known to close all together. The footlogs over Carbon River may also wash out. Call ahead, or
check the Mount Rainier Web site for current conditions.

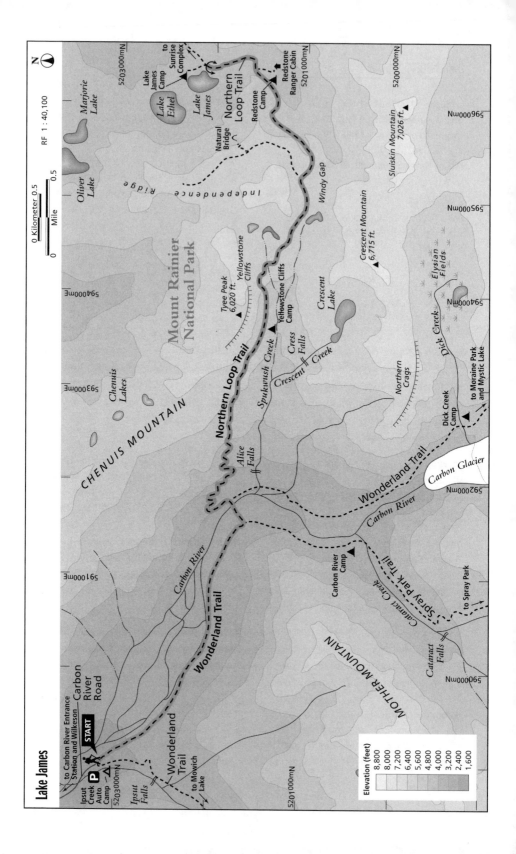

The Hike

From Ipsut Creek Campground follow the small connector trail south to the Wonderland Trail. The Ipsut Falls spur trail intersects to the right (west) shortly after leaving Ipsut Creek Campground. If you desire, take this spur trail to gently cascading Ipsut Falls. From the spur trail continue traveling south to the Wonderland Trail. The trail ascends very gently for the first couple of miles and crosses the silty waters of the Carbon River. Once on the east bank of the river, you will come to the Northern Loop Trail.

> ▶ Lake James was named for the son of Ranger Thomas O'Farrell by the Mountaineers in 1912.

The footlogs over Carbon River frequently wash out and sometimes remain washed out for weeks at a time. If fording the Carbon River seems too dangerous, follow the Wonderland Trail (southeast) for another mile, cross the Carbon River over the suspension bridge, then follow the Northern Loop Trail left (north) a little over a mile to reach the spot where you would have otherwise crossed.

Stay to the left (north) at the junction with the Northern Loop Trail, heading toward Yellowstone Cliffs and Windy Gap. The trail now takes a turn toward the sky. In about 3 miles, it climbs more than 3,000 feet, making this a long and very steep ridge. There are no views along the climb, save for the cooling foliage of the tall trees and lush low bushes, to distract you from the effort.

When the trees open up to reveal a steep mountain meadow covered with a variety of wildflowers, you know that you are near Yellowstone Cliffs. Almost immediately after entering the meadow, the trail forks. To your right (south), a small trail descends to Yellowstone Cliffs Camp. To your left (northeast), the main trail ascends toward Windy Gap. As you continue to switchback through fields of flowers, look to the north to admire Yellowstone Cliffs, a columned rock formation topped by Tyee Peak.

The switchbacks soon end in a subalpine clearing between two mountains and a ridge. About a mile beyond the junction to Yellowstone Cliffs Camp, an unmaintained trail spurs to the left (north). If you want to explore Yellowstone Cliffs, this trail travels over Tyee Peak to Bee Flat. Tread lightly, though: The subalpine meadow is fragile and susceptible to damage.

Back on the Northern Loop Trail, you enter Windy Gap less than 1.0 mile beyond the unmaintained spur trail. Nestled between Sluiskin Mountain and Independence Ridge, Windy Gap is a green meadow strewn with boulders. As you reach Windy Gap, you also come to the intersection with the Independence Ridge Trail, 6.5 miles into the hike. A clear stream, perfect for filtering water, bisects the gap. A great view of the northeastern section of the park awaits you.

Continue east along the Northern Loop Trail. The trail leads down Windy Gap, into a boulder field and through a forest for about another 2 miles. A mileage sign in the middle of the trail to the lake attempts to dissuade people from trampling the banks of Lake James. Overuse in the 1970s led to the destruction of the land around Lake James, but recent restoration efforts are proving successful. You can still fish at Lake James and the lake beyond it, Lake Ethel, but please avoid straying from the path. Take the trail to the left (northwest) and you encounter Lake James in less than 0.2 mile.

Miles and Directions

0.0 Start at the Ipsut Creek Campground. Follow the small connector trail to the Wonderland Trail.

0.2 A less than 0.1-mile spur trail to Ipsut Falls heads off to the right (west). Continue south on the trail to the junction with Wonderland Trail.

2.0 Turn left (northeast) onto the spur trail that crosses Carbon River.

2.3 Stay left (north) at the Northern Loop Trail junction and begin climbing up the steep ridge toward Yellowstone Cliffs.

5.1 A trail forks downhill (south) to Yellowstone Cliffs Camp. Stay left (northeast), traveling through the meadow.

6.1 To the left (north), an unmaintained trail goes over Tyee Peak to Bee Flat. Stay to the right toward Windy Gap.

6.5 A trail to Independence Ridge forks off to the north; you have reached the beginning of Windy Gap. (See Option for a possible side trip to Independence Ridge.)

8.4 Trail to Lake James. Try your hand at fishing or retrace your steps.

16.8 Arrive back at Ipsut Creek Campground.

Option: If you have the time and energy, take the side trip along Independence Ridge to the natural bridge. Do not continue on the unmaintained trail beyond the spur trail to the natural bridge, but do descend to the natural bridge. The arching rocks are a wonder of nature. It is only 0.9 mile to the natural bridge, so this side trip adds 1.8 miles to your hike.

Wilderness camping: Yellowstone Cliffs Camp has a fantastic view of, what else, Yellowstone Cliffs and has two nice campsites. Site 1 has a better view and proximity to water. Lake James Camp has three individual sites and one group site located

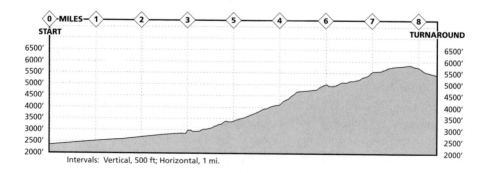

Intervals: Vertical, 500 ft; Horizontal, 1 mi.

far from the banks of Lake James. The water source is Van Horn Creek, a short trek back on the Northern Loop Trail toward Lake James.

Hike Information

Local Information

Mount Rainier National Park Web site, www.nps.gov/mora; twenty-four-hour visitor information, (360) 569-2211.
Mount Baker Snoqualmie National Forest, www.fs.fed.us/r6/mbs/.

Lodging

For a list of accommodations outside the park, visit www.nps.gov/mora/general/accom.htm.

Campgrounds

Ipsut Creek Campground, located 5.0 miles east of the Carbon River Entrance, issues campsites on a first-come, first-served basis. For no fee, Mowich Lake Campground, at the end of Mowich Lake Road, also offers walk-in campsites on a first-come, first-served basis. Campfires are prohibited.

58 Spray Park

A short, but steep hike takes you through beautiful forest and to a subalpine meadow dotted with colorful wildflowers. The open meadows of Spray Park provide spectacular views of Mount Rainier and Mother Mountain.

Start: Mowich Lake.
Distance: 8.0-mile out-and-back.
Approximate hiking time: 3.5 to 5.5 hours.
Difficulty: Moderate.
Seasons: Late-July through September.
Nearest town: Wilkeson.
Fees and permits: $10.00 vehicle or $5.00 individual entry fee (seven days); $30.00 annual entry fee. Wilderness Camping Permits free—reservations recommended ($20 fee).

Maps: USGS: Mowich Lake; Trails Illustrated Mount Rainier National Park; Astronaut's Vista: Mount Rainier National Park, Washington; Earthwalk Press Hiking Map & Guide.
Trail contacts: Wilkeson Wilderness Information Center, (360) 829-5127.
Trail conditions: www.nps.gov/mora/trail/tr_cnd.htm; weather, www.nps.gov/mora/current/weather.htm.

Finding the trailhead: From Wilkeson drive 9.0 miles south on Highway 165 until the road forks. Stay to the right (south) at this fork, the way to Mowich Lake. After 3.2 miles the road becomes a well-maintained dirt road, although it can be very slippery when muddy. Follow this road for another 8.8 miles to the Paul Peak trailhead on the right (south) side of the road. Pause to pay the entrance fee at the fee station here, then continue south and east another 5.3 miles to Mowich Lake, a total of 26.3 miles from Wilkeson. The parking lot is fairly big, although on weekends you might have to park along the road. *DeLorme: Washington Atlas and Gazetteer:* Page 48 A1.

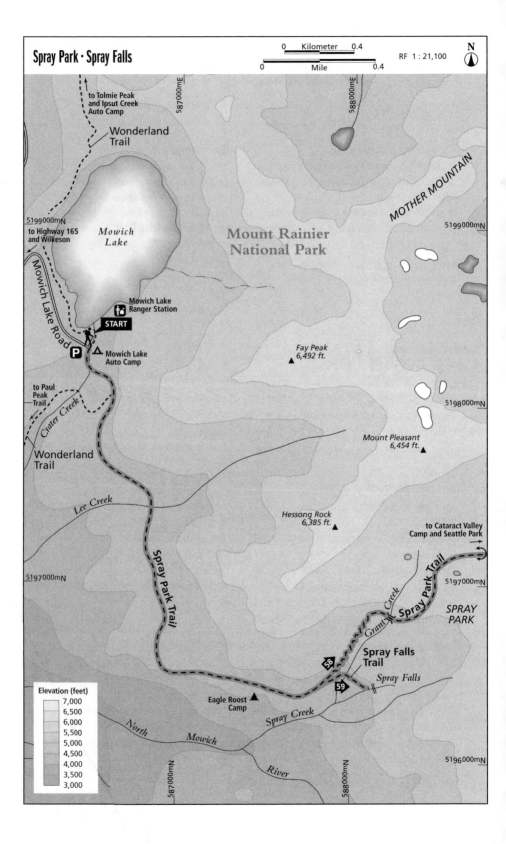

Spray Park · Spray Falls

Kilometer 0.4

Mile 0.4

RF 1 : 21,100

N

to Tolmie Peak
and Ipsut Creek
Auto Camp

Wonderland
Trail

5199000mN

to Highway 165
and Wilkeson

Mowich
Lake

Mowich Lake Road

Crater Creek

to Paul
Peak
Trail

Wonderland
Trail

Lee Creek

Mowich Lake
Ranger Station

START

P

Mowich Lake
Auto Camp

Mount Rainier
National Park

MOTHER MOUNTAIN

5199000mN

Fay Peak
6,492 ft.

5198000mN

Mount Pleasant
6,454 ft.

Hessong Rock
6,385 ft.

to Cataract Valley
Camp and Seattle Park

Spray Park Trail

5197000mN

Spray Park Trail

5197000mN

SPRAY
PARK

Grant Creek

58

59

Spray Falls
Trail

Spray Falls

Eagle Roost
Camp

Spray Creek

North

Mowich

River

Elevation (feet)
7,000
6,500
6,000
5,500
5,000
4,500
4,000
3,500
3,000

587000mN

588000mN

5196000mN

Special considerations: We recommend waiting until August to attempt this hike, unless you have well-tuned compass and navigational skills. Many hikers have lost their way in the snow-fields of Seattle Park, especially under foggy conditions.

The Hike

The Spray Park Trail is very popular due to the amazing views of Mount Rainier available from Spray Park. Views of Mother Mountain, Mount Pleasant, and Hessong Rock also bedazzle you, while hoary marmots and lupine fill the rocky meadows of Spray Park. The first 1.9 miles of the trail dip and climb over rolling hills; the trail then heads uphill all the way to the end of Spray Park.

Head to the south end of the Mowich Lake parking lot, past the restrooms and campground to the trailhead. Head south on the Wonderland Trail and travel down-hill for 0.2 mile to the first junction. Go left (southeast) where the Spray Park Trail forks off from the Wonderland Trail. A short spur trail about a mile from the junction leads to a viewpoint over Eagle Cliff, a total of 1.5 miles into your hike. You can see the North Mowich Glacier clearly from the viewpoint.

When you have traveled 1.7 miles total, you will see the signs for Eagle's Roost Camp, which is less than 0.1 mile away and south of the Spray Park Trail. Just beyond the spur trail to Eagle's Roost Camp is the junction with the Spray Falls Trail. This is a worthy option. If you choose not to go to Spray Falls, stay left and head north-east up the trail. There is no official beginning for Spray Park, but it probably begins when the forest thins and Hessong Rock appears to the south of the trail.

Spray Park continues for 1.2 miles to its highest point before the trail reaches several snowfields and starts descending into Seattle Park. Continuing uphill, you come to several snowfields. The number of snowfields you encounter depends on the time of year, although at least one lingers year-round. Flags, painted rocks, and cairns help you through the snowfields, but we recommend waiting until August to descend into Seattle Park, unless you have well-tuned compass and navigational skills to prevent you from losing your way. Hikers have been known to become temporarily lost in this area, especially under foggy conditions. You can travel into the green meadows of Seattle Park as far as you desire and then head back the way you came.

Miles and Directions

0.0 Start at Mowich Lake. Head to the south end of Mowich Lake, past the restrooms and Mowich Lake Campground to the Wonderland Trail. Go south on the Wonderland Trail for a little over 0.2 mile to the junction with the Spray Park Trail.

0.2 At the junction with the Spray Park Trail, go left (southeast) onto the Spray Park Trail.

1.8 The junction with the spur trail to Eagle's Roost Camp leaves the trail. Stay to the left, heading east.

1.9 At the junction with Spray Falls Trail, stay left (northeast), continuing on the Spray Park Trail. (See Option for a possible side trip to Spray Falls.)

2.8 As you leave the forest, you have entered Spray Park.

4.0 The beginning of Seattle Park roughly coincides with the time you traverse the snowfields and begin descending. Now retrace your steps.

8.0 Arrive back at Mowich Lake Camp.

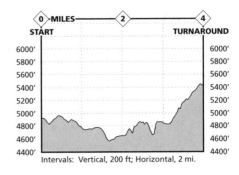

Intervals: Vertical, 200 ft; Horizontal, 2 mi.

Option: Take the side trip to Spray Falls, only a short 0.1 mile up the Spray Falls Trail. The misty falls are fascinating. At the junction with the Spray Falls Trail, go right (southeast) and follow the trail to the falls.

Wilderness camping: You can stay at Eagle's Roost Camp. The camp only allows stoves, as with all backcountry campgrounds. There are seven sites and one pit toilet. The only water source is Grant Creek, a little more than 0.1 mile from the camp.

Hike Information

Local Information
Mount Rainier National Park Web site,
www.nps.gov/mora; twenty-four-hour visitor information, (360) 569–2211.
Mount Baker Snoqualmie National Forest,
www.fs.fed.us/r6/mbs/.

Lodging
For a list of accommodations outside the park, visit www.nps.gov/mora/general/accom.htm.

Campgrounds
Ipsut Creek Campground, located 5.0 miles east of the Carbon River Entrance, issues campsites on a first-come, first-served basis. For no fee, Mowich Lake Campground, at the end of Mowich Lake Road, also offers walk-in campsites on a first-come, first-served basis. Campfires are prohibited.

59 Spray Falls

This short, relatively flat hike travels through beautiful forest to striking Spray Falls. From the top of these tall falls, water sprays out, leaving the air misty and raining down on the colorful wildflowers lining Spray Creek below the falls.

Start: Mowich Lake.
Distance: 4.0-mile out-and-back.
Approximate hiking time: 1.5 to 2.5 hours.
Difficulty: Easy.
Seasons: Early July through September.
Nearest town: Wilkeson.
Fees and permits: $10.00 vehicle or $5.00 individual entry fee (seven days); $30.00 annual entry fee. Wilderness Camping Permits free—reservations recommended ($20 fee).

Maps: USGS: Mowich Lake; Trails Illustrated Mount Rainier National Park; Astronaut's Vista: Mount Rainier National Park, Washington; Earthwalk Press Hiking Map & Guide.
Trail contacts: Wilkeson Wilderness Information Center, (360) 829-5127.
Trail conditions: www.nps.gov/mora/trail/tr_cnd.htm; weather, www.nps.gov/mora/current/weather.htm.

Finding the trailhead: From Wilkeson drive 9.0 miles south on Highway 165 until the road forks. Stay to the right (south) at this fork, the way to Mowich Lake. After 3.2 miles the road becomes a well-maintained dirt road, although it can be very slippery when muddy. Follow this road for another 8.8 miles to the Paul Peak trailhead on the right (south) side of the road. Pause here to pay the entrance fee at the fee station, then continue south and east 5.3 miles to Mowich Lake, a total of 26.3 miles from Wilkeson. The parking lot is fairly big, but on sunny weekends you might have to park along the road. *DeLorme: Washington Atlas and Gazetteer:* Page 48 A1.

The Hike

This hike (see map on page 276) has no significant elevation gain, but it trundles over rolling hills all the way to Spray Falls. A trail construction crew named Spray Falls in 1883 because they felt that the cascading falls broke "into a mass of spray." The well-maintained, heavily used trail winds through beautiful forest. Expect to see many other park visitors; please reduce your impact by staying on the trail.

Head to the south end of Mowich Lake, past the restrooms and Mowich Lake Campground to the Wonderland Trail. Go south on the Wonderland Trail for a little over 0.2 mile to the junction with the Spray Park Trail. Go left (southeast) when the Spray Park Trail forks off from the Wonderland Trail. About a mile after the junction, a short spur trail from the junction leads to an overlook from Eagle Cliff, a total of 1.5 miles into your hike. You can see the North Mowich Glacier clearly from the lookout.

After traveling 0.3 mile past the lookout, you will see the signs for Eagle's Roost Camp. Eagle's Roost Camp is less than 0.1 mile away and southwest of the Spray Park

Trail. Just beyond the camp is the junction with the Spray Falls Trail. Go right (southeast) onto the Spray Falls Trail, which goes 0.1 mile to Spray Creek and Spray Falls.

The falls drop roughly 160 feet. At the top of the falls, the water sprays off the mossy rocks, leaving the air misty and cool. Lewis and yellow monkeyflowers line Spray Creek, adding to the beauty of this natural wonder.

Miles and Directions

0.0 Start at Mowich Lake. Head to the south end of the lake, past the restrooms and Mowich Lake Campground to the Wonderland Trail. Go south on the Wonderland Trail for a little over 0.2 mile to the junction with the Spray Park Trail.

0.2 At the junction with the Spray Park Trail, go left (southeast) onto the trail.

1.8 On the right, the spur trail to Eagle's Roost Camp leaves the trail, heading south. Stay to the left (east).

1.9 Turn right, heading southeast at the junction with Spray Falls Trail.

2.0 The trail travels next to Spray Creek; Spray Falls lies at the end of the trail. Enjoy the falls before retracing your steps.

4.0 Arrive back at Mowich Lake.

Option: Hike farther up to Spray Park, which begins only 0.9 mile from the junction with the Spray Falls Trail. This will make your trip roughly 2.0 to 2.5 miles longer, depending how far you decide to hike up Spray Park. (See Hike 58: Spray Park.)

Wilderness camping: Eagle's Roost Camp allows only stoves, as with all backcountry campgrounds. There are seven sites and one pit toilet. The only water source is Grant Creek, a little more than 0.1 mile from camp.

Hike Information

Local Information

Mount Rainier National Park Web site, www.nps.gov/mora; twenty-four-hour visitor information, (360) 569-2211.
Mount Baker Snoqualmie National Forest, www.fs.fed.us/r6/mbs.

Lodging

For a list of accommodations outside the park, visit www.nps.gov/mora/general/accom.htm.

Campgrounds

Ipsut Creek Campground, located 5.0 miles east of the Carbon River Entrance, issues campsites on a first-come, first-served basis. For no fee, Mowich Lake Campground, at the end of Mowich Lake Road, also offers walk-in campsites on a first-come, first-served basis. Campfires are prohibited.

◀ *Spray Falls.* Marika Engelhardt

60 Chenuis Falls

Despite its shortness, this hike takes you through a variety of natural wonders. The hike begins by traversing the wide, pebbly riverbed of Carbon River and continues through an old-growth forest to beautiful, cascading Chenuis Falls.

Start: Chenuis Falls trailhead.
Distance: 0.4-mile out-and-back.
Approximate hiking time: 30 minutes.
Difficulty: Easy.
Seasons: May through October.
Nearest town: Wilkeson.
Fees and permits: $10.00 vehicle or $5.00 individual entry fee (seven days); $30.00 annual entry fee.

Maps: USGS: Mowich Lake; Trails Illustrated Mount Rainier National Park; Astronaut's Vista: Mount Rainier National Park, Washington; Earthwalk Press Hiking Map & Guide.
Trail contacts: Wilkeson Wilderness Information Center, (360) 829-5127.
Trail conditions: www.nps.gov/mora/trail/ tr_cnd.htm; weather, www.nps.gov/mora/ current/weather.htm.

Finding the trailhead: From the Carbon River Entrance Station (see Getting There), drive 3.5 miles to the Chenuis Falls trailhead, located on the left (north). Limited parking is available. *DeLorme: Washington Atlas and Gazetteer:* Page 48 A2.

Special considerations: Check ahead to make sure the footlogs over the Carbon River have not washed out before starting this hike.

The Carbon River Road may be open only to high-clearance vehicles after washouts have eaten up portions of the road. This road often washes out and has been known to close all together. Call ahead, or check the Mount Rainier Web site for current conditions.

The Hike

From the trailhead descend the steep side of the riverbank to the first crossing of the Carbon River. There may be up to seven footlogs crossing the many channels of the Carbon River, but the location and number changes according to how the river reroutes itself. Continue traveling northeast toward the north bank of the river, making sure to look up the riverbed toward Mount Rainier for fantastic views of Crescent Mountain in front of Mount Rainier.

The trail, consisting of gray sand and river rock from the Carbon River, is sometimes difficult to follow, even though the Park Service tries to outline it in rock. If you continue heading toward the footlogs, it will lead you all the way to the north bank. At this point the trail heads into beautiful old-growth forest with ferns, devil's club, and lichen-covered trees lining the path. Continue hiking along the trail. You will pass an unmaintained trail to your left, but continue hiking north along the main trail to a small overlook with a view of Chenuis Falls. The unmaintained trail

Chenuis Falls.

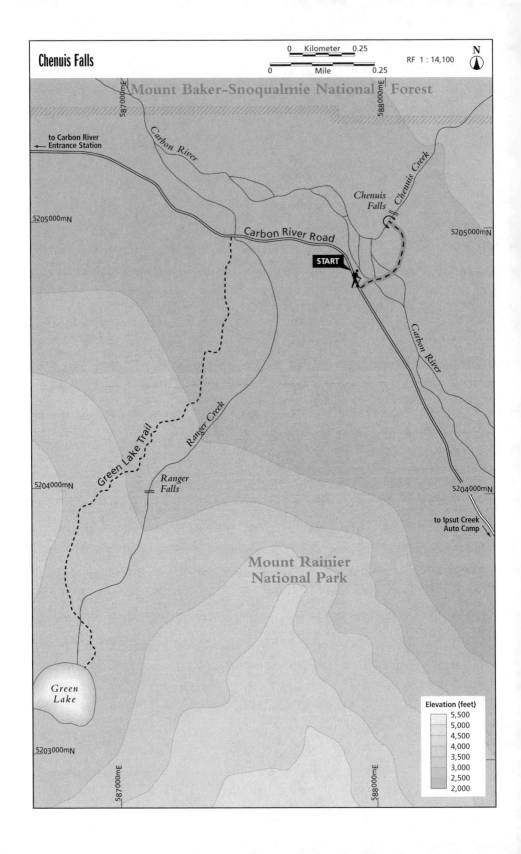

Chenuis Falls

Mount Baker-Snoqualmie National Forest

0   Kilometer   0.25
0   Mile   0.25

RF 1 : 14,100

N

to Carbon River
Entrance Station

Carbon River

Chenuis Creek

Chenuis
Falls

Carbon River Road

START

587000mE

588000mE

5205000mN

5205000mN

Carbon River

Green Lake Trail

Ranger Creek

Ranger
Falls

5204000mN

5204000mN

to Ipsut Creek
Auto Camp

Mount Rainier
National Park

Green
Lake

5203000mN

587000mE

588000mE

Elevation (feet)

5,500
5,000
4,500
4,000
3,500
3,000
2,500
2,000

that you just passed also takes you to the falls; many people take that trail on their return trip, making the hike a lollipop.

Take the time to enjoy the clear waters of Chenuis Falls as they cascade down the smooth rocks. The falls are at a gentle slope, allowing the waters to weave between large rocks. Just past your viewing point, the clear waters from Chenuis Creek join the silty waters of the Carbon River.

Miles and Directions

0.0 Start at Chenuis Falls trailhead. Hike through the riverbed to the north side, using the footlogs as your guide.

0.1 Enter the forest. You will immediately pass an old, unmaintained trail to the right, heading east. Continue north. You will pass another unmaintained trail to your left; continue to the right (north).

0.2 The trail takes you to a small overlook with a view of Chenuis Falls. Either retrace your steps or make a small lollipop by taking the unmaintained trail back to the main trail.

0.4 Arrive back at the trailhead.

Hike Information

Local Information

Mount Rainier National Park Web site, www.nps.gov/mora; twenty-four-hour visitor information, (360) 569-2211.
Mount Baker Snoqualmie National Forest, www.fs.fed.us/r6/mbs/.

Lodging

For a list of accommodations outside the park, visit www.nps.gov/mora/general/accom.htm.

Campgrounds

Ipsut Creek Campground, located 5.0 miles east of the Carbon River Entrance, issues campsites on a first-come, first-served basis. For no fee, Mowich Lake Campground, at the end of Mowich Lake Road, also offers walk-in campsites on a first-come, first-served basis. Campfires are prohibited.

Wonderland Trail

The renowned Wonderland Trail encircles magnificent Mount Rainier. This lengthy trail allows you to indulge in all the natural wonders the park offers. The trail travels through strikingly different landscapes, allowing you to view the rich and diverse flora and fauna of Mount Rainier National Park. The trip begins at Mount Rainier's largest mountain lake but immediately drops in elevation, bringing you through Mount Rainier's only rain forest, filled with old-growth Douglas fir and red cedar. You continue on to pass the snout of a glacier and hike through pristine subalpine meadows sprinkled in colorful wildflowers, all while experiencing the land change before your eyes and under your feet. From here you will experience dramatic elevation gains and losses that take you through a variety of landscapes guaranteed to fulfill every hiker's inner dream. The Wonderland Trail grants you the unique opportunity of viewing all twenty-five glaciers carved into the mountain, with majestic Mount Rainier enchanting you behind its veil of glaciers.

Because the Wonderland Trail commands a considerable amount of time, up to two weeks, hikers tend to rush through this hike like a race-trek. Our advice is to allot yourself enough time to savor the landscape, like a delicious meal. Moreover, keep in mind that you will be carrying a very heavy pack and that there are extreme elevation changes throughout the hike. Some persons finish the hike in nine days, averaging 10 miles per day; we recommend taking twelve to thirteen days, averaging 7 to 8 miles per day.

Potentially, you can begin the Wonderland Trail at any point you can find a trailhead with ample parking. The majority of hikers begin the Wonderland Trail from the Longmire Historic District, which provides access to services, rangers, supplies, and the Longmire Inn. Additionally, a tour bus makes a stop at Longmire, and it is closest to the busy Nisqually Entrance Station. We have chosen to write the Wonderland Trail starting at Mowich Lake for several reasons. First, starting the Wonderland Trail at Mowich Lake allows you to access the services and facilities at Sunrise and Longmire during the hike, rather than waiting until the end of the loop. Second, though quite a drive up a gravel road, Mowich Lake lies in the northwest corner of the park, nearest to the closest metropolis to Mount Rainier: Seattle,

Washington. Third, because the government outlaws shipment of fuel in the mail, you will probably want to pick some up at Longmire before the final leg of the trip. Finally, you can reward yourself for completing the mountain loop and refresh yourself for the drive home by jumping into Mowich Lake. High demand for specific campsites may give you little choice in where you begin the loop, and no matter where you start, you face severe ascensions and elevation drops.

The Wonderland Trail is often unnavigable until mid-July and closes again the end of September due to snow coverage, yet snow levels vary year to year. Call (360) 569–HIKE (4453) or visit the Web site for current conditions. It may be possible to start your hike earlier.

Wilderness Camping Reservations

This ever-popular route experiences a considerable influx of hikers every year, necessitating that you reserve campsites as soon as possible. (See Fees and permits for reservation information.) The park accepts reservations as early as April 1. By the end of April there are usually no reservable campsites left at either Summerland or Indian Bar Camp, making the excursion impossible. Moreover, cross-country camping is not an option for hikers doing one-third or more of the Wonderland Trail. You might want to plan a couple of alternative routes before you submit your reservations.

Food Cache System

As you can imagine, carrying all your supplies for such a lengthy hike can be rather overwhelming. The National Park Service has devised a food cache system that allows you to store food at various intervals throughout your hike. You can store food caches at the Longmire Wilderness Information Center, Sunrise Ranger Station, White River Wilderness Information Center, Ohanapecosh Visitor Center, and Mowich Ranger Station. The guidelines for this system are listed below, but be aware that changes often occur in the procedure. It is always a good idea to send for additional information or to check out the current restrictions and guidelines at www.nps.gov/mora/trail/wonder.htm. If you are a late- or early-season hiker, some of these stations may be closed.

- All caches must be packed in rodent-proof containers (sealed hard plastic preferred).
- Fuel may not be mailed or shipped to the park, nor may it be included in any food cache. Either carry enough fuel for your hike with you, or plan on purchasing fuel at the Longmire Gift Shop.
- All caches must be dropped off or sent to the Longmire Wilderness Information Center, Sunrise Ranger Station, White River Wilderness Information Center, Mowich Ranger Station, or Ohanapecosh Visitor Center only. Park staff will not transport caches from one area of the park to another.

WHERE TO SEND FOOD CACHES: Refer to visitor facilities for directions to and more information on each food cache site.

Longmire Wilderness Information Center

Mount Rainier National Park
Longmire Wilderness Information Center
General Delivery
Longmire, WA 98397

Mowich Ranger Station

Mount Rainier National Park
Wilkeson Wilderness Information Center
P.O. Box 423
Wilkeson, WA 98396

Ohanapecosh Visitor Center

Mount Rainier National Park
Ohanapecosh Ranger Station
208 Ohanapecosh
Packwood, WA 98361

Sunrise Ranger Station or White River Wilderness Information Center

Mount Rainier National Park
Sunrise Ranger Station (or White River Wilderness Information Center)
70002 Highway 410 East
Enumclaw, WA 98022

- Longmire Wilderness Information Center and Sunrise Ranger Station are near the Wonderland Trail for easy cache pickup. Ohanapecosh Visitor Center and White River Wilderness Information Center are not along the Wonderland Trail and require a side trip. Before mid-June and after early September, White River Wilderness Information Center and Ohanapecosh Visitor Center may be your only options on the east side of the park.
- Use the U.S. Post Office or UPS to ship your package. Allow at least two weeks' delivery time.
- Caches will be held at White River Wilderness Information Center until Sunrise Ranger Station opens around July 1. Make sure the food cache arrives at

White River Wilderness Information Center one week prior to the hiker pickup date at Sunrise.

- If you want to pick up a food cache at Mowich Ranger Station, allow an extra week for transfer when you drop off or send your food cache to Wilkeson Wilderness Information Center.

- All caches must have the following information printed outside, separate from the shipping label:

FOOD CACHE FOR: (YOUR NAME)
FOR PICKUP AT: (NAME OF CACHE STATION)
FOR PICKUP ON: (DATE)

61 Wonderland Trail

This spectacular, nearly 90-mile loop completely encircles Mount Rainier, presenting a challenge to the ablest hiker and a comprehensive taste of Mount Rainier. This hike involves dramatic elevation changes, taking you from the calm of old-growth forests to the openness of subalpine meadows with breathtaking views of Mount Rainier.

Start: Mowich Lake.
Distance: 89.9-mile loop.
Approximate hiking time: 9- to14-day extended backpack.
Difficulty: Strenuous.
Season: Mid-July through September.
Nearest town: Wilkeson.
Fees and permits: $10.00 vehicle or $5.00 individual entry fee (seven days); $30.00 annual entry fee. Wilderness Camping Permits free—reservations recommended ($20 fee).
Maps: USGS: Golden Lakes, Mount Rainier East, Mount Rainier West, Chinook Pass, White River Park, Sunrise, Mowich Lake, and Mount

Wow; Trails Illustrated Mount Rainier National Park; Astronaut's Vista: Mount Rainier National Park, Washington; Earthwalk Press Hiking Map & Guide.
Trail contacts: Longmire Wilderness Information Center, (360) 569–HIKE (4453).
White River Wilderness Information Center, (360) 569–6030.
Wilkeson Wilderness Information Center, (360) 829–5127.
Trail conditions: www.nps.gov/mora/trail/tr_cnd.htm; weather, www.nps.gov/mora/current/weather.htm.

Finding the trailhead: From Wilkeson drive 9.0 miles south on Highway 165 until the road forks. Stay to the left (south) at this fork, the way to Mowich Lake. After 3.2 miles the road becomes a well-maintained dirt road, although it can be very slippery when muddy. Follow this road for another 8.8 miles to the Paul Peak trailhead on the right (south) side of the road. Pause here to pay the entrance fee at the fee station, then continue 5.3 miles south and east to Mowich Lake, a total of 26.3 miles from Wilkeson. Although there is a big parking lot, you might have to park along the road on a sunny weekend. *DeLorme: Washington Atlas and Gazetteer:* Page A1.

Special considerations: Historically, the western part of the park experiences numerous washouts due to glacial outburst floods. Footlogs across rivers or streams originating from glaciers frequently wash out. The National Park Service does not advise fording glacial rivers due to the high concentration of debris and the risk of large glacial boulders in the water. If you must cross, the Park Service recommends crossing early in the day and using fallen logs that span the channel. Try to choose a large tree with bark for traction—and use extreme caution! Also, always wear your boots to protect yourself from any debris suspended in the river.

▶ *Mowich,* name of the largest lake in Mount Rainier National Park, is a Native American term for deer.

Do not filter water from creeks or rivers cloudy with glacial silt, called glacial flour, suspended in them; it will ruin your filter. Bring iodine tablets and an extra filter along in case your filter fails.

The Wonderland Trail.

The Hike

From the Mowich Lake parking lot, locate the trail that runs along the west side of Mowich Lake. There are several paths down to this trail; continue heading north on the only trail that runs north–south along serene Mowich Lake, the Wonderland Trail. Head north on the Wonderland Trail. The first 0.5 mile continues along Mowich Lake and then slopes gently uphill to the top of Ipsut Pass. Near the top of Ipsut Pass, the Tolmie Peak Trail splits left (west). Stay right (northeast), traveling on the Wonderland Trail.

The first 0.5 mile down Ipsut Pass is very steep and open with salmonberry bushes lining the path. You can see Castle Peak to your right (east) towering above the valley. After 0.5 mile of steep downhill, the trail levels out and heads into the cool forest. The trail continues downhill for about 3 miles until you reach the spur trail to Ipsut Creek Campground. You will cross several clear streams on the descent, in case you need to filter water.

The next couple of miles to the Carbon River Camp climb gently along the Carbon River, which runs brown from an abundance of glacial silt. Do not try to filter this water; it will ruin your filter. As the trail opens up, the hulk of black stone above you is the north side of Mother Mountain. When you reach the junction where a small connector trail heads over the Carbon River to meet the Northern Loop Trail, stay to the right (southeast), proceeding along the Wonderland Trail. You will cross the Carbon River on a suspension bridge about a mile away. Bushes line the trail along the river, and in August the thimbleberries are ripe for the picking.

If you do not plan to camp at Carbon River Camp, follow the Wonderland Trail east across the suspension bridge over the Carbon River. This bridge offers a fantastic view high above the Carbon River. Its source, the massive Carbon Glacier, lies only 0.4 mile upstream. On the other side of the Carbon River, stay to the right (southeast), ascending toward the glacier and Dick Creek. The easy grade gives way to a steep pitch. The trees open up to reveal the Carbon Glacier, with Mount Rainier standing high above. Rubble and debris carved from the earth litter the blue ice of the Carbon Glacier. Do not be surprised to hear the echoing crashes of falling rocks as chunks of the glacier fall off into the silty waters below.

▶ In 1903 Army engineer Eugene Ricksecker was working on the road from Longtime to Paradise. His boss suggested creating a 100-mile loop of the mountain to reach the "snout of each glacier . . . in turn," but the Mountaineers objected. It was agreed that the north side of the mountain would remain roadless.

Carbon Glacier is currently undergoing a minor retreat, yet it has experienced a total retreat of only 0.6 mile since the last ice age. With a thickness of 700 feet and a volume of 0.2 cubic mile, Carbon Glacier claims the greatest measured thickness and volume of any glacier in the contiguous United States. In the 1970s park visitors saw the glacier actively advancing and witnessed it crush vegetation caught in its path.

The trail climbs steeply, paralleling Carbon Glacier, all the way to Dick Creek Camp. This allows you ample viewing time to admire the glacier. Spend some time appreciating the Northern Crags over the Carbon Glacier before heading into the forest. After the trail leads through Dick Creek Camp, it climbs through forest, switching back and forth for about 2 miles. The grade lessens when the path begins to run along Moraine Creek. Keep in mind that this is bear country. In fact, a fellow hiker said that she has not come here without seeing a bear. When we were here, we came across a small black bear that was not easily deterred by loud voices, banging pots, and shrill singing.

Beyond the streambed you come to a rockfield, then into the fields of Moraine Park. On a sunny summer day the mountain tops off your view of this large mountain meadow dotted with colorful wildflowers. At this point you have only two small hills to climb before beginning the descent to Mystic Lake. The lake rests in a valley between Mineral Mountain and the appropriately barren-looking Old Desolate. The beautiful view, however, cannot be seen from Mystic Lake Camp, 0.2 mile down the trail, but you can glimpse one of the best views of the mountain from the front porch of the Mystic patrol cabin.

The next established camp, Granite Creek Camp, is only 4.0 miles beyond Mystic Lake Camp, but in order to get there you must circumvent the Winthrop Glacier. After leaving the cozy subalpine forest near Mystic Lake, an easy 1.0-mile descent skirts the Winthrop Glacier, leading to Winthrop Creek. Cross the prepared log to the other side, and begin to climb your final big hill before reaching Sunrise. Hike 2.0 miles uphill with a few sporadic switchbacks to Granite Creek Camp. These 2.0 miles run along the Winthrop Moraine, providing an excellent glimpse of the glacier, before turning west toward forest. If you plan to pass the camp and move on toward Sunrise, stay on the Wonderland Trail, heading east through camp.

Less than 2 miles of nicely graded, long switchbacks lead to a saddle below Skyscraper Mountain, with views in all directions. You can see several trails convening and converging. More than 19 miles into your hike, you come to the Northern Loop junction. However tempting this 33.0-mile hike may be, you have your own loop to worry about: Stay on the Wonderland Trail toward Sunrise. In almost a mile you reach the junction of five trails near Frozen Lake. Signs clearly point you east and then southeast toward Sunrise Camp. If you need to go the Sunrise Ranger Station to get supplies or devour some decadent fries at the snack bar, you may want to take the Sourdough Ridge Trail for the best views. Otherwise, head downhill toward Shadow Lake and Sunrise Camp.

The trail heading east, to your left, is somewhat of an administrative road. Instead of taking this road to the Sunrise Complex, head right (south) and travel until you reach Sunrise Camp. From Sunrise Camp you must take the Sunrise Rim Trail to the Wonderland Trail. The Sunrise Rim Trail begins to the south of the camp, heading east toward Shadow Lake. The trail wraps around Shadow Lake, heads east then starts down toward the White River Campground. The Emmons Vista and Silver Forest Trail splits off from the Wonderland Trail just before you begin your descent. Stay to the right (south), or you may end up on a dead-end trail amid windblown firs. You leave the alpine meadows of Sunrise for the shade of the fir and cedar forest as you snake down to the river.

▶ Glaciers are really moving rivers of ice, which advance when snow accumulates faster than it melts. The weight of the snow squeezes the air out, packs down the snow, and compresses the glacier into ice. Even when the summer snowmelt exceeds the winter snowfall, causing the terminus of a glacier to recede, the main body of the glacier always continues moving downhill. As glaciers travel they displace rock debris and carve out U-shaped canyons. Frequent frosts burst the waterlogged rock walls along the glacier. These bursts cause large rocks to break away and join the glacier.

▶ At least eleven explosive eruptions, dozens of large lava flows, and repeated mudflows have occurred here over the past 10,000 years. These mudflows were large enough to reach densely populated areas in the Puyallup, White, and Nisqually River Valleys. Triggered by the collapse of Mount Rainier's summit, the Osceola Mudflow flowed through this area, pouring across the Enumclaw Plateau and onto the present-day Seattle 5,700 years ago. This massive mudflow, the largest known to Mount Rainier, reduced the mountain's summit from 16,000 to 14,410 feet. Little Tahoma stands as a formidable remnant of the original summit. Native Americans testify to another mudflow, coined the Electron Mudflow, which rapidly covered the forested areas of Puget Sound as recently as 500 years ago. Within three hours the foothills were buried 100 feet deep. It is postulated that debris was 30 feet deep at Orting, Washington. The volume of Mount St. Helen's mudflow was only a small fraction of the Electron Mudflow.

More than 3 miles of steep, downhill switchbacks bring you to Loop D of the popular White River Campground. Walk either way around Loop D to the other side, marked by a large picnic area with a fantastic view of Mount Rainier and White River. Look for a sign that marks the resumption of the Wonderland Trail, and start down toward the river. Cross the river over several hatched logs and bridges, and then enter the forest. The trail remains relatively flat for the next 2.7 miles to the Fryingpan Creek Trail junction. Ignore any intersecting trails to the road to Sunrise and the sound of cars zooming along until you come to the intersection with the Fryingpan Creek Trail. At this intersection stay to the right (south), following the Wonderland Trail.

Heading south from the Fryingpan Creek Trail junction, the trail climbs gradually through woods. A few switchbacks indicate that you are nearing the Fryingpan Creek crossing. Just beyond the creek you enter a gap in the forest that allows for a good glimpse of Mount Rainier. The trail then gets steeper. When the trail turns south, you have only 1.0 mile of switchbacks to go until you reach Summerland, 31.0 miles into the hike. In the Summerland area you stand in fields of wildflowers with a fantastic view of Mount Rainier and Little Tahoma atop her shoulder, the rocky holdout from a massive explosion.

After the trail crosses the water source for Summerland Camp, the fields of subalpine flowers give way to rockfield—you are entering alpine terrain. The mountain looms over you as you pass an iceberg lake and Panhandle Gap, a saddle between two rocky rises. At this point you have reached the apex of the entire length of the Wonderland Trail.

In this area, snow is a constant. Prepare to cross several steep and slippery snowfields, even in the heat of late summer. Route-finding in this area may prove very difficult in bad weather. As you descend along a ridge flanked by cliffs and falls on one side and a flowered valley on the other, you have just 1.5 miles to go before you reach Indian Bar Camp. Many switchbacks lead down to a mountain meadow covered with lupine and magenta paintbrush. The Indian Bar Shelter is across the meadow. If you are camping here, follow the sign that points left (east) to an available site. Otherwise, continue south along the main trail.

From Indian Bar the trail climbs steadily, gaining 1,000 feet to the top of a mountain known colloquially as "5930" its total elevation. Make sure you look behind you, because you once again have a great view of Mount Rainier. The top of the knoll makes for a good photo opportunity if the weather cooperates. The descent from the top leads to a wooded ridge, eclipsing Mount Rainier. Walk along this ridge, the Cowlitz Divide, 3.0 miles to a fork in the trail.

At the fork head right (southwest) toward Nickel Creek. Bloodthirsty mosquitoes frequent the snowfields in this area in midsummer, so come prepared for the onslaught. Soon after taking the Wonderland Trail toward Nickel Creek, you leave any remaining snowfields, descending quickly along steep switchbacks. The trail flattens as you approach Nickel Creek Camp, 2.0 miles beyond the intersection to the Cowlitz Divide Trail. If you do not plan to stay here, follow the Wonderland Trail around the camp. You cross a small stream before crossing Nickel Creek along a prepared log. Only 0.9 mile more of gradual downhill, and you come to Box Canyon.

Stay to the right (northwest) along the small Box Canyon Loop. Years of glacial erosion have smoothed the surfaces of these rocks. Plants struggle to survive. You soon come to the bridge over the Cowlitz River. Water churns below. The trail almost immediately forks beyond the bridge. Stay to the right (southwest) along the Wonderland Trail. The trail ascends a bit before crossing Stevens Canyon Road over a tunnel. Less than 1 mile from the road crossing, you come to the Stevens Creek Trail junction. Stay to the left (west), once again along the Wonderland Trail. Cross the bridge where Stevens Creek churns over gray, black, and turquoise boulders.

Another mile of hiking on relatively flat terrain brings you to Maple Creek Camp. Reaching Maple Creek Camp, 45.5 miles from where you began, means that you have traveled more than halfway around the Wonderland Trail. Unless you want to explore campsites or use the pit toilet, stay to the right (northwest) toward a deceptively narrow part of the trail. The trail will widen and cross a stream along a small log. While crossing, look up and to your left to see Maple Falls, which you may find difficult to spot as a result of its distance from the path.

Sylvia Falls, less than 1 mile beyond Maple Falls, is obscured by large trees, but what is visible is engaging. It appears as though the water shoots directly out of the land from no source. A small clearing that looks out upon Sylvia Falls makes a nice, cool lunch spot for summer hikers.

A gradual ascent begins here and continues 1.0 mile to Martha Falls, the most impressive of the five falls on this stretch, if just for its size. The gradual ascent soon becomes a steep ascent for 0.7 mile of switchbacks. The sound of cars tells you that you are near Stevens Canyon Road. The trail continues directly across Stevens Canyon Road.

The ascent continues for 1.0 mile before you catch sight of Louise Lake through the trees. If you would like a closer look, follow the marked and maintained trail to the sandy beaches of Louise Lake. Park rangers report decent fishing here. Permits are not required to fish in the national park, and there are no limits on most fish. You may not fish for bull trout, an endangered species listed by the Environmental Protection Agency. After you've had your fill of the lake, continue along the main trail, which widens—a sign of more frequent use. A more gradual ascent leads to the junction with the Lakes Trail. Turn left (south) to once more encounter Stevens Canyon Road.

When you reach Reflection Lakes, the trail ends. You must hike 0.1 mile along the road until the trail resumes on the west side of the lakes. Stay on the trail until you cross Stevens Canyon Road and are on the Wonderland Trail again. The trail slopes down and then slightly up to the beginning of a set of downhill switchbacks. It is 1.3 miles from Stevens Canyon Road to the junction with Narada Falls Trail.

We recommend hiking the short jaunt to the glistening waters of Narada Falls before continuing on the Wonderland Trail. Go right (north) less than 0.1 mile to view the falls, or go left (southwest) if you are too tired or in a hurry. You will hear the Paradise River flowing directly to your right and will soon cross it. You will pass Paradise River Camp on your left, a little over 0.5 mile from the Narada Falls Trail.

Three bridges take you over the relatively calm forks of the Paradise River. About 0.5 mile from here is Madcap Falls, where Tatoosh Creek flows into the Paradise River. Instead of dropping straight down, Madcap Falls flows at a diagonal. The water gushes over the rocks to create an amazing white wonder.

Carter Falls is 0.2 mile after Madcap Falls. A sign reaffirms that the gorgeous waters you see dropping straight down are in fact Carter Falls. You might come upon a number of people here, considering the proximity to Cougar Rock Campground.

The next 1.1 miles are a pleasant walk along the Paradise River, despite some metal drain pipes and power lines along the trail. Then a set of bridges crosses the Nisqually River. The waters of the Nisqually River originate from active glaciers that deposit silt and grind glacial flour into the river—making the water extraordinarily muddy. The wide, pebbly Nisqually River valley is scattered with debris and downed trees from previous floods.

After you cross the bridges, climb up to the Longmire-Paradise Road. The Wonderland Trail continues to your left (southwest). In less than 0.25 mile, you come to another junction. The trail to your right (north) goes to Cougar Rock Campground; the old horse ford for the Nisqually River is to the left. Continue heading southwest on the Wonderland Trail until you reach a junction. To go to the Longmire Historic District, go left (west); otherwise go right (north). You will cross Longmire-Paradise Road 0.1 mile after this junction. The Wonderland Trail continues on the other side of the road, heading north up to Rampart Ridge.

You are about to begin the part of the Wonderland Trail coined "the piecrust" due to the extreme elevation changes. Be prepared for steep elevation oscillations.

After traveling for 1.6 miles from Longmire-Paradise Road, you come to the junction with the trail to Van Trump Park, heading east. Stay to the left, heading north, and arrive at the junction with the Rampart Ridge Trail in just 0.2 mile. The next mile to Kautz Creek is relatively level and a break from the uphill. Due to continual washouts, Kautz Creek has been recently rerouted, but you might still have to ford this river.

On the other side of Kautz Creek, the trail ascends to Pyramid Creek Camp, 0.7 mile away. The trail continues steeply, taking you through dense forest all the way to Devil's Dream Camp. After Devil's Dream Camp the trail continues uphill, but it is not as steep. You pass Squaw Lake about 0.3 mile from Devil's Dream Camp. The Kautz Creek Trail junction, in the center of Indian Henry's Hunting Ground, is 0.8 mile away.

Iron Mountain and Copper Mountain are visible to the right of the trail as you head toward the picturesque meadows of Indian Henry's Hunting Ground. This area was named for Indian Henry (Sutelik), a Native American who taught James Longmire about the trails in Mount Rainier. Indian Henry's Hunting Ground is filled with lupine and a variety of other colorful flowers in August. On a clear day you have fantastic views of the southwest side of Pyramid Peak and Mount Rainier, as well as the Sunset Amphitheater.

Mount Rainier's oldest patrol cabin, still in use, appears to the right of the trail, nestled in the meadow just after you pass the Kautz Creek Trail on your left (southwest). The trail is relatively level as it travels through Indian Henry's Hunting Ground. You will pass the Mirror Lakes Trail on your right (northeast) 0.2 mile beyond the Kautz Creek Trail.

After the Mirror Lakes Trail, the trail begins to descend to Tahoma Creek. This part of the trail has steep switchbacks and travels through pleasant forest to the suspension bridge, 1.5 miles from the Kautz Creek Trail. From the suspension bridge there is an amazing view of Tahoma Creek. If it is not too windy, take the time to look up the creek. Tahoma Creek continually experiences glacial outburst floods. If you hear a loud, roaring sound, immediately head to higher ground.

Just after you cross the suspension bridge, look for a sign for Tahoma Creek Trail on the right, heading west. The Tahoma Creek Trail connects with Westside Road in 2.1 miles. As the sign indicates, the trail is not recommended for use. The Wonderland Trail takes off uphill at this point and travels up steep switchbacks until it leaves the forest. You will hike over the South Tahoma Moraine as you head up to Emerald Ridge.

The top of Emerald Ridge is an emerald-green meadow filled with wildflowers in mid-July. The scent of lupine wafts in the breeze. A plethora of hoary marmots live in the meadows. Do not feed these wild animals; they need to remain self-sufficient to survive in their natural habitat.

The Tahoma Glacier and its moraine are directly to the left (north). If you look up at Mount Rainier, you will see the top of Tahoma Glacier, accompanied by the

South Tahoma Glacier on its south side. To date, twenty-three glacial outburst floods have burst from South Tahoma Glacier. Between the two glaciers rests Glacier Island. Mountain goats can often be seen grazing on Glacier Island, a green haven in a sea of glaciers. If you look closely, you can see fields of lupine.

From the top of the ridge, it is 1.7 miles down rocky trail to the intersection with South Puyallup Trail. The trail along the north side of Emerald Ridge has washed out many times. You'll be hiking a steep, unstable ledge; be very careful. Take the new trail that crosses the ridge diagonally. This part of the trail has an up-close view of the Tahoma Glacier Moraine. Tahoma Glacier resides in a land scar carved out by a previous mud slide. At the South Puyallup Trail junction, the South Puyallup Trail heads left (west) toward South Puyallup Camp, 0.1 mile away. The Wonderland Trail is to the right (north). Cross the silty waters of South Puyallup River and start heading uphill. The trail is extremely steep and brushy for the next 2.2 miles to St. Andrews Park.

▶ Puyallup (*pyoo-AL-uhp*) is composed of two Native American words—*pough,* meaning generous, and *allup,* meaning people. The Puyallup tribe was known to be fair and honest traders with other Native Americans.

The meadows of St. Andrews Park are beautiful. In mid-July, avalanche lilies, lupine, and magenta paintbrush fill the meadows with their splendor; Mount Rainier towers above it all. Hike through the colorful meadows, and pass over a rocky ridge to St. Andrews Lake.

Previous hikers have greatly impacted the lake by creating numerous social trails along the fragile banks of this subalpine lake. Minimize your impact by admiring the lake from the designated trail. You can also see a west-side climbing route that many climbers have used to attempt the summit. Fortunately the trails do not entirely take away from the beauty of the deep-blue waters of St. Andrews Lake.

As much as you will hate leaving St. Andrews Lake, Klapatche Park Camp is only 0.8 mile away and just as amazing. The trail slopes downhill the rest of the way. Beautiful wildflowers fill the meadows of Klapatche Park and surround Aurora Lake in mid-July. Aurora Lake is only a shallow pool of snowmelt, but it looks astonishing with Mount Rainier towering above it. If you are staying at Klapatche Park Camp, it is located at the south end of the lake.

The descent from Klapatche Ridge is long, steep, and brushy. Watch your step; the trail has an unstable ledge that drops straight off. On a clear day you have a great view of Mount Rainier, Tokaloo Spire, and the Puyallup Glacier from the ridge.

At the bottom of Klapatche Ridge, you come to the North Puyallup Trail, next to the group site of North Puyallup Camp. If you're not staying here, cross the North Puyallup River via a prepared log. As you cross the river, make sure to look down at the raging white waters of the North Puyallup River and up at the Puyallup Glacier. Soon after you cross this river, you reach the individual sites of North Puyallup Camp. The trail descends slightly before it resumes climbing for the next 4.0 miles to Sunset Park. At the edge of Sunset Park, the hillside is filled with ghost trees, the

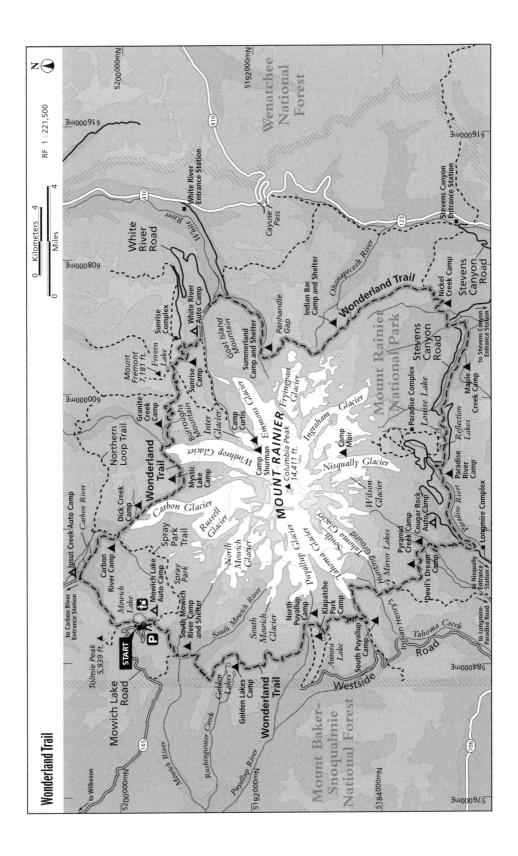

eerie remains of a fire many years before. Magenta paintbrushes and avalanche lilies fill the meadows of the park in mid-July.

A 0.5-mile descent from Sunset Park brings you to Golden Lakes Camp and the Golden Lakes Ranger Station to the left. Wildflowers, such as shooting stars and avalanche lilies, line the lakeshore. You can filter water here, but the water is thick with bugs and dirt. A mile from Golden Lakes Camp, you reach the top of a ridge covered in bear grass and Columbia lilies in mid-July. Hike over the ridge and begin the descent down steep switchbacks to the North and South Mowich Rivers. The next 5.1 miles are all downhill, with no water source.

When you reach the South Mowich River, you will notice the river bar scattered with debris and crushed trees due to the ever-changing south fork of the Mowich River from previous glacial outburst floods. When we hiked this trail, one of the three bridges over the South Mowich River was washed out, which it apparently does several times a year. Be aware that it is a tricky ford, and glacial boulders in the river are a possible hazard. It is a good idea to call ahead to the Wilkeson Wilderness Information Center to find out if the bridge is down so that you can prepare accordingly, but understand that the bridge might be washed out regardless, because washouts are unpredictable.

After crossing the South Mowich River via three bridges, you come to South Mowich River Camp and the South Mowich Shelter. Hike through lush forest to the North Mowich River, which you cross via two bridges, and start climbing to Mowich Lake. The next 3.6 miles of trail are very steep, ascending through old-growth forest. When you reach the junction with Spray Park Trail, you know you only have 0.2 mile left to go until you reach the refreshing waters of Mowich Lake. In warm weather consider taking a dip before heading back into civilization.

Miles and Directions

0.0 Start at Mowich Lake. Locate the trail that runs along the west side of Mowich Lake. There are several paths down to this trail, but continue heading north on the only trail that runs north-south along Mowich Lake, the Wonderland Trail.

1.5 Near the top of Ipsut Pass, the Tolmie Peak Trail splits left (west). Stay right (northeast), traveling on the Wonderland Trail.

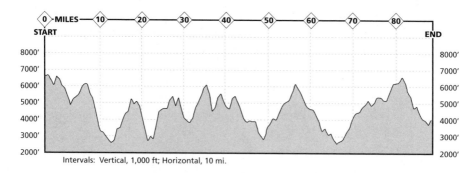

5.1 Stay to the right, continuing on the Wonderland Trail, heading southeast at the junction with the spur trail to Ipsut Creek Campground.

6.8 A small connector trail to the Northern Loop Trail jets off to the left (east); stay to the right (southeast) along the Wonderland Trail.

7.7 When you reach the Spray Park Trail, stay to the left, following the Wonderland Trail east across the suspension bridge over the Carbon River.

7.9 Stay to the right (southeast), heading toward Carbon Glacier. In less than 0.5 mile you will begin to view Carbon Glacier to the right (south) of the trail. This spectacular view continues until you reach Dick Creek Camp.

8.8 After Dick Creek Camp, the trail heads into the woods and climbs steeply.

10.5 As the trees slowly disappear to give way to mountain meadows, you have reached the beginning of Moraine Park.

12.0 Arrive at Mystic Lake.

12.6 After skirting the lake, leave its banks and head into forest; soon come to the trail to Mystic Lake Camp on your left (north).

16.5 From Mystic Lake, hike down a ravine, around a moraine, over a river, and back up the ravine to Granite Creek Camp. The trail goes through the camp.

19.2 At the junction with the Northern Loop Trail, continue east on the Wonderland Trail toward Sunrise.

20.0 A fenced-off lake, known as Frozen Lake, marks the convening of five trails. Follow the signs to Sunrise Camp along the Wonderland Trail.

20.6 Sunrise Camp appears on your right (southwest), and Shadow Lake sits to your left (east). If you have not reserved a camp here, stay on the Wonderland Trail, which curves south toward White River Campground. If you need supplies or to access your cache, follow the Sunrise Rim Trail to the Sunrise Complex.

24.0 The trail snakes down a steep slope to Loop D of the White River Campground. The Wonderland Trail continues on the other side of the loop; go either way and you will see the trailhead marked by many picnic tables at a viewpoint over the White River.

26.7 After crossing the White River over hatched logs, follow the trail, bypassing two spurs to the White River Road, to the Fryingpan Creek Trail junction. Go right (south) toward Summerland.

30.9 The trail to Summerland Camp appears on your left (east). If you do not plan to stay in Summerland, continue south on the Wonderland Trail toward Indian Bar.

32.3 Panhandle Gap marks the zenith of this east-side section; It's all downhill to Indian Bar.

35.4 You can see Indian Bar Shelter across the meadow to the right (west) of the trail. The spur trail to Indian Bar Camp goes left (east).

40.1 At the Cowlitz Divide Trail junction, stay to the right (southwest) toward Nickel Creek.

42.1 If you are staying at Nickel Creek Camp, take the trail to the left (south). Otherwise stay on the Wonderland Trail toward Box Canyon.

43.1 A short descent from Nickel Creek leads you to the Box Canyon Wayside Exhibit. You could forgo the Box Canyon Trail and hike along the road, but it is safer and more picturesque to check out the canyon. Hang a right onto the Box Canyon Trail, loop around, and cross the road over a tunnel.

44.5 Just one more downhill to the intersection with the Stevens Creek Trail and you begin heading uphill again. At the junction stay to the left (west) along the Wonderland Trail.

45.5 After hiking on relatively flat terrain, reach Maple Creek Camp. Unless you want to visit the camp or plan to camp here, stay to the right (northwest) toward the hatched log over Maple Creek and a view of Maple Falls.

48.2 After passing several waterfalls, arrive at Stevens Canyon Road. The trail continues toward Louise and Reflection Lakes on the other side of the road.

49.3 A sign marks the trail to Louise Lake on your right (north). Although you can see the road from the lake, the tarn has sandy beaches and relatively decent fishing.

49.5 Continue along the Wonderland Trail to reach the Lakes Trail. Take a left (west), along the lower part of the loop around Reflection Lakes.

49.6 The trail leads you along Reflection Lakes, then once again to Stevens Canyon Road. When the Wonderland Trail splits from the Lakes Trail, cross the road rather than heading right (north) toward Paradise.

51.5 At the junction with Narada Falls Trail, stay to the left (southwest) on the Wonderland Trail.

52.2 When the spur trail to Paradise River Camp appears on the left (south), stay to the right, heading southwest. Pass Madcap Falls on your left.

53.0 Just after Madcap Falls, Carter Falls is on the left. Stay right on the Wonderland Trail, heading west.

54.1 A small spur trail heads to the Longmire-Paradise Road. Continue southwest.

55.6 A spur trail to Longmire Historic District heads off to the left. Unless you need to pick up a food cache at Longmire, stay to the right and cross the road to continue on the Wonderland Trail, heading north.

57.4 At the junction with the Rampart Ridge Trail, stay right and continue north on the Wonderland Trail.

58.4 When you reach Kautz Creek, it is possible that the footlog has been washed out; you may have to ford the river.

59.1 Reach Pyramid Creek Camp not long after you cross Kautz Creek.

61.4 Arrive at Devil's Dream Camp.

62.5 At the Kautz Creek Trail junction, stay to the right, heading north on the Wonderland Trail. You will pass a trail to Mirror Lakes soon after you pass the Kautz Creek Trail. Stay to the left (north).

64.2 A suspension bridge takes you over Tahoma Creek. Afterward, continue hiking uphill on the Wonderland Trail.

66.3 After traversing the rocky terrain of South Tahoma's moraine, reach the top of Emerald Ridge.

67.9 At the junction with South Puyallup Trail, stay to the right, heading north.

71.1 Reach St. Andrews Lake; the trail travels around the east side of the lake. You will pass the St. Andrews Trail before you reach Klapatche Park. Stay to the right, heading north on the Wonderland Trail

71.9 Arrive at Klapatche Park Camp and Aurora Lake. The trail skirts the west side of this small lake. Continue traveling north on the Wonderland Trail.

74.7   At the junction with North Puyallup Trail, stay to the right, heading north.

79.7   Reach the Golden Lakes and Golden Lakes Camp.

85.8   Just before the South Mowich River Camp, cross the South Mowich River. The footlogs over this river often wash out; you may have to ford parts of the river.

86.7   At the junction with Paul Peak Trail, stay to the right, heading north toward Mowich Lake.

89.7   The Spray Park Trail diverges to the right (east). Stay left (north).

89.9   Arrive back at Mowich Lake.

Wilderness camping: Fires are not permitted in any backcountry camps. Following is a list of camps along the Wonderland Trail from start to end. Depending on how you decide to take on the Wonderland Trail and the availability of sites, you will choose from the following options.

Carbon River Camp: A camp located just off the Carbon River nestled in old-growth forest. There are four individual sites and one group site. The first two have excellent tent sites but are not very private. Sites 3 and 4 are more secluded with slanted tent sites; Site 4 is the most remote. The water source for this camp is Cataract Creek, a good 0.1 mile from all the sites.

Dick Creek Camp: One of our favorite backcountry camps, it has two nice individual sites. Site 1 has an unbelievable view of the Carbon Glacier. Dick Creek, the water source, is only a short walk away.

Mystic Lake Camp: Unfortunately this camp is located quite a distance from Mystic Lake. An established camp along the Wonderland Trail, it has a whopping seven individual sites and two group sites, all with good tent sites but little privacy.

Granite Creek Camp: The two individual campsites and one group site at Granite Creek have no view but quite a bit of privacy. Granite Creek makes a nice water source.

Sunrise Walk-in Camp: There are eight individual sites available, plus two group sites. None of the sites are very private, but Site 8 is the most secluded. Try to snag Site 5 or 6 for a great view of Shadow Lake.

Summerland Camp and Shelter: This camp has five individual campsites and one group site. We recommend camping at either Site 3 or 4, even though these sites are farther from the toilet than the other sites (except Site 5, which has no view). Both 3 and 4 have the best views. The water source for all sites is a stream that's south along the main trail.

Indian Bar Camp and Shelter: Three lovely, private individual sites and one group site with bunks within the shelter.

Nickel Creek Camp: A large, flat area for camping includes three individual campsites and one large group camp. Nickel Creek provides a good water source.

Maple Creek Camp: Four individual sites and one group site are situated very near the pit toilet. The National Park Service is currently establishing another camp here. Take Site 4 for the privacy and view, although it is farthest from water and the toilet.

Paradise River Camp: Its three individual sites and one group site are small and flat. Site 2 is the most secluded, but it overlooks Site 1. Site 3 is nearest to the toilets and directly off the spur trail. The Paradise River is the water source for this backcountry camp. The Park Service closes the Pardise River Camp periodically to protect a pair of spotted owls seen nesting there. Should this happen, Wonderland Trail hikers with reservations are moved to Cougar Rock Camp.

Pyramid Creek Camp: The camp has two sites and a pit toilet; its water source is Pyramid Creek, less than 0.1 mile north on the Wonderland Trail. Both sites are flat and nice; Site 2 is more private and more spacious.

Devil's Dream Camp: This camp, nestled in the forest, has seven individual sites and a group site, all of which are very nice and flat. Sites 5 and 6 offer the most privacy. There are two pit toilets, and the camp is often filled with Wonderland Trail hikers. Be careful when you use the toilet near Site 4—it is likely that the residents at Site 4 can see you! All the other sites are next to the trail, spacious, and flat. Usually the water source for Devil's Dream Camp is near Site 1, but it often dries up in late summer. If this is the case, you will have to hike about 0.25 mile to Squaw Lake or to the creek directly after Squaw Lake, depending on where you prefer to obtain your water.

South Puyallup Camp: There are four individual sites at South Puyallup Camp and one group site. Site 1 is probably the best campsite. It is private, with a close water source. Be forewarned that the toilet is 0.1 mile from all the campsites. Site 2 also has its own water source with good tent sites. Sites 3 and 4 have just been improved, and if seclusion is your primary concern, Site 4 is your best bet.

Klapatche Park Camp: The campsites here will spoil you. There are four individual sites. The toilet is near all the sites, although the food storage pole is too close. Site 1 is closest to the lake and has an incomparable view. Watching the sun rise and reflect Mount Rainier in Aurora Lake will astound you. You cannot see Mount Rainier clearly from any of the other sites, but the view down the north side of Klapatche Ridge from Sites 2, 3, and 4 is also very pleasant.

North Puyallup Camp: The camp is along the North Puyallup River, although you do not see the river from any of the sites. Tucked away in the forest, the camp has three individual sites and one group site. All sites are flat but small and directly next to the trail. The group site is rather spacious and open, but still near the trail. The group site is separate from the three individual sites and located across the footlog over the North Puyallup River.

Golden Lakes Camp: There are five individual campsites and one group site. The camp also has a food storage pole to hang your food. Sites 1, 2, and 3 are near the toilets and far from water. The group site and Sites 4 and 5 are near the lake. You have a fantastic view at Site 5, as well as a close water source. The group site is closest to the lake; Site 4 is on top of the ridge and looks down into the valley on the other side of the lakes.

South Mowich River Camp and Shelter: This camp has four individual sites and a group site. (The South Mowich Shelter is considered one of the individual sites.) Sites 3 and 4 are closer to the South Mowich River. Sites 1 and 2, along with the group site, are crunched together and near the trail. There is an outhouse.

Hike Information

Local Information

Mount Rainier National Park Web site,
www.nps.gov/mora; twenty-four-hour visitor information, (360) 569-2211.

Lodging

For a list of accommodations outside the park, visit www.nps.gov/mora/general/accom.htm.

Campgrounds

Ipsut Creek Campground, located 5.0 miles east of the Carbon River Entrance, issues campsites on a first come, first served basis.

For no fee, Mowich Lake Campground, at the end of Mowich Lake Road, also offers walk-in campsites on a first-come, first-served basis. Campfires are prohibited. Sunshine Point Campground is located in the southwest corner of the park, 0.25 mile inside the Nisqually Entrance. Register at the campground. Cougar Rock Campground is located in the southwest corner of the park, 2.3 miles north of the Longmire Historic District. Reserve a site at Cougar Rock Campground online at http://reservations.nps.gov, or call (800) 365-CAMP (2267) 7:00 A.M. to 7:00 P.M. PST.

Appendix A: Zero Impact

Going into a national park such as Mount Rainier is like visiting a museum. You obviously do not want to leave your mark on an art treasure in the museum. If everybody going through the museum left one little mark, the piece of art would be quickly destroyed—and of what value is a big building full of trashed art? The same goes for a pristine wilderness such as Mount Rainier National Park, which is as magnificent as any masterpiece by any artist. If we all left just one little mark on the landscape, the wilderness would soon be despoiled.

A wilderness can accommodate human use as long as everybody behaves, but a few thoughtless or uninformed visitors can ruin it for everybody who follows. All wilderness users have a responsibility to know and follow the rules of zero-impact camping. An important source of these guidelines, including the most updated research, can be found in the book *Leave No Trace*. See Appendix C for ordering information.

Nowadays most wilderness users want to walk softly, but some are not aware that they have poor manners. Often their actions are dictated by the outdated habits of a past generation of campers, who cut green boughs for evening shelters, built campfires with fire rings, and dug trenches around tents. These "camping rules" may have been acceptable in the 1950s, but they leave long-lasting scars. Today such behavior is absolutely unacceptable. The wilderness is shrinking, and the number of users is mushrooming. More and more camping areas show unsightly signs of heavy use.

A new code of ethics is growing out of the necessity of coping with the unending waves of people who want an enjoyable wilderness experience. Today we all must leave no clues that we have gone before. Canoeists can look behind the canoe and see no trace of their passing. Hikers, mountain bikers, and four-wheelers should have the same goal. Enjoy the wildness, but have zero impact on the landscape.

Three Falcon Guide Zero-Impact Principles

1. Leave with everything you brought in with you.
2. Leave no sign of your visit.
3. Leave the landscape as you found it.

Most of us know better than to litter—in or out of the wilderness. Be sure you leave nothing, regardless of how small it is, along the trail or at the campsite. Pack out everything, including orange peels, flip tops, cigarette butts, and gum wrappers. Also pick up any trash that others have left behind.

- Follow the main trail. Avoid cutting switchbacks and walking on vegetation beside the trail.

- Do not pick up "souvenirs," such as rocks, antlers, or wildflowers. The next person wants to see them, too, and collecting such souvenirs violates park regulations.

- Avoid making loud noises that may disturb others. Remember, sound travels easily to the other side of lakes. Be courteous.

- Carry a lightweight trowel to bury human waste 6 to 8 inches deep, and pack out used toilet paper. Keep human waste at least 300 feet from any water source.

- Finally, and perhaps most important, strictly follow the pack-in/pack-out rule. If you carry something into the backcountry, consume it or carry it out.

Practice zero-impact principles—and put your ear to the ground in the wilderness and listen carefully. Thousands of people coming behind you are thanking you for your courtesy and good sense.

Appendix B: Being Prepared

Backcountry Safety and Hazards

Boy Scouts and Girl Scouts have been guided for decades by what is perhaps the best single piece of safety advice: Be Prepared! For starters, this means carrying survival and first-aid materials, proper clothing, compass, and topographic map—and knowing how to use them.

Perhaps the second-best piece of safety advice is to tell somebody where you are going and when you plan to return. Pilots must file flight plans before every trip, and anybody venturing into a blank spot on the map should do the same. File your "flight plan" with a friend or relative before taking off.

Close behind filing your flight plan and being prepared with proper equipment is physical conditioning. Being fit not only makes wilderness travel more fun, it makes it safer. To whet your appetite for more knowledge of wilderness safety and preparedness, here are a few tips.

- Check the weather forecast. Be careful not to get caught at high altitude by a bad storm or along a stream in a flash flood. Watch cloud formations closely so that you are not stranded on a ridgeline during a lightning storm. Avoid traveling during prolonged periods of cold weather.

- Avoid traveling alone in the wilderness.

- Keep your party together.

- Study basic survival and first aid before leaving home.

- Do not eat wild plants unless you have positively identified them.

- Before you leave for the trailhead, find out as much as you can about the route, especially any potential hazards.

- Do not exhaust yourself or other members of your party by traveling too far or too fast. Let the slowest person set the pace.

- Do not wait until you are confused to look at your maps. Follow them as you go along, from the moment you start moving up the trail, so that you have a continual fix on your location.

- If you get lost, do not panic. Sit down and relax for a few minutes while you carefully check your topographic map and take a reading with your compass. Confidently plan your next move. It is often smart to retrace your steps until you find familiar ground, even if you think it might lengthen your trip. Many people get temporarily lost in the wilderness and survive—usually by calmly and rationally dealing with the situation.

- Stay clear of all wild animals.

- Take a first-aid kit that includes, at a minimum, the following items: sewing needle, snakebite kit, aspirin, antibacterial ointment, two antiseptic swabs, two butterfly bandages, adhesive tape, four adhesive strips, four gauze pads, two triangular bandages, two inflatable splints, moleskin or Second Skin for blisters, one roll of 3-inch gauze, CPR shield, rubber gloves, and lightweight first-aid instructions.

- Take a survival kit that includes, at a minimum, the following items: compass, whistle, matches in a waterproof container, cigarette lighter, candle, signal mirror, flashlight, fire starter, aluminum foil, water purification tablets, space blanket, and flare.

- Last but not least, do not forget that the best defense against unexpected hazards is knowledge. Read up on the latest in wilderness safety information.

Geologic Hazards

Since Mount Rainier is considered an active volcano, it is important to be aware of geological hazards. Eruption is the most obvious hazard, but other more common hazards such as landslides, glacial outburst floods, and rockfalls can be more dangerous and can occur without warning. Before an eruption occurs, the frequency of earthquakes rises dramatically. Mount St. Helens, the youngest and most active of the Cascades, experienced thousands of earthquakes per week before its eruption. Mount Rainier, second in geological activity to Mount St. Helens, experiences only thirty earthquakes every year.

You are more at risk to geological hazards when you are camping due to longer exposure and greater reaction/evacuation time. The National Park Service considers the danger of geological incidents to be relatively low, but you personally must assume the risk of staying overnight at any backcountry campsite or any automobile campground.

The park also advises that if anytime you are near a river and notice a rapid rise in water level or hear a roaring sound coming from up valley—often described as sounding similar to a fast-moving train—move quickly to higher ground. The National Park Service suggests moving to a location 160 feet or more above river level to remove yourself from the path of a glacial outburst flood.

In Mount Rainier National Park, the South Mowich River, Kautz Creek, Carbon River, and West Fork White River continually experience glacial outburst floods. Footlogs across these waters are frequently washed out. The National Park Service does not advise fording glacial rivers due to the high concentration of debris in them. Large glacial boulders are always a potential hazard. If you must ford, the Park Service recommends crossing early in the day and crossing on any fallen logs available, but only if they are steady and secure. Also, always wear your hiking boots to protect yourself from any debris suspended in the river, but you might want to take your socks off before crossing to keep them dry.

Detailed information about geological activity in Mount Rainier National Park is available from the USGS Cascades Volcano Observatory.

USGS Cascades Volcano Observatory
5400 MacArthur Boulevard
Vancouver, WA 98661
Web site: www.vulcan.wr.usgs.gov/

Springtime Hiking

Snow is found on most trails through June and lingers on some trails throughout summer. If you are planning to hike in spring or on higher elevation trails, you should anticipate the hazards of hiking in snow and take the necessary precautions. Here is a list of safety tips to assist you:

- Snow-covered trails are harder to follow. Hikers must have a reliable map and possess compass skills to travel through many areas of the park. Known problem areas: Panhandle Gap, Spray Park, Seattle Park, St. Andrews Park, and Ipsut Pass.
- Avoid crossing steep, snow-covered slopes where a fall could be disastrous. Turn around instead. Comet Falls and Pinnacle Peak trails have hazardous slopes during spring.
- Falling through thin snowbridges is a hazard anywhere streams remain snow covered. Stay alert for the muffled sound of running water.
- Falling into snow moats around trees and adjacent to logs and rocks can cause injury. Avoid getting too close.
- Avoid stepping on wet, slippery rocks, especially those near rivers and waterfalls. Common hazard areas: Narada Falls and Silver Falls.
- Avoid stepping onto snow cornices, which may collapse under your weight.
- Stop by a wilderness information center or park visitor center for details about current trail conditions, or visit the park Web site: www.nps.gov/mora.

- Be prepared for wet, cold weather at any time; snow can fall in Mount Rainier National Park during any month of the year.

Hypothermia: The Silent Killer

Be aware of the danger of hypothermia—a condition in which the body's internal temperature drops below normal. It can lead to mental and physical collapse—and ultimately death.

Hypothermia is caused by exposure to cold and is aggravated by wetness, wind, and exhaustion. The moment you begin to lose heat faster than your body produces it, you are suffering from exposure. Your body starts involuntary exercise, such as shivering, to stay warm and makes involuntary adjustments to preserve normal temperature in vital organs, restricting blood flow in the extremities. Both responses drain your energy reserves. The only way to stop the drain is to reduce the degree of exposure.

With full-blown hypothermia, as energy reserves are exhausted, cold reaches the brain, depriving you of good judgment and reasoning power. You will not be aware that this is happening. You lose control of your hands. Your internal temperature slides downward. Without treatment, this slide leads to stupor, collapse, and death.

To defend against hypothermia, stay dry. When clothes get wet, they lose about 90 percent of their insulating value. Wool loses relatively less heat; cotton, down, and some synthetics lose more. Choose rain clothes that cover the head, neck, body, and legs and provide good protection against wind-driven rain. Most hypothermia cases develop in air temperatures between thirty and fifty degrees, but hypothermia can develop in warmer temperatures.

If your party is exposed to wind, cold, and wet, think hypothermia. Watch yourself and others for these symptoms: uncontrollable fits of shivering; vague, slow, slurred speech; memory lapses; incoherence; immobile or fumbling hands; frequent stumbling or a lurching gait; drowsiness (to sleep is to die); apparent exhaustion; and inability to get up after a rest. When a member of your party has hypothermia, he or she may deny any problem. Believe the symptoms, not the victim. Even mild symptoms demand treatment, as follows:

- Get the victim out of the wind and rain.
- Strip off all wet clothes.
- Dress the victim in warm clothes and a warm sleeping bag. Place well-wrapped water bottles filled with heated water close to the victim. If the victim is only mildly impaired, give him or her warm drinks.
- If the victim is badly impaired, attempt to keep him or her awake. Put the victim in a sleeping bag with another person—both naked. If you have a double bag, put two warm people in with the victim.

Cougar Safety

Although there has never been a reported cougar attack in Mount Rainier National Park, there have been sightings. It is important to be prepared for an encounter. The most important safety element for recreation in cougar country is simply recognizing their habitat. Deer are the primary prey of cougar, and these ungulates are a key element in cougar habitat. If you are not experienced at observing deer or at recognizing their tracks or feces, talk to locals, park rangers, or state wildlife biologists. Fish and wildlife agencies usually have good information about deer distribution from population surveys and hunting results.

Deer tracks can be found easily on dirt roads and trails. If you are not familiar with identifying deer tracks, seek the advice of someone knowledgeable, or refer to a book on animal tracks such as Falcon's *Scats and Tracks* series.

Safety Guidelines for Traveling in Cougar Country

1. Travel with a friend or group.
2. Keep small children close.
3. Do not let pets run unleashed.
4. Try to minimize your recreation during dawn and dusk—the times cougars are most active.
5. Watch for warning signs of cougar activity.
6. Know how to behave if you encounter a cougar (see below).

What to Do if You Encounter a Cougar

In the vast majority of cougar encounters, these animals exhibit avoidance, indifference, or curiosity that doesn't result in human injury. However, it is natural to be alarmed if you have an encounter of any kind. Try to keep your cool and consider the following:

1. Recognize threatening behavior. A few cues may help you gauge the risk of attack. If a cougar is more than 50 yards away and directs its attention to you, it may be only curious. This situation represents only a slight risk for adults, but a more serious risk to unaccompanied children. At this point you should move away, while keeping the animal in your peripheral vision. Look for rocks, sticks, or something to use as a weapon—just in case.

If a cougar is crouched and staring intensely at you less than 50 yards away, it may be assessing the chances of a successful attack. If this behavior continues, the risk of attack may be high.

2. Do not approach a cougar; give the animal the opportunity to move on. Slowly back away, but maintain eye contact if close. Cougars are not known to attack humans to defend young or a kill, but they have been reported to "charge" in rare instances. Best choose another route or time to venture through the area.

3. Do not run from a cougar. Running may stimulate a predatory response.

4. If you encounter a cougar, be vocal and talk or yell loudly and regularly. Try not to panic: Shout in a way that others in the area may understand, to make them aware of the situation.

5. Maintain eye contact. Eye contact presents a challenge to the cougar, showing you are aware of its presence. Eye contact also helps you know where it is. However, if the behavior of the cougar is not threatening (if it is, for example, grooming or periodically looking away), maintain visual contact through your peripheral vision and move away.

6. Appear larger than you are. Raise your arms above your head and make steady waving motions. Raise your jacket or another object above your head. Do not bend over—this will make you appear smaller and more "preylike."

7. If you are with small children, pick them up. First, bring children close to you; maintain eye contact with the cougar, and pull the children up without bending over. If you are with other children or adults, band together.

8. Be prepared to defend yourself and fight back, if attacked. Try to remain standing. Do not feign death. Pick up a branch or rock; pull out a knife, pepper spray, or other deterrent device. Remember, everything is a potential weapon; individuals have fended off cougars with blows from rocks, tree limbs, and even cameras.

9. Defend your friends or children, but not your pet. Adults have successfully stopped attacks on children. However, it is very dangerous and risky; physically defending a pet is not recommended.

10. Respect any warning signs about cougars posted by agencies.

11. Teach others in your group how to behave in case of a cougar encounter. Anyone who starts running could bring on an attack.

12. If you have an encounter with a cougar, record your location and the details of the encounter, and notify the nearest park official, landowner, or other appropriate agency. The land management agency (federal, state, or county) may want to visit the site and, if appropriate, post education/warning signs. Fish and wildlife agencies should also be notified because they record and track such encounters.

If physical injury occurs, it is important to leave the area and not disturb the site of attack. Cougars that have attacked people must be killed, and an undisturbed site is critical for effectively locating the dangerous animal. See Falcon's *Lion Sense* for more details and tips for safe outdoor recreation in cougar country. (Ordering information is available in Appendix C.)

Be Bear Aware

Bears are wild animals, and you should treat them as such. Never feed a bear; it is detrimental to the animal's survival skills. Also, a fed bear is more likely to be aggressive, increasing dangerous encounters.

Nobody likes surprises, and bears dislike them, too. The majority of human-bear conflicts occur when a hiker surprises a bear. Therefore, it is vital to do everything possible to avoid these surprise meetings. Perhaps the best way is to know and follow these five rules for reducing the chance of a close encounter with a bear to the slimmest possible margin.

- Be alert.
- Do not hike alone.
- Stay on the trail.
- Do not hike in the late evening or early morning.
- Make lots of noise. Singing, whistling, and hand-clapping work well.

If you do see a bear, freeze and begin to slowly back away. Let the bear know you are there by clapping or talking to it in a loud voice. Never run from a bear—it might consider you prey. Nine times out of ten, the bear will take action to avoid you.

The National Park Service has established food storage poles at every wilderness camp. Park regulations require that you hang your food at night. Remember to keep a clean camp and use a minimum of odorous food to avoid attracting bears. For additional information on how to be bear aware and camp in bear country, Falcon publishes an excellent book, *Bear Aware*. (See Appendix C for ordering information.)

Appendix C: Further Reading

Following is a list of helpful FalconGuides to help enrich your hiking experience. You can order these books online at www.falcon.com or by calling (888) 249–7586.

Bear Aware
by Bill Schneider

Lion Sense by Steve Torres	*Wilderness First Aid* by Gilbert Preston, M.D.
Avalanche Aware by John Moynier	*Wilderness Survival* by Suzanne Swedo
Backpacking Tips by Russ Schneider and Bill Schneider	*The Rocky Mountain Berry Book* by Bob Krumm
A Field Guide to Scats & Tracks *of the Pacific Coast States* by James Halfpenny, Ph.D. Illustrated by Todd Telander	*Western Trees* by Maggie Stuckey and George Palmer Illustrated by Keith Bowers
Leave No Trace by Will Harmon	

About the Authors

Mary Skjelset and Heidi Schneider are still the youngest author team to complete a FalconGuide. Heidi is currently studying medicine at Oregon Health Sciences University, with a strong commitment to community service. Her childhood was spent exploring the wilderness in and around Montana. Heidi continues to derive strength and spirituality from nature. Also from Montana, Mary appreciates the wild side of life. After graduating college and working with an environmental organization in the Czech Republic, she settled in Oregon and now attends law school at Lewis and Clark College.